Reclaim Your Right to Heal

The ancient women healers knew that the body is more than what is seen. They respected the wholeness of body, emotions, mind and spirit, saw the goddess as within all Be-ing, and treated their patients with respect and caring. Healing was a three-way agreement between healer, goddess and the person being healed, and healing was an active choice. Such partnerships and participation are missing in today's modern medicine, along with the concepts of wholeness and respect. The great secret of healing—that anyone can do it and can choose it—goes back to the worldwide traditions of the women healers, back to ancient matriarchal cultures that valued the goddess and women, valued life. Despite modern allopathic medicine's denial of this secret, denial of the concept of wholeness, and denial of the goddess-within, the secret is still fact. Anyone can heal, and anyone can choose well-being. By learning and using the ancient skills of healing, many dis-eases of the body, emotions, mind and spirit are preventable, or are easily transformed before they become matters for allopathic medicine. The skills of the ancient healers are available, powerful and very much alive right now.

Women's healing, which is healing for the benefit of women and men, children, animals and the planet alike, includes such skills as aura and chakra work, colors, creative visualization, meditation states, laying on of hands, psychic healing and crystals and gemstones. These ancient and universal knowings are elemental, and though long submerged, they have never been lost. Receiving increasing attention in the New Age and Women's Spirituality movements, healing is being re-learned and re-claimed. *The Women's Book of Healing* demystifies, explains and teaches these skills in ways that anyone can learn and use. It teaches basic healing, then applies those skills to healing with crystals and gemstones—a beautiful, effective and empowering aspect of the ancient women's healing methods. Healing and well-being in these ways are within choice and reach, for the benefit and good of all.

About Diane Stein

Diane Stein is the author of *The Kwan Yin Book of Changes*, the first women's I Ching, and *The Women's Spirituality Book*, published by Llewellyn Publications in 1985 and 1986 respectively. She has been involved in the women's movement since 1969 and involved with women's spirituality since the early 1970's. Coming from a background of women's movement activism and theoretical writing, and women's spirituality work as a writer, healer and priestess, she has been involved with women's spirituality for many years and has been active and instrumental in its growth into a worldwide movement. With a publishing and writing reputation in the women's movement that extends for over fifteen years, her writing is well-known and respected in the women's network of writers and women's spirituality workers. She has been active in the anti-Vietnam movement, the women's rights movement, anti-nuclear and disability rights movements, lesbian activism, and women's spirituality as an aspect of all of these. With the publication of *The Kwan Yin Book of Changes* and *The Women's Spirituality Book,* Diane Stein has become a well-known public figure in the women's movement.

To Write to the Author

We cannot guarantee that every letter written to the author can be answered, but all will be forwarded. Both the author and the publisher appreciate hearing from readers, learning of your enjoyment and benefit from this book. Llewellyn also publishes a bi-monthly news magazine with news and reviews of practical esoteric studies and articles helpful to the student, and some readers' questions and comments to the author may be answered through this magazine's columns if permission to do so is included in the original letter. The author sometimes participates in seminars and workshops, and dates and places are announced in *The Llewellyn New Times.* To write to the author, or to ask a question, write to:

Diane Stein
c/o THE LLEWELLYN NEW TIMES
P.O. Box 64383-759, St. Paul, MN 55164-0383, U.S.A.
Please enclose a self-addressed, stamped envelope for reply, or $1.00 to cover costs.

ABOUT LLEWELLYN'S NEW AGE SERIES

The "New Age"—it's a phrase we use, but what does it mean? Does it mean the changing of the Zodiacal Tides, that we are entering the Aquarian Age? Does it mean that a new Messiah is coming to correct all that is wrong and make Earth into a Garden? Probably not—but the idea of a *major change* is there, combined with awareness that Earth *can* be a Garden; that war, crime, poverty, disease, etc., are not necessary "evils."

Optimists, dreamers, scientists . . . nearly all of us believe in a "better tomorrow," and that somehow we can do things now that will make for a better future life for ourselves and for coming generations.

In one sense, we all know "there's nothing new under the Heavens," and in another sense that "every day makes a new world." The difference is in our consciousness. And this is what the New Age is all about: it's a major change in consciousness found within each of us as we learn to bring forth and manifest "powers" that Humanity has always potentially had.

Evolution moves in "leaps." Individuals struggle to develop talents and powers, and their efforts build a "power bank" in the Collective Unconsciousness, the "soul" of Humanity that suddenly makes these same talents and powers easier access for the majority.

Those who talk about a New Age believe a new level of consciousness is becoming accessible that will allow anyone to manifest powers previously restricted to the few who had worked strenuously for them: powers such as Healing (for self or others), Creative Visualization, Psychic Perception, Out-of-Body Consciousness and more.

You still have to learn the 'rules' for developing and applying these powers, but it is more like a "relearning" than a *new* learning, because with the New Age it is as if the basis for these had become genetic.

The books in the New Age series are as much about ATTITUDE and AWARENESS as they are about the "mechanics" for learning and using Psychic, Mental, Spiritual, or Parapsychological Powers. Understanding that the Human Being is indeed a "potential god" is the first step towards the realization of that potential: expressing in outer life the inner creative powers.

Other Books by Diane Stein

The Women's Spirituality Book, Llewellyn, 1986
The Kwan Yin Book of Changes, Llewellyn, 1985
innocence/experience, Woman Prints Press, 1981. A book of short
   stories.

Tapes:
Rachida Finds Magic
Meditation On The Goddess Within/Meditation On The Chakras:
   The Rainbow
I Ching Workshop Tape
Crystal Healing Workshop Tape

Forthcoming books:
Stroking the Python: Women's Psychic Experiences

Llewellyn's New Age Series

THE WOMEN'S BOOK OF HEALING

★ Crystals and Gemstones
★ Auras and Laying On of Hands
★ Chakras and Colors

by

Diane Stein

1987
Llewellyn Publications
St. Paul, Minnesota 55164-0383, U.S.A.

International Standard Book Number: 0-87542-759-6
Library of Congress Catalog Number: 87-45748

First Edition, 1986
First Printing, 1986

Library of Congress Cataloging-in-Publication Data
Stein, Diane, 1948
    The women's book of healing.

    (Llewellun's new age series)
    Bibliography: p.
    Includes index.
    1. Mental healers.   I. Title.   II. Series
RZ401.S8118   1987   615.8+52   87-45748
ISBN 0-87542-759-6

**Cover Painting: Ruth Zachary
Interiors: Merle Insinga
Photography: Frank Schneider
Book Design: Terry Buske**

Produced by Llewellyn Publications
Typography and Art property of Chester-Kent, Inc.

Published by
**LLEWELLYN PUBLICATIONS
A Division of Chester-Kent, Inc.**
P.O. Box 64383
St. Paul, MN 55164-0383, U.S.A.

Printed in the United States of America

Dedication

**for
Laurel Wise Ela**

Acknowledgements

I would like to thank Lee Lanning and Nett Hart for their comments and critiques of this book in process. Their time, effort, interest, caring and discernment have been greatly respected and appreciated. I would also like to thank Susan Sheppard and David Speer for healing information and feedback, Kay Gardner for encouragement, Nan Hawthorn and Jim Tedford for the long work of indexing, and the people of Llewellyn Publications: Carl Weschcke, Julie Feingold, Terry Buske, Phyllis Galde, Nancy Mostad, and Steve Bucher for making my books possible and being friends besides.

Credits

Special thanks go to these people who provided services or rocks for our photo section: Muriel Deneen; Berg's Rockhound's Paradise, Prescott, Wisconsin; Terry Buske; Phyllis Galde; and Julie Feingold.

CONTENTS

Preface

In these times of great global change and upheaval, many ancient healing techniques are surfacing in teachings from a myriad of spiritual disciplines. Healing is the recognition that wholeness comes when our physical, mental, emotional, spiritual and psychic senses are in balanced relationship. In this balance lies the holiness and perfect health both of individual and of Earth.

Woman as Mother has been healer from the beginnings of humanity. As "bringer of life," Woman has known which runes to speak, which magic chants to sing, which healing touches to apply, which images to visualize and which herbs and stones to gather for treating the imbalance of dis-ease.

In the West during the Middle Ages, women were excluded from the new patriarchal medical schools. As a result of patriarchal religious persecution, we were burned and tortured for our healing wisdom.

After being forced underground for centuries, women healers are re-emerging in the 20th Century to take our rightful, ancestral places at the forefront of all healing practices.

Diane Stein's comprehensive text, *The Women's Book of Healing,* brings a wealth of healing knowledge from women's tradition and culture. A thorough exploration of how our unseen energies flow through and around our bodies leads to a complete, practical guide for applying that healing knowledge with our hands, psychic energy and gemstones. Stein's book is an important addition to the libraries of both beginning healers and professional practitioners.

May the compassion and wisdom of Woman continue to bring healing and wholeness to all.

Blessed Be . . .

Kay Gardner

Gender in Language and Thought

*There are no generics in English. Terms such as **people,
persons, individuals, children, workers, officers,** et
cetera, are used to cover the absence of women as agents
and our all too frequent presence as patients.**

—Mary Daly

Women healing women does not exclude men in practice, though as in other books I use the *she* pronoun exclusively. The usage is both personal and political, a re-cognition of the erasure of women in (at very least) the English-speaking culture. There is no descriptive word in the language, with the exception of *people,* that includes every/body, and all of the words are male gender. Women in the West have grown up with the overt and subliminal concept of *he* as meaning *people,* and themselves not included.

In every book on every subject women read about *he. He* is active, goes out and builds buildings, becomes a doctor, makes decisions, has adventures and love affairs, makes a living and makes a world. *She* is not mentioned. Though she is assured (if only recently) that *he* means everyone, it does not and never has. *She* is not who goes out and makes the world, *he* is. *He* is not a generic but a reinforcing of sex role stereotypes and the patriarchal system. *He* can, *he* does, *he* is. She is excluded, nonexistent; she *can't,* she *doesn't,* she *isn't.* Written out of the language, of the generic, told from the beginnings of patriarchy that women are to be silent, the message comes through loud and clear. Instead of being active, women are trained to be passive and are reinforced in that. Being a doctor is a man's job, women are to become nurses. Being a builder is a man's job, women are decorators instead. God is male, and women are not "in His image."

Even the words for women, virtually every one of them, are words containing the root word *men. She* contains *he,* and there is *female, woman, women, human, human*kind, *man*kind, *he*rs. In the women's community, some have taken on alternative spellings for women (womyn, womoon, wimmin, etc.) to point out and include the

---

*Mary Daly, *Gyn/Ecology, The Metaethics of Radical Feminism,* (Boston, Beacon Press, 1987), p. 326. The idea is referenced to Julia P. Stanley.

xiii

feminine. In culture and language, women under patriarchy have been erased.

There are punchlines to this. If being a doctor is a male job now, medicine and healing were originated by women, and it was not until the burning times that men in the West became doctors at all. Building and contracting are male jobs in today's society, but every archaeological evidence and the current records of Native American and African cultures show women to be the builders in their societies, and probably the originators of building. In the words for male and female, the origin of the word *man* is Norse and means *woman,* is a word derived from *moon* in Sanskrit. Moon of course is the goddess, and has been so for cultures throughout the world.* Divinity under patriarchal religions is male, but this has been only for the last 5,000 years. Traditional esoteric thought places all that is Earth and of the Earth, all that is physical, as feminine. Reflecting that the Earth is goddess and goddess is female, all bodies are female (and all life), whether they are women's bodies or men's.

Using *she* to mean every/body makes women look at themselves as people, as active creators of the universe and of their own Be-ing and lives. If this seems new to some women and men, it is actually very old. Until the patriarchal order it was daily life, accepted as the *he* in language is accepted today. Before patriarchy, divinity was goddess and women were not excluded in the matriarchies, they were women's children and had their respected place in the goddess' law, in society and in natural world order. The advent of patriarchy was a world revolution in which the conquered, colonized people of the old way—women and the matriarchies—were sacrificed, submerged and controlled for the new order to survive. Women were removed from divinity (goddess became god), from medicine, from building, from literature and from the very language of the cultures and civilizations they had headed and designed.

Women in patriarchy are trained to look beyond themselves, rather than at themselves. They birth, teach, nurture and support others, value others, without looking at, teaching, nurturing and supporting themselves. Women have been told that our bodies are to be hidden, made to take up as little space as possible, are not clean, are never good enough, are sexual objects only and reproductive machines. Women's spirituality and this book say that women's bodies

---

*Barbara G. Walker, *The Woman's Encyclopedia of Myths and Secrets* (San Francisco, Harper and Row Publishers, 1983), p. 574.

are part of the rest of them, are one with emotions, minds and spirits to create a valued whole that is an image of goddess divinity. Men have always known that for themselves, seen that in themselves, women haven't. To talk about this idea in terms of *people's bodies,* in a language that has excluded women from being people, misses the point entirely, telling women to again look beyond instead of at or within. By using *women's bodies* and *she,* the point is not missed, and no one is excluded.

There will be no gender equality on goddess Earth until women re-claim, re-value and dis-cover their feminine creative goddess identities. By using *she* instead of *he* to mean *people,* women are re-minded of their own Be-ing, their own goddess-within divinity, their own active creativity, their own physical and otherwise great worth and value. By using the female pronoun, women are made to re-cognize, see and affirm themselves as goddess Be-ings (*human beings* in the old grammar), right along with men. If that changes the order of male superiority/supremacy *everyone* is raised with, so much the better.

Using the *she* pronoun does not erase *he,* unless men reading it choose to let it. Women have read *he* and fought to see themselves in it for thousands of years, even ironically knowing that it was women who developed writing to begin with, in the goddess temples. Women have learned to mentally change the pronouns, *he* to *she,* to include themselves and men can surely do the same. It's a consciousness-raising exercise for men (and women) who haven't thought of it before, but something women under patriarchy have never known differently. 90 per cent of this book involves material valid for men as well as for women, if men will accept the feminine aspects of them-selves and change the pronouns, will accept the oneness of their own bodies, emotions, minds and spirits, their goddess-within. Using *she* and *women's bodies* is inclusive of men, while it strongly and actively affirms women.

For women and men both, the use of *she* to mean *every/body* to mean *all of us,* to mean *people,* to mean *goddess-within* and *Be-ing,* is a political and personal affirmation of things missing in modern life for women and men both. It's an attempt to notice and right an imbalance and inequity that has existed since the northern patriarchal peoples descended upon and conquered the goddess matriarchies. If the usage seems extreme, it makes a point, raises consciousness, and affirms and establishes women's identities—extremes that need reinstating. Until women re-cognize themselves and establish the extremes of feminine aspects within themselves, there can be no balance, no equality of gender. Using the *she* pronouns, excluding by implication *he,* making the reversal in language, opens the way for internalizing the idea of goddess-within, of female divinity and Being in men and women both. There will be no balance, no equilibrium, no peace between men and women or in the world without it.

In Oriental philosophy, yin and yang, the concepts of active and receptive, light and dark, summer and winter, male and female are dualities. Neither exists without the other, and the roots of each are present intrinsically in the other. Therefore, the active, light and summer are existent in women, and the receptive, dark and winter are a part of men. Since there are no words in the patriarchal English language that re-cognize that, that include both men and women equally, and since the words being used are words that exclude the feminine and women totally, reversing the process by *she* pronouns is a movement toward balance. "In the yin and yang symbol, the important part is the circle that unites them."* Western culture and language have excluded *women* and *she* for too long. Using the *she* pronoun and *women's bodies* is an attempt to re-cast the circle.

Diane Stein
11/30/86
darkest moon

---

*Gail Fairfield, *Choice Centered Tarot* (Seattle, Choice Centered Astrology and Tarot 1982), p. 30.

Introduction

Women Healing

For women to heal ourselves is a political act ... To call upon the natural healing ways is to say "No" to the patriarchal obsession with controlling, directing and enacting "cure." To heal ourselves is a reclamation of the power we all have as living beings to live in harmony with the life energy and to fulfill our potentials as creatures among many on this planet. *

Women have always been healers of ourselves and others, and are re-claiming that empowerment as part of the women's spirituality movement today. Connecting the earliest midwives, witches and wisewomen to today's medical activists, body workers, herbalists, psychics and crystal/gemstone healers is a long line of women's healing tradition. This tradition, going back to ancient Egypt and Sumeria, and suppressed by the male establishment since patriarchy's takeover of goddess, is a known and vital fact of herstory. Women are the healers of the universe and Earth, the positive civilizers, inventors, comforters and homebuilders of the planet, the guardians of peace and well-being, and the mothers, care-givers, listeners and priestesses of the life force.

Women contain the powers of life and healing in their own goddess Be-ing, women *are* this healing power, and women and men once knew it planetwide in the ancient goddess matriarchies of early civilizations. Women in these matriarchies were the inventors of culture, medicine and government, were the images of goddess-divinity creation, and they lived in peace, health and balance with the Earth and their societies. For the last five thousand yars of earth HIStory, women's power, wholeness, goddess values, learning and healing have been repressed, denied and partially lost to patriarchal power-over

---

*Chellis Glendinning, "The Healing Powers of Women," in Chalene Spretnak, Ed., *The Politics of Women's Spirituality* (New York, Anchor/Doubleday Books, 1982), p. 291.

that's brought harm and dehumanization on women and men alike.*
Modern patriarchal medicine, with its fragmentation of body and
spirit and its heavy-handed "cures" is not a positive experience for
women's health or bodies, for anyone's well-being. Women's healing,
by contrast, with its emphasis on wholeness and gentleness, on the
unity of body, emotions, mind and spirit, on the seen and unseen and
on choice, is a powerful and hopeful alternative.

The meaning of women's power in this book comes from the
latin *podere,* "to be able,"† the ability to act, create and self-determine,
the ability of choice. Women's healing and knowledge, women's culture,
has been destroyed deliberately in the past and much is forever lost,
much stifled before it had a chance to flower in countless women's
lives in every culture and continent over fifty centuries. The matriarchal
reverence for life and birth, for the inter-relationship of parts of the
self and of the self with the planet, is eroded worldwide by patriarchal
conquest, competition, mechanization, corporate mentality and death
worship negativity. There is clear and present danger to women and
to men, to the planet and the life force by these attitudes.

Women today are re-claiming, re-gaining and dis-covering‡
women's peaceful power-within wholeness through politics, scholar-
ship, art, spirituality and healing. The philosophies of women's healing
renaissance, this re-claiming of women's heritage, women's medicine,
well-being and the life force goddess are philosophies of power-
within as opposed to power-over. Power-within is to be able, as in
natural childbirth or laying on of hands; power-over is to be dominated
and passive, as in birth by thousands of unnecessary caesarean sections
or "cures" by mastectomies and hysterectomies. Power-within is
shared healing by gemstones, massage, crystals, aura work and one-
to-one caring; power-over is mega-doses of improperly re-searched
drugs with their high costs and often dangerous side effects.

All forms of health—physical, emotional, mental and spiritual—
are power-within. It's the wisdom to visualize a well world in flow with
natural law and the ability to create that visualization on an individual
and universal basis. It's an external world where air, oceans, streams
and rivers are clean, where whales and seals live safe and free, where

---

*For further material on goddess and matriarchy, see Diane Stein, *The Kwan Yin Book of Changes,* and *The Women's Spirituality Book* (St. Paul, Llewellyn Publications, 1985 and 1986).

†Starhawk, *Dreaming the Dark: Magic, Sex and Politics* (Boston, Beacon Press, 1982), p. 2. The concepts of Power, power-within and power-over are Starhawk's work.

‡Hyphenated word concepts are owed to the work of Mary Daly: Be-ing, Re-claiming, Dis-covering, etc. See *Beyond God the Father* and *Gyne/cology* (Boston, Beacon Press, 1973 and 1978), throughout.

trees grow tall and green, where fuel is generated cheaply and without danger or pollution, where guns, rape and Pershing missles are inconceivable, where people of every variety and color care for and about each other, and where racism, classism, agism, sexism, hunger, poverty, anti-semitism, incest, child abuse and ablism cannot exist. It's an internal world where a woman through free choices creates her own life and well-being, gets what she wants and needs on all levels, and has abundance and goodness for herself and for all. It's a world where health and healing are chosen, and are participated in mutually by the healer and healed working together. It's a world where respect, love and caring are extended also at the time to die.

Individually and cross-culturally, women's healthy power-within skills and values, her lost, ignored and repressed knowledges are being re-learned, re-claimed and re-gained—and are being found able. Specific to women's dis-covery of whole Be-ing health, or at least to vital (living) parts of it, are women's healing skills and techniques: the sciences of herbs and massage, of psychic development, body work, music therapy, dreamwork, and women's-only space. Specific also to women's healing and health, basic skills and the subjects of this book, are the re-claiming and dis-covery of energy flows and auras, chakras, color work and thought forms, laying on of hands and creative visualization, psychic healing, meditation states and the powerful and empowering uses of crystals and gemstones.

Women's healing is herstory and women's heritage, as well as women's power. It reclaims the lost goddess and the goddess-within, the power-within of women and men, the ability to choose and create self-positive, whole and healthy lives. It re-claims herstory and women's learning and worldwide cultures, and applies these tried-and-true knowledges to the birthing, creating, nurturing, caring-for, healing and uniting of women's bodies, emotions, minds and spirits with the Earth. If women as healer-practitioners are the beneficiaries of this re-claiming, so are children and men, and the good is for the power-within affirmation of the planet.

Women's re-claiming of health is a dis-covery of women's bodies and functions, of respect for their goodness and rightness, of respect for the goddess-creation within all women. It's a re-claiming of menstruation, sexuality, birth, breast-feeding and menopause. It's a re-turn to ancient (and present and future) women's healing roles, that of one-on-one sensitivity and caring, of woman-to-woman as equals whether healer or being healed, and of woman in control of her self and her own well-being. Women's healing is a re-turning to inner power, to power-within, a refusal of the medical patriarchal system's split between total power-over of the doctor and total powerlessness and passivity for the patient. Since doctors are overwhelmingly male and patients in this system overwhelmingly female, the roles reflect patriarchy profoundly. It's a radical political act for women to assert healing and self-healing in the face of things as they are, and doing so is a major step toward women's health. The act benefits women and men both, and is for the good of all.

A personal example of the contrasts: I traveled from doctor to doctor with chronic, debilitating migraines. I was offered asprin, then various other drugs to break the pain cycle, but the drugs failed or worsened it and had side effects. I was put on anti-depressants, since I must have been neurotic, and refused help in breaking the addiction to them when the migraines continued and the side effects increased. After a difficult year of withdrawal from the anti-depressants, the migraines escalated to incidents of passing out and seizures. I was referred from emergency room to psychiatrist; I wasn't taking the drugs so I had to be crazy. An article in a magazine said that some women develop migraines from computer screens, and, working in the women's secretarial ghetto, I took the question to a doctor who first scoffed at it, and then admitted it, without doing anything else. Psychiatric "sanity" tests revealed dyslexia, and a strong possibility of the computer screen theory. I lost my job for refusing to use computers, after proving thoroughly to myself that they were the cause. Without money or hospitalization insurance, I couldn't afford more pills and doctors, and tried to heal myself alone. The migraines lessened and passing out stopped, but stress and headaches continued. It was a time of change.

I went to the Michigan Women's Music Festival for four days in August, and talked to women healers there. I had my first massage and felt my body as real and part of me, as an ally in well-being for the first time in my life. I learned about nutrition, vitamins and herbs for migraine, and ways to alleviate stress, a major migraine and headache cause. I learned meditation techniques, biofeedback with crystals and uses of gemstones, and began to understand the concept and politics of women's versus patriarchal health care. At home I made an inexpensive and nonaddicting mixture of herbs: chamomile, hops, scullcap and catnip, a tea that relaxes tension and relieves pain, prevents simple headaches from becoming migraines and relieves the early headaches. I took no other drugs, not even asprin, had no need to, and became a vegetarian, conscious of sugar, caffeine, additives and nutrition. I used meditation nightly to relax and sleep, and wore an amethyst. Crystal work at the start of pain ended it and left me feeling clear and connected, as did (and does) crystal work at the start of tension. I opened psychically and learned psychic self-healing, discovered it alone without a name for it—the ability to stop a headache or other dis-ease when I felt it first begin. I worked with the learnings and gained in skill.

With a few month's time and effort, I felt good. I had no more pain, no migraines and few headaches, gained weight and health, slept well, could read again, had relaxed noticeably and lived without fear of passing out. I began writing *The Kwan Yin Book of Changes* and found healthier jobs. With a few days' help and training from a variety of women healers, none of which had charged a fee, and with my own active experimentation, work and continued learning, I took back my power-within and took control of my own health. I am not neurotic or psychotic, and know that I never was. I am strong and whole. I went back to Michigan the next year to teach what I had learned to other women, became a priestess of the goddess craft, and three years later began this book.

Since the loss of the women healers in the witch burnings, male medicine has learned science mechanistically, without women's sensitivity or healing skills and without input from the wide realm of the psychic. Little degree of personal caring or respect for the patient and her needs remains. High tech medicine works to defeat nature, rather than to cooperate with it, replacing natural organs with plastic ones or with organs belonging to someone else, or cutting out non-crucial organs completely. High tech interest in birth puts conception in a test tube and searches for total doctor control of delivery. In routine daily medicine, women are seen as patients but are seldom heard. They are given little or no understanding of or participation in their care, and often not informed of consequences, risks or choices when a doctor chooses treatment. The abuses extend to men, but since women are patients more often than men, women are more often medicine's victims. In women's and psychic healing, the patient heals herself from the cell and aura level, cooperating with a healer and with her own goddess-within.

In male medicine, there is little or no re-cognition of woman (or man) as a unified combination of body, emotions, mind and spirit, or that treating dis-ease means treating the whole person on all of her levels. Given this world view physically, a woman judged "sick" in her body is given drugs for her symptoms, not their underlying causes, or the offending (usually female) organs are cut out. If she is judged "sick" in her mind or is old or poor, is lesbian, Hispanic, Black or disabled, she is dismissed with tranquilizers to keep her quiet or hospitalization to "put her away" or out of sight. None of these are true in women's healing, a system based on personal caring between individuals. A woman with a physical illness is taught to look for and heal its causes, while relieving symptoms and pain. A woman with emotional discomfort is shown her own power and invited to take that power-within to make of her life what she wills. In patriarchal medicine, a woman who is psychic—and everyone has that potential—is seen as mentally "sick"; in women's healing, she is trained to her full capacities, and is honored. In patriarchal medicine, the reasons for a woman's dis-ease may never be dis-covered; in women's healing, knowing the reason is part of the healing, and the patient dis-covers or re-cognizes it for herself.

Women healers today attempt to return power and power-within, goddess-within, to women and to men. An outgrowth of feminism and the radical women's movement, of the New Age and women's spirituality, women re-search and re-claim the ancient caring methods, including psychic methods. They combine these things with allopathic medicine and goddess matriarchal pride to heal and prevent dis-ease from its source. The emphasis is on Be-ing and wholeness, the quality of life, caring, active choice and total participation, natural law and the interconnectedness of body, emotion, mind and spirit. The focus is on learning and understanding, then on teaching others freely.

In thealogian Sally Gearhart's philosophy, re-claiming women's healing is a re-sourcement. "To re-source is to find another source, an entirely different and prior one, a source deeper than the patriarchy."* It's a new way of seeing and utilizing energy to work for and with women instead of against them, and women's healing methods of laying on of hands, psychic healing, crystal and gemstone work, auras, visualization and meditation are new/old ways of seeing literally and figuratively. Re-sourcement is a re-valuation of things lost or

*Sally Gearhart, "Womanpower: Energy Re-Sourcement," in Charlene Spretnak, Ed., *The Politics of Women's Spirituality* (New York, Anchor/Doubleday Books, 1982), p. 195.

repressed in women's culture, the "women's work" skills so long denigrated by patriarchal men, the life-giving, nurturing, caring and sharing roles without which women or men could not survive. That source of energy and strength begins with the self, the individual, with women's power-within. It becomes inter-personal between women. Going within to goddess-within, to power-within, to re-claiming individual strength and self-determination leads outward eventually; women healing themselves begin to heal others and the Earth. Attunement to the self leads to attunement with others, leads to attunement with the universe/goddess/Earth, and attunement means health and well-being. This is

> a source or kind of power qualitatively different from the one we have been taught to accept or operate with; . . . the development of that source and the allowing of it to reach full dimensions could mean the redemption of the entire globe from the devastation of (patriarchy).*

Re-sourcement is a re-turn to respect for the Earth and for women's bodies, for the life force and life herself, for women and the goddess. It's re-turning life to the planet, fighting apartheid, cleaning up the lakes, saving the whales and seals, refusing nuclear involvement and nuclear plant building. It's re-claiming the work and learning of lost women, naming and honoring women of the past and of today for their contributions to civilization and culture. It's re-turning to the goddess and the goddess-within, to power-within instead of power-over. Re-sourcement is a re-claiming, dis-covering and building-upon of the knowledge of pre-patriarchal and witch-midwife women healers, an adding to science in medicine rather than a denial of it. It's a re-turn to more humane values and methods in medicine and healing, to personal responsibility and participation of healer and healed, and to relationships of respect and caring of every sort. It's women working together to heal themselves, each other and the Earth.

Women's healing is a re-sourcement not only for women but for women's children and for men, for the planet as goddess Be-ing. Growing from feminism, the women's radical health movement and women's spirituality, women are becoming aware of their power-within to heal themselves and others, to create and sustain life including their own, to protect and heal the world. Women can accept this

---

*Ibid., p. 196.

power, the "women's work" re-sourcement and healing, or refuse it, and either choice has far-reaching consequences for the survival of life and the Earth. Women can say "no" to a patriarchy that destroys, and affirm instead a matriarchy that cherishes and heals. They can say "no" to war and nuclear waste, to oppression of peoples, to racism, sexism, ablism and poverty by taking back power-within and using it wisely and well. They can refuse ill health and mis-treatment and take well-being for themselves and for all. Women accepting re-sourcement accept the re-turn of goddess values, women's matri-archal values, women's Be-ing and freedom, healing and peace. The choice is here and now, clear and present. By learning and using the skills, sharing the skills and accepting and protecting women's power, women can be what women truly are—well and strong.

This book is a "no" to patriarchy and a "yes" to women and to goddess-within healthy men. It teaches some starting skills in the direction of peace of the women healers. Laying on of hands, psychic healing, aura and color work, visualization, the powers of crystals and gemstones are all things the woman healer knew before patriarchy and male medicine power-over. The journey of re-sourcement, of re-claiming and Be-ing, of power-within, are dis-coveries of goddess and goddess-within, of women, women's selves and well-being.

THIS EARTH
What She Is To Me

This earth is my sister; I love her daily grace, her silent daring, and how loved I am, *how we admire this strength in each other, all that we have lost, all that we have suffered, all that we know: we are stunned by this beauty,* and I do not forget: what she is to me, what I am to her.

Susan Griffin, *Woman and Nature: The Roaring Inside Her*
(San Francisco, Harper and Row Publishers, 1978), p. 219

CARING FOR OURSELVES

Healing is a journey within oneself to reunite body, mind and spirit. The life energy connected with all living things is channeled through one so as to release blocked energy. Exercise, fresh air, sunshine, healthy diet, adequate rest, free expression of emotions all open the passages.

Lee Lanning and Vernette Hart,
Ripening: An Almanac of Lesbian Lore and Vision
(Minneapolis, Word-Weavers, 1981), p. 127

When we give power, our energy, we are nurturing without limiting, caring without controlling. This is true of our relationships with each other, with nature, with the earth.

When we are in need, we are nurtured without being controlled, we are cared for without feeling powerless. We are cradled in plenty.

Lee Lanning and Vernette Hart,
Ripening: An Almanac of Lesbian Lore and Vision
(Minneapolis, Word-Weavers, 1981), p. 134

PART I

BASIC HEALING

Body, Emotion, Mind and Spirit: The Aura

WOMEN'S HEALING, like women's spirituality, is a connecting of the seen with the unseen, and women's sensitivity to the unseen, her psychic ability and knowledge, is healing's greatest hope today. Women's use of psychic sensitivity, of intuition or aura awareness, has been laughed at and repressed in Western patriarchy, but is recognized and respected in Native America, Africa, India, China and South America—many still matriarchal and goddess cultures. Women are re-claiming and re-sourcing the lost skills in the West that the witches knew, paying attention to inner knowledge and inner health. Like other "women's work," "women's intuition" has real things behind it, and is a wisdom for survival and well-being. Inner awareness, sensitivity, attunement, intuition are available to all and are women's keys to the goddess and goddess-within, to healing and to self-healing power-within. By connecting and making conscious the four parts of Be-ing, the physical, emotional, mental and spiritual, women use Be-ing and the aura to heal.

Surrounding a woman's dense physical body is her unseen body, the aura, composed of layers of energy. The physical self first has an energy-layer double, called the etheric body. Health begins here, is mirrored here, and this is where dis-ease manifests first, before it reaches the physical flesh. The emotional/astral body is the next aura layer, woman's feeling level, her connection between body

The Aura

and mind. Her mental body, the next layer beyond the emotional, has two aura levels, the lower and higher mental, or rational and intuitive thought. The spiritual body's three aura levels, the lower, middle and higher, are a woman's spirit or soul, her connection with the goddess and the universe. A woman's aura is composed of the four energy bodies, the physical/etheric, emotional, mental and spiritual, which are in turn seven layers or levels. More discussion on them follows. A "silver cord" of life energy connects the unseen bodies, and connects a woman to Be-ing and non-Being (life to death).

In simple examples of using the unseen bodies for healing, a woman holds an amethyst in her hand, and opening to its energies, she uses the stone and her powers of emotion and mind—her etheric, emotional and mental unseen bodies—to relax herself into sleep. Medicine calls this biofeedback. In another instance, she holds a crystal over an inflamed foot. She uses the crystal and laying on of hands, her own aura's etheric body, connects spiritually with the goddess and visualizes and wills the swelling and redness gone. The pain and inflammation disappear overnight. In the same way, she uses the energy of her hands (etheric body) and a crystal with another woman, and the woman's three-day headache goes away. She can do the work with only her body and aura—her physical hands and etheric double directed by her mind via emotions, and relaxed into spiritual level calm—or she can do it with her hands and gemstones using these aura levels as well. When working with another woman, both women's auras are affected. Medicine calls the results spontaneous remission or the placebo effect; it cannot explain it and dis-counts this, but the woman and the women together know that they did it themselves and how. Healing is using the unseen aura bodies, the energy bodies, to change conditions on the seen and earthly plane.

Male medicine and patriarchy fragment the parts of woman's Be-ing. They not only separate the seen from the unseen whole, but separate the physical self. One doctor treats the back and another the heart, a different one the uterus and ovaries. None treats the whole woman or re-cognizes her energy bodies, the unity of her whole Be-ing. The power-over system denies the non-physical, the non-scientifically measurable, the psychic and irrational, as it denies the female with her connection to these things. It refuses to acknowl-edge, derides and represses the emotions, mind and spirit in healing, and cuts itself off from studying or making use of them.

The earthly physical body is accepted as fact, is provable,

measurable and treatable, but is also seen in Judeo-Christian patriarchy as "evil," as something to be punished or dominated with
force. Medicine to this day holds this attitude. The aura's physical
body/etheric double bond is not recognized. Its emotional/astral
level is not considered. The mind and mental body is downgraded to
physical brain, and the spirit is left to male religions that fail to satisfy
or fulfill it. Science denies and ignores the teachings of thousands of
mystics, psychics and healers across all cultures and times. In addition it denies women's inherent aura intuition and even the Bible,
both of which describe the aura and four bodies. It also denies the
"silver cord," the life thread that connects the four bodies to earthly
flesh and existence. By doing so, male medicine loses valuable re-
sources and treats dis-ease in only a fraction of the patient, on her
earthly flesh plane only. Its "cures" are partial and ineffective, are
traumatic and drastic—and could be much better and easier.

A woman with insomnia, for example, is given barbituates to
deactivate portions of her brain. She comes to depend on them, can
no longer put herself to sleep alone, but needs the pills to do it for her.
A woman with an inflamed foot is given drugs to kill the infection,
instead of using her own aura and bodies to remove it herself. The
"cure" takes more than a week, the cause of infection is not gone, and
the drugs leave her body resistant to them and without immunities. A
woman with a headache takes another aspirin, and her pain is gone
for four hours. She has had it for three days and it returns.

Women's healing is psychic healing; it includes a woman's physical body, her etheric double, her unseen emotions, mind and spirit. It
includes her will and her whole Be-ing. The skills of visualization,
meditation, psychic healing, crystals and gemstones bring the
unseen to affect the physical, and bring the invisible energies into
conscious reach of solid mass. The methods work with free will, with the
goddess and natural law, with the aura, the dense physical body and
power-within, to achieve cell-source healing in harmony with all the
levels. It works where male medicine often fails because it connects the
four planes of existence: the body, emotions, mind and spirit; connects
the seen and unseen, the mass and energy levels of the life force.

A woman's energy aura is an electrical forcefield, the easily felt but
usually unseen energy that envelopes the earthly physical body. It contains seven mirror layers or energy ring levels, and these make up the
four bodies. Each of the aura layers has in turn seven levels of its own for
a total of forty-nine levels. The next chapter describes the seven major

chakra or energy centers located in the etheric double, the physical layer of the aura. There are also forty-nine total chakras, including smaller centers, and the seven major chakras correspond to the seven major aura layers. Only the major levels and chakras are fully considered in this book.

Of the seven major levels of the aura:

> The first ring reveals her state of health (etheric double), the second (astral or emotional body) her emotions, the third her intellectual makeup, the fourth her higher mind (both together are the mental body), . . . the fifth her spirit, or the link between the individual and the cosmos (spiritual body), and the sixth and seventh reveal cosmic aspects (also the spiritual body).[1]

The etheric double contains the chakras and is the level of psychic diagnosis and laying on of hands; the emotional or astral body is the one of changing colors that women who can see or sense auras are aware of, and healing requires emotion; the mental body is made up of two aura bands, the intellectual and intuitional levels, and is the place of creative visualization/mental healing; the spiritual body is three aura layers, the maiden/mother/crone aspects of the goddess, the highest of which is woman's connection with divinity and the universe. Women connect with the goddess and their spiritual bodies for healing through meditation states.

The mental and spiritual auras are the levels least likely seen by women who sense auras, but the ability to see or sense the physical aura/etheric body and the emotional/astral levels can be taught. The physical aura is usually sensed as a very thin bluish or clear line around the earthly body, above and below the etheric double, and is part of it. The etheric double is a reddish black, lined ribbon between layers of light. The emotional/astral body is the wider, color changing vibrant band that starts about four inches from the body and that varies with the woman's emotions and thought forms. Thought forms are transmitted by the lower mental body and can sometimes be seen as shooting colors or lights inside the emotional aura.

The visible, physical, *earthly flesh body* that the aura envelopes is dense, low-vibrating matter, and each of the unseen aura levels and aura bodies vibrates at a faster rate above it. The earthly dense body is the woman seen; it eats, breathes and talks, digests and eliminates, menstruates and experiences life by the earthly senses of sight, sound, touch, smell and taste.[2] Male medicine treats and works totally on this earth plane, on reactions that are measurable and empirical to science by cause and effect. It treats mass, where women's healing treats energy, and its expectations are based on norms and averages, rather than on the individual patient's responses, chemistries or astral dimensions. Acting on the lowest energy vibration, it is the crudest level for healing effectiveness, the site of surgeries and drugs. The earthly dense body is the only reality that male medicine accepts, and a partial one, until science dis-covers the aura that's always been there.

The newest theories of physics and body chemistry have some interesting ideas on the seen body's makeup, theories that scientifically verify what psychics and healers have said for thousands of years but doctors still laugh at, and that give scientific credence to the aura levels. Dr. W. J. Kilner's chemical screens made the etheric double visible to anyone and a tool for diagnosis as early as 1911, and Kirlian photography makes visible the auras surrounding people and animals, plants, crystals, and inanimate objects. The science of x-ray crystallography is a growing specialty, pioneered by woman scientist Rosalind Franklin in the 1950's.

Quantum physics' dis-coveries of the structures of the atom posit great empty spaces between atoms and atom parts, which are energy field (aura) areas. Even the densest matter is composed mostly of empty space. In the explanation of healer/science writer George Meek, the solid portions (mass) of the human body are composed of 75-80 percent water, and the distance between atoms in that very solid matter/flesh makes the body 99+ percent void! The example is that if an atom in the body were the size of an apple, the next closest atom to it would be 1,000-2,000 miles away.[3] The idea of this is that solid human flesh on the earth plane is composed mostly of energy, of the spaces between atoms, and healers cross-culturally know that energy is what composes the four bodies and the aura, and is what they use to heal with. Medicine treats the little bit of solid matter that exists.

Another scientific theory that dis-covers healing is the composition of the water molecules that make up most of the earthly seen body. The body is mostly water, and water is an unstable compound of hydrogen and oxygen that is changeable to almost any form of energy. Healing energy in laying on of hands and in crystals and gemstones is an energy that can transform water's bonding structure and change growth in the body's enzymes,[4] thereby explaining the change from dis-ease to health. Sister Justa Smith in Buffalo, with several other American scientists and many more outside the United States are working to measure and document these changes. A healer using laying on of hands creates changes in the unseen energy bodies of the aura, and also changes in the earthly "solid" material flesh by changing its water composition and the energy balance between atoms. More on crystals' part in this and laying on of hands later.

A third interesting theory scientifically verifying the work of healers is the new knowledge of cell intercommunication and rapid changeover. "Most of the 60,000,000,000,000 cells of the physical body . . . are linked by a highly perfected communications system,"[5] and cells are generators of living energy and DNA. A single cell from any body part can be used in cloning an entire new organism; this is fact and not science fiction. Each cell contains the full blueprint of the individual. Cells die and are replaced by new cells at a rate of 5,700,000 per second. Protein, the major body component after water, is also being replaced continuously, the matter of the lungs, brain, bone, skin, muscles, in varying amounts of time from days to months.

> Only the *design* of our bodies, changing slightly with the passing years, remains constant . . . If the healer and the patient can help these new cells to be born in a state of health and perfection, rather than as a facsimile of the diseased and ailing cells which died, then the body is on its way back to health.[6]

The seen human body is totally new every six months by these cell changes and replacements, and each cell is an aware microcosm of the whole body mass. Changing the information of the cell from dis-eased to healthy, by healing energy of laying on of hands, by creative visualization and thought forms, by the energies of crystals and gemstones, brings dis-ease back to well-being rapidly, far more rapidly and thoroughly than the trauma of surgical recovery or drugs. Dis-ease is written out of the actual cell-source blueprint by women's healing methods, and allopathic medicine is failing its patients by not investigating and making use of it. The cell theory is one known to Eastern healers since before Christianity and Judaism, and before Christianity and Judaism were the goddess matriarchies of women's healing.

The *etheric double* is the unseen mirror of the earthly physical body, its next dimension. It's the first level, the life force band of a woman's aura, and interpenetrates the earthly dense body. Also called the physical aura, health aura or bioplasmic level, its purpose is to maintain life by distributing energy, and to connect the earthly body to the astral/emotional plane.[7] The chakras are located in this level (discussed more thoroughly in the next chapter), and the etheric double is responsible for the intake and use of prana (vitality and the life force), the energy sent and utilized in crystal work and laying on of hands. Changes made in the etheric double or the chakras by creative visualization, gemstones or absent healing work can remove dis-ease, reprogram the etheric body and transmit the changes to the dense earth level, to the cells and organs. Like the root chakra that this aura band has correspondence with, its color is black or red, its circle direction is north, and its element is earth.[8] Beginning gemstones for this level are garnet and black tourmaline.

A woman sees her own etheric double. She sits skyclad on a dark rug floor, candles lit on her altar, no other light in the quiet nighttime room. She breathes deeply and rhythmically and relaxes her physical body step by step, holding a crystal in her left hand to help. Casting a circle if she wishes or inviting the goddess' presence, she asks to see. Looking at her leg or arm lit against the dark background, she clears her mind and holds her eyes steady on one spot. If she wears eyeglasses, she takes them off, allowing her physical vision to unfocus and her third eye, her aura vision, to open. Slowly and elusively the aura appears. When she blinks it wavers but returns; she does not move her eyes.

The woman sees a very thin line of light at the edges of her skin and following her body's contours. The line is a quarter inch or less wide,* and connected to it and above it is another line, a flat red/black band. The dark band has lines or striations through it and is the texture of grosgrain ribbon. The ribbon is her etheric double, following the contours of her body and the thin line of light between it and her skin. It is a half to one inch wide. Above the etheric double is another band of light, wider this time, bluish, silver, rainbow-like or clear. In her quiet meditative state, the light band is one-half to two inches wide, or may be as wide as several inches. It's of even width all around her body, and shimmers, seeming to be there and not-there.

Healing takes place in the etheric double before it manifests in the earthly body, and dis-ease both manifested and pending is visible in the etheric double. W. J. Kilner's 1911 book, *The Aura,* was the first to scientifically observe both healthy and dis-eased physical auras in women, children and men. He used lenses coated with the chemical dyes dicyanin and carmine to make the etheric body visible.

Kilner recorded and described changes in the physical aura/

---

*This varies with the individual, her health, level of energy and with viewing conditions. Descriptions here are personal ones. Women of color may wish to experiment with neutral, rather than dark backgrounds.

etheric double, the differences of age, sex, health and condition. He could distinguish the difference between very early pregnancy and the impending onset of menstruation in women by changes in the aura shape and texture.[9] He could detect dis-ease before the patient "got sick," and the extent and duration of the coming or manifested illness. He noted the wider and more highly developed auras of healthy women as compared to healthy men, of girl children as compared to boys, and the ages at which a child's aura becomes an adolescent's and then an adult's. He noted the changes in the aura during pregnancy. He was able to make accurate diagnoses of specific illnesses, and to distinguish between physical and emotional dis-eases, all by observation of the patient and her aura through chemically coated lenses that made her etheric double visible. He noted that subjects, especially women, could cause changes in their physical auras by willing them to happen, and that "auric force" from one person could be sent or willed to give another vitality (prana or healing). This is the principle of laying on of hands and psychic healing, and crystals and gemstones focus and amplify the energy. Kilner's work with complementary colors is also used by woman healers today in color work and chakra balancing, and with colored gemstones. Though the book's illustrations and descriptions are not as clear as they might be, the work is important and bears modern study.

Kilner was not a psychic and had medicine's distrust for psychic phenomena, but he made the unseen etheric double visible for measurement. He died in total disgrace and discredit for his pioneering work that male medicine refused to take seriously, work that verified to science what healers have known and seen for centuries. A great many of the patients who helped and participated in Kilner's experiments were women, and it was healers and psychics after his death who dis-covered and validated his findings. Annie Besant and Helen Blavatsky were two contemporary psychics working from the side of the unseen who did work in the etheric double and the aura. Their work and Kilner's was germinal, but of course science took no notice of it. Kilner attempted to bring scientific methods to psychic healing, something not tried again until recently, and something that needs to be done more.

The etheric double is crucial in women's healing and crystal/gemstone work for several reasons, one of which is the chakras, the body's major energy centers that are located at this level. Along with the chakras are the nadis and meridians, the nerve ending centers used in acupuncture and acupressure techniques. Significant emphasis in healing is placed on clearing and balancing the chakras and meridians for a free flow of energy and use of prana. The etheric double takes in, stores and distributes prana through the chakras and meridians, and the chakras are the immune system of the body to dis-ease. Prana is the vital force, the "rays" sent in laying on of hands, and therefore much healing is both sent and received from the etheric double. Kundalini energy, the serpent fire goddess Shakti, is also located at this level. Each body of the aura is a connective link to the levels below and above it, and the etheric double is the bridge between the physical dense body and the astral plane, between mass and energy. Death in simple definition is the stopping of the etheric double, the life force level of the aura.

The *emotional/astral body* is the second aura layer or ring, its color orange and corresponding to the belly chakra, its circle direction west and its element water.[10] Beginning gemstones are carnelian and orange/red coral. This is the body of feeling, emotion, desire and passion—the subconscious level. The emotional body of woman's aura is the half to two-foot light band beyond the etheric double and the one usually visible to women who see or sense auras. Its colors change with emotional changes and are connected to thoughts, but are not the thought-form patterns of the mental body that come next. While the emotional rainbow shifts and changes, there is usually a predominant color or two colors that are individual for each woman, and the colors that appear in the emotional body have a universal key. They are the colors used in healing and color work, are the chakra colors, and are major guidelines in choosing a stone for gemstone healing. Though the corresponding color for this body is orange, the emotional aura expresses all the colors of the chakra spectrum.

Recent popular appeal of the rainbow in art and greeting cards is a reflection of the universal colors of the emotional aura body. The colors are the basic spectrum, short (red) to long (violet) light rays in the order of red, orange, yellow, green, blue, indigo and violet. All of these colors mixed together as light are white light; all of them mixed together as pigment are black. The clarity and refinement of the color in the emotional aura, or the color sent in healing, is the degree of refinement and development in the woman seen, or in the healing effects sent.

From the work of Annie Besant, C.W. Leadbeater and S.G.J. Ouseley: clear red in the emotional aura is affection, life, passion and love; rose tones are higher and unselfish love, universal love or healthy self-love. Clear orange is good health, pride and ambition, the color found in outgoing, tactful people with leadership qualities. Clear yellow denotes intellect, intelligence and reason, cheer and optimism. Clear green in the emotional body is sympathy and adaptability, success, prosperity, individualism and independence. The lighter blues and blue/greens are women of devotion and inspiration, loyalty, self-reliance and self-confidence; light blue is associated with the goddess and the moon. Clear indigo, a darker blue, is spirituality and integrity, creativity, inspiration and idealism. Clear violet is the highly developed color of priestesses and indicates transcendence, higher spirituality, oneness, affection, devotion, true greatness and wisdom. Colors less than clear denote less positive characteristics: greys for depression and fear, green/greys for deceit and jealousy, lurid dark reds for anger, and heavy yellows for selfishness. Stronger colored shades indicate stronger emotions. When used in healing, only clear and vibrant color tones are sent.[11]

Gemstones carrying a particular color carry that color's attributes, while clear crystal can be programmed for any color as it contains all of them. Examples of gemstones for the aura color attributes are: red, ruby; orange, carnelian; yellow, amber or topaz; green, jade or peridot; blue, lapis lazuli; indigo, sapphire; and violet, amethyst. The all colors of light that are white light are found in clear quartz crystal, and the all colors of pigment that are black are found in black tourmaline or black onyx.

In the higher spectrum ranges, from blue through violet, the colors and attributes blend into each other, and this is also true though less so for the lower ranges. The spectrum colors of the emotional/astral body correspond to the seven aura levels and to the colors of the seven major chakras. Much more will be said about them in every aspect of healing. To *will* a particular color into the emotional body, or to use a colored gemstone, is to cause mood and attitude changes in the self or others that greatly affect health and well-being.

Many women sense the emotional aura and its colors without physically seeing them, and the skill can be trained to both sense and sight. The moods and attributes of the emotional/astral body are the messages of "women's intuition," realized as colors or not. They create first impressions that are usually accurate when not analyzed, but are discounted by male science as "irrational." Tuning into these impressions and color values, becoming aware of and noticing them, is to stimulate psychic development.

To see the emotional aura visually, have a woman sit or stand still in front of a white background, light coming from in front of her. The softness of candle light is a good light source. The woman wishing to see sits a few feet away, and puts herself in a meditative state by deep breathing and body relaxation, as in observing the etheric double. She casts a circle if she chooses to, perhaps holds a crystal or moonstone in her left hand to stimulate her third eye, and asks to see auras. Staring steadily at the forehead/third eye of the woman being seen, she allows her physical eyes to unfocus and her third eye to open, her brow chakra and middle spiritual aura layer. If she wears eyeglasses she removes them, since this vision is not physical sight. The aura first appears as clear light, shimmering and moving faintly, usually a glow around the head. It appears as a dim haze, then it brightens. Colors, or a personality predominating single color, appear after longer watching, and after willing it to happen or asking for it. When the woman blinks, the colors or light wavers but does not disappear, as long as both women hold the meditative state and keep still physically.[12] Workshops with Kay Gardner are wonderful for learning to see auras, and also to connect colors to musical tones. Many children see auras naturally, believing that everyone does, until they're told otherwise or laughed at. The skill is then repressed or lost, and has to be relearned. Experiencing auras non-visually is discussed later.

A personal experience: relaxed in the audience at a women's music concert I saw clear light auras of up to a foot high appear around the working musicians' heads. The group was a five-piece women's band, standing on a stage with a light background. In the audience I began deep breathing, unfocusing my eyes, holding my vision steady on the cloud of light around one of the performers. Color came slowly when asked for, first sensed and then seen, a lovely blue/green.

I appreciated and thanked them, then moved my vision to another band member, until rose-colored light appeared around her when asked for. I appreciated and thanked the rose and the woman wearing it, then moved my attention to another musician, a woman surrounded by silvery blue light. Another band member had a golden yellow halo. The color around the head and shoulders of the group's vocalist was a wonderful violet. I appreciated and thanked each color, each woman in turn for the gift that came with their music.

As I watched the entire stage again, the colors remained with each performer, but dimmed slightly, surrounding the head, shoulders and upper body of each. Meeting the group after the concert, I made warm friends with them, but was too shy to tell them what I saw. Ever since when thinking of the women's band, I see them as a rainbow, and thinking of each member, see her particular color while hearing her individual sound.

The emotional/astral body is one of the more beautiful wonders of women's Be-ing. In its function as a bridge between bodies it connects the conscious mental level above it to the etheric double below it, and connects the body to the mind. Since the body cannot be healthy unless the emotions are, and since the thought forms of the mental body have great effect on emotional well-being, the inter-relatedness of the body's four levels and their effects on each other begin to be apparent. Color and gemstone work are most powerful on the emotional body's subconscious level and are important elements in women's healing. The colors transmit downward from the emotional body to the etheric double and then to the earthly physical level. They transmit upward from the emotional body to the mental.

Next is the *mental body*, composed of two aura bands, and divided into the intellectual and intuitive aspects, the conscious and super-conscious. The lower mental body is the rational, intellectual, thinking mind, corresponding with the color yellow, the solar plexus chakra. Two of its stones are amber and topaz, its element is fire and circle direction south. The higher mental body is the imaginative and intuitive superconscious mind, the higher self or causal body, corresponding with the heart chakra, with the colors green or rose, the element air, and circle direction east.[13] Some stones for this level are aventurine, jade and rose quartz. A.E. Powell defines the difference between the layers as the difference between form-thoughts and formless thoughts, the concrete and abstract.[14] The lower mental body creates thought forms that women who see or sense auras may perceive along with the single colors in the astral/emotional body.

Two major healing ideas are connected with the mental body: that the mind is not the brain, and that thoughts and attitudes are crucial to well-being and health. To start with the second of these, thoughts and emotions together (two bodies), are what Theosophists call the kama-manas (desire-mind), and create much of the atmosphere for health or dis-ease. The kama-manas can be consciously programmed. To put it in modern terms, negative thoughts or the mental/emotional image of illness brings illness, and positive thoughts or the mental/emotional image of health and well-being bring health and well-being. Thought-form healing involves both bodies, plus both levels of the mental body.

"Thoughts are things," and the things that thoughts are, (both concrete and abstract), are tools for healing.[15] Telepathy and empathy skills are begun in the higher mental body and are used in psychic healing, as are dreams and the self-or-others healing of creative visualization and meditation in the lower mental body.[16] Creative visualization is the conscious, planned impressioning (programming) of the emotional body with an idea to be transmitted above it to the mind and below it to the physical level. Chosen thoughts are transmitted from mental to emotional levels, through the etheric double, and into the dense physical body to cause healing changes. Like other forms of healing and self-healing in this book, creative visualization is a learning skill, a part of women's power-within for creating or re-gaining women's health. Affirmation or creative visualization is the process of self-healing, and is the absent or "psychic" healing used with others not present. Just as the etheric double is the energy level for laying on of hands, and the emotional body is the place of color healing, so creative visualization and psychic healing occur in the two levels of the mental body. Their effects in the mental body are linked inextricably with the emotional/astral subconscious level, with the kama-manas.

The difference between the mind and physical brain is the other relevant idea here, and the mental body is not the physical mass of the body-part brain. The brain does not heal or cause dis-ease, the mind does. The human brain is composed of 80 percent water, ten or twelve ounces of the loose chemical H_2O bonding. Male scientific medicine and psychiatry have not located in that brain any exact cell, section or place that is the actual mind, the place of rational or non-rational thought.[17] Yet the non-medical healers that science scorns, healers of all cultures from the Navaho and Hopi to Hawaiian Huna, from Egypt and Africa to Tibet and the women healers, have used the levels of the mind and emotions to heal the body for untold centuries. Hawaiian Huna's use of the mind in healing puts Western psychiatry and medicine to shame.

If the mind is not the brain, then what is it? The earlier idea of matter and energy, the space between atoms, is part of the explanation, the seen and unseen. If the brain is composed of energy spaces between atoms of mass, then the mind or the mental body is the unseen energy force that directs the cells of the physical dense brain. The four unseen bodies are energy levels, moving at increasingly faster vibration rates. Thought is energy (as are the four bodies), and what energy is follows individual belief. Science calls it simply "energy"; some call it the self or higher self, others call it soul or spirit, god or goddess, life or Be-ing. Thought is the process that determines a species' level of development—"I think, therefore I am"—and thought is not dissectible in physical mass.

The mind channels thoughts to the physical brain through the emotional subconscious and the etheric double, and channels health and well-being (or dis-ease and illness) by way of thoughts and thought forms. If 70 percent of all dis-ease is mind-related and science agrees to this, then mind-related healing is what's needed for it—but mind depends on emotion, too. Healers everywhere recognize that the *desire* to be well is required before a woman *is* well, and also that she have the emotional belief that wellness is possible. Desire and thought, kama-manas, the subconscious, conscious and super-conscious are inextricably linked, the emotional and mental bodies bearing force on the etheric double and the earthly dense physical. All dis-ease originates in the mind (mental body), and all healing and healing processes originate there, but healing does not happen there alone.[18] Thought forms are powerful "things" used in healing, the rational and imaginative mind to eliminate dis-ease, with spectacular results that male medicine cannot explain and refuses to make use of—since male medicine refuses the unseen.

Annie Besant and C.W. Leadbeater's book *Thought Forms* is a metaphysical classic filled with color plates and psychics' attempts to describe the thought patterns of the mental body to artists. There are strange and familiar shapes, geometrics, streaks, cones, flowers and projectiles in the rainbow colors discussed in the emotional body section. Positive thought forms are beautiful things, while negative ones are not. Thoughts affect the self and others at conscious and nonconscious levels, and are energy vibrations that affect the emotional body below them. The emotional body that they affect in turn affects the etheric double and the physical dense body, the brain.

To describe an experience of seeing thought forms: Kay Gardner's emotional aura, a glow of silver/white light around her head and shoulders as she demonstrated music and healing in a workshop, flashed suddenly and amazingly with rose and yellow rapidly moving projectiles. She was performing "Awakening," her flute composition for the solar plexus chakra from A Rainbow Path. The process of seeing thought forms is the same as for seeing the emotional aura, but results come less often and less easily. As in other manifestations of aura, the colors and vision were breathtaking, were reflections of the woman-within. W.J. Kilner experimented with these through his chemical screens, and in Besant and Leadbeater's words also on the subject,

> The mental body is an object of great beauty, the delicacy and rapid motion of its particles giving it an aspect of iridescent light, and this beauty becomes an extraordinarily radiant and entrancing loveliness as the intellect becomes more highly evolved . . . [19]

These same thought forms, the energy bodies of the two-level mind/mental body, are used in healing and preventing dis-ease. Along with the emotional level colors, they are used to transmit mood changes and optimism, full and glowing health through creative visualization. The process changes attitudes, emotions, actions and health. Use of creative visualization is a basic skill of the goddess and women's spirituality. Since each aura body transmits impressions to the body above and below it, is a bridge between two bodies, changes in the mind filter down through the emotions and chakras, influencing and changing them, and eventually reach the material physical level— the woman's outward health. Thought forms used wisely change dis-ease to well-being, prevent well-being from submitting to dis-ease. The power of planned positive thinking is no joke, is a healing skill to utilize. Thought forms can be used to heal even cancer, (or better yet to prevent it), if the patient has the desire and optimism to do so:

> the patient's own psychosomatic process in a positive mode can be utilized to restore the healthy condition which that same process in a negative mode was previously destroying.[20]

By choice, desire, positive thinking and power-within, a woman heals herself through thought forms, kama-manas, and the mental body/ mind. This is psychic or mental healing.

The last of the four unseen bodies, the highest vibrating energy level, is the spiritual body, composed of three aura layers. Because of its rapid vibration rate, this body is not often perceived visually, but is felt in experiences of oneness and transcendence. The level as a whole corresponds in the circle to aether or spirit,[21] the transformative cauldron of the center. It's the place for will, inner knowing and higher understanding, for experiencing interconnectedness with others and with all that lives, for experiencing the goddess.

The lowest spiritual body level, linked with the will, corresponds to the throat chakra and the color light blue. It's the center for communication, creativity and self-understanding, and one of its gemstones, lapis lazuli, is a lower spiritual level gemstone. On the middle spiritual plane is the brow chakra, place of clairvoyance and psychic sight, instant and intuitive higher knowing, connection and oneness with others. Its color is indigo, and blue sapphire is a corresponding gemstone. The highest spiritual aura band is the fastest vibrating of all, and is woman's connection to the goddess/universe, to Be-ing. In the Hopi world view, this center that corresponds to the crown chakra is the fine thread of life that connects the individual to the goddess. The Hopi concept of *kopavi* compares to the silver cord, the thread of life in Eastern metaphysics that connects the four bodies to each other and the dense physical, and is severed at death. The silver cord becomes visible in astral projection work (through the emotional/astral body), and is a part of the life concept in cultures worldwide. It is equivalent to the African concept of *sekpoli,* is the Eastern lotus, and is developed in the Theosophical concept of the three outpourings.

The highest spiritual layer corresponds with the color violet, or in some systems, white with a gold center; a healing stone for it is amethyst. Where the middle spiritual level's circle direction is below or the planet, the connectedness with others and the Earth, the higher spiritual's direction is above or the universe, the connection with the goddess. In casting the circle, these are recognized and honored by saluting the Earth and the sky before invoking the other directions. They are Mother Earth and Father Sky in some Native American traditions. The three aura bands of the spiritual body are the realm of the soul or spirit, the highest abstraction of the unseen.

Theosophical philosophy corresponds the three levels of the spiritual aura to the three-part divinity/goddess and three "outpourings" or "life waves" of creation. The first aspect manifests on the higher spiritual level, the second on the middle spiritual level, and the third on the lower spiritual body or aura.[22] The three parts are not separable from the oneness of the goddess, but are parts of her, and are the Maiden, Mother and Crone (or in patriarchy's version, the

Father, Son and Holy Spirit). The three levels of the spiritual body, of the spirit or soul, correspond to the three levels of divinity/goddess. They are a description of the goddess-within, since the goddess or creative energy, the life force, is part of each of the three spiritual levels of woman's Be-ing.

In the three outpourings, life force/creation/goddess travel from the goddess/source through all the four bodies and to all the levels of individual and universal Be-ing. The first and second outpourings endow life to all, from crystals to women, before returning to the goddess. The third outpouring is pure light/goddess/energy, touching spiritual essence but not touching matter.[23] The three outpourings are the energy that brings life to all the four bodies and to the seen earthy plane. They are the energy spaces between atoms in quantum theory. The spiritual body of the aura and Be-ing is goddess creation in all forms, and is women's oneness with that creative force.

The spiritual body is the channel of Be-ing and energy, and with connection to it woman's health has peace and well-being, a sense of purpose and rightness in her life. The channel of the goddess and the three outpourings are the channel of inner nourishment and without it dis-ease filters down through the bodies to the earthly level.[24] The name of divinity doesn't matter. The woman may call it goddess or god, Isis, Mary, Mawu, Great Mother or Christ, call it energy, her higher self or the Intelligence of the Universe. The principle is important, not the name. When she calls upon it for healing, attunes with it to heal herself or to channel healing to others, she receives and transmits the goddess through her spiritual body and is rarely denied. Able to make contact with spiritual essence/goddess/healing, she channels it from the spiritual to mental levels, from the mental to emotional body, from the emotional/astral to etheric double, and from the etheric double to dense physical matter. She does this in herself and in whomever she heals. The healing takes place level by level, healing each body in turn.

George Meek comments on the child-simple spirituality, the oneness with god or goddess, that he finds among all great healers crossing religious denominations and countries, and that same quality that often exists in patients who are healed successfully by them. The qualities of "empathy, harmony, unselfishness, devotion, tenderness, consecration, kindness, love and compassion" are evident in the men and women healers he works with.[25] They are all spiritual level qualities, oneness of self with others and the goddess, power-within, and are also "women's work" attributes of caring, mothering, nurturing and loving. The connection with goddess/spirituality/the spiritual body, the feeling of transcendent oneness with the world and universe, is a major energy force in women's healing.

The major way for connecting with this experience of oneness, with the spiritual body as a channel for oneness and healing, has been known to all esoteric cultures and is called meditation.[26] An aspect of creative visualization, meditation as the experience of oneness is a starting point for every healing technique known. Other terms for it are attunement, deep relaxation, trance, alpha states or altered states of consciousness, and it's the basis for circle work or magick in women's spirituality as well.

Meditation is easily learned with perseverance, and does not mean giving up free will. It's a self-controlled means of connecting the four bodies. Science in studying sleep and dreams has learned to measure meditation states by electro-encephalograph. Meditation changes the frequency of brain wave vibrations, of thought patterns/ thought forms, from the rational awake beta to the meditative high power alpha levels. Alpha or meditation states are the states of con- sciousness that healers work in. With the brain in the alpha state, the mind is susceptible to positive suggestion (creative visualization), and this is the state that connects the four bodies for impression of healing sent or received.[27] Women who are healers learn to use their spiritual bodies to enter this plane of awareness, and healing causes alpha state changes in those being healed by them as well. The spiritual level skill of reaching oneness with others and with the goddess, materially measured as alpha states and attained by meditation, is a key to all women's healing. As with the other bodies, changes made from the spiritual filter down through each of the energy levels to the mass earthly physical, and women's healing works to connect the four bodies to the physical plane with positive growth and changes.

The seen is dependent upon the unseen, as is described in this chapter, and earthly physical health or dis-ease is affected by far more than the physical mass of the body. Woman's body is both mass and energy, and in healing, both mass and energy are brought into focus and balance. Where patriarchal medicine treats only the mass, the earthly physical dense body, it ignores the rest of Be-ing. Women's healing re-cognizes the importance of the unseen levels, of the etheric double, emotional/astral, dual mental and triple spiritual bodies in preventing dis-ease or in healing all of Be-ing through its own energy. The connection of the four energy bodies with each other and with physical mass is the goal of women's healing techniques, of all non-allopathic healing since the matriarchies. Its methods recognize more than the seen, and re-cognize that healing takes place on all four levels before well-being on Earth manifests.

Women healers reach the four unseen bodies to affect the seen physical by laying on of hands, crystals and gemstones, color work, creative visualization, meditation and psychic healing. The methods are inter-related, as all of oneness with the goddess is inter-related. An understanding of the energy aura, the four bodies and the chakras is essential to an understanding of how healing works.

THE AURA AND FOUR BODIES[28]

Aura Layer	Body	Attribute	Healing Area	Chakra	Color/Stone	Direction
1. Dense Body and Physical Aura/ Etheric Double	Physical	Life	Laying on of Hands	Root	Red/Black Garnet/Black Tourmaline	North/ Earth
2. Emotional/Astral	Emotional	Feeling/Desire (Subconscious)	Color Work	Belly	Orange Carnelian/ Orange Coral	West/ Water
3. Lower Mental	Mental	Intellect (Conscious)	Creative Visualization	Solar Plexus	Yellow Amber/Topaz	South/ Fire
4. Higher Mental	Mental	Intuition (Superconscious)	Creative Visualization	Heart	Green/Rose Jade/Peridot/ Rose Quartz	East/Air
5. Lower Spiritual	Spiritual	Will The Crone	Psychic Healing	Throat	Blue Lapis Lazuli	Center/ Spirit
6. Middle Spiritual	Spiritual	Oneness with Others The Mother	Meditation	Brow	Indigo Blue Sapphire	Below/ Planet
7. Higher Spiritual	Spiritual	Kopavi/Oneness with Goddess The Maiden	Meditation	Crown	Violet/Purple Amethyst	Above/ Universe

FOOTNOTES

1. Diane Mariechild, *Mother Wit: A Feminist Guide to Psychic Development* (Trumansburg, NY, The Crossing Press, 1981), p. 37.

2. Keith Sherwood, *The Art of Spiritual Healing* (St. Paul, Llewellyn Publications, 1985), p. 20. For full book treatments on the four bodies, see A.E. Powell, *The Etheric Double, The Astral Body, The Mental Body, The Causal Body and the Ego* (Wheaton, IL, Quest/Theosophical Publishing House, 1978-84, originals 1925-27).

3. George W. Meek, *Healers and the Healing Process* (Wheaton, IL, Quest/Theosophical Publishing House, 1977), p. 196-197.

4. *Ibid.,* This is a mind-blowing book.

5. *Ibid.,* p. 195-196.

6. *Ibid.,* p. 196. For a wonderful science fiction/fantasy treatment of this subject, see Madeleine L'Engle, *The Wind in the Door* (New York, Dell Publishing Co., 1973).

7. A.E. Powell, *The Etheric Body, The Health Aura of Man* (Wheaton, IL, Quest/Theosophical Publishing House, 1983, original 1925). The passage quotes the work of woman healer/psychic Annie Besant.

8. A.E. Powell, *The Mental Body* (Wheaton, IL, Quest/Theosophical Publishing House, 1984, original 1927), p. 221.

9. W.J. Kilner, *The Aura* (York Beach, ME, Samuel Weiser, Inc. 1984, original 1911), p. 291-304.

10. A.E. Powell, *The Mental Body,* p. 221.

11. Annie Besant and C.W. Leadbeater, *Thought Forms* (Wheaton, IL, Quest/Theosophical Publishing House, 1969, original 1901), p. 22-24. S.G.J. Ouseley, *The Science of the Aura* (Essex, England, L.N. Fowler and Co., Inc., 1982, original, 1949), p. 19-29.

12. Diane Mariechild, *Mother Wit,* p. 38-39.

13. A.E. Powell, *The Mental Body,* p. 221. Colors here follow the systems of Ouseley and Kay Gardner. There are several color systems for the chakras and bodies to choose from.

14. *Ibid.,* p. 1. Much of Powell's work on thought and thought forms is based on the work of Annie Besant.

15. Annie Besant and C.W. Leadbeater, *Thought Forms,* p. 6.

16. Chapter IV is on creative visualization, meditation and colors. See also Diane Stein, *The Women's Spirituality Book,* Chapter VI.

17. George W. Meek, *Healers and the Healing Process,* p. 197.

18. *Ibid.,* and Keith Sherwood, *The Art of Spiritual Healing,* p. 23.

19. Annie Besant and C.W. Leadbeater, *Thought Forms,* p. 8.

20. George W. Meek, *Healers and the Healing Process,* p. 160.

21. A.E. Powell, *The Mental Body,* p. 221.

22. C.W. Leadbeater, *Man Visible and Invisible* (Wheaton, IL, Quest/ Theosophical Publishing House, 1980, original 1925), p. 21-27. He credits Helen Blavatsky for her work here.

23. A.E. Powell, *The Causal Body and the Ego* (Wheaton, IL, Quest/ Theosophical Publishing House, 1978, original 1928), p. 70-71.

24. Keith Sherwood, *The Art of Spiritual Healing,* p. 24.

25. George W. Meek, *Healers and the Healing Process,* p. 226.

26. More on meditation in Chapter Three. Also see Diane Stein, *The Women's Spirituality Book,* Chapter VI.

27. Keith Sherwood, *The Art of Spiritual Healing,* p. 38-43.

28. A.E. Powell, *The Mental Body* (Wheaton, IL, Quest/Theosophical Publishing House, 1984, original 1927), p. 221; S.G.J. Ouseley, *The Science of the Aura* (Essex, England, L.N. Fowler and Co, Inc. 1982, original 1949), p. 17-18; C.W. Leadbeater, *Man Visible and Invisible* (Wheaton, IL, Quest/Theosophical Publishing House, 1980, original 1925), p. 21-27; and A.E. Powell, *The Causal Body and the Ego* (Wheaton, IL, Theosophical Publishing House, 1978, original; 1928), p. 70-71.

The Chakras

The Rainbow of the Chakras

WOMAN'S ETHERIC double contains the chakras, the seven rainbow energy centers that correspond to the seven aura layers, the four bodies. The seven major chakras and four of the smaller ones are used in healing. Like the silver cord, the chakras are a connective link between the bodies. They are present on each of the four body levels: the physical, emotional, mental and spiritual; but affect healing the most from their source level, the etheric double. On the physical plane, they correspond to places in the central nervous system, and to the seven ductless glands. Each chakra vibrates at an increasingly higher energy and color rate, and each corresponds to different physical, emotional, mental and spiritual attributes. The colors of the emotional aura body are the chakra rainbow. Each chakra is stimulated by a particular musical note, vocal sound syllable for chanting, its own and a complementary color, and a range of gemstones for specific uses. The correspondences are the basis for healing on the etheric level and beyond.

Known to India, Tibet, Egypt, the Native American Pueblo peoples, Hebrew Qabalists and other cultures, the chakra system in the West is influenced by a variety of sources, mostly Eastern. Chakra colors vary from system to system, as do positions and number of centers, but the attributes are very close cross-culturally. Some Eastern systems delete the belly chakra, or vary its location, while Tibetan healers combine the third eye with the crown.[1] The Hebrew system recognizes ten centers which correspond to the ten sephiroth (roses) of the Qabalistic Tree of Life. Each system has its own names for the chakras. The material and correspondences used in this chapter come primarily from the combined works of S.G.J. Ouseley, Kay Gardner, C.W. Leadbeater, Diane Mariechild, Amy Wallace and Bill Henkin. Where sources contradict or intuition merits changes, the choices and interpretations follow Gardner or are personal ones. Women reading this book use what works for them, this system or any other. As in any healing or goddess work, a book is only the starting place for women's experimentation and personal choices and development.

"Chakra" in Sanksrit means "wheel," and the Hindus describe the chakras as revolving wheels of light and color. They are also described as lotuses, flowers with ascending numbers of petals, an idea echoing the Qabalistic roses. The chakras are visible to many women who can see or sense energy levels, and the skill can be developed. Much of psychic healing depends on visualization of and "reading" or assessing the chakras, which is also taught in this book. The energy centers usually appear as luminous circles, wheels or discs, the chain of them strung like brightly colored beads in a row or column from the crown (head) to root (genitals) or from the feet to the top of the head.

Colors are the rainbow spectrum of the emotional body aura: red, orange, yellow, green, blue, indigo and violet. The sizes and brightness of the wheels vary with individual development, with physical condition and energy levels, health or dis-ease and the location of illness, physical, mental or emotional stress. Different centers in the same woman can be different sizes, affected by all of these factors, and she can will changes in the sizes and brightness to control their effects and aspects.

The root chakra is located at the genitals, the belly chakra between the genitals and navel (this varies in some systems), the solar plexus just above the navel, the heart chakra at the breastbone, the throat chakra at the base of the throat, the brow center above and between the physical eyes, and the crown chakra at the top of the head, slightly to the back. The root chakra's color is red, the belly is orange, the solar plexus yellow, the heart center green or rose, the throat chakra light blue, the brow indigo or dark blue, the crown center violet. There is a major chakra beyond the body several inches above the crown. This is what Kay Gardner names the transpersonal point, and its color is clear, white or rainbow, all colors of light combined.

There are smaller centers in the hands and feet. Listed here are more beginning gemstones for the chakras to add to those in the first chapter: for the root chakra, smoky quartz; for the belly chakra, orange/brown agate; for the solar plexus, citrine; for the heart, emerald; for the throat center, aquamarine; for the brow chakra/third eye, moonstone; for the crown center, selenite/desert rose; and for the transpersonal point, diamond.

To see or sense the chakras and begin to open them, sit or lie comfortably on a soft-rugged floor, or sit in a straight-backed chair. Unless you wish to fall asleep, avoid doing meditations in bed. Loosen clothing or work skyclad (in the nude) if warm enough. Candles or casting a circle of protection are recommended, but are optional. Get very comfortable, physically and emotionally. Arms and legs are straight, never crossed. Take several deep breaths, deepening and slowing normal breathing into a rhythmic pattern. Air enters every part of the body from head to feet, relaxing and vitalizing it. Begin relaxing each part of the body step by step, starting from the toes, clenching them, then letting go and relaxing them. Keeping the toes relaxed, move to the ankles, clenching and relaxing them in the same way. Then do the calves, knees, thighs, genital area, each in turn, first clenching and then relaxing it before moving on to the next. Once one part is relaxed, keep it relaxed. Clench and relax the abdomen, lower back, diaphragm, middle back, chest, breasts, shoulders. Clench and relax each part in turn, moving relaxation upward through the body and continuing rhythmic breathing. The breathing becomes automatic after a while. Clench and relax the fingers, make a fist, and clench and relax the hands, wrists, forearms, biceps, shoulders. Next go to the neck, and then the jaw, the muscles of the cheeks and face, tensing and relaxing each set of muscles. Go to the eyes, the muscles around the eyes, clench and relax them, then to the forehead and scalp.

When totally relaxed, continue breathing deeply and feel deep breaths entering every part of the body. Imagine the air turning to clear light, see it or imagine it, and breathe it in and out, staying very relaxed all over. Imagine with each inhaled breath that light enters through the top of the head and travels through the body until it leaves at the feet with each exhalation. Breathe the light into and through the body for several deep breaths.

Now on an inhaled breath, breathe clear light to enter the crown of the head.[2] Feel the light remain steady for a moment and feel, see or imagine it lighting up a round, glowing disc at the crown. The light is a vibrant circle, flower or wheel, luminous and beautiful, just at the top of the head. Exhale and appreciate the light, and on the next inhaled breath, the crown center still lit, breathe the light in a line or column to the forehead, and see or feel a round, glowing wheel of light appear at the forehead or brow. Appreciate the lovely wheels and the light between them for a couple of breaths, keep them both bright, and then breathe them brighter. On another inhaled breath, breathe the light in a column or line to the throat, breathing light into the throat chakra, and keeping the crown and brow centers lit brightly.

When the wheel of clear light is strong at the throat, brighten it more, then breathe the column of light further down, using it to light the center at the heart. Keep the already lit centers still glowing and beautiful, and brighten them. Breathe the light column downward to the solar plexus, just above the navel, and breathe that center into glowing brightness. Brighten it more, then carry the light further down, and breathe the belly chakra into light, a luminous wheel of bright light. Brighten it and all the other centers. Breathe light into the root, the genitals, and see that center glow and waken into a bright wheel or disc. Take time for several breaths to appreciate the light in all the centers and the column of light that connects them, to brighten it even more, and then on inhaled breaths, breathe light into hands and feet. A smaller brightness appears at the palm of each hand, and finally at the sole of each foot.

Breathing in, breathe light through the column and chakras from the crown to the feet, feeling it leave the body through the feet. Continue for several breaths, keeping each center bright, then on an inhaled breath, draw light into the feet from the Earth, breathing it into the genital center, and filling the root chakra with a lovely, clear ruby red. See the color, sense it or imagine it. Appreciate the color and the beauty; pay attention to it, and notice the center's size, color, and qualities for several breaths. On an inhaled breath again, breathe color into the belly chakra, filling it with a luminous clear orange. Pay attention to and appreciate the clear orange color, before breathing clear golden yellow into the solar plexus. After appreciating and noticing the solar plexus, its clear bright color, its size and qualities, breathe clear green or rose color into the heart, and pay attention to the qualities of the heart chakra for several breaths. Next breathe clear sky blue into the throat center, then indigo/midnight blue into the brow. Breathe several more deep breaths to appreciate each clear color before moving on to the next chakra, and keep all of the colors brightly lit. Breathe clear violet into the crown, appreciating the connection with the goddess, the beautiful color and qualities, and pay attention to the halo of clear or rainbow light beyond the crown chakra, beyond the body completely. For several breaths, appreciate the colors, light entering from the feet and leaving the body through the crown and transpersonal point, lighting and filling each color with clear beauty on its way. Breathe light to the palms of the hands, and notice what color/s they fill with. Breathe light to the soles of the feet and notice the colors there. These vary with individuals.

When this is finished, and enough time and breathing have been spent on the colors, breathe the colors clear again with inhaled breaths, drawing light through the crown again. The colors can be changed one by one or all at once. When all the colors are clear light, allow the glowing wheels to fade into the general glow of the body or the column connecting them. Allow the column and the aura of clear light around the body to fade, as well.

Remain quiet, without moving yet, and come back to daily consciousness. Open and focus the eyes, move a little, but get up only very slowly and when ready to. Pressing the palms to the floor, allow any excess of light or energy to leave through them and feel it leaving. Spaciness can happen, but fades in a little while and is not unpleasant. You will feel good, feel vitalized, rested and refreshed.

Dis-covering and opening the chakras, learning about them and seeing, imagining or sensing the colors, is the beginning of psychic healing. To make doing the meditation easier, learn it before starting or tape it.[3] If a circle is cast, open it and thank the directions and the goddess. Say "blessed be." As the chakras awaken, they grow in size and brightness, and psychic development occurs. Repeat this meditation as often as wished.

The chakras draw prana or vitality into the four bodies through the solar plexus and distribute it to all the energy centers (chakras) of the physical central nervous system. Prana is made from sunlight and air, in the Hindu concept, and the increase of these in summer and decrease in winter explains women's higher summer energy levels. Prana, the seven-atom "vitality globule," is easily visible. Women looking out toward a distance can see bright specks of moving light against the sky. They are tiny, quick changing, quick moving, and nearly colorless, of white or slightly golden tint.[4] Drawn into the four bodies through the solar plexus chakra in the etheric double, the seven atoms that compose prana separate, and each travels to the chakra it nourishes. The solar plexus operates as the hub of a ten-spoked wheel, distributing the prana color rays, which are the chakra colors or slight variations and combinations of them. Women who see the chakra colors as something different from the schedule given in this chapter may be seeing the colors of prana by Leadbeater's system rather than the chakras themselves. A personal example: seeing the usually green heart center as rose, the color Leadbeater lists as energizing and calming the entire nervous system.[5] Some systems list the heart chakra color as yellow. There are a variety of color systems to choose from, and Leadbeater's follows Helen Blavatsky's work in *The Secret Doctrine.*

When prana is drawn into the solar plexus in normal amounts and distributed in normal flow through the chakras, the woman is in a state of balanced energy and has good health. Where there is too much or too little prana flowing through a given center or through all the centers an imbalance occurs, manifesting as dis-comfort or dis-ease in a form that depends on which chakra/s are out of harmony. Well-being is a state of balanced energies, and dis-ease is dis-harmony, blockage or imbalance of prana. Healing is the process of changing an imbalanced situation to free-flowing balance and harmony, the change from dis-ease to health. On the chakra level, this can be done before dis-ease manifests in the earthly physical body. The woman doing chakra dis-covery meditation or gemstone work becomes familiar with her chakras, and able to immediately see or sense disharmony, a block, imbalance or change. By willing the chakras to be in balance or using gemstones or other means to balance them she improves her health, balances prana and the chakras in a number of possible ways. She directs more color to a faint or clouded chakra, stimulates it with crystal or the proper colored stone, or directs an overactive chakra to "shut down" a little. She takes power-within control to regulate the flow, and her physical mass body follows the changes made in the unseen energy levels.

A woman can also transmit prana to herself or someone else by color work, crystals or gemstones, or by laying on of hands, with no loss or harm to her own energies. Prana is directed and made to flow through quartz crystal, in any of the colors or in all of them. Learning the normal attributes of each chakra is important for learning the healing processes that follow.

Prana also extends through the chakras to the nadis or meridians that are the basis for acupuncture treatment, and these are extensions of the chakras. Hiroshi Motoyama, a doctor in Tokyo, has developed computerized sensors to measure the energy levels of the meridians in the physical body and their connecting organs. Shafica Karagulla, a woman MD, has scientifically proven the chakra system and the chakras' connections to dis-ease and wellness.[6] Science eventually catches up with ancient knowledge; the Chinese system of acupuncture is at least 5,000 years old, and comes from the time of the Wu, the Chinese women healers.

In Sanskrit, prana means "absolute energy." It is the force that pervades all Be-ing, the life force that comes from the goddess, connecting all living things and all energy matter.[7] It is the energy spaces between atoms. Laying on of hands is pranic healing, transmission of prana from the healer to the woman being healed to balance energies in the etheric double. Crystal and gemstone work is *directed* pranic healing, transmitting colors and balancing energies through the chakras and the stones. Pranayama is the science of breath, the use of breathing/meditation techniques to increase vitality, to direct maximum prana to all of the chakras and to change imbalances of energy in the chakras where there are any. Proper breathing, according to this discipline, causes increased amounts of prana to enter and flow, and increases the powers of healing, balance and well-being.[8] Prana is an important and basic concept.

Another important chakra concept is the energy channel called kundalini, the serpent fire. Less used in healing, kundalini may be awakened by it, and women healers need to know what it is. Because of its sexual aspects and extreme power, there are lots of kundalini jokes and warnings, but not enough real information. Kundalini properly channeled is positive enlightenment, oneness with the goddess and connection of the four bodies, but it must be prepared for, sometimes over several incarnations. It should not be awakened intentionally in others or the self without knowledge and understanding of its process.

Kundalini is energy that rises through the chakras and the spine. The chakras are visualized on the front surface of the body, but they extend through it and are rooted in the spinal column/central nervous system. Think of them as cones or spirals, tornado shaped, with the wider end a whirling concave disc at the front, and the point of the

Kundalini

cone as penetrating the spinal cord. At the base of the spine, the root chakra, lies dormant feminine energy described usually as a sleeping snake. The snake, serpent or dragon is an archetype goddess symbol, representing eternity in the Western craft. She is Aido Hwedo, the great goddess of Haiti and voudoun, and the lucky dragon life force in China. The awakening of the dragon at the Chinese New Year (around the time of the wiccan Candlemas) is the return of life to the Earth, the rebirth of spring. The sleeping dragon or snake at the kanda or base of the spine in kundalini is called Shakti, the goddess of fire.

When awakened, through extended meditation, pranayama breathing, chanting or some other forms of care-ful chakra work, Shakti activates.[9] She rises and hisses as the snake, then travels upwards through the spinal column via the chakras, to the brain. Reaching the brain, she makes union with Shiva, her polar opposite duality, in a oneness that merges the physical with the spiritual, and is the oneness of all life. This is often defined in sexual terms, but is much more than sexual union. The result of the merging is physical/spiritual integration, total balance and harmony of Be-ing, and the release of intense healing energy. As Kundalini rises through each chakra, this is the process:

> at the first, or Root chakra, she brings physical vitality and earthly protection. When she comes through the second, she brings sexual prowess; through the third self-confidence and strength of identity. These first three centers make up the personality. When Kundalini awakens in the fourth, the heart center, she manifests as Shakti, the creative female power of heat and passion. She brings compassion and an open heart, the ability to channel healing energy and to express universal love. When the fifth center awakens, the throat opens, becoming "oracular"— bringing through a direct transmission of divine knowledge and information. When the sixth opens, the third eye becomes active, and reality is truly seen ... The seventh center is the Crown; when it awakens, one experiences union with the Divine ... [10]

The dangers of kundalini and the warning about it are given because of its intensity. The power can heal, but opened before one is ready can result in harm. Natural opening of the centers for safe kundalini awakening can take lifetimes to prepare, and Shakti's rising before the chakras are open channels can have negative outcomes. The process has both a rising and a return of Shakti to the kanda. If the chakras are blocked on her way upward or are unable to handle the intense power of the return trip, there is danger of intense pain,

loss of consciousness, sexual or psychological aberrations, even madness or, in the extreme, death.

Kundalini can also awaken spontaneously, or, in healing, as an intense rush of one-way energy that takes it from the root chakra through the spinal column and out through the crown. It's a powerful upward rush of electricity that may cause unconsciousness, psychic vision, or temporary mental disturbance, but usually does no real harm. Psychic powers often awaken with the experience, and the woman can be frightened by this.[11] If this begins during healing work, Shakti should usually be quieted and restrained. A bodyworkers' technique for stopping kundalini that awakens during massage is for the healer to run her hand along the spine from neck to root, pushing the energy back gently.[12] A psychic healer or gemstone worker's method is to use the healer's hands, whether the woman being healed is present or not, to do the same through the woman's energy field. The healer should not be frightened by this, but should understand it: no harm comes to the woman being healed, but only good.

The energy of kundalini and Shakti's rising is connected to the nadis (meridians) and to the system of chakras:

> The principle nadi is that known as sushumna, which runs inside the spinal column and through the brain to the crown of the head. It is the Hindu life force known as prana, flowing through the sushumna, that is the kundalini.[13]

This is the same prana, at its maximum, that is used in healing and is necessary for actual life. Opening the chakras, clearing them and making them free-flowing and balanced for the channeling of prana is also to make them ready to experience kundalini safely. Kundalini moves from chakra to chakra upward through the spine, and the union with Shiva is the union of energy with consciousness. Once this union occurs, Shakti returns down the spine to her place at the root, a goddess of the sun that has merged with the goddess of the moon. She vitalizes all of the chakras with intense solar/lunar energy as she passes downward through them again. The merging unites the life force with the goddess, and absorbs the lower three chakra centers with the crown,[14] merges the physical, emotional and mental bodies with the spiritual centers.

Attained in one life, kundalini enlightenment must be learned again in each new reincarnation, as the body is a new one. Once learned, however, it happens again easily. The channels once opened and prepared remain open. Opening and clearing the chakras and channels in healing is safe and positive, and a beginning preparation to go further. The science of this energy is called kundalini yoga, and anyone wishing to pursue it should seek a teacher. No woman would try to hold a high voltage wire in her hand without protection, and this is what Shakti's force is. It's another side of prana, the healing energy, another side of the goddess and goddess-within.

Studying the individual chakras begins with the *root chakra,* called *muladhara* in Sanskrit. The root chakra is located at the genitals on the front of the body, and the base of the spine, the coccyx or tailbone, to the back.[15] The front and back ends of the chakras are connected in the front and back of the body, the cone and tail of the spiral. The center is the sexual/genital area, the gateway of birth and the uterus. It's the root beginning, and also the place of elimination. Its color is *clear red*, denoting heat, the life force, physical existence, strength, energy and vitality. In traditional correspondences from India and Tibet, its sound is C major and its chanted sound syllable is Ooo (ways vocally or musically to stimulate the center). Kay Gardner's ductless gland correspondent is the ovaries, though personal choice corresponds this chakra to the uterus (not a ductless gland) and connects the ovaries to the belly chakra. Some systems connect this center with the adrenals. Kay Gardner uses the square as a representative symbol, where Leadbeater uses the equal-armed cross. The element and circle direction for the root chakra are earth and north, and the wheel or flower appearance contains four petals, divisions, spokes or rays, related to the vibration frequency. The numbers of petals are traditionally Eastern and Tibetan correspondences, psychically derived. Like the etheric double aura band it mirrors, the root chakra has the lowest energy vibration rate of the chakra system. It's the center closest to dense matter, the physical mass of the body, and having the most to do with the material plane.

The root chakra's basic skill is survival, mostly survival on the dense physical level and the ability to adapt and make changes. If a woman is very frightened and feels threatened, if survival or emotional survival issues are at stake (anything from stagefright to being broke at rent time, to actual threat of physical harm or threatening dis-ease), the root chakra opens to its widest, and offers the energy and reflexes necessary for life-saving action. When the crisis ends or the reaction is inappropriate, what Amy Wallace and Bill Henkin call "running on survival,"[16] the chakra sometimes needs help to slow down. Too much root chakra red is ungroundedness, fear, panic, unnecessary survival struggle, nervousness. Too little of the root chakra's activities, not enough red, results in lethargy, depletion, feeling cold and resistance to changes.[17] A good balance is that of stability, energy, alertness and security, enough warmth without overheating and the ability to adapt. To reduce the effects of the root chakra, close it slightly in the chakra meditation to perhaps one quarter open, regulate it till it feels right, but never shut it down completely. See the chakra disc or wheel as a camera lens with a spiraling eye on the front of the body at the pubic bone, and regulate the width of the opening. Use black grounding gemstones to reduce the chakra also. To boost its energy, visualize the chakra widening to half, or use red gemstones.

This meditation for stimulating (opening) the root chakra is from Kay Gardner's album, *A Rainbow Path:*

> *Visualize scarlet red light while intoning the syllable "Ooo." Bring the color through your feet and up to the base of your spine; let the red light swirl in a figure-eight spiral slowly up through your body until it spouts through the top of your head like a fountain then flows down to your sides and into Earth again.*[18]

As with any meditation, use rhythmic breathing and step-by-step physical relaxation before starting the passage. On completing it, put the hands on the ground to release excess energy. A visualization with red is highly energizing.

Women with clear red in their emotional auras are strong of will, mind and sexuality. They are ambitious, courageous, passionate and affectionate, strong leaders with charisma. Red is the color of heat and the life force, and its color less clear manifests negatively as anger, selfishness or impatience. The clearer the color, the more positive the attributes. Women with red as their predominating aura color, or as one of their colors, are strong, interesting and dynamic.

Some root chakra gemstones are ruby or garnet for heat, circulation and vitalizing, bloodstone to decrease bleeding, smoky quartz for fear, and black tourmaline or black onyx for grounding. Black light is less used in color healing, but send red to warm, increase energy, for life, passion and reproductive organ healing. Avoid using red where there is any sort of infection or inflammation (sources conflict on this), or for burns, anger, overheating or over-excitement. Send green for these instead, red's complementary color, or send blue.

The second chakra is the *belly chakra*, called *swadhisthana* in Sanskrit, and its color is *clear orange*. The center is frontally located in the lower abdomen, between the root chakra and the navel, and corresponds to the pancreas gland for Kay Gardner, or to the ovaries in women and the spleen in men (following Diane Mariechild). The chakra is rooted in the spinal column at the first lumbar vertebra. Sexual and generative energies are located in the belly chakra, and this is the place where sexual feelings originate and are acted upon. It's interesting that Leadbeater moved this chakra to the spleen, contrary to the Easter system, saying that sexuality should not be aroused. He notes that in Egypt, steps are taken to keep this center dormant.[19] The orange chakra's musical tone is D, sound syllable Oh, and symbol the delta triangle, all correspondences from Kay Gardner. In C.W. Leadbeater, the symbol is the crescent moon. Where the physical sense correspondent for the root chakra is smell, for the belly chakra it is taste. Its circle direction and element are west and water, and there are six petals or spokes to the orange chakra flower or wheel.

The basic attribute associated with the belly center is flowing—in emotions, sexuality, or feeling others. Impressions and images of all sorts are stored here on subconscious levels. Proper balance in this chakra means the ability to flow with emotions freely and to feel and reach out to others in proper perspective, sexually or not. Too much orange or this chakra too open becomes clairsentience to a discomforting degree; too little or too closed is repression, drying and hardening, the dis-ease of arthritis, hardening of the arteries and sexual dysfunction. Correspondent with the emotional/astral body and the emotional band of the aura, feelings happen and are regulated here; emotions, passions and desires in whatever degree. This chakra's psychic skill is clairsentience, the ability to feel with others, a skill that requires control and is usually not opened intentionally. The heart is developed instead. A woman who is clairsentient feels with others to the point where their feelings become her own. She links with her friend's fear and is frightened, not always knowing why; doing healing work for others, she takes on the symptoms she is healing. Moderate amounts of clairsentience are positive, but the chakra held wide enough to cause problems needs to be shut down. Visualize it in meditation, and close it to one quarter if needing to feel others less; open it to half if wanting to feel others more. Free-flowing of emotions is the goal, not holding back or holding on. Use orange gemstones to increase the effects of the belly center, to open it, or its complementary color and colored stones (blue, aqua or indigo) to decrease it. Orange is a warm color, expressing the life force and solar energy.

A meditation on orange, the feeling and flowing warmth of the belly chakra, comes from S.G.J. Ouseley's book *Colour Meditations.* Do it with lit orange candles, after entering deep relaxation. Notice the mood and physical changes that occur.

> *See in your mind a glorious October carpet of newly fallen foliage. The brown earth is spread with a deep rich cover- ing of warm russet and copper, crimson, orange and red— thickly scattered leaves of all delightful shapes; thrown down here and there, in wonderful patterns of warm colors, are maple and oak leaves of gold, orange, red and green.* [20]

Ouseley directs that looking for color and flavor in life, sexually or emotionally, causes women to find it and empowers them. Use it in positive and balanced, free-flowing ways. As with any meditation, and particularly those using warm colors, be sure to ground the energy.

Women with orange in their emotional auras are warm, giving, active and energetic, outgoing leaders and women of strong personal pride. They are self-confident and positive, and convey that positivity to others. They are women of feeling, creativity, sureness, energy and optimism. Orange is a vitalizing color, a warm to nearly hot color, expressing life energy as does red in the root chakra. In its duller, less clear tones, there can be too much pride and some selfishness, but at its best these are lively, live-wire women without power issues.

Orange is a color important in healing, stimulating the belly chakra to give energy to someone depleted or ill. It is associated with wisdom and reasoning ability, as well as with feeling, energy, sexuality and emotion. Some belly chakra stones are carnelian for painful menstruation, orange coral to energize and purify the blood, and the orange/brown jaspers and agates. The brown-toned stones ground and balance orange energy, decrease it, while the bright orange stones increase it. As in using red, avoid orange where the woman is over-volatile and use indigo instead. Never use on burns, high blood pressure, or where there is over-heating or over-excitement. Wallace and Henkin use orange as their most general healing color.

Next is the *solar plexus* chakra, the center for balance and power, and the seat of personality. Its color is *clear yellow*, its Sanskrit name *manipura*, its frontal location just above the navel, and its spinal location at the eighth thoracic vertebra. Yellow denotes energy and vitality, thought, intellect and mental concentration. The center is the place of ego and power-within, of passions, impulses, anger, strength and freedom/ability to act.[21] The chakra and color correspond with the lower mental body, the kama-manas, seat of consciousness influenced by desire and emotion. In traditional uses, its musical tone is E, chanting syllable Aw, and gland the adrenals. Keith Sherwood connects this chakra to the pancreas,[22] and most sources to all the processes of digestion except elimination (which is located in the root chakra). The yellow center's physical sense is sight, and its symbol is the circle for Kay Gardner and the triangle for C.W. Leadbeater. Its element and circle direction are fire and south.

Psychics note ten spokes to the solar plexus flower or wheel, and these are the spokes that radiate prana throughout the body, drawing it in and distributing it in balance to each chakra. Food, physical nourishment and maintenance are also processed and distributed through this center, and the balance between emotion and intellect (kama-manas), happens at the solar plexus. In addition, this is the center for distribution of the psychic senses, what Amy Wallace and Bill Henkin call "a sort of psychic energy pump."[23] It's the center for astral travel and astral influences, receptivity to spirit guides and receptivity to psychic development, the chakra of psychic balance. Too much yellow or the solar plexus opened too wide is nervousness, disharmony, disruption of digestion, eating disorders, psychic disturbances, and mental instability. Too little yellow or the chakra too closed results in lethargy, apathy, tiredness, mental stagnation, obesity, closure of psychic abilities. Balance the center for harmony, good use of nourishment and prana, mental and emotional peace, self-confidence. The solar plexus is the place of the personality and of ego equilibrium.

A meditation with yellow for drawing energy:

Sit on a yellow rug, mat or towel and do deep relaxation to enter the meditative state. Place the sun card from a tarot deck in front, several clear crystals, and hold a topaz or citrine in the left hand. Draw yellow through the stone and into the body, breathe yellow in and out. Draw it in through the solar plexus, upward through all the centers, then down and out through the root chakra or the feet. When feeling thoroughly warm and energized, stop the flow and return to now.

Use yellow candles or perform outdoors in sunlight, and be sure to ground the energy thoroughly. Stop when there's enough and before too much. This is a good meditation to do before studying or writing, but is not recommended at bedtime.

Women with yellow in their emotional auras are highly intelligent, positive, psychic and capable in business. They are high-spirited and sometimes restless, often teachers or students formally or informally. Yellow is the color of confidence. Gold in the aura is beginning spiritual development and psychic development. Less positive qualities present when the yellow in the aura is not a clear yellow are jealousy, impracticality and suspicion, and power issues. When the color is clear, these are positive women, capable, intelligent, sensitive and lively.

Solar plexus stimulating stones are topaz, amber, citrine and yellow jade, all highly energizing gemstones. Use for physical, mental and psychic stimulation as a mood lifter and tonic. For nervous people (women with too much solar plexus activity), decrease and balance it with violet—its complementary color. Very anxious women or women with insomnia or high blood pressure would benefit from wearing an amethyst. Avoid using yellow or yellow stones before sleep.

The fourth center is the *heart center*, the center that connects the higher with the lower levels. Its colors are *clear green* or *clear rose*, and its Sanskrit name is *anahata*. At the front, the heart center is located between the breasts, at the lower edge of the breastbone; at the back its location is the first thoracic vertebra between and below the shoulder blades. Qabalistic theory lists a sephira or chakra/rose at each shoulder, and names them severity and mercy, with the heart in between. The attributes of this center are love and compassion. Green denotes healing, sympathy and success. Rose is love and positive self-love, the warming ability to care for the self and for others. The heart center corresponds to F major in music and the chanting syllable Ah; its ductless gland is the thymus located at the center of

the chest. The center's physical sense is touch; its symbol for
Gardner is the equal-armed cross, and for Leadbeater it's the Star of
David, (two equal triangles crossed). Its element is air and the circle
direction east. There are twelve petals to the flower. Green is a cool
color; rose is warmer but not highly energizing. Both are soothing
colors.

The heart chakra corresponds to the higher mental body, the
green band of the aura, the place of intuition and nonrational
thought, formless or imaginative thought. The center is the meeting
place of the three upper (spiritual body) and the three lower (physical,
emotional and mental body) chakras, the place of reaching below
and above to heal the whole woman. Vicki Noble describes this as the
"place of union, where the head and the body can come together as
the one organism you are."[24] Healing comes from the heart center as
does love and self-love, unselfish caring that includes all. This is the
chakra to develop (rather than the clairsentience of the belly chakra)
for true empathy with others, but the heart chakra opened too much
can produce some of the symptoms of clairsentience—what Diane
Mariechild calls a "savior complex."[25] Too little heart chakra energy is
a loss of connection with others, loss of caring, or inferiority feelings
in the self. Proper balance of the center is love and oneness, within the
self and beyond. It is sympathy and reaching out beyond the self, the
ability to heal and self-heal.

A meditation for green, from Ouseley:

> *Picture mentally the refreshing greenness of a meadow of
> young grass after a shower of rain. It gleams like a new car-
> pet of emerald velvet—bright, soft, tender. Above, the blue
> morning sky is fringed with flushed clouds—a cosmic har-
> mony of ethereal turquoise and rosy-gold, blessing and
> glorifying the day.[26]*

Ouseley reminds us that the negativities and troubles of life cannot
overwhelm life's goodness, its joy, beauty, contentment and
harmony—women's power-within to manifest the positive and goddess. Women use green for healing, blessing and peace. For a meditation with rose:

> *Imagine a perfect pink rose, create and appreciate it, then
> watch it turn into rose colored light. Breathe the light in
> and out, and watch it become an aura, an envelope or*

glow surrounding you. Breathe the love, self-love, peace, joy and beauty of the rose for as long as wished. Open your heart chakra wide to it, and draw it within.

Women with green in their emotional auras are individualistic, sympathetic, successful and caring. They are independent, versatile, able to adapt to changes, intelligent and thoughtful. Green is the color of ideas, growth, regeneration and new life. Unclear green tones show deceit and jealousy. Rose in the aura is love for others and a healthy love for the self, a woman of great caring, giving, devotion, sympathy, tenderness. She is modest and refined in type, and loves too often and too much, with times of heartache that she needs to heal. She is gentle and unselfish, but negatively may lose herself in others and be stubborn. She is artistic, joyous and beauty-oriented. These are good women to know and to love.

In healing, green and rose gemstones are used for ungrounded-ness, their harmony bringing peace and balance, for loneliness and love-loss. Green stones are antiseptic and cooling to use for inflammations and burns. They are good for infections and headaches, especially the blue/green stones that overlap with the next higher chakra, the throat. Green jade, aventurine, green tourmaline, emerald and peridot/olivine are examples. Rose stones are for heartache, loneliness and love-loss, for love and self-love. They are soothing and slightly warming, providing a comforting glow. Rose quartz is the major gemstone for this, but also use rose jade or watermelon tourmaline (rose and green). The woman who sends rose in healing sends joy and love.

The fifth center is the *throat chakra,* called *vishuddha* in Sanskrit, and is *clear light blue*, the color of the daytime sky. When the throat overlaps with the heart chakra, the color is blue/green or aqua. The throat is the center for all forms of creativity, communication, expression, speech and hearing. What women tell others, tell themselves, and women's self-image is from this center.[27] The throat chakra is located in the front at the base of the neck, at the hollow of the collarbone, with its spiral rooted in the third cervical vertebras at the back, the spine at the base of the skull. Musical correspondence is G to G sharp and the chant syllable is Eh; this is a chakra quite responsive to sound stimulation. The ductless glands, following Kay Gardner, are the thyroid and parathyroids, and there are sixteen spokes or petals to the flower or wheel by Eastern thought. In the circle, the throat chakra represents aether or spirit and the center, the cauldron of transformation and change. For Kay Gardner, its symbol is the crescent moon, for C.W. Leadbeater, the circle, and its physical sense is hearing. Blue is cooling and calming, the color associated with the goddess as Mary, Yemaya, Isis or Kwan Yin.[28]

Psychically, the throat chakra corresponds to the lower spiritual body, the crone level of the maiden/mother/crone triad. It's place of hearing the inner goddess voice or spirit guide. The psychic skill is clairaudience, psychic hearing. The center corresponds with speech, communication, hearing and creativity, so that when it is too tightly closed or blocked, saying what a woman means is hard for her to do. By opening the throat, things that need expressing get said, and words are no longer stuck there. A too closed throat chakra, words unsaid that need saying, results in sore throats and laryngitis. Amy Wallace and Bill Henkin list a closed or blocked throat center as a "universal ailment,"[29] and a bane to healing. The three spiritual level chakras and the transpersonal point eighth chakra can never be opened too widely. Opening the throat chakra for free-flowing of energy opens creativity of all sorts, from singing ability to writing and dancing. It opens communication, meaningful listening and speaking with others.

A meditation on light blue, from Kay Gardner:

> Visualize sky blue light while intoning the syllable "Eh."
> Bring the color through your feet and up to your throat; let
> the blue light swirl in a figure-eight spiral. When your fifth
> chakra has been bathed, allow the light to spiral slowly up
> through your body until it spouts through the top of your
> head like a fountain and then flows down your sides into
> Earth again.[30]

Women with light blue in their emotional auras are artistic, creative and spiritually oriented. They are loyal and sincere friends and lovers, expressing a great deal of intensity in relationships. They are self-confident and self-reliant, qualities that vary in amounts with the strength of color. Stronger blue in the aura has a stronger development of these qualities. Unclear blues can be selfish devotion, spiritually or in relationships, or fetish worship. The goddess moon and the feminine, the goddess-within are associated with light blue as a clear color, and blue/green.

Blue gemstones are used for cooling, inflammations, infections and swellings, for sore throats, burns and fevers. The color is an antidote to too much red, orange or yellow in the lower chakras.

Some blue/green stones used for headaches (their positions disputed with the heart chakra) are aquamarine, chrysocolla and turquoise. Blue aventurine stimulates creativity, and blue quartz is good for burns. Lapis lazuli is a major stone for both the throat and third eye, and stimulates creativity, speech and singing. Lapis is an all-healing stone of great power.

The third eye or *brow chakra* is one of the more talked about chakras in women's spirituality, and its color is clear *indigo blue,* the color of the midnight sky. Its Sanskrit name is *ajna,* and in the Eastern tradition there are ninety-six petals to the center's flower or wheel, a large jump in vibration rate from the sixteen of the throat. The chakra is located frontally just above and between the physical eyes, and at the first cervical vertebra of the spine at the back. Its musical tone is A, chant syllable Ih, and the gland is the pituitary (Ouseley says pineal; most sources place pineal at the crown). Kay Gardner's symbol for the brow chakra is the Star of David, two interlocking triangles, while C.W. Leadbeater gives the center no form symbol at all, moving it beyond form entirely. The center corresponds with the middle level of the spiritual body, the sixth aura band, and the mother in the three-form goddess triad. It represents the planet or below in the circle.

Vicki Noble places psychic intuition and knowing reality/truth as women's use of the brow chakra; men's use for it being the projecting of thought or control. She comments that women need to develop their will and power in connection with this center, combining it with heart chakra caring, while men need to work on their ability to surrender and know.[31] The brow's color indigo is purifying and electric, astringent rather than warm or cool. Extra-earthly sight is the center's sense, all the senses without physical correspondence, hearing, seeing, feeling from goddess-within. The color and chakra are involved with knowing in the spiritual meaning of the word, with nervous, mental and psychic forces. Distinguishing what's real internally or externally is an aspect of this center's abilities.

Psychically, the brow chakra is the place of clairvoyance, far-seeing and instant knowing/intuition. Developing the third eye stimulates creative visualization, empathy/telepathy links, seeing auras and psychic healing skills. Keith Sherwood comments that "channeling rays from both the brow chakra and the heart chakra simultaneously is an effective way to transmit healing from a distance."[32] The brow needs the heart for balance, or else is unfeeling and cold. It's the center for understanding the inter-connection of all that lives, becoming one with others in a universal wisdom or all-knowing perception, understanding beyond the rational or even imaginative mental levels. The place of ideals and idealism, the brow chakra is knowing the unseen and spiritual, women's intuition, power-within, healing, and touching the cosmos/goddess. For Diane Mariechild, it's "the space where conscious and unconscious knowledge join,"[33] the lunar/feminine night. A closed third eye or a blocked one often results in headaches; an open and active one tingles and vibrates with "headiness" and awareness.

A meditation on indigo from Ouseley:

> Picture mentally the earth lying veiled in the mystic sleep of night. A light diaphanous vapour wraps the wet grass and the silent trees, which seem like intangible brooding shadows. The silver floating mist, like the aura of a spirit, is all woven through with white moor light, and high above the earth in her astral dream, hangs the indigo sky, jewelled thickly with scintillating stars. No sound disturbs the breathless quietude but the rhythmic falling of dew from unseen leaves. The cosmic beauty is almost too ethereal for mortal mind, but its balm sheds on the soul a radiant blessing beyond all words.[34]

Reach out in this meditation to connect with others, and feel their hands touching yours. Indigo is the balance and harmony of the psychic night.

Women with indigo in their auras are highly developed spiritually. They are intuitive and psychic, high of integrity and loyalty, deeply sincere. These are idealistic women, trusting and open, sensitive and magnetic. The color itself rejects negativity, and has no clouded or unclear form.

Gemstones for the third eye are moonstone and blue sapphire, star sapphire and dark aquamarine. Moonstone is sometimes designated for the crown, and Tibetan systems combine the third eye and crown centers. Lapis lazuli, a throat designated stone, and sodalite are also for the brow center and nervous balance, the balance of darkness with light, yin and yang, healing and stimulating all the senses, to raise positivity and intuition. Use these stones where there is too much orange, its complementary color. Use them to develop psychically, to aid visualization and healing work, and to encourage psychic links with others.

The seventh and furthest physical chakra, corresponding with the higher spiritual aura level, the maiden of the goddess triad, is the *crown center*, and its color is *clear violet*. *Sahasrara* is its Sanskrit name; the Native American Hopi call this chakra the *kopavi*, and in Africa it's the *sekpoli*. There is no spinal location for this center, and its physical front and back location is at the top of the head, slightly to the back. Gland correspondence is the pineal for Kay Gardner and the pituitary for S.G.J. Ouseley; most sources list the pineal. The crown chakra has no physical body sense, and is the symbol of the lotus for Kay Gardner, with no form symbol at all for C.W. Leadbeater. Tibetan psychics designate 960 petals or spokes to the center's outer ring, and within it is another inner ring of twelve more divisions. Leadbeater colors these rings glowing white for the outer and gold for the center of the flower, and describes the developed chakra as a "crown of glory."[35] He combines it with Gardner's transpersonal point. The musical sound for the crown chakra is B, the chant syllable Eee, and the element and circle direction are the universe and above. Violet is the highest spirituality color and vibration, denoting power-within, psychic and inner development, influence and transcendence. Like indigo it is an electric/magnetic color, rather than being cool or warm.

Peace and connection with the goddess are the skills and attributes of the crown center, the higher spiritual aura body. This is the place of pure knowing and pure intuition, of meditation, trance-work and spiritism. The *kopavi* is women's connection with the goddess, a channel of pure wisdom which if kept open is the channel for the goddess-within. The crown is the center for psychic skills far beyond any of the other chakras. Using the crown center, information comes direct from the source, and from the goddess for healing, profound changes and inner peace. This channel with the goddess, which the Hopi describe as a life thread connection with Spider Woman, is the state that spirituality seeks to attain in every system and religion since the matriarchies. It is total well-being in every sense: physical, emotional, mental and spiritual. The crown opens to the goddess, is connected with the goddess, then healing and self-healing enter and are channeled. The violet crown chakra is the psychic woman's intuition skill of knowing the goddess and goddess-within.

To meditate on violet and the woman-goddess channel:

Enter the meditative state holding an amethyst in the left hand. Cast a violet aura of peace and protection all around you, invoking the goddess and asking to know. Within the violet light create her image, in any terms and descriptions that are personally meaningful, and see the connection between your Be-ing and her essence. Ask her for wisdom, for peace and understanding, and listen to her message. Draw her into your heart or crown chakra—she is you and you are she.

Women with violet or purple in their aura's emotional body express the goddess in a variety of ways, in ritual or in mothering, in writing or relationships, in everything they are and in everything they do. There are no negative attributes to this color. Women with violet in their auras may also have red, the root color, since the circle at this level is complete and rebegins. Lighter tones of violet denote goddess consciousness and a developed love and respect for others. Deeper tones of purple and purple/blue are idealism and transcendence, often with strong inspirational creativity.[36] Violet is the color of priestessess, and women with violet in their auras are highly developed spiritually, aware and manifesting the goddess within.

Purple/violet gemstones are headed by amethyst, the colored quartz that calms, eases the nerves and generates sleep. Translucent white stones, moss agate, chalcedony, moonstone and selenite/desert rose are also crown chakra stones, as are purple garnet and alexandrite, and violet fluorite. Some sources call this the outermost chakra level and combine its stones with those for the transpersonal point. In healing, violet reduces stress and all stress dis-eases, as well as mental disorders, tumors and dis-eases of the head and skull, and high blood pressure.

An eighth chakra, located beyond the physical and spiritual and having no correspondences to the spine, glands, organs or senses, is the *transpersonal point.* Its color is *clear* or *white light,* the combination of all colors of light taken together. It's perceived as the rainbow, and reference here comes from the work of Kay Gardner, who uses a circle of light rays to represent it symbolically. The center's location is beyond the body, several inches above the crown chakra. Place a hand there, and a tingling in the palm identifies the center. Its musical sound is silence, the sound of all notes together as one, and the beyond-aura level of this chakra is the goddess, the source herself. Her element is all elements and she is the entire circle, all the women within it. The sound syllable for chanting is the universal Om, and the psychic skill for this level is oneness. All women have clear/white/rainbow light in their auras, and are the goddess.

To meditate on the transpersonal point chakra, on the attributes of this center for "divine liberation, love and light,"[37]

> *Visualize rainbows becoming white light while silently intoning the mantra, "Om." Bring the light through your feet and slowly into each succeeding chakra, letting the white light swirl in figure-eight spirals. When each chakra has been bathed in light, allow the light to spout from the top of your head like a fountain and then flow down your sides into Earth again.*[38]

All the colors of the goddess are within.

In healing, clear quartz crystal is the most representative stone for this chakra. It contains all colors, can be used for any center, any healing. Other transpersonal point/goddess stones are rutilated clear quartz (rutile), diamond and zircon. Use rutile to open, energize and reflect on each color, on all the colors in turn; use the electricity of diamond to intensify and magnify rainbow energy; and use clear quartz for all healing. White light is used and over-used in women's spirituality, but is appropriate in making contact and in unifying at the end of healing, and for working with the aura energy field. For specific dis-eases and chakras, color is more directive than clear/white light, and don't forget black as connecting with the Earth. Program clear quartz crystal for any chakra color needed by directing it to transmit that color.

Two smaller sets of chakras used in healing are the centers in the palms of the hands and soles of the feet. The foot chakras are women's connection with the Earth, and are used for grounding, drawing energy, and returning it. The chakras in the palms of the hands are developed to send energy in laying on of hands (pranic healing). The palm chakras are highly sensitive and grow more so with use. Both of these chakra pairs have colors varying with the individual. They may be different for the left and the right, and may be the colors of other chakras or not. The foot chakras are usually earth tones. The hands, in addition, contain chakras at the tips of each finger, and these can be used and developed. Various sources list other small chakras, less important to women's healing. The lips and eyes are also chakra centers.

With information on all the centers and their colors and correspondences in mind, begin a meditation to balance the chakras in yourself. Start with the chakra opening meditation at the beginning of this chapter. Set the tone and mood with an altar or candles (white, green or blue ones are good), and cast a protective circle in a safe, quiet, uninterrupted space. Enter the meditative alpha state by rhythmic breathing and deep relaxation. Visualize and light the chakras, fill them with their colors as in the earlier meditation, and notice the qualities and sizes of each chakra in turn, how each center looks and feels.[39] Is it too wide or too closed? Is it clear of color, or clouded and blocked? These ideas have individual meanings, feelings, appearances and symbols. Does a center appear tilted, wobbly or out of place? Does it have "gunk," stickiness, images, blots or blotches in it?

Beginning with the crown and working downward, see that the four highest chakras are opened wide (the crown, brow, throat and heart centers). Pay special attention to the throat. Unless suffering a "savior complex," the heart is not too wide, however widely it is opened. To open a chakra wider, send light in its color brightly to it, or see it as a camera lens and spiral it open wider. Use a gemstone for each color to send that color's light. Below the heart is the solar plexus chakra. If nervousness is an issue this chakra may be too wide, so spiral it down to about a quarter open. If more energy is needed, send it yellow or topaz and open the lens to half. Pay attention to how it feels, and decide if the width is right, then leave it or change it to what feels good. See the color brighten to gem clarity before moving down. Do the same for the orange belly chakra: regulate its opening size and send clear color to it. Remember clairsentience and adjust it for what's comfortable, neither too far opened nor too closed. At the root, check again for width and clarity, and if "running on survival" without needing to, adjust the center. If needing more root energy, open it or send it ruby light. If the hands and feet chakras were not opened in the beginning meditation, open them now. Run an umbilical cord from the root chakra and ground it in the goddess Earth, then go back to the solar plexus:

Imagine that any unsavory energy, pictures or clutter of any kind which is stored there will be flushed down from your third chakra to your second, where it will collect any stuff in that chakra, and then down to your first, repeating the process. Flush whatever you collect in these chakras down your grounding cord and into the earth.[40]

See the energy entering Earth changed to things she can use. Repeat this in a continuing, cleansing flow until the root, belly and solar plexus chakras are clear, bright and without blocks, each spiraled to the size that's comfortable. If a chakra seems out of alignment, tipped, drooping or uncentered, mentally right it and put it back in place.

Then go to the heart center and repeat the sequence, but send the goo, gunk and stickiness upwards from the heart to the throat, throat to third eye, and third eye to the crown. See it all leaving the body and the chakras in a flowing stream by way of the crown/*kopavi* center, becoming harmless energy to be recycled by the universe as it enters her. Repeat until all of the chakras are gemstone-color clear, bright, beautiful, unblocked and opened wide, aligned in their places and glowing. When this is so for all of the centers, including the hands and feet, intensify each of their colors once more, then allow the colors to turn to clear crystal light. When you are ready, stop the energy flow, and dissolve the grounding cord.

Return to now, and slowly come out of the trance state. Thank the goddess and open the circle, blow out the candles and rest until present, here and now. Move slowly for awhile. Remember to ground the excess energy by running it through the palm centers to the Earth. This is important. What's needed remains within—it won't be lost. You feel good: clean, clear, rested, energetic, calm and well. You have completed your first psychic healing using the chakras, colors, gemstones and four bodies. Skills to further develop this healing ability using meditation, creative visualization and color healing are discussed in the next chapter.

Chakra Correspondences[41]

Chakra	1. Root	2. Belly	3. Solar Plexus	4. Heart
Color	Red	Orange	Yellow	Green/Rose
Sanskrit	Muladhara	Swadhisthana	Manipura	Anahata
Spinal Location	Coccyx	1st Lumbar Vertebra	8th Thoracic Vertebra	1st Thoracic Vertebra
Ductless Gland	Ovaries (Or Adrenals	Pancreas Ovaries/Spleen	Adrenals or Pancreas)	Thymus
Aura Body	Etheric Double	Emotional/ Astral	Lower Mental	Higher Mental
Musical Tone	C	D	E	F
Chant Syllable	Ooh	Oh	Aw	Ah
Skill	Survival	Clairsentience	Balance/ Astral Travel	Love/Compassion/Joy
Physical Sense	Smell	Taste	Sight	Touch
Spokes/ Petals	4	6	10	12
Temperature	Hot	Warm	Warm	Cool
Symbol	Square	Triangle	Circle	Equal-armed Cross
Element/ Direction	Earth/ North	Water/ West	Fire/ South	Air/ East

Chakra Correspondences

Chakra	5. Throat	6. Brow	7. Crown	8. Trans-Personal Point
Color	Light Blue	Indigo	Violet	Clear/White/Rainbow
Sanskrit	Vishuddha	Ajna	Sahasrara	_____
Spinal Location	3rd Cervical Vertebra	1st Cervical Vertebra	(none)	(none)
Ductless Gland	Thyroid Parathyroids	Pituitary	Pineal	(none)
Aura Body	Lower Spiritual	Middle Spiritual	Higher Spiritual	Goddess
Musical Tone	G	A	B	Silence, All Sound
Chant Syllable	Eh	Ih	Eee	Om
Skill	Clairaudience	Clairvoyance	Pure Knowing/Spiritism	Oneness
Physical Sense	Hearing	All Senses	(none)	(none)
Spokes/Petals	16	96	960+12	Infinity
Temperature	Cool	Electric	Electric	Electric
Symbol	Crescent	Star of David	Lotus	Light Rays
Element/Direction	Aether/Center	Planet/Below	Universe/Above	Goddess/The Circle

Chakra Correspondences

Chakra	1. Root	2. Belly	3. Solar Plexus	4. Heart

Attributes	Life Force
	Heat
	Strength
	Will
	Ambition
	Sexuality
	Affection
	To Warm
		Solar Energy
		Emotions
		Tastes
		Appetites
		Pride
		Sexual
		  Desires
		All Desires
		Lungs
			Intellect
			Balance
			Nourishment
			Psychic
			  Center
			Nerves
			Personal
			Power
			Self-
			  Confidence
			Stimulation
				Love/Self-
				  Love
				Empathy/
				  Caring
				Healing
				Individualism
				Success
				Higher
				  Intelligence
				Adaptability
				Nervousness

Healing Uses	Circulation
	Depression
	Infertility
	Bring on
	  Menses
	Anemia
	Frostbite
	Neuralgia
	Paralysis
		Coughs
		Exhaustion
		Intensify
		  Emotion
		Menstrual
		  Cramps
		Arthritis
		Mood Ele-
		  vation
		Sexual
		  Disorders
		Kidneys
			Vitalizing
			Learning
			Mood
			  Elevation
			Dispel Fears
			Exhaustion
			Digestion
			Constipation
			Psychic
			  Development
				Ulcers
				Eyes
				Sunburn (green
				  then blue)
				Love loss/
				  Loneliness
				Harmony and
				  Balance
				Soothing/
				  Refreshing
				Headache
				Antiseptic
				Infections

Beginning Gemstones	Garnet
	Black
	  Tourmaline
	Smoky
	  Quartz
	Ruby
	Bloodstone
	Black Onyx
	Obsidian
	Jet
	Black
	  Tourmaline
	  Quartz
		Carnelian
		Coral
		Orange
		  Sapphire
		Brown Jasper
		Jacinth
		Agate
			Topaz
			Amber
			Citrine
			  Quartz
			Yellow Beryl
			Yellow Sapphire
			Yellow Jade
			Tiger Eye
				Jade (Rose or
				  Green)
				Peridot/Olivine/
				  Chrysolite
				Rose quartz
				Green
				  Aventurine
				Green
				  Tourmaline
				Watermelon
				  Tourmaline
				Pink
				  Tourmaline
				Emerald
				Green Quartz

Chakra Correspondences

Chakra	5. Throat	6. Brow	7. Crown	8. Trans-personal Point
Attributes	Communication Speech Creativity Artistry Spirituality Loyal Sincerity Self-Confidence Independence	Intuition Knowing Perception Psychic Healing Telepathy Empathy Spirituality Idealism Connection with Others	Spirituality Royalty Tran-scendence Power Influence Psychic Develop-ment Connection with Goddess Source	"Divine Liberation, Love and light" (Gardner) The Soul
Healing Uses	Cooling Burns Pain Sleep Calming Headaches Inflammations Infections Swellings Fevers Throat Menstrual Cramps	Ears Eyes Nose Mental & Nervous Negativity Mind Clearing Inspiration Pneumonia Reality	Sleep Inducing Stress Stress Diseases Nervousness Cataracts Calming Mental Disorders Scalp and Skull Tumors	Clearing Making Rapport Vitalizing Protection Unifying
Beginning Gemstones	Lapis Lazuli Aquamarine Blue Quartz Chrysocolla Turquoise	Blue Sapphire Moonstone Lapis Lazuli Sodalite Dark Aquamarine Blue Star Sapphire	Amethyst Selenite (Desert Rose) White/ Precious Opal Chalcedony/ Moss Agate	Clear Quartz Crystal Diamond Zircon Rutile Quartz

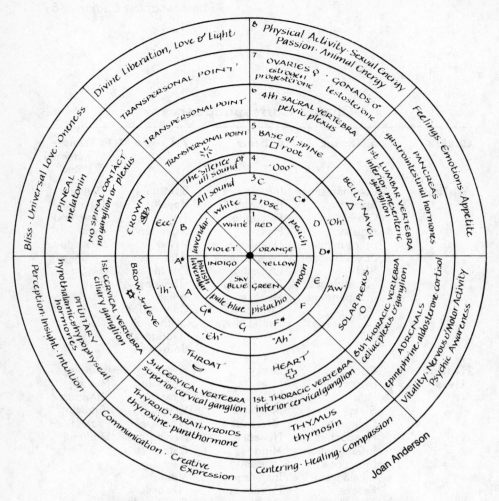

A CHART OF COLOR, SOUND AND ENERGY CORRESPONDENCES

1. COLORS (1st Octave)
2. COLORS (2nd Octave)
3. TONES (Chromatic Scale)
4. SYLLABLES
5. CHAKRAS (Energy "Wheels")
6. NERVOUS SYSTEM CONTACTS
7. ENDOCRINE GLANDS & HORMONES
8. ESOTERIC ATTRIBUTES

By Kay Gardner, M.Mus. from
The Rose Window, Healing Through the Arts, Inc., Stonington, Maine, Spring issue, 1983.

FOOTNOTES

1. Amy Wallace and Bill Henkin, *The Psychic Healing Book* (Berkeley, CA, The Wingbow Press, 1985, original 1978), p. 26.

2. This meditation is adapted from Melita Denning and Osborne Phillips, *The Llewellyn Practical Guide to Astral Projection* (St. Paul, Llewellyn Publications, 1984), p. 70-78.

3. The meditation is available on tape, Diane Stein, *Two Meditations,* (St. Paul, Llewellyn Publications, 1986).

4. C.W. Leadbeater, *The Chakras* (Wheaton, IL, Quest, Theosophical Publishing House, 1985, original 1925), p. 53-54.

5. *Ibid.,* p. 56. Leadbeater lists the prana colors as violet/blue, yellow, green, rose and orange/red.

6. George W. Meek, *Healers and the Healing Process* (Wheaton, IL, Quest/Theosophical Publishing House, 1977), pp. 204-206.

7. Keith Sherwood, *The Art of Spiritual Healing* (Llewellyn Publications, 1984), p. 67-68.

8. *Ibid.*

9. Mary Coddington, *In Search of the Healing Energy* (New York, Destiny Books, 1978), p. 129-134. Much of the material on kundalini is from Coddington and much is from Vicki Noble.

10. Vicki Noble and Jonathon Tenney, *The Motherpeace Tarot Playbook: Astrology and the Motherpeace Cards* (Berkeley, CA, Wingbow Press, 1986), p. 64-65.

11. C.W. Leadbeater, *The Chakras,* p. 116-117 and personal experience.

12. Personal communication from Adriadne, bodyworker at the Michigan Women's Music Festival, August, 1985.

13. Mary Coddington, *In Search of the Healing Energy,* p. 131.

14. Vicki Noble, *The Motherpeace Tarot Playbook,* p. 65.

15. Sources for correspondences are: Kay Gardner, "A Chart of Color, Sound and Energy Correspondences," in *The Rose Window* (Healing Through the Arts, POB 399, Stonington, ME 04681), Spring, 1983; S.G.J. Ouseley, *The Science of the Aura* (Essex, England, L.N. Fowler and Co., Inc., 1982, original 1949), p. 19-25; Diane Mariechild, *Mother Wit: A Feminist Guide to Psychic Development* (Trumansburg, NY, The Crossing Press, 1981), p. 42-43; Amy Wallace and Bill Henkin, *The Psychic Healing Book* (Berkeley, CA, Wingbow Press, 1978), p. 27-31: C.W. Leadbeater, *The Chakras* (Wheaton, IL, Quest/Theosophical Publishing House, 1985, original 1927), p. 10-51, 78-80. Where sources contradict, choices are personal ones or follow Kay Gardner.

16. Amy Wallace and Bill Henkin, *The Psychic Healing Book,* p. 71-71.

17. Diane Mariechild reverses these, but other sources and personal experience interpret it as given.

18. Kay Gardner, "Processional: The Root Chakra," Liner notes to *A Rainbow Path.* This is a magnificent album both musically and spiritually.

19. C.W. Leadbeater, *The Chakras,* p. 7 note.

20. S.G.J. Ouseley, *Colour Meditations, With Guide to Colour-Healing* (Essex, England, L.N. Fowler and Co., Inc., 1981, original 1949), Meditation 30, p. 47. Slightly adapted.

21. Vicki Noble and Jonathon Tenney, *The Motherpeace Tarot Playbook,* p. 69.

22. Keith Sherwood, *The Art of Spiritual Healing,* p. 60.

23. Amy Wallace and Bill Henkin, *The Psychic Healing Book,* p. 28.

24. Vicki Noble and Jonathon Tenney, *The Motherpeace Tarot Playbook,* p. 70.

25. Diane Mariechild, *Mother Wit,* p. 43.

26. S.G.J. Ouseley, *Colour Meditations,* Meditation 2, p. 27-28.

27. Vicki Noble and Jonathon Tenney, *The Motherpeace Tarot Playbook,* p. 71.

28. S.G.J. Ouseley, *The Science of the Aura* (Essex, England, L.N. Fowler and Co., Incl., 1982, original 1949), p. 22.

29. Amy Wallace and Bill Henkin, *The Psychic Healing Book,* p. 29.

30. Kay Gardner, "Castle in the Mist: The Throat Chakra," Liner notes from *A Rainbow Path.*

31. Vicki Noble and Jonathon Tenney, *The Motherpeace Tarot Playbook,* p. 72.

32. Keith Sherwood, *The Art of Spiritual Healing,* p. 61.

33. Diane Mariechild, *Mother Wit,* p. 43.

34. S.G.J. Ouseley, *Colour Meditations,* Meditation 26, p. 44-45.

35. C.W. Leadbeater, *The Chakras,* p. 15.

36. S.G.J. Ouseley, *Colour Meditations,* p. 25.

37. Kay Gardner, "A Chart of Color, Sound and Energy Correspondences," in *The Rose Window,* Spring, 1983.

38. Kay Gardner, "Fountain of Light: Transpersonal Chakra," Liner notes from *A Rainbow Path.*

39. This meditation is combined and adapted from two exercises by Amy Wallace and Bill Henkin, in *The Psychic Healing Book,* p. 70-72, and 122-123. Also see Diane Mariechild, *Mother Wit,* p. 44-45.

40. Amy Wallace and Bill Henkin, *The Psychic Healing Book,* p. 122.

41. References are from: Kay Gardner, "A Chart of Color, Sound and Energy Correspondences," in *The Rose Window* (Healing through Arts, Inc.), Spring, 1983; C.W. Leadbeater, *The Chakras* (Wheaton, IL, Quest/Theosophical Publishing House, 1985, original 1927), p. 10-15, 78-80; Diane Mariechild, *Mother Wit: A Feminist Guide to Psychic Development* (Trumansburg, NY, The Crossing Press, 1981), p. 42-43: S.G.J. Ouseley, *The Science of the Aura* (Essex, England, L.N. Fowler and Co., Inc. 1982, original 1949), p. 19-25; and Amy Wallace and Bill Henkin, *The Psychic Healing Book* (Berkeley, The Wingbow Press, 1978), p. 27-31. Where sources contradict, choices are personal ones, and usually follow Kay Gardner.

Basic Healing Skills— Meditation, Visualization and Color Work

WOMEN'S HEALING has three basic types: laying on of hands or pranic healing, psychic or mental/visualization healing, and spiritual healing. The types involve working with the chakras and four bodies, and begin with three basic learning skills. Meditation, creative visualization and color work are the skills of this chapter, connected to spiritual healing, psychic healing and laying on of hands respectively. The three skills are used in all three types of healing, whether using crystals and gemstones or not, and crystals and gemstones are used in all three types. Pranic healing or laying on of hands occurs on the level of the etheric double, and color work in the etheric and emotional bodies. Psychic healing and creative visualization occur on the thought form or mental level, involving the kama-manas, and spiritual healing occurs in the three aura levels of the spiritual body. The higher the aura level that a healer and the woman being healed can reach together, the more profound the change to wellness. Since change or well-being filters down from the higher to the lower bodies or from the lower to the higher,* all of the bodies experience change, and connecting the unseen bodies is the important goal. Meditation, visualization and color work effect changes in the spiritual, mental and emotional bodies to change dis-ease at the etheric double and dense physical levels.

---

*The aura levels and bodies are not a hierarchy but are parts of the whole. They are arranged in levels, like layers on a cake, and higher to lower is the clearest way to describe and visualize them. There is an order of placement, not a higher to lower value of worth.

63

The skills of meditation, visualization and color work are known in women's spirituality for their part in ritual, divination, contact with higher knowledge and contact with the goddess. Creative visualization is the way to manifest wishes on the physical plane, to invoke the directions and cast the circle. Colors, easily expressed in matching candles and altar decor to the seasons, directions or request, set the tone and establish the mood, and appeal to the emotional body. Colors and visualizations combined with meditation states are the keys to connection with the goddess, to opening the spiritual levels for raising power and inviting the presence and wisdom of devas, guides or goddesses to the ritual. Meditation and visualization are the channeling of power-within, the connection with the goddess that brings the above to below, brings goddess-within through the self to the earth plane for knowledge and healing of every sort. These uses connect the four bodies in a different way than healing does, but they do connect them just the same. "As above, so below" is the goddess' law. Meditation, creative visualization and color work are also skills that unlock psychic development, and are made much more powerful with crystals and gemstone work. These are learning skills, fun to dis-cover and bring about major results, and though kept secret by male systems since patriarchy sent them underground, they are available to anyone who chooses to learn them.

Eastern mystic Ramacharaka lists the three forms of healing and their effects on the unseen bodies and the physical. The first is *laying on of hands,* magnetic or pranic healing, "the sending of prana or vital force to the affected parts"[1] to stimulate changes through the etheric body and the chakras to the cells of dense physical matter. The changes made in laying on of hands cause dis-eased cells to regenerate into healthy ones, eliminating pain or dis-ease electrically from the microcosm, from the energy spaces between atoms. Science is dis-covering and measuring this force, in instances where it acknowledges it at all. Crystals and gemstones are used in pranic healing to direct energy and colors, and to amplify and intensify energy sent from the small chakras in the hands. Color work involves the chakra colors, using gemstones or light. Laying on of hands is taught in Chapter Five, and is an ancient skill of women healers.

Ramacharaka's second form of healing is *psychic or mental healing,* or creative visualization, "by which is meant the control of cell-minds,"[2] the programming of the inter-communication between cells. This is another universal theory of healing that science is beginning to notice and prove. Each part of the body, each cell that comprises each organ and each organ, bone, gland or blood vessel is a microcosm of the whole body and has the aspect of conscious mind that woman's Be-ing as a whole does. Any cell from any part of the body can be used to regenerate an entirely new Be-ing—the process of cloning has been done successfully with amphibians since the 1950's and with plants since the 30's. Taken outwardly, cell minds or cloning is science fiction unreality or the male quest for sons without women's wombs, but taken inwardly to healing, the idea is logical. Studies on psychic phenomenon in Russia have worked with the electrical and communication abilities of the human cell in scientific ways, and there is also the factor of rapid cell turnover,[3] already discussed. In healing, this means that changes made on the cell level are changes made in the entire body. In laying on of hands, crystal or gemstone work, the changes are made by energy/prana, the aura's electrical field. In mental healing or creative visualization, the changes are made by changing the mind's blueprint for the cells through the electricity of thought forms. An image of well-being and health impressed on the mind/mental body becomes well-being and health impressed on the physical, through every cell's blueprint of Be-ing.

As was discussed in the material on the emotional and mental bodies, thoughts are things, electrical energy with the power to shape and change reality. In psychic healing, creative visualization, thought-form healing, affirmation, mental healing (call it any of these), thoughts are used to effect changes on the physical as transmitted from the mental levels through the emotional body (kama-manas/desire-mind) to the etheric double and then the dense physical plane. The woman doing a healing for herself or another chooses them carefully. The woman being healed agrees, but is present or not, and distance is irrelevant. With over 70 percent of all dis-ease caused by a mental or emotional thought factor,[4] the changing or reprogramming of these negative factors is a powerful healing tool. The results of creative visualizations used in psychic healings are spectacular, as self-healings or distant ones, and make changes and repairs that male medicine cannot duplicate or explain. The power of this form of healing can't be over-emphasized. Creative visualization is the beginning skill, and its use in full psychic healing continues with the next chapter.

The third form of women's healing is *spiritual healing,* the connection of the individual with the goddess, becoming a channel to heal or self-heal. The spiritual level is reached nonrationally through the skill of meditation, and a meditative or contemplative state is necessary for any of the forms of healing. Ramacharaka lists this type of healing, direct from the source or goddess, as being extremely rare. Personal feeling says otherwise, believing that all forms of healing are a connection and channel with the goddess. Healing is a skill that is taught and developed, and connection with the source can use any name. No particular belief system, name or concept of divinity is required to heal or to be healed by any of the forms of women's healing. Spiritual channeling can be called goddess, god, the higher self, the mind, the Intelligence of the Universe, the self, energy. It can be called under any of the thousand goddess names, her thousands of recorded or imagined aspects, faces and world cultures. The woman healing or being healed does not have to directly believe in the goddess, in any divinity or in healing itself for the process to work, but she does have to link with some aspect of source and be open to it, want to be healed, believe that she can be, and connect through altered states in some form.

The woman doing the healing recognizes that she is a channel for the goddess or source, that she is not doing the healing herself, but simply conducting the energy for it through her own Be-ing. An ego situation obstructs healing—something male medicine needs to learn. Anyone can do healing and anyone can be healed, if she chooses. Anyone can be the channel. The healer does not do healings, she directs energy from the goddess that helps the person she is healing to heal herself. Energy is prana or the electrical field of the aura, the spaces between the atoms of dense matter. The woman being healed chooses to use the energy or rejects it, consciously or not, and a woman being healed that does not choose to heal herself is not healed. The healer takes no credit for a healing, has a responsibility to teach and share her knowledge, and does so with love and compassion. She often takes no pay for her work, and her ability to channel healing power grows with these attitudes and perspectives.

Healing is a cooperative act between healer and goddess, and between healer, goddess and the woman being healed. It requires all three Be-ings for success. The form of healing used, laying on of hands, crystals and gemstones, psychic or visualization work, meditation/spiritual healing or a combination of these, is open to choice and circumstance, and to the women involved. All are channeled from the goddess and from the goddess-within. No woman who has done a healing and seen it work, or has experienced and participated in a healing for herself and has been healed, can deny the power-within of her Be-ing, or deny her goddess-within. Healing is a linking with the source, with the goddess, as is all women's Be-ing.

Virtually all forms of healing, across cultures and across time, have understood the link with divinity or a higher source as the healing channel. Every esoteric society has some system for attunement with that source, for reaching that consciousness or energy, some setting up of the channel. Patriarchal religions call it prayer, but have diluted prayer's meaning and removed its power from lay people, perhaps as another form of removing the goddess/divinity, the direct channel, from women.

The connection most often used in Europe and North America for channeling the goddess is that of *meditation*, which has a number of various methods and forms. Meditation as most women know it was brought to the West from India, China and Tibet, but is known and practiced in every culture. Its basic universal goal is the altered state of consciousness through which the channeling of inner changes, enlightenment and healing occur. Changes in meditation are chosen and made in the self by free will, whether they are changes in mood, awareness, brain wave patterns or in physical condition/ healing. Changes are made intentionally, via woman's will, knowledge and power-within, and via the goddess and goddess-within. Entering a trance state does not mean losing contact with reality; it means taking power over inner and outer realities by choice.

The meditative state is basically a condition of inner stillness and awareness of Be-ing. In it a woman slows her mind, clears it of everyday worries and busy-ness, and allows her own Be-ing to surface into consciousness. The process of stilling the mind also stills the body, relaxes it completely through breath control (pranayama) or tension release of the muscles and parts. Mantras or focusing keys are used to bore the intellectual/rational mind, the lower mental body, so that it loses interest and the nonrational levels can come through. Visualizations in pictures, touch or sounds, in sense images rather than word concepts, allow the emotional and higher mental bodies to be felt. Total stillness, oneness, reaches the spiritual body, reaches women's connection with the goddess, and the woman pays attention to them, notices and understands her inner Be-ing. The process, familiarly, connects the four body levels, the physical, emotional, mental and spiritual, and unites them.

The processes of stilling the mind and body and uniting the levels in meditation develop skills of concentration and creative visualization. Attunement, the connection of the bodies in the self, the oneness of the self with the oneness of the goddess, combines with concentration and visualization as healing tools. With the body, mind and spirit made one, concentration and visualization are used deliberately to make changes in that oneness. The changes may be physical control, as in biofeedback, emotional control as in mood changes or stress release, or wellness control, as in changing pain or dis-ease to good health. The woman doing a meditation is always in total control of the changes going on in her seen and unseen bodies.

The alpha brain wave state has been mentioned, the change in brain activity that happens in meditation, in dreams and in deep concentration/creativity. This is a scientifically measurable change in the dense body. Healing, changes in the connected oneness of Being on all the four levels, occurs at the alpha state, and this is the brain level that meditation enters consciously. It is also the level of seeing auras and of ritual work, and the place where the chakra meditations of the last chapter happened. Analyzed more fully here, the sequence of doing meditation is the same as for doing a group or individual ritual, and the process is discussed in those terms.

Meditation is a cumulative skill and a pleasant one, but like tennis or typing does not reach pro-status on the first try. Set aside some quiet and unhurried time every day to do it; either first thing in the morning or last thing at night is suggested. Some women do it after work, as a means of changing roles from job to homelife. Meditating in the morning means that the mind is already clear of worries and relaxed; meditating at night or after work clears it of the day's worries that have gone before. Doing it daily, the skill develops and grows without measuring it or forcing the process. It grows slowly, but each day's work adds to well-being, to the sense of calm and power-within, the ability to manifest wishes on the physical plane, and connection with the goddess and goddess-within. When you need the meditation link for healing, for yourself or others, it's there for you, and you have only to ask the source and to do it. The power is within, where it's been all along.

To begin, find a place to meditate, a quiet and uninterrupted spot that feels safe and comfortable. If you have an altar, seated in front of it is a good choice. Disconnect the phone. The room should be neither too warm nor too cold, have a straight-backed chair to sit in or a soft rug for sitting on the floor, and needs to be a place alone. Work in loose comfortable clothing or skyclad. Meditation is best after a shower or bath has washed the cares of the day away. Several hours after a meal is the best time, not soon after eating. Arrange candles and crystals in front and in sight (white or violet are good candle colors), and a crystal or gemstone held in each hand or the left hand is optional but good. Other meditation stones are jade, amethyst, sapphire, emerald, aquamarine or moonstone. Keep the arms and legs uncrossed. If sitting on the floor, the lotus position is good when it's comfortable, but is not necessary. Sitting instead of lying down prevents falling asleep, but meditation can be done lying down, too. Light the candles and shut off the room lights, hold the gemstones and get comfortable.

Once seated and ready, focus your concentration on the candle flame, until with the eyes closed the image of the flame remains. Take several full deep breaths to slow and calm the body, and clear the mind intentionally of all the day's concerns. Emptying the mind of all thoughts is the goal of some forms of meditation, but takes practice and time and may not happen fully at the beginning. Invoke the four (or six, seven or eight) directions, and cast a circle of protection if wished, formally or not. Seated in the circle, you leave the physical plane for be tween the worlds, the meditative state. If circle casting isn't used to reach this state of Be-ing, clear the mind by will, letting go of worries step by step, acknowledging and releasing each and letting it go in turn. Imagine a violet or indigo bag, and store each worry in the bag for later—or see it dissolve as each worry enters the bag. Alternately, say aloud, "I am worried about _____" and then say, "the worry is gone." Rhythmic breathing and step by step relaxation are the tools to use next.

To start rhythmic breathing, a pranayama exercise, breathe deeply and fully and establish a pattern to the breaths. Breathe in for a count of six heartbeats, hold the breath for three heartbeats, breathe out for a count of six heartbeats and hold it again for three.[5] Listening to your inner rhythm and feeling your heartbeats is a part of the process. If a count of breathing in and out on four beats and holding it for two in between, or a count of breathing in and out on eight heartbeats and holding it for four are more comfortable and natural, this is the pattern to use. Experiment and find what's pleasing and feels good, never forcing it. If, when you are beginning the exercise your normal breathing is faster, start with breathing in and out on four beats, holding for two, then slow both breathing and heart rate slightly to breathing in and out on six and holding for three. When this feels comfortable, slow it still more to breathing in and out on eight beats and holding for four. The rhythm is important, not the number of beats, breathing and then holding; use the increasing length of breaths to slow down. Breathe in and out twice the number of beats than the holding number of beats. Notice the changes and notice how it feels, and notice the ability to make the changes by *will* simply by doing them. It's that easy. By breathing slowly and gently in this pattern, breathing in and holding, breathing out and holding, easily and without forcing it, you become calm in your body and mind. Your thoughts and muscles relax, and you feel alert, energetic, rested and well. The pranayama pattern becomes automatic, and balances energy to the chakras. Pay attention to the changes.

Now physically relax each part of the body step by step as described in the beginning of the chakra meditation. Tense and release each part of the body, from toes to crown, continuing rhythmic breathing. By the time this is done, you are completely relaxed. Once you are used to doing meditations, you may not need to do all of the exercises each time; either circle casting, worry lifting, breathing or body relaxation may be enough alone. Now try a color meditation, or a series of colors for the chakras. First breathe in red to every part of the body, then each color in turn, orange, yellow, green (or rose), blue, indigo and violet. End with clear light. Pay attention to how each color feels, and to what it feels like at the end of all the colors. You can choose to use only the cool and calming colors, avoiding red, orange and yellow, or you can choose to use only the warm ones. Another idea is to choose a single color whose attributes are desired and breathe this color into all the parts of the body. This is color work, and a good color for stimulating meditation is violet.

Try a visualization exercise. Remember the gemstone or crystal held in the hand. Without looking at it, create a mind picture of it, not in words but in colors, shapes, textures, sounds and feelings. Imagine or invent a crystal if none is really there, or pick any other object that's familiar, in or out of the hand. Use as many of the senses as possible to create it. Keep the eyes closed and use the mind for this. Some women are sight-oriented, while others are sound or touch-oriented.

Create the crystal, gemstone or object and pay attention to its shape, weight, warmth or coldness, smoothness or roughness. Does it have a sound-connotation? Is it clear or colored? What colors? And what do those colors awaken by thinking of them? If the stone is clear quartz crystal all the colors are there—picture each of them and what each color means personally. Is it a temperature, scent, shape or sound? Does violet smell of lilacs, and indigo of starlight and forests? Is rose warm like feathers and does green smell like grandmother's garden in the rain? Does light blue mean peace or a particular symphony? Is orange growing poppies or marigolds, and red a favorite beach? What does yellow mean? Does it sound like a cello or a rock guitar? Is black positive and deep? Allow imagination to run free and appreciate the images; they are personal, individual and intuitive. If the stone is a colored gemstone or a non-gemstone object, start with its own color, but there is no need to be limited. Create it in any color. If you lack some particular sense, use your other senses, and visualize on your own terms. A color has temperature or texture; a sound may be a visual image. All the images, sounds, textures, impressions, and colors are the right ones.

Allow the crystal or gemstone visualization to fade. Next, cast either a clear aura around your Be-ing, or rose colored or violet, or blue, and again breathe the color that was in the image of the stone. Notice how it feels as you breathe it, and see yourself feeling always as good as you are feeling now. You are calm and relaxed, in tune and knowing joy. Woman's purest state of consciousness is joy. Draw the sounds, colors, textures, impressions within you; allow them to fade from your vision and your view, and open your eyes.

Return slowly and come back to now. Sit or lie still for a few moments. Notice the surroundings and the present, the candles on the altar and stones still held in the hand. Pay attention to feeling, breathing, mood, self and the room. Come back slowly, without moving yet. Notice what changes there have been since starting the meditation, and how much time has passed. Open the circle and thank the directions, and the goddess for her help and presence. Put the stones down and place the palms to the floor, feeling the excess energy leaving, entering the Earth to be recycled. Hold the hands there long enough. Get up slowly when ready, and return to now.

The next day at the same time and in the same place, try it again. Duplicate the conditions. The ability to enter and leave the alpha state grows with practice and happens more quickly in time. Full breathing routine, full body relaxation are needed at first, but become gradually shorter and easier. Eventually the concentrating key of the candle flame or crystal, the place, time, quiet and surroundings are enough by themselves to *will* entrance to the meditative state. Try using the crystal as a focusing key, looking into it instead of into the flame, or looking at the flame through the crystal. Eventually healings can be done anywhere at any time, the alpha meditation state triggered quickly with a crystal or a few deep rhythmic breaths. This process is called centering or deepening, becoming still inside at any time.

The visualizations at the middle of this meditation have infinite varieties. Colors and healings, chakra work, divination and guided journeys are only a few of them. An excellent basic book of meditations is Diane Mariechild's *Mother Wit: A Feminist Guide to Psychic Development,* and various meditation tapes are available including the author's. The work with the crystal, learning about its colors and qualities, can be used to gain information about any gemstone and its uses, what it is and how to heal with it. Meditate on its color and shape, and let the images come. The breathing exercise can be combined with chanting or mantras, or use Kay Gardner's chant syllables listed for the chakras. Pranayama is a major tool for releasing stress. Clearing the mind of all thoughts totally can be the object of a meditation, letting each thought go, until there is total stillness. When the stillness is complete, joy and oneness enter to be appreciated. Be sure to ground after every meditation or healing; do it every time at the end. This is extremely important.

The skill of creating an image, whether of an object or color, of the chakras, people, energy flows or of things that the woman wishes to make happen in her life, is the skill of *creative visualization.* It's the process of choosing a thought form, creating it in the lower mental body, then transmitting it downward and upward through all the body levels. A thought moves downward from the conscious mental level to the emotional/astral body, then to the etheric double and lastly to the dense physical. It moves upward from the lower to higher mental levels, then to the lower, middle and higher spiritual auras, the spiritual body. Other names for the skill are imaging, picturing, creating, imagining, affirmation or suggestion. Thought forms are not word concepts but are symbols, pictures, sounds, scents or touch images, images of kama-manas. Only the conscious mind, the lower mental body, understands words; the other bodies need pictures or other sense imagery to understand the language with. Creative visualization is a powerful means of connecting the four bodies. By doing it in the meditation state, carefully selected changes in the dense body or even in external events can be created and made manifest on the physical plane.[6]

Creative visualization is "the power of positive thinking," and means that literally. Creating a positive image or thought creates a positive result, while creating a negative image or thought creates a negative one. The woman in the meditation created a crystal and that's what she got. If she had created a rotten egg, she would have gotten a rotten egg, alive and smelling ripe. If she asked for "not a rotten egg" she would have gotten the rotten egg again—the nonconscious mind knows the picture "rotten egg," but the word-concept "not" has no meaning to anything but the rational mind. "Not" doesn't transmit to the higher mental or to the emotional body, nor to the etheric double, the physical level or the spiritual. The image becomes reality, and has to be a positive one in present tense, an image she wants to create and manifest in the now.

In healing, picture full glowing health, the woman smiling and active. Never picture the woman with her broken leg (self or otherwise), see her running with the cast off to create the image in reality and in her aura. Picture what is wanted, and visualize it exactly as if it exists right now—astral/psychic time is timeless, what will be already is. Take care in what is visualized, as it manifests as it's created. Avoid visualizing fears, or letting your imagination run wild with all of the negatives that could happen in the dis-ease. By doing that, you only create them and make them be. When healing yourself and others, think and speak in positive terms to create only positive images and thought forms. Visualize what you want to exist, full, glowing, active health, and create it by doing so. The image of perfect health at the end of any healing is extremely important, and is a safeguard.

If, in your meditation/visualization you want a ruby, visualize a ruby, not an emerald, but you can change it to an emerald at will. If you want one of your chakras closed or opened in some amount, or the soreness in your throat removed, picture it happening as you direct it. Picture your aura or another's as it is, see what's out of balance, and change it to balance and health. What you visualize and will, you create. If you are unable in the beginning of this work to actually see the thing happening or being created, imagine that it's there, or speak a description of it aloud until the skill develops, but train the mind pictures, too. A woman who does not see visually or is not sight-oriented makes the images in personal terms, in sound, feel, scent, texture or temperature images that represent to her the object and event. No disability or orientation prevents visualization, despite its name and emphasis on sight. This is a skill that grows easier with time and use, and comes more quickly to some women than to others, but is available to all. One hint of it is that in learning to read, children learn to translate pictorial/sensory images into word concepts, and learn to use their rational, lower mental minds. In creative visualization (something that was real and active in everyone before they learned to read), a woman learns to turn the images back again. In a word-oriented society, it's a skill that needs relearning, just as in a science and rationality-oriented society, children un-learn that they can see auras. Word concepts are the language of the rational mind; visualizations are the language of the unseen bodies, the energy levels of Be-ing. The word "visionary" is related.

"Thoughts are things," to quote Annie Besant and C.W. Leadbeater.[7] They are capable of affecting the individual who creates them and by them a woman creates her own reality. Thoughts are capable of changing reality, changing dis-ease to health, and a woman's positive thoughts directed in a meditative state create positive objects. Thoughts also affect others: a happy, confident, well woman entering a roomful of others makes everyone else feel happy and confident and well. The opposite is also true. Thoughts can be sent to others if the other is receptive to them, and used to help another woman to heal herself. There are three classes of thought forms:

1. Thoughts that transmit the thinker's image: A woman who thinks of herself as being elsewhere, sends an image of herself there. A woman who thinks of herself as happy and well, becomes happy and well.

2. Thoughts that transmit another's image: When a woman thinks of someone else, she forms an image of that person in her own mental and emotional bodies. When she thinks of that person being healed, she creates the thought form of that person being well.

3. Thoughts that transmit their own forms: A thought of love and well-being for a woman sends love and well-being to her, and helps to heal and protect her. Thoughts of illness reach her only if she is open to them, including such thoughts of her own making.[8]

Every thought and feeling creates a vibration in the energy spaces between atoms, and these have a permanent effect on the woman's Be-ing and aura. Every time that thought is repeated, it becomes easier to accept in the emotional/astral body, and becomes a habit and easier to manifest on the dense physical level. Thought is energy, and thought forms are an electrical means of creating or changing energy. A woman who has thought of herself continually as powerless (what patriarchy tells women) believes that, and makes it true by her own actions that are manifested through her belief. When the woman creates thought forms of herself as power-ful (what matriarchy is), and repeats them often enough in the alpha state for the vibration in her emotional body (her kama-manas), to make it a habit, she begins to see herself as power-ful, with power-within. As she sees herself, so she acts and becomes. A woman who sees herself as well and healthy has a ready-built protection against dis-ease. And if disease manifests, she changes its image, the thought form to wellness in her unseen bodies, and her physical body becomes well again.

A woman feeling tired and run down uses thought forms. She enters the meditative state by which thoughts are transmitted through the bodies. When completely relaxed, she visualizes herself as being well. She brightens, clears and aligns her chakras, protects herself with a healing gold aura, and comes out of the meditation feeling strong, energized and well. She is well physically down to her very cells, and well on her unseen levels, on the blueprint energy level of those cells. She is and remains well. A woman feeling tired and run-down that sees herself as a tired and run-down woman has created a thought form that makes it so. By changing the thought form, she changes her condition from dis-ease to well-being. Likewise, a woman whose friend is tired and run-down and who asks for help is visualized, and seen as healthy, glowing, happy and vital. The woman helps her friend to relax completely, to balance her chakras, sends her light to protect, heal and energize her in the colors and gemstones she needs, and her friend (either present or a thousand miles away) feels well again. The healer does this only with the other's permission, cooperation and choice.

Patriarchal culture is filled with negatives and negative thought forms, "thou shall not" or "women can't," and filled with directives of authority that only the doctor or expert can heal or "cure" a dis-ease. The fact is that women can and do cure themselves, and the only person that cures a dis-ease is the person who has it. No medicine, healing or surgery will cure a patient who has chosen to die; no healer can remove a pain or dis-comfort from a woman who chooses to keep it, or who cannot realize that she has the power to make herself well. Choices are involved here and habits, conscious and unconscious conditioning and free will. When a woman takes power-within and understands the use of thoughts and thought forms, she understands that she can heal herself, despite the years of being told otherwise, and that she can also heal others.* To put it scientifically, "thought is a form of energy," on and in a body that's energy, and "thought fields can interact."[9] The means of making the change is in creative visualization—in carefully choosing what thought forms to transmit to the bodies and transmitting them in positive, present tense, "I can" terms through the meditative alpha state. The change connects one woman's bodies or aura with another's, and connects women to the goddess source.

Creative visualization at the highest level of potential can control bleeding, remove pain and stress, shrink tumors, clear infection and knit bones, all in a time frame considered impossible by medical science.[10] It creates changes of condition that go to the cell-source levels in the dense body, by way of the electrical energy system between the atoms of the cells and the cell minds, and does so as easily as the woman in the pranayama exercise changed her rate of breathing, metabolism and heart rate to relax her body and mind. If 70 percent of all dis-ease is caused by negative thought patterns, then creative visualization is the way to change those patterns and re-turn women's bodies to health. Visualizing the crystal or the clearing and balancing of a woman's chakras are only examples, and beginnings of a whole healing universe.

Visualization will not "cure" disabilities and inborn dis-eases, or substitute for normal care—good nutrition, daily bathing, a body free of drug, tobacco or alcohol abuse, enough rest—but every evidence says that women can have good health, can choose it and do it, simply by using visualized well-being techniques in the controlled alpha state, by the simple awareness of thought forms, thoughts and the body as energy, and the method of creative visualization,

> Each person, without use of any medication, can avoid as many
> as 4 out of 5 minor illnesses, (coughs, colds, flu, headache, some
> allergies, asthma, etc.) and major illnesses (including many types

---

*A medical dis-claimer is required for this book: healing and medicine are two different things, complementary things in patriarchy at best. In medical difficulty seek medical attention, no claims or prescriptions of "cures" can legally be made.

of cancer, non-malignant cysts and tumors, many types of heart trouble, stomach and intestinal disorders, mental and emotional breakdowns, etc.)[11]

Most dis-ease causing thought patterns can be changed by visualization and power-within choice, and most healing for the self and others is mental or psychic healing, or uses visualization as colors or in some other way. All healing begins with the meditative state as a means of connecting the four bodies and reaching the goddess within. The woman who does this work before dis-ease begins, who appreciates and nourishes her body with positive thought forms and a self-image of good health, goes a long way toward preventing disease. When dis-ease manifests, the woman changes the thought form, and changes her health. The power is immense, and women recognize the need always to use it and all healing only for good, and in accordance with free will.

An aspect of creative visualization that has been mentioned often and will continue to be is *color work* done with gemstones, laying on of hands or with use of light. By understanding the chakras and chakra correspondences, doing the chakra meditations to feel the colors, the woman using this form of healing has good guidelines for what colors to use and when. Color surrounds sighted women, and even grade school art and design classes contain information on colors that are used in daily life and carried into healing. Women sighted or not are aware that colors have temperatures and other non-visual attributes, and that colors and their temperatures cause mood effects. Few women paint their bedrooms red, for example, because it's hot in summer and keeps them up at night. Bedroom choices are frequently light greens, blues, violets; softer, cool tones that aid quiet and sleep. Kitchens in most homes are given bright, warm, wake-up colors; often yellows and bright yellow-greens. High school browns are depressing to live in at school or the office all day, as is grade school grey or muddy green. Women choose clothing colors that consciously or not match their moods and auras. Colors that look well together are pleasing and harmonious, while colors that clash are agitating to live with or to wear. The colors that surround daily living are the colors used in healing.

Scientifically, light is composed of the seven colors of the chakra rainbow, and all of the colors taken together are white light. In pigment, all of the colors taken together are black. In light or pigment there are three primary colors that the seven major colors are made from: in light these colors are red, green and blue/violet; in pigment they are red, yellow and blue.[12] All other colors are made from these. Each color also has its complementary color, made by combining the other two of the triad. Combining any two of each three gives the third's complement. In the chakra spectrum, each color/center has its complementary shade that balances too much of that center. Red (root) and green (heart) are complementary colors; orange (belly) and blue or indigo (throat or brow) are complements: and yellow (solar plexus) and violet (crown) are complements. Color is light's vibration rate, each color with its own vibration, increasing from red to violet. All of these are used in healing, and used with gemstones of the needed color or complementary shade. Each chakra's color correspondence is a stimulant or depressant for dis-eases whose origins are in that chakra. When using colors for healing or mood altering, visualize them entering the aura in only their clearest, brightest tones.

Beginning with the root, *red* is a hot color, energizing and heating. It stimulates the life force and the nervous system, increases blood circulation and red blood cells, and aids anemia.[13] It stimulates sexuality, brings on menses and reduces depression. Gemstone healer Mellie Uyldert lists red for relieving pain, but personal choice prefers green or blue for this. Use red to activate and rouse, to stimulate the liver, for AIDS, paralysis, leukemia, cancer, neuralgia, frostbite, exhaustion, burn out, fear. This is the color of incarnation and life, to use on women needing life energy. Uyldert uses it to prevent miscarriages and premature births. Avoid on nervous, restless, angry women, but women of this type needing red energy respond to black gemstones without increasing their nervousness or pain. Black light is not often used in healing (more on this later), but instead use the black stones and visualize red, or use the complementary color green. Visualize the woman that needs red's attributes, and cast an aura of pure ruby light around her. Send red in laying on of hands. In the doctrine of signatures, red stones carry the attributes of red energy, and among the hot stones, ruby is the strongest example. Hold a ruby in the hand to generate the visualized red aura; it sends bursts of intense red light.

Orange is also a hot/warm color, cooler than red, but almost as stimulating and energizing. This is the color of the belly chakra. Use orange in healing for sending warmth, for exhaustion, weakness, intensification of emotions, for depression, epilepsy, the lung dis-orders of asthma, bronchitis, phlegm and coughs (also indigo for these). The color aids digestion and orgasm, brings on menses, helps menstrual cramps and ovarian cysts. It's good for the kidneys and varicose veins, for arthritis and joint dis-eases that need warming, stimulates the thyroid and depresses the parathyroids. Orange is a respiratory stimulant, and also increases breast milk. Amy Wallace and Bill Henkin in *The Psychic Healing Book* use orange as their primary healing color for psychic/visualization healing.[14] Nearly as stimulating as red, however, it is not suitable for all women or all situations. It's a good color for sending energy and vitality.

To use orange in healing, cast an aura of it around the self or woman needing the color. Direct the color to the specific pain area, to an arthritic shoulder, for example, by visualization and laying on of hands. Use orange stones, orange jacinth or carnelian to cast the aura with. Wrap a chilled woman in a blanket of orange light to warm her and return her energy. Put a carnelian in her hand. Blue is the complementary color, and uses for specific gemstones are con-tinued in later chapters.

The third healing color, corresponding to the solar plexus chakra, is *yellow*. In healing, this is a warm solar color, another stimulant, and connected with the assimilation of prana, nutrition, and mental understanding. Yellow dispels fears and exhaustion, and lifts depression. It stimulates the voluntary muscles and nervous sys-tem, the lymphatic system, the digestive tract, and depresses the spleen. Use it for diabetes, constipation, gas, skin problems, and for stomach upsets. It's a purifier. *Gold*, its electrical counterpart, pro-tects and strengthens the heart and entire aura. Healer Susan Shep-pard uses gold as her primary color.[15] Yellow is gentler in its heat and intensity than is red or orange, and gold is extremely powerful. Topaz is a representative gemstone for both colors, electrical and volatile but also soothing. Yellow's complementary color is violet.

Heart chakra *green* is an all-round balancer and harmonizer. It's the first of the cool colors, the most neutral color in temperature. It builds muscles and tissues, regenerates, salves, and is an antiseptic against bacteria and infections. Green is good for the nerves, eyes and heart. It helps high blood pressure, calms and soothes physically and emotionally. Mellie Uyldert uses green and green stones for flu, headaches, neuralgia, migraine, venereal dis-eases, heart dis-eases, the kidneys and cancer, as well as for stomach ailments.[16] Use it for ulcers, burns, sunburn and for nervousness. For burns and sunburn, use it first, then switch to blue, indigo or violet. For migraines, try aqua, the blue/green colors and stones. Greens stabilize and bring down inflammations and swellings, and blue does this as well. Green stimulates the pituitary, according to Ray Buckland.[17] Most stones for digestion are green or yellow/green stones, and green as the color of abundance and the Earth is the shade to use where poverty is an issue in women's health. Use it in visualizing or in laying on of hands.

Emerald, peridot and green jade are some typical green energy gemstones for healing. The possibilities in green and blue/green gemstones are great, with many good choices available. Green light stimulates healing of every sort; it's the color of spring and new life. Its complement is red, for the life force.

The heart chakra's alternate color is *rose*, used in cases of depression, grief, broken heart, lovelessness/love loss. It stimulates the thymus for love and self-love, creativity, joy and trustfulness. Rose is a major healing color, as dis-ease is so often a lack of love or self-love manifested in the physical body. Use rose for hearing loss and skin ailments, palsies, kidney trouble, heart ailments, for trauma, cancer prevention and recovery from child abuse. Rose quartz and pink tourmaline are good rose healing stones. A rose aura cast around the self or another comforts, warms, loves and heals. It protects, balances, brings hope, and rejuvenates the entire nervous system. A blanket of rose light makes sweet sleep and dreams, and rose is a major stone for self-healing.

Blue/green is the intermediary color between heart center green and throat chakra blue. Blue/green, aqua or turquoise light is a connector of the physical and mental with the spiritual aura bands, and it harmonizes and balances, calms. It decreases brain activity, and helps to remove worries and overactive thoughts from the mind, helps with skin problems, migraines, headaches, nutritional disorders, is a tonic, and stimulates breast milk. Turquoise is a soothing color or gemstone, good as a complement to too much orange. Use it on women who are hypersensitive, too clairsentient, irritable and hypercritical. It's good for the eyes and eye problems, for swelling in the brain or any part of the body, for high blood pressure, for inflammations, infections, burns. Other gemstones to use when casting blue/green light are aquamarine or chrysocolla. They are major stress-reducing stones. Susan Sheppard calls aqua an electric/cool color.

Clear *blue* light from the throat chakra is the coldest color and probably the most major one for all types of healing. It overlaps with blue/green. Blue is an antidote for red, the red of inflammations, burns, swellings, wounds, bleeding and fevers. Blue cools and relieves pain, reduces blood flow and high blood pressure, calms and relieves headaches, and induces sleep. Blue is antiseptic and it disinfects, cools sunburn, ulcers, skin rashes. Use it also for diarrhea and dysentary, hemorrhages, menstrual pain, sore throats, vomiting, insect stings, goiter, colic, and rheumatism that is hot. It soothes and relaxes. Blue heals all and relieves all suffering. A blue aura sent in healing is the most universal healing visualization. Concentrate it on pain or wound areas, and use it for any healing where the color is unknown and over-cold is not a factor. Lapis lazuli is the most ancient and representative blue gemstone, a powerful stone for most healing work, and another antidote for too much of blue's complementary color, orange.

Indigo is the brow chakra color, and is astringent and electrical, rather than cool or warm. It's a sedative and pain reliever, slows blood flow, and builds white blood cells for immunity and fighting infection. It increases function in the parathyroids and decreases function in the thyroid glands. It decreases breathing and causes contraction, drying, thickening and hardening. Use indigo for the eyes, ears and nose, for the lungs, asthma, bronchitis, tuberculosis, pneumonia. It helps with hearing loss, breathing diffficulties, cataracts (also violet), upset stomachs, mental and nervous dis-orders, and is another complement to orange. Mellie Uyldert lists indigo for infants' convulsions, delirium tremens, depression, hypochondria, manic-depressive disorders and dementia, mental upsets, epilepsy and Parkinson's disease.[18] Blue sapphire is a stone which can be used with this aura, as is sodalite or dark aquamarine. Many healers use lapis lazuli for the brow center and indigo. Indigo is a spiritual cleanser that clears the mind and rejects negativity—things that creative visualization, color work and women's healing are all about. An indigo aura is vitalizing and calming at once.

Violet is the fastest vibrating visible color ray, connected to the higher spiritual body and the crown chakra. This color in healing is sleep inducing and stress-removing, good for all stress-related diseases including migraine and high blood pressure, and for all troubles of the head and mind. It calms, relaxes, slows the motor system and heart rate, decreases lymph activity, builds white blood cells and stimulates the spleen. Ray Buckland lists the deeper purple tones as increasing function in the veins, expanding the blood vessels, and decreasing kidney function.[19] Violet is a sexual inhibitor, drunkenness inhibitor, and lowers body temperature. It decreases sensitivity to pain. Cataracts and brain tumors are helped with violet or purple light and gemstones, meningitis, hair loss, concussion, colds and stuffed sinuses. Mellie Uyldert connects it also to creative thinking and inspirational greatness, and S.G.J. Ouseley uses it for mental and nervous dis-orders that are non-chemical in nature, for epilepsy, neuralgia and/or rheumatism. The most representative stone for casting a violet light aura is amethyst.

Some final colors to list are *silver,* used by Susan Sheppard in her work to knit broken bones, *white* for increasing breast milk in nursing women (white rather than clear/rainbow), *brown* for grounding. Brown stabilizes and connects with the Earth, and is often a color of the chakras in the soles of the feet. *Magenta* or any reds stimulate the heart. *Clear/white/rainbow* is all of the colors of light together and is used for protection, for making contact with a woman's aura, and for unifying a healing before leaving the aura at the end. Clear quartz crystal is used for this light, and is also used for any of the other colors. Simply program it to send the color desired, visualize the color, or use it when the color is unknown without programming it at all.

When colors in this way are combined with the concept of creative visualization, the woman has a fair idea of how to begin doing psychic healings. Colors are used in laying on of hands as well. The healer enters the meditative state, assesses what's needed by the conditions of the chakras and aura, and chooses a color. She sends the color, surrounding her aura or the woman she is healing with light in that tone, or uses a gemstone of the color and attributes needed. Where there is a specific site of illness, she focuses the color on that spot. She may use one color or a color series, or run through the whole rainbow spectrum. Before leaving the aura, Susan Sheppard surrounds her patients with gold; Amy Wallace and Bill Henkin use orange, and many other healers use blue or green. Sheppard warns against using rose for healing others as it creates a bond between the women, but where caring already exists or for self-healing, definitely use rose light or gemstones. Visualize perfect health, change the color to clear/white, and withdraw. When in doubt of what color to send, use intuition; ask the woman being healed, ask the inner self, a spirit guide or the goddess-within. If the healer is still in doubt, choose between warm and cool energy and go from there, and if still unsure, use green or blue light that can never harm. As in most healing, with the basic information understood, expand it and develop it in personal ways. Women's intuition and imagination in healing, her aura sense and sense of the unseen bodies, is virtually always guided and right. Remember the meditative state, the linking with the goddess, and remember that what is visualized happens.

Colors are also used in colored light or candles, their light rays in a room or focused on the area to be healed. There is no other light in the room, and it is only the light itself that touches the aura or skin. Use this for fifteen minutes twice a day, and combine it with color breathing. Colored bulbs to fit any lamp are available in lighting stores or supermarkets for about a dollar. Candles are available in card shops in a wide range of colors, and cost about a dollar also. Color breathing is done as a pranayama exercise, breathing in and out the color desired, and doing so in a rhythmic way. Colors and individual gemstones are dis-covered later, as well for their uses in pranic healing and in gemstone essences/elixirs.

Brief mention is needed here on the sources women link with for healing. Some women heal by looking within themselves and/or connecting directly with the goddess in meditation. Others work, again in the meditative state but a state often deeper, by way of inner voices or direction, discarnate entities that communicate through their Beings. The healing help surfaces when the woman asks for it or needs it, or seeks it in altered states. These energies are called spirit guides, and are a central concept in Native American, some African, South American, and many other traditions. Either way is powerful, positive and right—and is effective.

Seeking within or reaching to connect with the goddess is called *animism,* and is the experience of most Western women healers. These women seek the goddess as a Be-ing within as well as beyond themselves, the goddess as all of life and all of life's processes everywhere. Working with spirit guides is called *spiritism,* and many women who are clairaudient are in contact with healers on other planes. Women who heal through discarnate helpers are called mediums, and may do it by entering very deep altered states.[20] Many of the famous healers being studied in the Philippines and worldwide are mediums, and many women who are healers in the women's community are aware of psychic help. Some healers who know what to do without knowing *why* are in contact with spirit guides, and may not be totally aware of it. They receive information it seems impossible to have. Luisah Teish's wonderful account of "She Who Whispers" is an example of spirit guides.[21] The guide may offer a name or not, and the woman can seek her name/s. Some simply call her "goddess." If wanting to meet with a spirit guide, the woman asks for her appearance and help in the meditative state.

Whether working from animism or spiritism, the woman healer is aware of the goddess and goddess-within, aware of her power-within to heal from whatever source, to heal herself and others. She uses the tools of meditation, creative visualization and color healing to right imbalances, alter moods and negative thought patterns, to protect, energize, calm, cleanse and to heal. By this time in the process and reading, the woman who knows auras, chakras and colors is already a healer. Applying what she knows is powerful and rewarding, and the subject of the next chapters. Then crystals and gemstones follow.

Color Work

Red	Orange	Yellow	Gold	Green
Root Chakra	Belly Chakra	Solar Plexus	Solar Plexus	Heart
Hot	Hot/Warm	Warm	Electrical	Cool/Neutral
Complement:	Complement:	Complement:	Complement:	Complement:
Green	Blue/Indigo	Violet	Silver	Red
energizing	energizing	energizing	energizing	soothing
heating	warming	warming	warming	cooling
stimulant	stimulant	stimulant	stimulant	sedative
life force	weakness	prana	strengthening	harmonizing
red blood	exhaustion	mental	protection	muscles
cells	intensify	fear	whole aura	tissue growth
circulation	emotions	exhaustion	heart	regeneration
anemia	epilepsy	muscles		antiseptic
sexuality	asthma	nerves		infections
liver	bronchitis	lymph glands		nervousness
paralysis	phlegm	digestion		eyes
leukemia	coughs	diabetes		heart
AIDS	orgasm	constipation		diseases
cancer	digestion	gas		high blood
neuralgia	bring on	skin		pressure
frostbite	menses	upset		flu
exhaustion	ovarian cysts	stomachs		headaches
burnout	kidneys	purifier		migraine
fear	veins	urinary		venereal
preemie	arthritis	infections		diseases
births	cramps			kidneys
	breast milk			stomach
				ulcers
				burns
				sunburn

Color Work, Continued

Rose	Aqua	Blue	Indigo	Violet
Heart Chakra	Heart/ Throat	Throat Chakra	Brow Chakra	Crown Chakra
Warm	Electric/ Cool	Cold	Electric	Electric
Complement: Light Green	Complement: Orange	Complement: Orange	Complement: Orange	Complement: Yellow

Rose	Aqua	Blue	Indigo	Violet
soothing	soothing	soothing	soothing	soothing
warming	cooling	cooling	energizing	sedating
sedative	sedative	sedating	pain	energizing
depression	connecting	inflammations	bleeding	stress
balancing	brain activity	infections	white blood cells	insomnia
broken heart	worry	burns	immunity	migraine
grief	skin	viruses	infection	high blood pressure
love loss	migraine	swelling	breathing	head
loneliness	hadache	wounds	contractions	mind
self-love	nutritional	bleeding	spasms	brain
love of others	tonic	fevers	drying	calms
creativity	breast milk	pain	eyes	slows
joy	hyper- sensitivity	high blood pressure	ears	white blood cells
hearing	hypercritical	headaches	nose	veins
skin	clairsentience	sleep	lungs	blood vessels
palsies	irritability	antiseptic	asthma	sexual inhibitor
kidneys	calming	ulcers	TB	drunkenness inhibitor
abused childhoods	eyes	skin rashes	bronchitis	pain
trauma	eye diseases	diarrhea	mental/ nervous	cataracts
acceptance	swelling	menstrual pain	fits	brain tumors
opening	high blood pressure	sore throats	delirium tremens	meningitis
endocrine glands	inflamma- tions	vomiting	depression	hair loss
cancer prevention	infections	insect bites	hypochondria	concussion
sleep	burns	rheumatism	hysteria	colds
throat		colic	epilepsy	mental/ nervous (non chemical)
sinuses		goiter	Parkinson's	epilepsy
gums			upset stomach	neuralgia
nose				rheumatism
high blood pressure				pancreas

FOOTNOTES

1. Yogi Ramacharaka, *The Science of Psychic Healing* (Chicago, Yogi Publication Society, 1937, original 1909), p. 33.

2. *Ibid.*, p.33-34.

3. George W. Meek, *Healers and the Healing Process* (Wheaton, IL, Quest/Theosophical Publishing House, 1977), p. 195-196.

4. *Ibid.*, p. 169.

5. Melita Denning and Osborne Phillips, *The Llewellyn Guide to Creative Visualization* (St. Paul, Llewellyn Publications, 1983), p. 44-45.

6. See Diane Stein, *The Women's Spirituality Book* (St. Paul, Llewellyn Publications, 1986), for ritual and non-healing uses of visualization.

7. Annie Besant and C.W. Leadbeater, *Thought Forms* (Wheaton, IL, Quest/Theosophical Publishing House, 1969, original 1901), p. 6.

8. *Ibid.*, p. 26-28. Not a direct quote.

9. George W. Meek, *Healers and the Healing Process*, p. 181.

10. *Ibid.*, p. 171-172.

11. *Ibid.*, p. 172.

12. Ray Buckland, *Practical Color Magick* (St. Paul, Llewellyn Publications, 1985), p. xii.

13. Color correspondences are from S.G.J. Ouseley, *The Power of the Rays* (Essex, England, L.N. Fowler and Co., Inc., 1951), p. 69-80; Ray Buckland, *Practical Color Magick* (St. Paul, Llewellyn Publications, 1985), p. 76-81; and Mellie Uyldert, *The Magic of Precious Stones* (Great Britain, Turnstone Press, 1981), p. 56-61.

14. Amy Wallace and Bill Henkin, *The Psychic Healing Book*, p. 23, and several other mentions.

15. Personal Communication, June 29, 1983.

16. Mellie Uyldert, *The Magic of Precious Stones*, p. 58.

17. Ray Buckland's gland correspondences vary with chakra sources at times but are noted here. The thymus is the gland for the heart center. Women are urged to experiment and use what works for them.

18. Mellie Uyldert, *The Magic of Precious Stones*, p. 59.

19. Ray Buckland, *Practical Color Magick*, p. 80-81.

20. Amy Wallace and Bill Henkin, *The Psychic Healing Book*, p. 16.

21. Luisah Teish, *Jambalaya: The Natural Woman's Book* (San Francisco, Harper and Row Publishers, 1985), p. 43-46.

22. Sources: S.G.J. Ouseley, *The Power of the Rays* (Essex, England, L.N. Fowler and Co., Inc., 1981, original 1951), p. 69-80; Ray Buckland, *Practical Color Magick* (St. Paul, Llewellyn Publications, 1985), p. 76-81; and Mellie Uyldert, *The Magic of Precious Stones,* (Great Britain, Turnstone Press, 1981), p. 56-61.

PSYCHIC HEALING

SITTING BEFORE an altar, hold a clear quartz crystal in each hand, cast a circle and ask for the goddess' presence to heal. Do rhythmic breathing, deep body relaxation, and enter the meditative state. Run a grounding cord from the root chakra into the Earth, and cast a circle of light and protection (blue, gold or clear/white) around the self. A friend who is not there has asked for healing; focus attention on her (or in self-healing on the self). First visualize the woman, who may appear in silhouette, then visualize the woman's unseen energy bodies—her aura. Pay attention to the colors, size of the aura bands, amount of light. The full rainbow will seldom appear, but usually a light haze and one or two emotional body colors. Are there any gaps, breaks, discolorations in the aura? Is the aura wider or smaller on one side, or at the back or front? Most healthy auras are egg shaped, the narrow end of the egg towards the feet and the wider cone of light around the head and shoulders, tapering from the waist. Is there a pain area on her body? How does it appear?

Visualize the woman's chakras, light them up and fill in their colors, read them as in the meditations before. What are the chakra sizes? Are any too open or too closed? Is there gunk, goo, blotches or pictures in any of the chakras? Is the woman's heart center wide or constricted? Her throat center? Her root? Is one or more of the centers out of line, tipped, cracked or disconnected? The disc or spiral at the front tapers into a tornado tip that connects with the spinal column at the back. Go to the known-about pain area, a red blotch, aura hole, cold or dark spot. Pay attention to what the pain is and visualize it. How big is the area? Is it concentrated or spread out, sharp or fuzzy in outline? What are the color/s or dis-color/s? Does more than one pain area appear, other areas not known about and that might be surprising? What does the woman need to clear the areas? Accept what is given, remember it, and accept whatever ideas come as to what the woman needs. If the beginning healer thinks she doesn't see all this, she imagines it instead, creates it and lets the images happen, images visual or otherwise. It feels funny at first, unreal, but is valid. She might receive instructions that she hears in her mind. Most women doing aura assessments or psychic readings for the first time are amazed at what comes, at how easy it is, and they learn to trust what they feel and see. If it doesn't come quickly at first, keep practicing in the meditative state. Be sure to ground at the end of each session, placing hands to the Earth and returning the excess energy.

The process of aura assessment just described is the first step of doing a psychic, visualization or mental healing. It works for self-healings beautifully, and works on healing women at a distance, either in the next room or thousands of miles away. Deep relaxation and the meditative state are the keys to receiving the information, visualization, and a concept of accepting and noticing that Keith Sherwood calls "paying attention."[1] Every woman is a healer, knows she can heal, trusts and believes in what comes. She learns to pay attention to the information offered, and by doing so learns how to use it.

The concept of paying attention is the concept of using the brow center, aura intuition and of understanding with the heart, rather than using the rational, intellectual mind. It is not analysis, but acceptance; a surrendering to the goddess-within, to being told what is real from nonrational sources. It is world love and heart centered empathy, detached rather than involved; it is not belly chakra clairsentience that participates, but is further removed and combined with third eye knowing. Paying attention or noticing is a willingness to be a channel and to heal, openness and trust in the goddess, operating on unseen levels. "Paying attention is a manifestation of the feminine."[2] To experience and understand it, the healer doing healing opens her heart center wide and works from that level and place. She opens her brow center, and combines it with the heart.

There are several exercises for learning to do psychic readings, assessing a woman's own aura or someone else's. A lovely one comes from Amy Wallace and Bill Henkin,[3] and a goddess Moon is substituted here for their use of the Sun symbol. Enter the meditative state, run a grounding cord and surround with protective light. On a viewing screen visualized if wished, or without one, create a rose. The rose is a symbol and can be in any color. It can be opened wide, closed as a tight bud, or verging on bloom. Create the rose and give it shape and color, leaves and thorns or no thorns. See it in a vase or on the bush or by itself. Make and dissolve several roses, each one different from the rose before.

Make another rose and name it with the name of the woman doing the meditation. How would she look if she were a rose? What color? What size? Blooming or in bud? Thorns or no thorns? On the bush, alone or in a vase? What kind of vase? Now put a Moon in the sky over the rose, leaving enough daylight to still see the flower. What phase is the Moon in? Is it waxing, full or waning? A psychic dark Moon? Is the Moon large or small, bright or dim? Are there clouds or no clouds around it? How is the Moon and her phases reflected in the woman doing the reading? How do the rose and the Moon symbolize her? How do they reflect her state of health or energy at the moment?

Dissolve the rose and make another one, giving it the name of a friend. What does this rose look like, and how is it different from the last one? Where is the Moon and in what phase? Think of the friend's Be-ing and health, and how her rose and Moon reflect that image. Do several of these, imaging/visualizing/picturing the rose as several other women. Pick a rose that's especially intense, and change it into a picture of the woman it symbolizes. What happened to the Moon? Is the woman holding her rose? What is she wearing or not wearing? Is she smiling or not? What do the images say about the woman's aura and health? Is there something in any of these roses or the visualization of the woman that you think needs changing, is negative or ill? Understand what is being shown, without changing it yet. Dissolve the image and the rose.

Create one more rose and Moon for the self, and notice on it anything that the woman wants to change. Mentally change it. Make the rose perfect and understand what was changed and why, and how it affects the woman's life or well-being. Change the phase, size, color and brightness of the Moon as well, if the woman wishes it. Give the

Moon a clear summer sky or make it full or waxing. If the rose is drooping, water it with green and watch it perk up, or choose another color that comes to mind. Don't analyze the color until later, or the images and their changes, but accept what rose and Moon are given and change them by intuition. Always make them better than they were before. Make the changes in a variety of ways: erase the painting and repaint it, pick it up and polish it with a polishing/healing cloth, wash away the negatives and see the perfect rose shine through, point a crystal at it and flow the changes through the crystal into the flower, flood the rose with healing light, say the changes aloud to make them happen. Surround the now-healthy rose with bright light in clear, blue, gold or rose color and draw the image within. Breathe it in through the heart or crown chakras. Come back to now.

Each rose is an aura assessment for the self or another. Try it again creating a gemstone. If a particular woman were a gemstone, what kind of stone would she be? What color, texture, shape, qualities? Is she raw, tumbled, gem cut, polished? Is she quartz crystal, clear or in colors? Are there sounds or musical notes connected with her gemstone or who she is? Create the stone with her name; create several of these visualizations. What stone complements her? If the stone is her but she should be a different stone, what stone should she be? Image the self and ask what gemstone is needed by the unseen bodies to make the woman healthier and more positive. Remember what is given, without analyzing it yet. Try the visualization given at the beginning of this chapter again, imaging the self or another woman. When this is completed, return to now. Understand what changes would help or heal, but do not make them yet. As in any visualization, meditation or other healing work, be sure to ground thoroughly at the end of it.

Some discussion of ethics is appropriate here. Women who are healers, particularly women just learning the skill, want to do the work and learn from it. Work on the self is fine and is the best place to practice and learn, but work on others *requires their permission*. Though common sense says that a woman who is not in good health wants healing and wants to be well, let the woman herself say so first. The easiest way to do this is to ask her, and to go ahead if she agrees. Be prepared for questions on what will happen, but *make no claims of promised cures*. If the woman refuses, she has every right to, and the healer is ethically bound to respect her decision. The woman may not understand or believe in what's going on, may not be open to the healer or the process, may want to hold onto her dis-ease. Every woman has the right to her own illness, and the right to say no. In offering healing, the healer should be prepared to explain and to teach.

When the woman being healed is not present, the issue becomes more difficult, but her permission is still required. If she can't be asked on the physical plane, ask her permission on the astral/unseen one. Go into the meditative state, visualize her, and ask her that way. Accept the answer received and be open to receiving it, whatever it is.

A technique that worked for healer Benjamin Bibb and was taught in classes by him is that of the "mental telephone."[4] He directed his students to enter the meditative state, then mentally pick up an imaginary phone. Dial the number or the imagined number of the woman, and when she answers asks her if she'd like healing energy. If she says yes, then ask her where her pain is, and go ahead. Bibb directed his students to keep a list of cards with names, addresses or cities, and health issues of a variety of people known and unknown. As an exercise, go through the cards, "phoning" each in turn and asking, making contact. In time it happens, and after a while becomes easy. If the woman contacted says no, thank her, wish her well, and withdraw. If the answer is yes, be ready to go ahead with healing, knowing that permission is granted. If not knowing what to do next, send an aura of gold or healing blue before withdrawing.

For Keith Sherwood, making contact and obtaining permission means creating a viewing screen and visualizing the woman to be healed on the screen. Held there with an open heart center, the healer's hand touches the hurting part of the woman being healed, and waits for her assent (something given and felt) before proceeding.[5] Assent is fully necessary; a woman choosing to refuse healing will not be healed, and going ahead without permission is a violation of her free will. Healing is power-within, and never power-over. There are emotional reasons for refusal—a woman may feel the need for self-punishment at this time: she may be getting something out of dis-ease that she needs, it may bring her needed attention that she wants to keep, it may bring her gains granted by others because she's in need. No one has the right to judge another or to violate her choices. This is hard to accept sometimes, but must be accepted. Seeing a woman suffer with menstrual cramps that could be relieved is hard to watch, especially when the healer knows that she can relieve

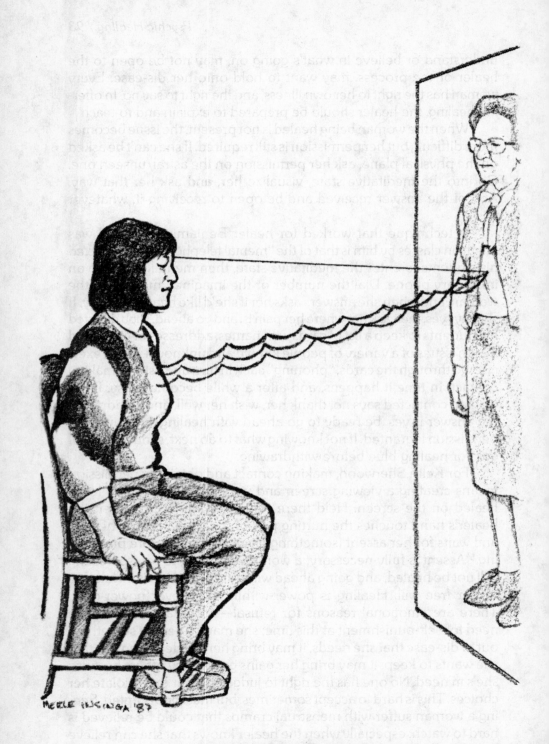

The Healing Screen

it permanently in a few moments. If the woman fears healing, distrusts it, blocks or refuses it, the healer can give her information but is bound to respect her choice. Such resistance can be conscious or not.

Healing is an immense responsibility and no place for ego. The woman doing healing is a channel for the goddess source. She works to the best of her knowledge and ability, but makes no claim that she does it alone. She is able to predict possible results but not to promise them, and she makes this distinction clear. She only promises to help. If the woman she is healing works with her, the two of them together make changes that bring well-being and good health. If the woman she is healing is unable to open to her, or if the connection with the goddess or goddess-within in the healer is not made fully, the meditative alpha state not achieved, or some other factor intervenes, if the woman being healed does not wish to be (consciously or not), the healing will not happen. If the healing is not meant to happen for some karmic reason, it won't. The healer knows she has power-within to help, and with the other woman's permission she does her best. She is simply a channel, however, and if it does not happen she accepts that. If healing occurs, she gives thanks and takes no credit for something that comes from the goddess/source. She respects the woman being healed and her choices, and honors her trust with caring, compassion and confidentiality. When the healer and woman being healed link energies and work together, create with the goddess a healing triangle of energy (healer, woman being healed, goddess), the results can be spectacular and profound. Every healing involves the personal choice to accept it, to make power-within changes in the self.

Along with ego issues, the healer also needs to remain uninvolved with others' pain, to love in universal ways, not participatory ones. She protects herself with an aura of light and a grounding cord from her root to the Earth at the start, and with grounding the energy through her hands at the end to prevent her from absorbing others' symptoms. If she takes on another's pain, she places her hands to the Earth again or places them in cool running water and feels it leaving her. She takes care in future healings that her belly chakra is not so widely opened, and that she heals from the heart center instead. Healing means protecting both the healer *and* the woman being healed. The results to both women are positive well-being, for the good of both and of all.

Once the healer has permission, she enters her friend's aura (or in self-healing, her own), and assesses what she sees, continuing in the meditative state, and paying attention. She uses her crystal as a magick wand to repair holes, tears, pain spots or imbalances in the aura, and sends the appropriate color/s. She casts crystal, gemstone or aura light around the woman being healed, in the proper color for the problem, watching the woman breathe in and use the color and energy. She goes into the chakras, brightens them, clears them of debris, and balances them. She adjusts the chakra opening sizes, puts a center out of place back into position, sends light to each center, and picks out whatever sticky goo may be blocking a center's prana. She visualizes taking the goo/pain/obstructions/pictures out with the thumb and forefinger, and drops the problems into a healing bag. When they are gathered up, she mentally burns the bag in a cleansing fire, or drops each dis-ease symbol into the fire as it's removed.* The red clots of pain in the throat chakra that are a sore throat may have to be picked out several times before they stay out. Send healing light, blue light to the center once the throat chakra is clear. Destroy or transform the sore throat goo in the fire so it doesn't come back or harm others. Getting rid of a dis-ease or a problem never means that someone else has to have it. If a chakra appears cracked, glue it back together; if cloudy, polish it. Imagining makes it happen, and tells the higher mind what to do.

Do the visualizations in personally meaningful ways; use symbols that have impact on the individual. The point is to create images that the unseen bodies can understand and accept as directions of what to program the cells for. Psychic healing is programming the four bodies, all the bodies, and it's only the lower mental that understands words. To reach the other levels, non-word pictures and symbols are required and the healer designs those symbols. Changes accepted by the higher mind and emotional body are in colors and ideas that can't be transmitted verbally. Non-word images tell these levels what to do, how to change the chakras, organs and cell minds of the physical body so that healing occurs from one level to the next. Full healing on all of the unseen levels and the seen dense body is the end result, the change from dis-ease to well-being. Use imagination to create the pictures wanted, to make the actions/changes happen. Remember that what's created becomes real, so create the images

---

*Many of these visualization techniques come from Benjamin Bibb or are based on his work. Each healer adapts them, uses them as suggestions, and does what works best for her.

carefully. Negative outcome from mishandled imagery is possible. Always visualize the woman in full perfect health at the end, and this is also a safeguard.

Thoughts are energy, and thought forms are transmissible from one woman to another. The idea of mind-to-mind communication is called telepathy, and is a fact of women's Be-ing. Most of male science, of course, dis-counts it, but women are aware of it, have always been aware of it, and are learning to become more aware and to train it. Telepathy is as valid a form of communication as the telephone, but the poles and wires are internal and unseen. Like women's intuition that telepathy is part of, it's a skill of the unseen bodies, of connection between one woman's higher mind and kama-manas and another's.

Science acknowledges that 90 percent of a woman's brain is involved in activities that are unknown and so far unmeasurable. Skills and powers exist for women that have been forgotten since the matriarchies or that women as yet have no knowledge of. Women's spirituality and women's healing attempt to train the unseen, dis-cover the potentials. The work after thousands of years of patriarchal repression is only beginning. Every woman has a story or stories about telepathy, particularly with someone she loves and cares about. Psychic healing uses telepathy and mental thought-form energy to help others heal themselves.

In self-healing, psychic/visualization work connects the lower mental to the other unseen bodies to make programmed and chosen changes. In healing for others, the contact is from higher mind to higher mind, one woman to the other by telepathy. The woman being healed accepts the thought form and uses it to transmit changes through her unseen bodies. The nonrational mind accepts these thought forms indiscriminantly, so the thought forms must be care-fully chosen and positive. The thought forms are symbols, rather than rational concepts or word concepts, since words are an unknown language to the higher mind. Any woman who has had a mind link or telepathy experience with another knows that physical distance is immaterial for achieving it. Distance is also immaterial in doing psychic healings. The links happen only when both women are open and receptive to them, and this is also true in psychic healing.

The unseen bodies operate on a feeling and emotional level, rather than an analyzing rational level, with the exception of the lower mental body that these symbols work for. Ideas are translated into pictures and symbols, the language of emotion and feeling. Kama-manas mind influenced by desire is in operation here, and emotions affect matter through it. Women under patriarchy have always been put down for the power of their emotions and intuitions. It was a power trained by the matriarchies and dangerous to the new order. The power of this emotionality and desire, combined with thought forms and transmitted as energy, is the power of mental or psychic women's healing. The energy of the exchange is the energy of the life force, the transformation and creative Be-ing energy of the unseen bodies, the spaces between atoms of dense matter. It is transmitted through the bodies via kama-manas.

The concept is connected to telepathy and is scientifically measurable. Healer Olga Worrall of Baltimore participated in the following experiment. Scientific measurement established the growth rate of rye grass seedlings at 6.25 thousandths of an inch per hour. Ms. Worrall was asked to send growth to laboratory seedlings at a specific time and on a specific date, and a strip chart recorder was attached to the seedlings. She was to begin at 9 pm, January 4.

> Exactly at 9 pm, the trace began to deviate upward and by morning the growth rate was 52.5 thousandths of an inch per hour, an increase of 840%. It gradually decreased but did not fall back to the original rate.[6]

Scientific safeguards against tampering were employed and the laboratory containing the seedlings was in Atlanta, 600 miles from Olga Worrall's home. Thought was the only energy applied; the emotional thought energy of a trained woman healer. Distance is no object in the telepathic transmission of this energy: the plants responded over a distance of 600 miles.

Many healers send this kama-manas energy in healings through aura work and transmitting healing as color and light. This is the example given by Keith Sherwood, Amy Wallace and Bill Henkin, and Susan Sheppard. Other healers make their visualizations and thought forms more precise. Along with color and energy, Benjamin Bibb used what personal imagination calls the "tinker-woman style of healing," and found it satisfying and effective. In this form, the healer goes into the aura and makes changes, cleans up, polishes, picks out dis-ease, zips up wounds and tears, fills in holes. The first form sends the woman being healed enough energy and color to take over and finish for herself. Color and light are transmitted through the bodies, and since woman's body in her natural state is well-being and joy, the energy is used to create that without further direction. For these healers, the image of wellness is the only specific instruction.

In the "tinker-woman" style, the higher self of the woman being healed is given precise instructions and diagrams of what is wanted, what changes are to be made and put into action. The healer works in metaphors but needs to know what to visualize, and knows it by intuition, knowledge of basic anatomy, and common sense. She watches her directions and images happen, supervises the process and controls it before leaving the woman's aura. Both systems begin with the meditative state and the grounding cord, with making contact and asking permission. Both systems end with flooding the woman's aura with healing or energizing light, and visualizing her perfectly happy and well. When beginning to learn healing, start with colors only, then move forward into "tinkering."

Healer Susan Sheppard and her friend Judy Burkhammer (the two often work as a team) do healing without visualizing graphic changes. They work primarily with colors and the aura bands, rather than with the chakras, and send light/energy instead of "tinkering." Their focus is less with the etheric body (the site of "tinker-woman" healings) and more with the higher mind and levels. After entering the trance state and grounding themselves and their subject, they go through the rainbow spectrum of colors, bringing the rainbow through themselves to energize their work and raise power. Then the healers surround themselves with a protective aura; golden or clear.

> We then imagine our subject standing before us. Strangely enough, we often see her/him as if in an x-ray vision . . . Often we just see an outline . . . We concentrate on damaged organs, swelling, afflicted tissue, strains, broken bones, etc. At this point we rely upon intuition to lead us. In the case of a young man with a bruised and swollen brain, we interjected a cool turquoise to bring down the swelling. After this is done, we may go to a basic green for rejuvenating purposes and then topped off with a brilliant yellow to energize the healing experience and rejuvenate tissue. If in doubt, the entire spectrum of colors is used. In the case of a young woman with leukemia, we were shocked by the amount of red absorbed during the healing: a color badly needed. It is very important not to have preconceived notions as to what color should be used before the healing.

>   After you feel that your healing is near completion, you
> again interject a pure gold into the afflicted areas. Imagine your
> subject standing before you completely healed and well...
> Cover the inner body and outer body with a protective shield of
> white light. As an extra measure, shield your own body with the
> chrysallis of white light. Say a small prayer in which you thank the
> higher power for assisting you. Now you can break your
> trance.[7]

A suggestion here is to use the rainbow or start with the expected
color for the dis-ease. The healer knows by intuition if this color is the
right one, or is shown what other color/s to use by moving through
the rainbow. In Sheppard's and Burkhammer's case, the color accepted
and absorbed is the color needed, and they go by that. Use this guideline, use women's intuition, and use what works. Always pay attention
to the woman being healed and let her responses and needs guide
the healing process. Knowing what color to use comes more easily
with experience.

Keith Sherwood's method is similar to Susan Sheppard's and
uses visualization of the woman being totally healed as the image
throughout. The healer sends light and colors, and watches the
woman's body absorbing and filling with the colors and energy. How
the woman uses this energy for physical dense body changes is her
choice. Sherwood visualizes the energy as being transmitted through
his hands to a subject appearing on a healing screen. He holds the
image on the screen with a combination of heart and brow chakra
opening and energy.[8] Women can visualize this energy as flowing
through hands, heart or a crystal, and visualize colors flowing
through gemstones. Hold the stones in the hand (the right hand is
usually the sending hand), pointed at the woman's aura, and simply
let their colors flow. End the flow by putting down the stone or shut-
ting it off. If no gemstone or crystal physically exists, create it; it's the
thought form that counts, and the thought form is as effective as the
real object to the unseen bodies. The energies of real stones have
great healing powers, and once these powers are understood they
can be visualized. Both of these healing methods operate on the level
of the higher mind.

Amy Wallace and Bill Henkin offer a technique from the etheric
double level, one moving closer to psychic "tinkering." In it they do
an assessment of the aura, visualizing the woman in silhouette, and
asking for pain and its source areas to light up as red spots. They note
in this that pain and its source may be at two different locations of the

body. A headache appears as red around the head, but if its source is the stomach, red appears there as well.[9] Pain can also appear in other colors: brown, reds, greys, or as dark spots of indeterminate color. The source of pain shows up in the chakras, to be treated there. Wallace and Henkin fill the red areas with healing color to dissolve the dis-ease and relieve the pain.

> When you have located the painful areas, pick one of them and imagine a glowing orange ball in the center of it. Imagine this ball slowly filling the spot of red until there is no red left. Do this with each red spot. If some spots will not turn orange, repeat the exercise. If they remain red, probably your friend will not allow these areas to be healed.[10]

Orange is the major healing color for Wallace and Henkin, yellow or gold for Susan Sheppard and Judy Burkhammer. Blue or green are other good healing agents, and used heavily by Ben Bibb. The healer experiments and does what works best for her, and is sensitive to individual situations.

A form of healing that does not involve the aura or chakras but is used with them and works through the rational mind is the form of mental healing used by Ramacharaka and mentioned often by George Meek. For a woman to be well, she must internalize the thought form image of wellness and see herself as well. The healer transmits wellness, that belief and thought form to women she does healing work with and to her own Be-ing, whatever her healing methods. This is true in both direct and distance healing, and positivity is the key. By thinking and visualizing in positive ways and refusing the power of negative thought forms, refusing fear and pessimism's power to create their impression, healing occurs or dis-ease never manifests to begin with. The technique borders on psychology as science, but is also known and practiced by women in ritual. Affirmations to make wishes come true is a use of this. What a woman states as fact comes into existence. She makes "I am" statements in the present tense and they manifest. The healer uses this for others, saying, "You are well," and visualizing her so, and the woman is helped to be well. She uses this technique in combination with other healing forms, as part of all healing work, and in the meditative as well as daily state. Positive healing statements made aloud and chosen in the rational mental body are transmitted to the other levels and are a part of psychic healing.

Negative thought forms bring disease, including cancer, and psychic healers working on cancer therapy have dis-covered a cor-relation between cancer and emotional factors, and the location of cancer sites with the type of negative thought patterns.[11] Healing consists in changing the thought forms, along with instilling the thought form of wellness and well-being. The healer visualizes the woman being healed as totally well, and visualizes herself that way. Several American healers are working from this angle. They comment that not only must the cancer patient change her thought patterns, but people around the cancer patient, her mate and family, must change theirs as well.

Women need to know that they deserve wellness, and that well-being is their natural, positive state. Too many years of patri-archy have told women that they have no right to exist, that their natural body functions are "sick," and such a mind set is a breeder of every sort of fatalism and dis-ease. Dis-ease in women's repro-ductive organs is a direct reflection of her believing from years of negative reinforcement that women's organs are sick, unclean or unvalued. She believes it and they become so. Add this idea to the amount of stress that women face in the patriarchy, stemming from the continually reinforced thought form that women don't measure up to men, and the ideas of positivity and believing in well-being become harder to maintain. In actual fact, the opposite is true: women from the embryo stage on are stronger than men, more advanced in physical, mental and psychic development in childhood and as adults, and women live longer and healthier lives.

Amy Wallace and Bill Henkin comment that people internalize a "havingness quotient," an estimate of what they believe they deserve, and they refuse to go beyond it, to allow themselves to have more (of health, money, love or whatever).[12] Women need to up their "havingness quotient," to accept well-being and whole-ness as their right and to take it, to wrest it from the patriarchy in whatever ways are necessary, and more importantly to wrest it from within themselves by power-within. This is the key to most dis-ease—cancer, reproductive, or any other dis-ease, and is the key to women's good health.[13]

A further thought is that stress is the root cause of perhaps 85 percent of women's ills,[14] including cancer, and that stress is a thought pattern. Changing that pattern, teaching women to

release tension and the negative images and self-images of patriarchy's attitudes is a major step in helping women to well-being.
Meditation is the greatest tool for stress reduction ever known, and
one in reach of every woman. Healing and self-healing, gemstone
work and visualization, laying on of hands, colors, chakras and
aura work are all stress-easing tools. When a woman does healing
for another, she reduces the stress levels in both of them; when she
does it for herself, she eases her own stress greatly, even when the
work is not specifically directed at stress. Psychic healing, creative
visualization, thought forms that add to women's "havingness
quotient," and images transmitted of health, joy, power-within,
self-beauty and well-being are crucial in stress reduction, too. A
woman gets what she asks for, and asks for the crystal instead of
the rotten egg. If she believes that dis-ease is how it has to be, she
gets dis-ease, but the woman who visualizes herself as well, happy,
relaxed and deserving to be, gets the power-within joy that is her
birthright. Visualizing wellness within, she is also immune to pres-
sures from without, to the ravages of stress and patriarchy, and to
most dis-ease. A further and necessary part of this is acceptance
and self-love of her body as perfect and right, which, contrary to
patriarchy's negative-bearing thought forms, it is. The woman
healer's emphasis on this deservingness and positivity is a part of
healing others and a part of healing herself. The image in psychic
healing goes a long way alone toward eliminating stress as a dis-
ease factor, and to combating patriarchy, as well.

The "tinker-woman style of healing" participates in these
ideas. This is a method described in vivid detail by Benjamin
Bibb,[15] and useful and adaptable for healing most dis-ease. In
cases of sending energy through the whole woman, Susan Sheppard's methods are the ones to use, and "tinker-woman" healing
employs this also. In cases where specific dis-ease is the issue, from
wounds to warts to colds, the graphic visualization method of "tinkering" is a powerful tool. The woman reading about these
methods learns to accept from them what parts work for her, to use
what works and also to create her own careful ways of doing
healings. Any book on healing is only a beginning, a basis for personal exploration and using women's power-within, knowledge
and aura awareness/intuition for the good of herself and for all.

Any of these healing methods also works well when enhanced
by crystals or gemstones—crystals to amplify and send light or

healing as a magick wand, and colored gemstones to amplify, direct and intensify color work and chakra healing.

As in other forms of psychic healing, you begin by entering the meditative state. At first you need to do this using the full exercise of pranayama breathing and tension/release body relaxation, casting a circle and going between the worlds. Do this before making contact with the unseen bodies of the women you wish to heal (or in self-healing with your own unseen bodies). Once meditation is familiar to you and you learn to enter it easily, you need only to do some rhythmic breathing, ask the goddess' presence to heal, and run a grounding cord or surround yourself with protective light before beginning. Instead of a grounding cord, healer Susan Sheppard visualizes planting her feet firmly into Earth for the grounding.[16] As this process of grounding and centering becomes easier and almost automatic, you can do healings virtually anywhere, but a quiet uninterrupted place, a safe-feeling place, is still necessary in most cases. Emergency healings may not offer this quiet, but women who are able to put their minds easily into the alpha state learn to do healings when and wherever needed, and they are effective.

In psychic healing when the woman being healed is actually there, sit before her with eyes closed and do the process in the same way as distance work. Ask the woman to do deep breathing and enter the meditative state as well, and ask her to ground herself. The process of a meditative state, grounding, making contact, asking permission, and positive thought forms are universal for all healings, absent or direct psychic healing, self-healing, laying on of hands, or healing with crystals and gemstones. The process of grounding at the end is also universal to all healing forms.

From the meditative alpha state, the healer contacts who she is healing and assesses the problem, then uses graphic visualization and colors to make mental repairs. The symbols and images are more usually the ones a mechanic would use than a doctor, but can be any sort of images that reach knowledgeable results. They tend to be mundane: a zipper visualized to close a wound by zipping it up, shrinking salve to reduce a tumor, washing out the plumbing to unstuff clogged sinuses. Tinker-woman images. The creative visualizations are symbols designed to tell the woman's nonrational mind, her higher mental body, what is wanted. When the mind understands what's being asked of it, it re-arranges the energy between atoms to accomplish the change. The healing is cell-source deep, is total, and occurs in a fraction of the time that medical means could effect. The images are made carefully and the body follows them.

In a personal example: I visualized a wart being pulled up like a gumband and snipped off, and the hole left filled in with goddess paint to make new skin. This was entirely imagined in the meditation. I did the visualization nightly and the wart sloughed off in a week's time. It was the author's first psychic and "tinker-woman" healing, done on myself, when I was totally inexperienced at doing psychic healings. The wart has not returned. In the case of a sore throat, sticky red blotches of gunk were picked out several times in the same meditation, putting them into an imaginary cleansing fire, until the blotches stayed away. I flooded the center with blue light, and the sore throat was gone in the morning.

Step by step, the process in its originator's words goes like this:

1. Contact the inner mind of the subject and observe the true nature of the injury or malfunction.

2. Use mental pictures to show the subject's inner mind how to correct this.

3. Supply healing energy and instruct the subject's inner mind how to obtain the energy necessary for it to perform and sustain the healing.

4. See the subject perfectly healed, then break contact gently and give it no further thought *at that time*, although the treatment may be repeated later.[17]

There is much leeway here for individual interpretation, for combining methods and using what works, and the healer does this. She pays attention to the woman she is healing and to her own inner intuition in knowing what to do specifically, what colors to use, what visualizations. Always ask permission when contacting another woman's Be-ing. Supply healing energy through crystals or gemstones, and/or draw it from the goddess Earth through the grounding cord, the goddess Universe through the crown chakra *kopavi*. Supplying healing energy means colors; the woman being healed accepts and uses this energy and the tinker thought forms to repair and heal her own Be-ing. Always visualize the woman being healed as perfectly well and happy before withdrawing from her aura. Susan Sheppard also imagines her subject standing before her five years from now, still totally well and free of dis-ease.

Surround the healer and the woman being healed with protective light, both before beginning the healing and before breaking contact at the end. This prevents unwanted absorption of symptoms by the healer and also keeps the healer from feeling drained after doing a healing. More on this in the section on laying on of hands. The healing needs no further thought; trust in the goddess that the work is done, that the healing has already happened. For entrenched conditions or serious ones, or when the healer is new and still finding her power, repetition is called for; do the healing again the next night or later in the day. A technique of Benjamin Bibb's for this is: before withdrawing, program the subject's higher mind to repeat the healing at specific intervals. This may be once an hour, every three hours, every twelve hours, once a day, depending on the seriousness of the dis-ease. The woman's higher mind takes over the healing, until healed or reinforced by another session, and the healing continues. Aura assessments in repeated healings show the woman's progress.

"Tinker-woman" images run to bad puns and verge on silliness, but their results are serious and amazingly effective. The healer's ability to create and transmit the telepathic thought forms grows with practice. It's a process so simple and logical that anyone can learn to use it, and this is true for most healing methods and processes. If the woman feels she cannot see the changes directly, she imagines them as happening—and they happen. She uses changes that reflect common sense knowledge of body processes. The system is based on visualization, but eyesight is not the issue; visualization can be done in any sensory symbols. Try feeling the broken bone knit or the cyst shrunk down to nothing and gone. Try sending a sound instead of a color. Be very aware of the free will of the woman who is being healed; ask permission and do not proceed without it. Inborn conditions may not be changeable, but healing results only in benefit and good. Healings have worked where medical science said it was impossible.

What traditional medicine calls the placebo effect has impact here. Visualization healing occurs in natural, spontaneous ways. The woman being healed may not connect her cold's going away to the psychic healing her friend promised to do for her that night from across the country. She believes that her cold would have gone away anyway, or perhaps it wasn't a cold to begin with, only a sinus condition that cleared itself up. The woman experiencing psychic healing at the time of an accident may never know that the foot was really broken, not just bruised as the doctor found it to be afterwards. The woman whose wart fell off could believe it was simply time for it to fall off, not that the visualizations had anything to do with it. Medicine has derided "spontaneous" healing, giving a patient colored water (what color?!) instead of chemical drugs, and finding her "cured" on the next visit. Women's healing uses this effect as a healing tool, instigates, catalyzes and controls it for healing, something male medicine could learn to do. Spontaneous remission is not lucrative, however.

Women's healing, being psychic healing that anyone can do and not coming from an "expert" or male doctor, is often not accepted or believed as real. The healer is not an example of a medical or patriarchal authority, licensed to cure. The woman who is healed by psychic healing may disbelieve that it happened. Healers need to be aware of this reaction, to know not to expect gratitude, or even feedback when they do healings. This is particularly true for distance work. No amount of arguing with the woman healed will change her mind in this case, but the healer knows what happened. The woman's non-belief doesn't matter; what matters is that she is free of dis-ease and dis-comfort.

Where two women can join together to do the healing for one of them, the results are intense, but this is less often possible in today's rational world. Women's spirituality, women's healing and teaching is making it more possible. Women aware of the potentials of psychic and visualization healing are healthier women all around. They are able to take control of the placebo effect, to use power-within for successful healing techniques to prevent dis-ease from ever entering their energy bodies or manifesting on the physical plane.

Here are some of the graphics and techniques of "tinker-woman" healing, based on the work of Ben Bibb.* In cases of a cut or wound, imagine a woman's work needle and thread and stitch the wound closed. Use a zipper to zip it shut, or goddess tape.† Flood the area with green or blue healing color. For bleeding, seal the cut blood vessels, then close the wound with tape. Pinch them shut with fingers or staple them closed with a stapler; tie them shut with string. When the bleeding has stopped, visualize the wound disappearing totally, see the skin as uncut, as healthy and smooth. First flood the wound area and then the woman's whole aura with light in the color needed,

---

*These are Ben Bibb's methods or based on them, revised by personal work. This type of graphic added to chakra healing and colors is a particularly effective combination. "Tinker-woman" healing reaches the dis-ease, but chakra work reaches the source.

†The idea is to visualize the result that you *want* to happen, and then *see* it happen in a very simple way. Make a simple visualization. This refers to goddess tape, goddess paint, etc.

gold, blue, green before withdrawing. If the cut is a deep one, instruct her unseen bodies to repeat the healing every six hours, more often for very serious wounds. For serious ones, repeat the healing again later, and again instruct the woman's higher mind to continue the process at intervals. Withdraw from the aura and break contact. Try again in the desired time space and check the woman's aura for progress.

For pain, use clear, blue or green light sent from the hands through a crystal or gemstone, from the heart chakra, or in any other way desired. Fill the pain area with color and light. For work with pain when the woman is present, laying on of hands is effective, and is soothing as well. Relieve the immediate pain with light, then go to the source of it and make repairs. If the source is unknown, visualize the woman's chakras and look for it in the centers. Ask her or her higher self why she hurts. Comfort the woman, soothe her nerves with caring. Use the healer's heart chakra and surround her with love if the pain is emotional: a rose aura. Comfort her heart with rose. Calm her with violet light. Leave her with a hug. Make sure the pain/source is healed so the pain won't return, but if she chooses to keep an emotional pain/source, just help her with pain. In cases of extreme hysteria, ground with black light. See her smiling before breaking contact, the emotional or physical pain relieved.

For infections, see the infection breaking up into fragments and pick them out or dissolve them with light. Use blue or green as an antiseptic, painting the area with goddess paint, and see green antiseptic healing circulate her body through the blood. Put the pieces of dis-ease into a cleansing flame. For broken bones, use goddess cement to glue them back together, or strong goddess tape; see the pieces aligned properly then fused. See the break line disappear, the cast gone, and the woman playing softball. Flood broken bones with silver energy, and the woman's whole aura with the color/s she needs. For swelling, send blue light to shrink it and see it gone; for cysts or tumors, visualize them growing smaller and smaller and then disappearing, or shrink them with shrinking salve. When not sure what to image, see the woman as totally well, telling her higher mind to function perfectly, to make all systems normal, the seen and unseen.

In cases of head colds, stuffed sinuses, congested lungs, visualize the dis-ease draining away to the outside (destroy it or transform the energy). Be sure to drain both sides and do them together. See the dis-ease leaving through hoses or faucets. When the lungs or sinuses are clear, fill the areas with orange or indigo light for drying, healing antiseptic energy. Use green or blue to soothe the tissues, if soothing is needed, then flood the entire aura with colors. Start with red and run through the rainbow spectrum, allow each color to flow until enough of it is absorbed—your intuition knows when that is. With the lungs, head or sinuses perfectly clear and healthy again, give the higher mind repeat orders: Do it again every three hours until fully healed. Check the chakras for blocks, surround the self and the woman being healed with a protective shell of light and color. See her fully well. Break contact.

For arthritis, first send the affected joints pain relief, and when assessing her aura pay attention to the appearance of calcium as roughness or grains in the joints. Healer Yolanda Scott's arthritis healing is quoted here:

> I cleaned the bones in the shoulder with sandpaper to take off the calcium. Then I put warm oil between the joints and sent white energy into the shoulder and upper arm to make sure all parts were properly healed. Finally I put her on automatic . . . I told her inner mind to send energy to this area each day for the next seven days . . . She tells me the pain never came back.[18]

Pay careful attention to the types of joint pain. Arthritis needs orange warming but rheumatism is hot and possibly inflamed, and requires blue to cool it. Some forms of back pain can be pinched nerves (inflate them with a bicycle pump and put a cushion under them, move them out of pressure, tie them in place). Some joint pains are injuries or swellings that are not from deposits. Make the "tinker-woman" repairs in whatever way is imagined, based on intuition and individual cases. Imagine sandpaper to remove joint deposits, and polish the bones with an imagined polishing cloth to make them smooth. Lubricate stiffness with an oil can of goddess oil for healing. For fluid in the joints or knees, drain it with a syringe and use the oil can again to soothe and heal. For slipped discs and dislocations, put them into place and tie them there with string, flooding the area with clear blue or gold.

To see the woman's body in its skeleton, simply ask for it, and visualize it when starting her aura assessment. After asking to see pain spots, ask to see them from inside. A cartoon visualization is as good as a medically correct photograph. The woman's higher mind needs a symbol, not a textbook, to understand what healing to do.

Since woman's natural state is health and joy, the higher mind works to achieve this, and once it knows how it succeeds. Use psychic healing along with traditional medical care, as well.

In skin problems, wash the skin with green goddess antiseptic and see it healed. For lesions and eczema, use sticky goddess tape. Stick the tape to the lesions and pull away to reveal clean, clear skin. Burn the tape and the lesions stuck to it. Send green or blue through the blood stream if the problem is systemic to flood the entire body inside and out with antiseptic and healing. With most blemishes and skin problems, flood the area with blue or green, visualize the red areas shrinking and fading until gone. Another method is to pick up the sores, warts, pimples, etc., drop them into a healing bag, and burn the bag. Then see the skin as new, clean and clear. Flood it with healing light: rose or green.

Another "tinker-woman" method is "stopping time."[19] This is used for repairs in cases where the organ needs to continue working throughout. The heart is an example. In working with a blocked or congested heart, use "stop time" by simply declaring it before going in to do repairs. Announce "stop time," go in and wash the heart with healing green to clear it of blood clots; treat blocked arteries by pushing a pencil through them to open the channels, repair tears or holes with goddess tape or needle and thread. When the repairs are completed, flood the organ with healing energy (red or blue is good for the heart), announce "end stop time" and visualize the blood returning, flowing normally, and the problem or blockages are gone. Don't forget to end "stop time." Use washing out to clear gall bladders, kidneys and urinary tract disorders, the uterus and other inside organs, including upset stomachs. Do the washing with a sponge or washcloth. Flood with blue or green healing light, yellow for the stomach or digestive tract.

These are enough suggestions to get the healer started. Expand them and add to them. The point is a simple visualization that tells the unseen bodies what to heal and shows her how to do it in very basic ways. The simpler the ways, the better. The work is one in the meditative state, using the same steps of other psychic healings. Combine it with other methods, and use what works. Always visualize the woman as well at the end of the healing. Use colors, light, tinkering, chakra and aura work separately or together, use them with gemstones and crystals, and use them for the good of all. After any form of healing work, be sure to ground.

A final concept in this chapter on psychic healing is the sources of dis-ease. When doing a healing, ask the woman why she is sick, and she usually knows. In a psychic healing she places her hand there, or the reason enters the healer's mind, and it enters the woman's as well. In a direct healing or when the woman is present, ask her directly. By asking and listening to her talk about it, the healer makes the woman self-aware, and awareness of the source is a major factor in healing and making changes. If 70 percent of all dis-ease is thought form related, then how much of dis-ease for women has its origins in living in a patriarchal world with its misogynist attitudes? If 85 percent of dis-ease is stress-related, ditto. Much of women's pain is the result of attempting and failing to internalize patriarchal concepts which are not healthy concepts anyway. Knowing that ulcers are anger, and eye and ear dis-orders are from things too hard to see or hear,[20] that sore throats are blocked throat chakras and the inability to say what needs said, makes a difference. Knowing that skin problems are usually lack of love or self-love and heart dis-ease a "broken heart" puts new light on dis-ease and why it happens. The idea gives women another way to take responsibility, power-within for their well-being, to recognize the emotional/nonrational/unseen sources and possible ways to change them. This is not in any way to "blame" any woman for dis-ease, dis-comfort or ill health. The unseen bodies work in symbols, and some of these symbols are puns in poor taste, but nevertheless women learn from them. The symbols and puns are similar to those that appear in dreams, and are the other side of using "tinker-woman" repairs to do healings.

Feelings of inadequacy, of women not feeling strong or good enough in a male world, are the root of headaches and migraines, of diarrhea, of the lack of vitality that is the real source of nervousness, or reproductive organ dis-eases. Inability to release anger causes teeth and mouth problems, ulcers, some skin problems, digestive disturbances, varicose veins, cancer or arthritis. Something that suffocates—a boss, job, poor relationship—is a source of asthma and breathing problems. Constipation is the inability to let go, and colds the inability to cry. Leg and foot problems are dependency issues; hand and arm problems, inability to grasp or manipulation questions.[21] Shoulder and upper back pain are from "carrying the world on her shoulders." The list goes on, and from it women look inside themselves, assess their health and dis-ease issues, understand their roots. Once understood, change the thought forms, the situations;

learn to release anger, understand patriarchal politics, and value women's self. Learn what to hold onto and what to let go of, when to speak and when to wait. In seeing what's hard to look at, make the changes, in the self and in the world. Open and let energy flow through without being stopped or blocked in any organ or chakra. Become a channel to heal, and self-healing follows.

Women who have gone this far in understanding healing have learned much in new insights, learned about their unseen bodies and how they work, and how the unseen affects the seen. In psychic healing, women learn to make changes, to visualize health and make it happen in themselves and in others. With the processes of visualization and colors understood, the symbols that communicate with women's auras, great good happens. Use crystals and gemstones in the visualizations. Send healing light through crystals, and use them as "tinker-tools." Send colors through crystals or gemstones, put stones into women's auras for their healing attributes and visualize the stones as catalyzing changes. Every technique of etheric and emotional body healing described in the gemstone and crystal chapters are useful in psychic healing. Direct healing and laying on of hands, actually working with a present woman's aura and doing healings together come next.

FOOTNOTES

1. Keith Sherwood, *The Art of Spiritual Healing* (St. Paul, Llewellyn Publications, 1985), p. 26.

2. *Ibid.*

3. Amy Wallace and Bill Henkin, *The Psychic Healing Book* (Berkeley, CA, Wingbow Press, 1985, original 1978), p. 100.

4. Benjamin O. Bibb and Joseph J. Weed, *Amazing Secrets of Psychic Healing* (New York, Parker Publishing Co., Inc., 1976), p. 18-19.

5. Keith Sherwood, *The Art of Spiritual Healing,* p. 83-84.

6. Jeanne P. Rindge, "The Use of Non-Human Sensors," in George W. Meek, Ed., *Healers and the Healing Process* (Wheaton, IL, Quest/ Theosophical Publishing House, 1977), p. 136.

7. Susan Sheppard, Personal Communication, April 9, 1986.

8. Keith Sherwood, *The Art of Spiritual Healing,* p. 86.

9. Amy Wallace and Bill Henkin, *The Psychic Healing Book,* p. 106.

10. *Ibid.,* p. 130.

11. George W. Meek, *Healers and the Healing Process,* p. 158-159.

12. Amy Wallace and Bill Henkin, *The Psychic Healing Book,* p. 119.

13. *Ibid.,* p. 119.

14. C. Norman Sheely, "Postscript," in George W. Meek, Ed., *Healers and the Healing Process,* p. 265.

15. Benjamin O. Bibb and Joseph J. Weed, *Amazing Secrets of Psychic Healing.* The basis for this material is from Bibb's work.

16. Susan Sheppard, Personal Communication, April 9, 1986.

17. Benjamin O. Bibb and James J. Weed, *Amazing Secrets of Psychic Healing,* p. 26.

18. *Ibid.,* p. 54.

19. *Ibid.,* p. 122-124.

20. Diane Mariechild, *Mother Wit: A Feminist Guide to Psychic Development* (Trumansburg, NY, The Crossing Press, 1981), p. 61-62.

21. *Ibid.* This is a brilliant and thought-provoking list.

Laying On of Hands: Pranic Healing

WHERE PSYCHIC healing techniques are mostly distant healing, not requiring the healer and woman being healed to be physically in contact, laying on of hands or pranic healing is usually direct, done as self-healing or more often in cooperation between two women. The techniques operate on the *etheric body level,* the closest unseen body to the dense physical. They send aura energy or prana from one woman to another, applying it directly to the woman's aura who is being healed or the pain area. The work can be done in groups, and in self-healing prana is transmitted from one part of the aura to another. The techniques of meditation states, creative visualization, colors and directing energy by positive thought forms all apply to laying on of hands, but not deriving from the mental bodies. This is a process less mental and more physical, involved with doing rather than creating. For this reason, many women find laying on of hands or pranic healing more here and now, more concrete in its processes and results than psychic healing.

Laying on of hands is the oldest form of healing, known to every religion and mystified by patriarchy, but having its origins in the basic female relationship of mother to child. The beginnings of laying on of hands are intuitive and instinctive—things women do to help without even thinking about it. Holding a bruised thumb with the unbruised hand, putting a mother's palm over a child's feverish forehead, stroking or kissing where it hurts, are all examples of pranic healing. The

115

place where the energy is transmitted from is the small rainbow chakras in the palms of the hands, and for some women it is the lips, eyes and tiny chakras in the finger tips. The palm chakras are the major source. As in other forms of healing, laying on of hands is available to all who choose to use it, and in using it the power to heal grows.

Women know the energy used in this healing by a variety of names. Prana is the Sanskrit term, and in China it is ch'i, in Japan ki; in Hawaiin Huna the energy is known as mana.[1] Christ called the force Light, and laying on of hands is mentioned often in both the Old and New Testaments. Biomagnetic waves, orgone energy and odic force are a few more recent names, and bio-cosmic energy, bioplasmic force, life force, vital force, animal magnetism and etheric energy are all names that have been used over time.[2] Dolores Krieger, a Ph.D. nurse working with this energy in hospitals and nursing school programs, calls the process of channeling it "Therapeutic Touch." Reiki healing and Touch for Health are teaching systems. Other names for working with it are laying on of hands, pranic healing, magnetic healing or magnetic passes, and faith healing. Author Mary Coddington, in her book *In Search of the Healing Energy*, traces a fascinating evolution of the method's use and development. Most women just call it healing.

The practice of laying on of hands has been known worldwide and across time. Early rock carvings in Egypt and Chaldea, and cave paintings in the Pyrenees that are 15,000 years old, portray pranic healing.[3] Written records of the process go back 5,000 years to the *Nei Ching* in China, believed to be the world's oldest book of medicine.[4] Laying on of hands in its various names was known in Africa, Tibet, South America and Native America, was known to the Romans and Greeks, and Egyptian healer queens and priestesses of Isis, the early Jews, and to the ruling families of Europe and Russia. Ramacharaka credits all of its systems and variations to ancient India, from which he says it spread by teaching to Egypt, Africa, Greece and other cultures.[5]

In Rome, Emperor Vespasian was known to heal with the palms of his hands, curing lameness, blindness, and nervous dis-ease. Hadrian used the chakras in his finger tips, and dropsy was his specialty. King Olaf of Norway used laying on of hands from the palms, and the "King's Touch" was known in England and France. The German Hapsburgs were said to be able to cure stammering with a kiss.[6]

As in other esoteric skills, patriarchy removed this power-within from its women originators and from laypeople, reserving it for rulers and the church. It was a women's skill in the matriarchies, and a skill known to women healers throughout time. The Spanish conquerors found it among Native American shamans and brujas, and North American Pentecostal congregations know about laying on of hands. Along with the voudoun-derived concept of spirit possession, pranic healing is an aspect of the African goddess religion. Healing in any form was a Middle Ages excuse for burning women at the stake, and in Europe and slavery the practice was submerged, as was much of women's healing. Something so natural cannot be lost, however, something so available to everyone, and the techniques survive. Every culture in every time has known this skill.

Laying on of hands is easily taught, and not the property of any religion, gender or ruling class. It relieves pain, calms and balances emotionally, and speeds the healing process. It eases emotional upsets and fear, ends headaches and menstrual cramps, soothes children and pets, cools burns, increases vitality, warms and is used to transmit colors.

The process seems ready-made for crystals and gemstones, and crystals used with laying on of hands enhance and focus its power immensely. Gemstones and laying on of hands send colors and healing through the aura. Combined with massage work and polarity balancing, laying on of hands or pranic healing is also amplified. Acupuncture makes use of the laying on of hands' pranic force by transmitting it from the chakra centers to the meridians and nerve endings.

Mary Coddington lists twelve principle attributes for the energy with so many names:

1. It can heal.
2. It penetrates everything.
3. It accompanies solar rays.
4. It has properties similar to other types of energy but is a distinct force unto itself.
5. It possesses polarity and can be reflected by mirrors.
6. It emanates from the human body and has been especially detectable at the fingertips and eyes.
7. It can be conducted by such media as metal wires and silk threads.
8. It can be stored inside inanimate materials such as water, wood and stone.
9. It can fluctuate with weather conditions.

10. It can be controlled by the mind.
11. It can cause things to happen at a distance, and enters into the dynamics of many paranormal phenomenon.
12. It can be used for good or evil.[7]

The force of laying on of hands is in a woman's aura, used directly or in distance (psychic healing) to make changes from dis-ease to well-being. Creative visualization is a controlling factor, and color work one of its media. Gemstones and crystals are media for directing its use. It is a force present and intrinsic in everyone, and everyone who chooses to can be taught to use it to heal. Any power, force, energy, skill has the possibilities for negative use, but women know the goddess' law: what's sent out returns threefold, and good sent is good received in return. No woman would consider damaging her own life or future lives, her karma, with using energy to harm.

To begin experiencing this energy, relax as completely as possible in a meditative state or not. Deep meditation is not necessary if you do some deep breathing and while seated comfortably, entering the state known as grounding and centering. Dolores Krieger has a simple and quick technique for this: from a seated position, place hands comfortably in the lap, palms open and up. Begin rhythmic breathing.

> Slowly move your body one to two inches from side to side two or three times so that when you stop you feel as though your spine is in postural alignment.

> Now tilt your body back about one to two inches. This should be a comfortable position; your vertebrae should be aligned so that they easily carry the weight of your body.[8]

With eyes closed, continue rhythmic breathing. Pay attention to any tension areas, and tense and release those areas. Feel balanced and centered. Run a grounding cord, an umbilical from the root chakra into the Earth. Notice how it feels.

Next lift the hands, rub them briskly together till they start to get hot, then hold the palms facing about three inches apart. Elbows and arms should not touch the body nor should the hands touch each other. Hold them steady and continue rhythmic breathing. Energy sensations that vary with the individual happen in a couple of

minutes.* The sensations are of heat or coolness, springiness or
bounciness, magnetism, waves, tingling, electricity or throbbing. Feel
this for awhile, then move the hands a little further apart. How far
away from each other does the palm sensation continue? Move the
hands in and out, still not touching. A feeling of springiness or bounciness results and the energy increases with playing it. As a last step,
place the hands together, palms touching, and notice the sensations.
There is an increase of energy, warmth, and feeling that can be surprisingly strong, or come in surges. This is the essence of laying on of
hands. Ground the energy by placing palms to the floor or running
them under cool tap water.

Try the exercise again, practice it anywhere and any time. Get as
centered and grounded each time as possible, and learn to do that in
a variety of places and conditions. How long does it take for the feeling of energy to fade when the palms are held together but not touching? How long does it take when they touch after raising the energy?
Rub the hands briskly together and try it again. End by placing hands
to the floor palms down to ground the energy or by running them in
tap water, then try it another time. Each practice session increases the
strength of the feelings and sensations. The energy comes from the
chakras in the palms of the hands, and is the same energy that makes
rugs spark static shocks in dry winter houses. Are the fingers tingling
as well? Remember the exercises for seeing the etheric double, the
black ribbon sandwiched between a line and band of light? The sensations in the hands are from feeling the etheric double, the aura
band's energy. Try the exercise holding a clear quartz crystal in the
left hand, in the right hand, or a crystal in each hand. So far the work
has been done alone.

Now with a partner, each woman raises the feeling of prana in her
own hands, moving her palms apart and back together, not touching,
until they feel like a springy ball of energy is moving between them.
One woman places her hand between the facing palms of the other
woman's hands without touching her. Feel the sensation that builds
after a few moments, and pay attention to it. How far away can the
woman who is using both hands move from the other woman's hand
and still feel the energy? How long does it take for the energy to fade?
If the woman has a cut on her hand, or her hands are stiff from
arthritis, what happens to the cut or pain? How does it feel after doing

---

* These techniques are detailed by Dolores Krieger, Diane Mariechild, and Richard Gordon. Personal early
teaching comes from healer Rebecca Crystal.

the exercise? What differences occur when the woman using both hands holds a crystal in one of them? In both of them? If the woman holding her hand between holds a crystal? In holding the stone, the crystal should be placed across the palm chakra, the pointed end facing the fingers. Hold it in place with the thumb at the base of the crystal, leaving as much crystal over palm exposed as possible. Hold a smaller crystal between the fingers if wished, point toward palm, or tape it in place on the palm of the hand. Any size crystal will do.

As a last move, the woman using two hands holds them against the woman's hand between hers, and keeps them there until the energy fades. Sometimes it takes a few moments for feeling to happen. The women switch roles, so that each experiences holding her hands around another's and each experiences placing her own hand between. Ground and center at the beginning, raise energy by rubbing the hands together, and ground the energy at the end.

In working alone as well as with a partner, notice differences in the energy flow from between the left palm and the right. Is the right hand stronger in sensation than the left, or is the left stronger? Is there a difference or no difference? The use of both hands sets up a polarity, a magnetic situation of energy giving and receiving, and both hands are needed in healing. For most women, the left hand receives energy, draws it in, and the right hand sends or transmits it. For some this is reversed, and other women may not perceive a difference, especially at first. As she practices and grows stronger in using laying on of hands, she usually dis-covers that she receives with one hand and sends with the other. (Since my left hand is the receiving hand, instructions here are based on this orientation. For women in whom this is reversed, adjust to individual needs.)

Polarity or magnetism has a strong effect in laying on of hands/ pranic healing. The cycle of energy requires both poles, positive and negative, or, as the Chinese call them, yin and yang. The concept does not in any way say that one is better than the other or stronger, only that they are complementary opposites. Almost everything on Earth or in women's spirituality is based on the concept of dualities,* on the opposites that match to make a whole. This is the case here as well; left and right are both needed, and are used in most healing. In laying on of hands, the magnetism of the healer's body is used to create a forcefield energy flow with the magnetism of the woman

---

*Some call this a trinity, as in maiden/mother/crone, taking the two opposites and the whole they become as three parts. This is how Z. Budapest expresses it, in her *Holy Book of Women's Mysteries Part II*.

being healed. The upper half of the woman's body is positive, and the lower body and feet are negative polarity. The right side of the body is positive, and women's left is the negative pole. In laying on of hands, the healer applies her left hand to the right side of the woman being healed, and her right hand to the woman's left side.[9] Try this with a partner doing the previous exercise: once the energy is raised, use only the left hand and place it over but not touching the other woman's right palm. Notice the feeling. One woman changes hands, and the sense of magnetism and energy flow becomes apparent. The left, negative hand usually receives, and the right, positive pole in healing is the sending hand for most women. For women whose finger chakras are active, the fingers have polarity charges, too. The thumb is neutral, but the index and ring fingers hold a negative charge, the middle and little fingers a positive one.[10]

Now take a clear glass of cool tap water and place it on the floor. Ground and center, and rub the palms together to stimulate energy. When the ball of springy magnetism grows strong between the palms, hold both palms over the glass of water. Keep the hands there, not touching glass or water, for as long as the healing energy continues. Magnetized water beside a control glass tastes slightly metallic.[11] The water contains pranic energy from the woman's hands, and calms or helps heal a woman who drinks it. Try the exercise with the water again. This time use color visualization to transmit red to the water. Feel the red entering the water through the palms. Notice the taste and the mood changes after drinking it, similar in effect to doing a color meditation using red. Try this with other colors, placing palms to the floor to ground the energy in between. At ending the exercises for a session, place palms to the ground again or run the hands under water to remove excess energy that could make the healer feel anxious or drained.

Using a glass of cool tap water again, place a crystal in the bottom and use pranic energy (the chakras of the hands and fingers) to magnetize the water. What are the differences between using the crystal and not using it? The water with the crystal contains stronger energy that the woman feels entering as she does the magnetizing. Try color sending through the hands again, in a variety of colors. For each, place a gemstone of that color in the glass, or direct the crystal to be each color in turn. In each case the water carries the healing properties of the gemstone as well as of pranic energy, and is called a gemstone elixir or essence. What impressions come as the woman sips the charged water slowly? Suggested dosage in healing with this water is "a wineglassful every half-hour for the first day, every hour for the second day, and a wineglassful three times a day to finish treatment."[12] The woman being healed does not have to be present at the time the water is magnetized to benefit from the energy, and the water can also be used for self-healing. Stored in a closed bottle, the energy in the water lasts about twenty-four hours. Combine magnetizing the water with the color work and gemstones to transmit the attributes of color and stones. This is a good technique for both energizing and sedating.

In similar work, take a wad of surgical cotton or an all cotton menstrual pad (mini or maxi) and hold the pad on the open left palm.[13] Hold the right palm over but not touching the cotton and keep it there for as long as there is sensation (the transfer of energy). It takes about two or three minutes with a woman beginning to heal from the time the feeling begins; longer for a woman more practiced at using and channeling energy. When the magnetizing is finished, place the pad face down upon a part of the body that needs healing. Put it over the wound for a cut, on the forehead for a headache while lying down. Do some deep breathing and relax completely while the pad is in place and notice the sensations. What happens to the cramps or headache after the sensations are gone? The pain in the cut?

Now try it again, deliberately willing a color to enter the cloth, but not telling a partner what the color is. Exchange pads, and hold a partner's charged cloth on the right palm, the left palm over it to feel the energy. Do not touch the cloth with the left palm. Notice impressions that come, however illogical, while sensing the pad. What color impressions happen? Other impressions? Ask the woman what she sent. If thoughts or pictures happen, ask the woman what she was thinking when she magnetized the cloth. Impressions can be thoughts, colors, sounds, pictures. Share them and compare. Try it again holding a crystal in the sending hand, or a crystal in each hand, one between the cloth and the palm. Be as grounded as possible at the beginning of the session. At the end of it, be sure to place the palms to the floor to channel out the excess energy, or run the hands in cool water. Stop before getting tired.

Practice these exercises daily until strong at them. A woman who does this feels the strength and length of her aura-power grow, as well as improves her ability to transmit colors. Use laying on of hands over houseplants and watch them sprout new growth and bloom. Send them green. Use it on dogs or cats and watch their reactions; pick a color to send them. An animal not in need of healing sometimes gets silly about it because it tickles. The dog or cat moves away. Dogs are usually more receptive than cats to energies not their own, but both will accept it when actual healing is needed, and psychic healing works well on animals, too. Practice sending colors with the energy, transmitting it through the palm chakras. Draw energy from the Earth to send it out through the hands, or draw it from the sky. Become a free flowing channel for energy entering and leaving. Feel it rise or fall through the chakras, a continuous flow. Always remember to ground at the end, and begin by grounding and centering, running a cord connecting the woman to Earth. Continue no longer than is comfortable; stop when becoming tired, and don't overdo it.

In a group situation, ground and center. Run a grounding cord and raise energy through the palm chakras. Feel the springy ball and play with it till it increases. Place the hands over the head of a partner, and find her transpersonal point, located several inches above her physical body. When the center is located by its tingling feeling, sense its energy for a moment, then separating the hands, palms facing the body but not touching it, run the hands along the energy beside the head and down the woman's body. Run the left palm along the woman's right side, while running the right palm along but not touching her left. The distance is three to six inches from her skin, maybe a little more. Feel the woman's aura from head to foot, not touching her dense physical body at all. Pay attention to areas where the energy flow changes, cold spots, spots of no sensation, holes, rough spots, ripply spots, spots where the energy is in any way different.[14] Notice these areas and remember their locations. Change places, and the woman being felt becomes the woman who feels her partner's aura. Notice the sensations of both feeling and being felt. Try it again holding a crystal in the left hand or crystals in both hands. Try it once more, attempting to locate each chakra, hands held at front and back of the woman's body but not touching her. Remember any impressions.

Concerning the places in the woman's aura that vary, the holes, cold or hot spots, rough spots, spots where the energy changes: ask the woman what each of these areas means to her. Is there pain there? Was there an old and healed injury or broken bone, a surgical scar? Is the heaviness over her pubic bone her menstrual period happening or about to come? Is the feeling of springy bulge over an otherwise unshowing belly an early pregnancy? (No harm to the fetus occurs with using pranic energy). Has she just had a full meal and is it noticeable in her aura? Is one of the cold spots her arthritis acting up? Is a hot spot a cut on her shin? An earache? Compare notes with each other as to what the differences in sensation meant. These vary with the individaul woman.

In psychic healing, the woman is viewed on a healing screen or in silhouette and the pain spots are asked to appear. These pain spots are the spots of different energy in the woman's aura in laying on of hands. The process of locating them and understanding the sensations grows with experience and is the pranic equivalent of an aura assessment. Pay attention to all impressions and also ask the woman what's there. In direct healing, the women work together closely. Stroking the woman's aura (not her physical body, this is done without touching her physically) from head to foot is soothing and calming; always work in this direction. Stroking slowly is sedating, while quicker movements are energizing and exciting.[15] Most healing work involves calming, moving the hands slowly from head to foot. Use both hands, one on each side of the woman's body, and move in a smooth, steady motion. The woman being stroked remains quiet and still, remains grounded and continues rhythmic breathing. The women switch places, so each can experience the exercise. Again notice the difference in sensations when holding a crystal or crystals.

Now go back to the spots that are different, with an understanding of what they are from the woman who has them in her aura. Find them again by stroking the aura from head to foot, but take much less time doing it this second time. Go to the spot highest on the woman's body, the one closest to her head. Hold both hands still, palms over the area but not touching the woman physically, until energy fades in the hands. Shake the hands in the air, flicking off anything absorbed from the pain area or from a different spot in the aura. Look for the spot again and feel how it's changed. Move to the next spot lower. Do each spot in this way, moving from head to foot, until each spot of different energy has been treated with laying on of hands and has changed. Shake the energy from the healer's hands after working with each spot.

Visualize while doing this: if the spot feels like a void, see the hole filled with light sent through the palms. Send warmth (red or orange) if the spots are cold ones, and send cooling (blue or green) if the spots are hot. Visualize sending smoothing if the spots feel rough; smooth them out. Keep the hands steady over the woman's body, and feel the energy from that position, then try using the fingers as combs to rake through the spots and break up any hard to change areas.[16] Stroke and rake with the fingers and palms, sending color and energy, temperature and light, until the different spots or pain areas become one with the rest of the woman's aura. Shake off after each spot changes, and release the energy from the hands. Ask the woman how she feels. Stroke her entire aura from head to foot once more.

At the end of using laying on of hands for each spot and of combing the woman's aura, pick one spot that feels particularly stubborn. Only with the woman's permission, physically rest both palms lightly on the area. Leave them there held still, and notice what happens. The sensation is usually one of heat, but could also be of cold; it may be of electricity or waves, or other forms of energy sensation. Its strength is surprising, particularly once the woman has gathered an amount of magnetism in her hands. It may take a few moments to happen, from the time the woman places her hands on the woman's body who is being healed. Hold the hands in place until the energy fades and stops. Use intuition to know when the healing's over.

Physical touch in laying on of hands is a powerful movement, and *should not be done without asking permission specifically,* even though permission to do healing was given before starting. As with the other exercises, try it with a crystal or crystals in each hand, or put the crystals down before touching, and be sure to stop before becoming tired. Ground at the end. The process of assessing the pain or spots that are different and changing them is one process of doing a laying on of hands healing. It does a good job of calming both healer and the woman being healed, and it balances the chakras. If they are not so at the beginning, both women are in an alpha meditation state by the end of the process.

The energy being used here is the etheric double, the closest of the unseen energy bodies to the physical dense body. This is the level that contains the chakras, so it is not surprising that balancing and smoothing the spots that feel different also balances the chakras, or that aura assessment reveals tingling over the chakra centers when this is asked for. In doing this and holding the palms over the chakras, notice the impressions that come. They are very similar to the ones gained in an aura assessment by psychic healing, but the impressions are a mix of visual and nonvisual ones. Use creative visualization techniques—send colors or light, cooling, warmth, whatever is needed to balance the blocks or places of pain or changed energy. Try doing aura assessments holding a crystal in each hand, and using the crystal in the left hand as a magick wand to send energy for changing the pain areas. When using crystals for healing, blow the negativity from them each time in the same way as flicking it from the palms. At the end of healing, run it under tap water point downwards when doing the same for the hands. Visualize all negative energy leaving the stone.

In doing psychic healing, see the hands as energy transmitters, and use laying on of hands techniques as psychic healing tools. In distant healing work, visualize running both palms along the woman's aura who is being healed. Make the same assessment of spots which are different that would be made if she were physically present. Change the aura blocks, the different or pain spots, the same way. Mentally visualize the changes happening and the healer using laying on of hands. The thought forms and aura energy are transmitted and the healing occurs.

Laying on of hands not only transmits across distance and penetrates distant matter, but it penetrates present matter as well. A woman being healed does not have to be undressed; the energy transmits easily through loose clothing. If she is wearing metal jewelry, however, it may interfere—metal conducts electricity and magnetic energies. Likewise, the healer's wearing of rings or other jewelry may or may not interefere with healing. The healer is aware of sensations and energy flows and judges for herself. Some healers use gold or silver intentionally for their conducting qualities. Silver is cool, lunar and flowing while gold is hot, solar and energizing. Copper is also a good conductor, containing both the components of silver and gold, and bronze or brass in alloys work, but alloys containing lead are to be avoided. Lead stops the energy flow entirely, and this is true for work with bare hands as well as pranic healing using crystals.[17] Crystal magnifies the energy transmitted, and gemstones worn or held during healings convey their individual qualities. Using the hands alone works well—the crystals, gemstones or metals are not required, but are enhancements to this form of healing.

Some scientific theory is available as to what happens in laying on of hands, what this energy is and does. Healing comes from the simple and proven fact that all life is surrounded by electricity and that most of life is composed of the energy spaces between atoms. The human body, as well as the dense bodies of animals, plants and inanimate objects, move in an envelope of electromagnetic energy at different levels. Recent science has named this energy the L-field,[18] and dozens of scientists worldwide have worked with it and accept it. With vacuum tube voltmeters, the energy is measurable, and with Kirlian photographic techniques it is visible. In George Meek's explanation,

> In the case of the human body, the electromagnetic fields operate in a complicated manner as the molecules in the cells are constantly being torn apart and rebuilt or replaced with fresh material from food we eat and the oxygen we breathe. But thanks to the controlling L-field, the new molecules and cells are rebuilt as before and arrange themselves in the same pattern as the old ones.[19]

When the L-field is "bent" (Meek's term), the new cells develop abnormally, and are in the blueprint of dis-ease instead of good health. Laying on of hands applies a polarity magnetism and electricity to rebuild the L-field. It repairs the "bent" places, the spots in the aura that feel different or are blocked, and changes those places to the normal healthy blueprint by restoring electricity and magnetism in normal form. The change is from disease to well-being. A "bent" L-field reproduces abnormal cells, but changed by laying on of hands, the new cells in the rapid process of cell replacement are healthy ones. The change takes place in the energy spaces between atoms, and is cell-source deep. The women who performed laying on of hands in ancient Egypt or India didn't *need* to know this, though they probably did. They only needed to know that it worked. Women today also know that it works, but want to know more. Modern medical science, with this sort of new information, will eventually accept pranic healing and begin to use what women have always used and known.

Scientific proof of what happens in laying on of hands/pranic healing came from the cooperation of the late Baltimore healer Olga Worrall. Using solutions of cupric chloride, a stable energy indicator, Worrall treated a solution specimen with laying on of hands. Compared to the control solution, Worrall's was a different color after two days' time, and showed significant chemical property changes. Laying on of hands changes the hydrogen bonding arrangement of the water molecule. This is particularly significant, since water is the major component of the dense physical body. Seedlings that Olga Worrall treated with laying on of hands grew faster than seedlings that were untreated and used as controls.[20] An experiment done in another laboratory and comparing wound healing in mice naturally and with laying on of hands treatments revealed significantly faster healing in the healer-treated animals.[21] Sister Justa Smith of Buffalo, reasoning that since healing occurs first by activating the enzyme system, studied the effects of laying on of hands on the trypsin enzyme. She found that pranic healing significantly increases and acitivates this substance necessary for physical healing, for the change from dis-ease to well-being.[22]

Dolores Krieger has used scientific testing to reveal that in laying on of hands there are changes in electro-encephalograph measured brain wave states, both in healer and healed, and in the hemoglobin of the woman's blood who is being healed. The amount of oxygen carried by the hemoglobin (red blood cell) molecule increases after a treatment of laying on of hands. Her studies with the electro-encephalograph reveal, not surprisingly, that both healer and woman being healed enter meditative states in the process. If, because of physical situations the healer is unable to enter this state, the healing is often unsuccessful. When the healer in the meditative state performs laying on of hands, the woman being healed (with no conscious intention) enters it as well.[23] The requirement of women's connection with the goddess/source is in effect here—the importance of meditation or of the lighter grounding and centering state in healing work.

The changes that occur in laying on of hands or pranic healing are beneficial for both healer and the woman being healed. The alpha meditation state is one of them, and with it comes a drop in the speed of speech and voice level of both women. Breathing and heart rate slow in both women, and both enter a state of significantly greater relaxation and calming. Krieger also notes a skin flush in the face and body, resulting from blood vessel dilation and added oxygen in the red blood cells.[24] Experience notes all of these changes in both women.

As far as healing results go, the woman receiving the healing feels a definite lessening or disappearance of pain, is greatly calmed and soothed, feels greater vitality and well-being, and a release of exhaustion and nervous tension. These are physical and emotional benefits that include stress reduction and aid every body system. Dis-ease symptoms often disappear completely without returning, and the healing rate of wounds, burns and broken bones is speeded up immensely. It ends headaches and menstrual cramps, reduces fevers, eases every sort of pain, induces every sort of healing and regeneration, can be used to cool or warm, and calms emotional episodes. The process is particularly effective on children and animals because they are so open to it. Adults who have no belief in laying on of hands are helped by it anyway, though occasionally someone who gives permission for healing will consciously or not block the process and prevent it from happening. As long as the healer works according to free will and with permission, pranic healing has potential for only the highest good.

To heal an individual pain area, full aura assessment and changing the spots that are different (the blocks) may or may not be desired. The woman doing healing has a choice here. In the case of a single pain area, she enters the meditative state or grounds and centers, runs a grounding cord to the Earth, and protects herself and the woman being healed with an aura of gold, clear or blue light. Then she raises energy in her hands by rubbing them together briskly, and holds her open palms or hands and crystals over the area to be healed. The healer does rhythmic breathing, and visualizes the changes she wants to transmit. She uses colors, visualizations, "tinker-woman" graphics, or whatever means occur to her for telling the woman's higher self what is wanted. She pays attention to the energy flows in her hands, and draws the energy from the Earth or sky, through her chakras, to send in the healing. Her heart center is open, and her third eye, but she sees that her belly chakra is not too involved. When drawing in the pranic energy she transmits, the healer is careful to bring it from the goddess Earth or universe, and not from her own Be-ing. Excessive tiredness, dizziness or hunger at the end of a healing suggests that she needs to draw more from other sources, and not from her own aura.

The healer pays careful attention to the woman she is working with, both to her spoken and unspoken responses. She obtains permission before beginning any healing process, and for women unfamiliar with laying on of hands, the healer's explanations of what's happening are useful and reassuring. Ask the woman being healed what she is feeling, as sensations felt are very individual. One woman feels heat and another cold from the same healer's hands. Energy sensations can be disturbing to a woman who has never felt them before. Some women (and healers) feel no energy at all, but the healing still takes place. The healer needs also to know if her energy is reaching where the woman hurts. In cases of nonvisible pain, and where the healer has not done an aura assessment, this is especially important. If the woman's cramps are under her pubic bone, healing at the level of her navel has effects, but the effects are greater if the healing is done where she needs it. Where no sensations are felt, the healer works on intuition and is usually right. There is no reason why the women can't converse while laying on of hands is being done.

When the energy sensations fade from the healer's palms and fingers, the woman being healed experiences them fading, too. From there the healer can do one of several things. She can end the healing there, or move her hands to the woman's head and begin clearing her aura, finding and changing the spots that are different feeling blocks. Stroking the aura from head to foot slowly is calming, very soothing and sedating. Moving in quicker strokes from feet to head is energizing and rousing. Ramacharaka suggests that sedating be done with the palms from about three or four inches away from the woman's dense body. Energizing ones are further away, at a distance of one to two feet.[25] The woman healer can also make passes across the body, suggested in cases of congestion. The hands are held sideways and swept outward across the body, palms brought back to face each other on returning. The healer holds her hands in a somewhat awkward way to do this, brushing the palms across the woman's body without touching.

Another movement which is particularly good when using crystals is to move the hands in clockwise circles over the pain area or spot that's different in the aura. The tips of the fingers can be used for this for women who feel the fingertip chakras activated. Ramacharaka also notes this movement as energizing and good for relieving congestions.[26] Movements of stroking, brushing or combing the aura are also effective.

Another technique a healer makes use of is actually touching the woman's physical body. Place your palms over the area being healed, feel the power in them raise and then fade before moving your hands. This can take several minutes; the energy sensations may not always rise immediately. Do this only with the woman's permission. Ask, "May I touch you?" and begin only after hearing a "Yes." This is not only true of more private body parts, but for extremities and headaches as well. Accept a woman's refusal as well as her affirmation. Use of actual touch is warming and very comforting for the woman who chooses to accept it. There may be intense surges of energy, usually pleasing but often surprising and strange with this movement. When the flow of energy stops, the healing is completed. The healer moves onto another movement, or withdraws from the woman's aura. Using actual touch is usually the last move in a healing, but not always. From there the woman healer may move into massage or polarity work, so closely related to laying on of hands/pranic healing. A healing consists of one of the possible moves, or several of them. Know when to stop, and do so before the healer or woman being healed becomes tired. When energy fades in the hands, the healing or that part of it is over.

Withdraw from the woman's aura and surround her and yourself with protective light. Break the trance state and place hands on the ground to release excess energy; send it transformed for recycling into Earth. The healer washes her hands in cool water if possible, and clears her crystals in running water as well. If water is unavailable, do the grounding with both hands, and blow through the crystals. Hold the crystals over the palms, or rest them on the woman's pain area to do the healing. In using gemstones in this way, be sure that the attributes of the stone/s match what the woman needs, and use them alone or in combination with crystals.

If you feel tired at the end of a healing, or dizzy or drained in any way, sit or lie flat on the ground for a moment and visualize drawing the energy to replenish from the Earth. Visualize this in any symbols that are meaningful: in colors, flows, pictures or sounds. Try the grounding cord again. The woman who has experienced the healing may be slightly dizzy, hungry, overly relaxed or feel the need to sleep. Changes have been made in her seen and unseen bodies and they take some time to readjust. Give her space to rest and encourage her to do so until she feels ready to get up. The feelings are not unpleasant ones. If you or the woman being healed feels hungry at the end of healing, eat something containing natural sweetness, but not white sugar. Fruit is a good choice; cookies or chocolate are not. The hunger fades and is nothing to be alarmed about. Vegetarians have easier times learning to sense and channel energies for healing. The use of alcohol, drugs or smoking can block or lessen this ability in some women.

In some cases, the healer may feel herself taking on the symptoms she has just finished healing. There is no need for this and if it happens, deal with it immediately. Take notice of the belly chakra and see that it is not opened wider than necessary. If this is a repeated problem in healing, each time before starting visualize and close the belly chakra to a proper perspective. Open the heart and brow centers instead, and heal from there. If symptoms occur, ground them immediately. Sit on the floor, palms to the Earth and visualize the symptoms flowing away, transformed to useful energy in the planet. Proper grounding and using the umbilical cord at the start of healing prevents most of this, and for women who tend to feel others' symptoms, the aura shell of protective light at the beginning and end of healing is particularly important. The healer who refuses to allow these feelings to enter prevents them from entering, or allows them to flow through her without harm.

In healing for a specific pain area, pay attention to the concepts of polarity. Hold the hands one on each side of the pain area, as in the example of the woman placing her hands between her partner's two palms. Remember, for most women the right hand sends while the left receives. Energy from the Earth or sky also enters the body through the left side in most women and leaves through the right. There is a continuous flow of energy entering and leaving, flowing through the healer, her hands, the pain area, and the woman being healed. The flow is a balancing of opposites or energies, a series of polarity situations. The energy comes from the goddess/source, from the Earth or sky and goddess-within. It enters the woman being healed through the healer's hands, then flows through the woman's body to be released by her again to the

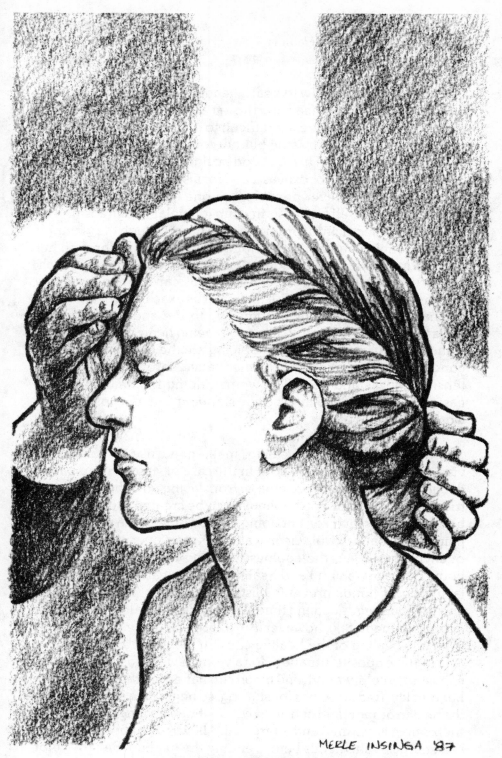

MERLE INSINGA '87

Healing a Headache

Earth or sky.

To establish this flow to heal a headache, place the right palm over the woman's forehead and the left at the back of her neck. For menstrual cramps, where it is difficult to place the hands front and back, place them side by side but not touching each other or the woman being healed. This is a good position for back pain, too, for other abdominal pain or dis-ease, and for working with constipation and diarrhea. Wherever possible, use one hand on each side, as this is the most effective setting up of polar magnetism. The polarity and electricity of pranic healing pass through the woman's body, through a hand or foot, shoulder, abdomen or through her head. Where the place being healed is an awkward one to reach, set up the polarity arrangement as well as can be, hands side by side or one on each side, even if they can't be exactly aligned. Moving the hands slightly and being sensitive to the energy, the healer finds the easiest position. The woman being healed can be sitting, standing or lying down. Sitting or lying are the best, and the most conducive to relaxation and the meditative state for the release of tension, blocks and pain. The woman doing the healing finds it easiest to reach and to move while standing, but any position that works is the one to use.

When doing pranic healing, make good use of colors and visualization in the energy flow. In the case of sunburn and burns, cooling is important. Since energy from laying on of hands is electrical and somewhat hot, cooling has to be created. Burns need to be cooled down quickly, but doing this too quickly is a shock and is painful. Visualize cool, clear water running over the burn and quenching its heat, the coolness running through the woman's body. Burns are painful and healing them can also be painful, but laying on of hands prevents blistering, reduces pain afterwards and greatly speeds healing time. The effects of healing may not be noticed immediately, however. Burns are one of the few examples in pranic healing of the healing causing pain.

In the opposite situation, for a woman with frostbite or over-exposure to cold, warmth and blood circulation are the issues. Warm her quickly. Red is too hot for starting, so begin with gold. Increase the heat to orange, and end with red. Continue healing with red until the woman is warmed and energized. Allow her to absorb as much red energy as she needs before ending the healing. See the color entering her body, circulating through it, and then leaving through her crown or feet. Where tissues are damaged by cold, warm them up first. Blue or green is used for inflammation later.

For headaches and migraines, move from green to blue/green or aqua. Migraines are one of the harder dis-eases to help. Try indigo or violet if aqua brings no calming response, and return to aqua once the woman has absorbed enough violet or indigo and calmed down. As in psychic healing, where there is pain, treat it first and then go to the source. This is also true in treating panic. A useful visualization of energy flow for pain is to see it breaking up into splinters, and the bits or splinters flowing through and out of the woman's chakras and aura. Be sure no splinters remain in a center or are left in the pain area. Flood the area with golden light or blue light once the pain is gone. Healing is an energy flow, a circuit between the healer's hands and flowing through her body, and a circuit flowing into and through the woman being healed. See pain breaking up, entering the flow, leaving and grounding in the goddess Earth or sky to be transformed.

In a few healings (burns and headaches the most frequent examples), there can be an increase of pain at the time of the healing. The increase happens because the process of working through the dis-ease is so greatly speeded up. The pain is never intolerable, but the woman experiencing the healing needs to know what's happening and that the increase is temporary. It generally lasts no more than a minute or two, and then the pain fades without returning. The woman being healed helps herself through it by deep breathing.

On some occasions, the woman being healed feels no different at the end of a healing than she did at the beginning. She returns to her activities, to dis-cover that in a few minutes, an hour, two hours, or the next morning, the pain is totally gone, or healing has progressed several days worth in an hour or overnight. After some healings, the woman has to be asked how she feels before she realizes that her pain is gone. These are all normal reactions. A few healings involve a temporary increase of pain. Some healings that seem unsuccessful at the time turn out to be extremely successful. When a healing provides no benefit, it is usually because the meditative state wasn't reached or because the woman being healed either blocked or refused the healing.

For a woman who needs her chakras balanced, dis-cover this in an aura assessment and balance the centers by opening the blocks and changing the different-feeling spots, smoothing and combing the aura. Where a chakra needs more energy, place the palms over that center and visualize the color needed flowing from palms and into the woman's aura. Where a chakra needs to be reduced, hold palms over the center again, sending the complementary color or simply willing the center closed to a proper size. *Never* close any chakra completely. Move from the crown to the feet, lighting up and balancing each chakra with laying on of hands. Stroke and smooth the woman's aura at the end. The woman leaves the healing feeling energized, calm and well. Where blocks or obstructions are felt in a center, use laying on of hands to dissolve them. See them breaking up as pain does, and stroke the aura to pull the fragments away. Be sure that you shake this energy from your hands and crystals before going on to the next move, and ground thoroughly at the end. If a woman needs more energy or her ungroundedness calmed, laying on of hands and aura work with colors are a powerful combination.

In all of these methods and combinations, the healer becomes a channel for the goddess and realizes that the woman she is healing is a channel as well. In the polarity example of how pranic energy works, positive and negative are both necessary. Without both there is no healing, or healing is greatly reduced. The same is true with the women; the healer and woman being healed are both necessary channels, and they work together. While laying on of hands/pranic healing is often done as self-healing, its best effects are in working with a partner. Energy is channeled by the healer, but it's the woman being healed who accepts it and does the healing in herself. No woman heals another; she only offers help, polarity and channeling. All healing is a power-within act of love, love of others, love of the goddess, love of goddess-within in the self. The healer is as much of a channel for this love as she is for healing, since both of the energies are one.

If the woman being healed is receptive to it and the healer is skilled in this direction, laying on of hands merges naturally with massage work, particularly the forms called polarity balancing or psychic massage. In this type of healing the principles of laying on of hands are used with touch and body positions to relax, heal and release blocks, to reduce stress, soothe and to energize for well-being. The movements and positions open the chakras and clear the aura, and are tremendously comforting.[27]

Massage work is an entire method of healing that cannot be discussed in detail here, but a couple of movements from Robert Gordon are especially effective with pranic healing work. Possibly the nicest is one he calls "the cradle."[28] To do this, raise energy in the hands by rubbing them together, and then place one palm on each side of the woman's head, thumbs just above the ears, index and middle fingers at the sides of her neck. The woman is lying down and the healer stands behind her. The healer's hands are close to the woman's physical body, but not quite touching her. She remains in the position for awhile to help with headaches, anxiety, panic and tension. This is an extremely soothing and love-sending movement.

Another position in polarity massage is called the "tummy rock."[29] The healer raises energy in her hands, then places her left palm on the woman's forehead (brow chakra), and her right hand over the woman's solar plexus, just above the navel. She uses the right hand to rock the woman's lower body for a couple of minutes, then holds hands still while energy flows from them. Touch is involved here throughout and the rocking is slow and easy. This is a powerful tension releasing movement, good before bedtime and recommended for children.

The tummy rock can be adapted for releasing a pain spot.* Place the right hand or one finger of the right hand on the brow chakra, and the left hand or one finger of the opposite polarity on a pain area. The brow chakra transforms negativity without being affected by it, and neutralizes the pain or block. Allow the hands to remain in the position until the energy flow stops or until you know that it's time. This is especially good for deep muscle pain, and can be used to open the chakras. The possibilities of massage work with pranic healing are valuable and worth looking into, but require partners to do the work.

The next chapters of this book apply healing techniques already learned to working specifically with crystals and gem-

---

* Personal teaching from healer David Speer, who directs that either hand will work for this and polarity is less important. Robert Gordon uses the left hand on the brow chakra, right on the pain area, and emphasizes polarity. The healer uses whatever method works for her.

stones. All of the material so far—psychic healing, color work, meditation, laying on of hands, visualizations, aura and chakra work are involved. Crystals and gemstones are tools for every sort of healing, and every sort of healing techniques benefit from their use and methods. Where Part I of this book is designed to teach women to be healers, Part II is designed to teach healers to be crystal workers. The methods interconnect in women's healing.

FOOTNOTES

1. Richard Gordon, *Your Healing Hands* (Santa Cruz, CA, Unity Press, 1978), p. 18-20.

2. *Ibid.*

3. Dolores Krieger, Ph.D., RN, *The Therapeutic Touch: How to Use Your Hands to Help or to Heal* (New Jersey, Prentice-Hall, Inc., 1979), p. 15.

4. Mary Coddington, *In Search of the Healing Energy* (New York, Destiny Books, 1983, original 1978), p. 16.

5. Yogi Ramacharaka, *The Science of Psychic Healing* (Chicago, Yogi Publishing Society, 1937, original 1909), p. 41.

6. *Ibid.,* p. 39-41

7. Mary Coddington, *In Search of the Healing Energy,* p. 16-17. Direct Quote.

8. Dolores Krieger, *The Therapeutic Touch,* p. 39-40.

9. Richard Gordon, *Your Healing Hands,* p. 24-25.

10. *Ibid.,* p. 101.

11. S.G.J. Ouseley, *The Power of the Rays: The Science of Color Healing* (Essex, England, L.N. Fowler and Co., Inc., 1981, original 1951), p. 66.

12. *Ibid.*

13. *Ibid.,* p. 65-66, and Dolores Krieger, *The Therapeutic Touch,* p. 28-29.

14. Again referenced by Dolores Krieger, *The Therapeutic Touch,* p. 45-46, and by Ramacharaka, *The Science of Psychic Healing,* p. 53-54.

15. Ramacharaka, *The Science of Psychic Healing,* p. 53-54.

16. Dolores Krieger, *The Therapeutic Touch,* p. 58. Krieger calls this process "unruffling the aura"; Ramacharaka calls it "longitudinal passes."

17. Uma Sita Silbey, "Crystal Tools, Not Toys", *Magical Blend,* (POB 11303, San Francisco, CA 94101), Issue 13, May, 1986, p. 34.

18. George W. Meek, "Toward a General Theory of Healing, in George W. Meek, Ed., *Healers and the Healing Process* (Wheaton, IL, Quest/Theosophical Publishing House, 1977), p. 198.

19. *Ibid.*

20. Jeanne C. Rindge, "The Use of Non-Human Sensors," in George W. Meek, Ed., *Healers and the Healing Process* (Wheaton, IL, Quest/Theosophical Publishing Society, 1977), p. 138-39.

21. *Ibid.,* p. 131-133.

22. *Ibid.*, p. 142-143.

23. *Ibid.*, p. 145 and Dolores Krieger, *The Therapeutic Touch*, p. 7, 157-161.

24. Dolores Krieger, *The Therapeutic Touch*, p. 75.

25. Yogi Ramacharaka, *The Science of Psychic Healing*, p. 54-56.

26. *Ibid.*, p. 56-57.

27. The best reference available for this work is Richard Gordon's book, *Your Healing Hands* (Santa Cruz, CA, Unity Press, 1978), and for more traditional massage therapy try Roberta DeLong Miller's *Psychic Massage*, (San Francisco, Harper and Row Publisher, 1975). Ramacharaka, in *The Science of Psychic Healing*, also has a good discussion of massage movements with laying on of hands (Chicago, Yogi Publishing Society, 1937, original 1909).

28. Richard Gordon, *Your Healing Hands*, p. 38.

29. *Ibid.*, p. 42.

PART II

CRYSTALS AND GEMSTONES

Clear Quartz Crystal

CLEAR QUARTZ crystal is the magick wand of women's healing. The choosing, cleansing and bonding of a new crystal is an experience of dis-covery and self-healing for the woman healer, and the use of clear quartz in healing work for the self or others is a powerful, rewarding tool. Crystal is a key for entering and deepening the meditative state, for grounding and centering, for forming and projecting visualization thought forms. It focuses and directs healing energy in laying on of hands or psychic healing, amplifies the light, colors, energy and images sent. Crystal transforms pain into well-being by transferring and transforming negative energies and repairing the aura L-field. Containing and able to transmit all colors of the aura rainbow, clear quartz crystal's power is controlled by the healer's unseen bodies, her kama-manas/desire-mind, and mental body. It operates on the etheric double level. No method of women's healing requires crystals for success, but every form of women's healing is aided, focused, magnified and blessed by its use. The power of clear quartz crystal—and of colored gemstones—is positive, versatile, strong and highly important in women's re-claiming of w/holistic healing and health.

Quartz is a natural formation, a gift of the goddess Earth, and is not to be confused with lead crystal, which is human-made and contains no healing powers. Natural clear quartz crystal is an oxygen and silicon bonded molecule, chemically designated as SiO_2, and poetically defined as petrified water, or as water frozen so hard that it never melts.[1] Actual formation is not of ice, but of fire, and the four directions and elements (earth, air, fire and water) are all involved in the process.

Clear quartz crystal takes over 10,000 years to form, and more than a third of planet Earth is composed of it.[2] Its hexagonal, symmetrical shape is a basic form in physics, geometry and atomic theory, and is seen as nature's most perfect form of dense matter. Naturally faceted, it never clouds or ripples, and is used for optical work and lenses. Its ability to vibrate and resonate makes clear quartz essential in communications devices, systems guidances and all computers. Its power for healing is demonstrated in the laser. Quartz is brittle but hard; hard enough to scratch glass; 7 on the Moh's scale. The U.S. Bureau of Standards uses clear quartz as a measurement constant. In crystal, poetry and science become one:

> Over 40 million years ago, crystals of gem quartz were formed deep in the earth. Pure elements of silica and oxygen combined under intense heat and pressure, aligning themselves magically to create crystals of stunning clarity with naturally precise faceting. This molecular ordering has made quartz the subject of ancient legend, the basis of modern electronic technology, and a rarity sought after for its enchanting beauty.[3]

The key to clear quartz crystal as a healing tool comes from what science calls its piezoelectric effect, and this effect, though less of it, is present in the colored gemstones as well. Crystal vibrates in tune with the Earth's core magnetic energy, and is a major component of the Earth's makeup. It partakes of the planet's polarity magnetism and of the Sun's energy radiation.[4] It absorbs, stores, transforms and transmits that energy. If these terms are slightly familiar, they should be, since women using laying on of hands are also participating in the Earth's polarity magnetism and their own. The sun's energy radiation, prana, is the energy that powers women's seen and unseen bodies. Crystal goes one step further: it resonates and tunes to women's auras, to the vibration rates of women's unseen bodies and aura energy levels. Its ability to absorb, store and transmit prana and polarity from the goddess Earth and universe, and to match these energies with the aura vibrations of a healer and the woman being healed, are its uses as women's tools. Like the pranic/laying on of hands' energy that it becomes part of, crystal energy penetrates anything but lead,[5] and takes the energies it transmits into a woman's unseen bodies. Clear quartz crystal energy enters the L-field (the spaces between atoms and energy of the aura bodies) with this resonance to transmit changes to the cell-source blueprint of regeneration. Directed as a complement to psychic healing or laying on of hands, quartz is the magick wand that changes dis-ease to well-being in powerful, positive ways. Mary Coddington's list of attributes for laying on of hands' energy also applies to clear quartz crystal healing work.

Where the power-over patriarchy sees crystal resonance in terms of microchips and laser weaponry, satellite communications and particle beam scanners, women and peace-loving men see it as the goddess' gift to healing. The legends of clear quartz crystal as a healing tool are worldwide, crossing every culture from Japan to Native America, from Africa to ancient Rome. Crystal and its uses in healing are as universal as the goddess, and extend to the legendary civilizations of Atlantis, Lemuria and Mu. As distant apart geographically as Siberia, Australia, North and South America and Africa, shamans and healers of various times and cultures all knew crystal work. Crystals and gemstones were known to early Judaism and Christianity,[6] and since both existed concurrently with goddess oriented religions, it's a good guess that the matriarchial religions knew crystals as well.

Egypt's structure of the great pyramids mirrors crystal theory, and the Great Pyramid is believed to have been capped with a giant quartz crystal. Sanskrit texts from 400 B.C. India discuss crystals and gemstones and their uses, and the Incas and Mayas knew crystal and gemstone work.[7] Native American Hopi shamans and wisewomen use crystals for dreamwork and healing, as do the Cherokee, Apache, Navaho and several other native peoples. Greece and Rome used quartz for cooling, and China called clear quartz "the essence of the dragon,"[8] the dragon being a symbol of the goddess life force. Women are working with and dis-covering it today as a major aspect of women's spirituality and healing.

Crystals aid psychic development and sensitivity, stimulate knowing and the intellect, induce dreams and visions, alter moods and consciousness, and are a biofeedback training device. Their resonance calms, grounds and balances, dispels and protects from negativity, dis-ease and harm, is an energy channeling tool and focus, and transmits heat for cooling or warmth. Crystals relieve pain, stimulate healing and regeneration, balance the aura, transmit colors, and enhance meditation and deep relaxation states. Clear quartz conducts electricity and magnetism, especially aura L-field electricity and magnetism, and future times and research will dis-cover it as a major and safe source for lighting and heating fuel.

Katrina Raphaell lists nine different types of clear quartz crystals, designated by shape and internal function. These include record keeper/library crystals, teacher stones, generator crystals, projectors, and the "tabbies" (tabular crystals, flat sided ones) that connect things and women to each other.[9] Many crystals used for healing would probably be "tabbies" by her system. Personal experience suggests that any crystal has characteristics of all types, with information and knowledge to teach the woman who used it, and any crystal is a healing crystal if it's used that way. The ability to work with crystals attracts some women more than others, some healers more than others, and is a learnable psychic skill within reach of any who choose it. DaEl, in The Crystal Book, classifies crystal attributes to: amplification and clarity, transforming, storage of information and energy, focusing, energy transference, and altered states of consciousness.[10] He does not divide the attributes into separate types of stones.

The great physical beauty and uniqueness of clear quartz, combined with its aura sensitivity and healing power, makes it a compelling tool for women healers. Many women feeling crystal energy for the first time are hooked on crystals ever after, and use them intrinsically in all their healing and spirituality work. Clear quartz crystal has an aura of its own, one visible by Kirlian photography, that resonates and matches a woman's aura and pranic energy.

The process of using crystals for healing begins with choosing a stone or stones, and clearing it of others' programming. Next, consecrate or dedicate it to healing, program it for healing, and learn about the crystal's individual attributes. Bond it to yourself as a very personal tool and working companion. Begin using the cleared and bonded quartz in healing work, learning about it continually, and the crystal itself will teach you how to use it to heal. With minimum care to keep its energies cleared and positive, women and crystals are a working team of the goddess and goddess-within.

Choosing a clear quartz crystal to work with, or a pair of them that match, is the first step in using crystals for healing. Sensing and feeling the stone firsthand, choosing by attraction and aura attraction, are desirable. Most cities have lapidary stores or rock shops, and these are sources for clear quartz, as are museum gift shops, and antique and gem shows. Magick shops and New Age bookstores sometimes carry crystals and gemstones or know of private dealers. The women's music festivals and goddess and wiccan gatherings are a prime source for good quality stones at reasonable prices, and these are usually stones chosen for healing. With growing concern over crystal strip mining in Arkansas and Tennessee (major North American sources for raw quartz; Brazil is another world source), increasing shipping costs, and increasing drain of mines by computer companies, prices are going up. Stones can run from less than a dollar for a very small or less attractive one, to thirty or forty dollars and up for the big ones that are clear, symmetrical and heavy.[11] Women who live in Arkansas or Tennessee can go to the mines and find their own, or pick them up from the goddess Earth at little or no cost. The mines sell them buy the pound, classed by size and clarity for as little as twenty dollars a pound, but most require a $100 minimum mailing order or sell only to businesses. Personal experience lists private dealers and the women's festivals as the next best sources and prices, and a good crystal of two or three inches in length should still be available for three to twenty dollars. As in other magickal tools, never haggle over prices. Women use the barter system, and crystals as a gift are gifts of love.

Mail order is possible for crystals and gemstones, and New Age publications list a variety of ads.* This is a less desirable source for women healers, but may be the only available one. No two crystals are alike and neither are two women's auras, and the goal is to match a crystal's aura to the individual healer. Crystal work, an aspect of laying on of hands, is based on touch and this is the sense that most women use to choose a crystal. When ordering by mail, write the letter by hand, stating that the crystal is for healing, and visualize receiving the perfect crystal till it comes. When it does, the bonding process may take longer than with a crystal chosen directly, but it happens with patience and time. Eventually, in most cases, the resonance adapts. When choosing a crystal for a woman not present, visualize her clearly, asking for the perfect stone for her, and pick the crystal that the woman choosing is drawn to as the right one. The woman receiving it then clears and bonds it herself.

In choosing a crystal from a room or boxful, work by touch and

---

*See Diane Stein, *The Women's Spirituality Book,* for more on clear quartz crystal, including non-healing uses. Please see the ads in the back of this book. Llewellyn Publications mail orders some beautiful crystals and gemstones for healing work, and *The Llewellyn New Times* lists crystal and gemstone dealers by mail.

sight. The crystal to which you are drawn visually is the one to investigate further by touch; but the prettiest crystal is not necessarily the most powerful or perfect for you. Use aura resonance—how the quartz feels in the hand to make the real choices. Handle and hold a stone to which you are attracted, and feel its energy as it rests against the chakra of the left palm. Hold it loosely, and wait for resonance to happen. This feels like the energies of laying on of hands, which it is, and raises in a few moments. The crystal that feels cold and alive, vibrant and active and joyous is the stone to choose. Notice the impressions, colors, sounds, feelings, mood changes that come from holding the stone. Pay attention to its shape and weight, its textures, and its temperature. The perfect crystal for you makes itself known to you, and is not necessarily the perfect quartz for someone else's choosing. No two crystals' auras or two women's auras are alike, nor is the match between the woman and a specific clear quartz crystal alike.

While some women are drawn only to very clear and symmetrical stones, and some crystal workers refuse a quartz with broken or chipped points, allow how the crystal *feels* in the hand to determine how individually right it is. The stone's appearance is secondary. Crystal and gemstone worker Serenity Peterson says the clearer the crystal the more direct the energy flow,[12] but stones with streaks, rainbows or clouds in them have other qualities equally desirable. A stone with mist inside it, water intrusions, has a gentle feeling, and those with colors transmit their rainbows and a sense of joy. A quartz with clouds can clear somewhat with long use, as pranic energy changes it in time. A crystal that's very clear can feel too intense or be hard to control. Avoid sharp edges in healing crystals, just for comfort's sake, or smooth them on concrete, but the smoothing changes the energies of the stone. Follow individual choice, what feels right, and follow your women's intuition. Pick the stone for healing that feels the most positive and good.

When choosing a pair of stones to match for healing work, pick them individually with that intent visualized, then hold them in the hands at the same time. Put one in the right and the other in the left, points toward the fingers for single terminated stones. Choose the pair by vibration and feeling, as in one stone, and also by how they feel as a pair together. Their weights and textures feel good in the hands, and both tingle with energy. When the stones feel balanced and good in position, try switching hands with them; one may feel stronger in the left or in the right. When choosing, you know by feeling and intuition which stone or stones are yours and for which hand's use by their aura resonance sensations.

The size of healing crystals is optional. For laying on of hands work, crystals that fit comfortably across the palms and hold easily are the right size. Personally, these are about three to three and a half inches long and fairly thin, but if a one inch quartz feels right, or a very thick one, use it. A crystal much larger than three or four inches is awkward or too heavy to hold, but can be perfect for placing under the bed or on an altar for meditation or directing energies. Crystals of an inch or smaller are usually crystals for wearing or are seed crystals for banishing pain. Crystals used in pairs can be of even size or not. Clear quartz comes in a limitless size range, from the minute Herkimer diamonds to the size that the pyramid capstone would have been. The limits are personal choice, what's available, and what feels good and comfortable to use.

The woman healer also has a choice between single or double terminated stones. A single terminated crystal is the most available, and has a point at one end and a flat-ended base. A double terminated stone has a point at each end. Clusters contain a number of points, facing in various directions, sharing a common center or base, and are often too large or prickly to hold for healings. They can be used for other work, for groups or changing room energy, for the centers of circles, if not suitable for holding in the hands. Single terminated stones transmit energy in one direction, in the direction of the pointed end. Double terminated stones transmit in both directions, sending and receiving. A single terminated crystal is fine for any healing work and for carrying or wearing. Double terminated stones are great for meditation, for chakra balancing and laying on of hands, but their power can feel too intense and spacey for wearing or keeping in the aura at all times. Use individual sensing to decide which crystal/s to choose, and follow intuition and experiment. Single terminated crystals have more balanced energy for grounding and calming, and double terminated are better for energizing and psychic development work. Both are strong protectors and healers of woman's aura.

Crystals held in the left hand are used for receiving energy, and crystals held in the right for transmitting and sending it. A single terminated crystal has positive charge polarity at the pointed end, and neutral charge at the flat base. A double terminated crystal is its own polarity pair, positive and negative charges. Intuition tells the healer which end sends and which receives in a double point stone. The points in a cluster are a mix of positive and negative charges, more difficult to control for polarity work and laying on of hands.

Protect the new crystal from chipping in transport (and when carrying or wearing it), and bring it home to clear it. Since clear quartz receives and stores energy, it comes with a past to neutralize. Clearing it is necessary before bonding takes place, and before using the stone for healing. Clearing is also necessary at intervals as the stone is used. A cleared, ready crystal feels positive and bright, tingly and cold to the touch. A crystal that needs clearing feels hot, heavy or drained, and is draining and ineffective to work with. Clearing a new crystal should be done at once, and there are a number of ways to do it.

Sea salt is the most traditional purifying agent in psychic work, healing, wicca and women's spirituality. It dispels any sort of dis-ease and negativity, and is a physical and psychic disinfectant. Place a new crystal in a cup or bowl of dry sea salt overnight, or in a solution of sea salt and water. Crystal worker Korra Deaver suggests avoiding sea salt with aluminum in it, and avoid using aluminum containers for crystal clearing.[13] Glass, china or ceramic is good for this, and so is wicker. Avoid any form of metal, and plastic is considered less desirable than glass. If sea salt is unavailable (try food co-ops and aquarium stores; it's very cheap), use table salt as second choice. Burying in the dry salt is stronger and harsher than in the salt water solution.

Various sources list varying amounts of time to soak or bury a crystal to cleanse it, from a few minutes or hours to overnight or three to seven days, to the time from the Full to the next New Moon. Waning Moons are good times to clear crystals, to dispel old energies, but any time works. The amount of time used varies with the sensitivity of the healer, the amount of material from which the stone needs cleansing, and the agent used for cleansing. When burying a stone, place it point downward. Sea salt is good for a new crystal, and is recommended for the first cleansing, but can be too harsh for subsequent clearing work. It can strip a stone of all its carefully built bonding, all its stored energies including the positive ones. There are other cleansing agents to try.

Running the crystal under cool tap water is a way to clear it, and a way recommended after using the quartz for each healing. Point the crystal downward, toward the drain, and visualize the water washing away all negativity. Visualize negativity in some simple term or graphic: perhaps see it as a bunch of minuses going down the drain. Mentally direct the crystal (if it's a bonded one) to let go of negative energies and dis-ease while retaining positive energies, memories and well-being. If the crystal is a new one, visualize it as new and positive, full of potential, and all its old impressions washed clean. Use only cool water, as crystal is fragile to temperatures and can shatter with heat. See the crystal as sparkly, tingly, cold and belonging to the healer.

Some women clear crystals by simply running their own aura energy through them, holding between their palms or in the right palm to send the visualization. A crystal can be buried in soil to clear it, again point down, and for a varying amount of time in personal choice. Outdoors, bury a popsicle stick with it, leaving enough stick showing to find the stone again. For apartment women, use a flowerpot, occupied or not, filled with soil.

A crystal placed in the Sun (not through windowglass) absorbs prana and solar energy and is cleared by it quickly.

Burying the stone in a cupful of dry herbs, any purification herb or positive drawing one, clears it as well. Suggested herbs for this are dried rose petals (personal favorite), sage, frankincense, myrrh, sandalwood. These are available at a low cost from food co-ops or herb stores. This is a gentle way to clear a crystal, and a nice way, but takes longer than salt or earth. The stone returns feeling very positive. A quartz used for dreamwork or psychic development can be cleared in mugwort. The time for the process varies; use intuition.

Blowing the breath sharply through a crystal, from base to point, is a way to clear it after healing dis-ease or negativity. Running water is more desirable, where it's available. A positive high energy environment also transforms negativity and dis-ease—place the stone on a goddess altar overnight or during ritual, on the stage through a women's music concert, in the center of a spirituality workshop circle, next to the bed when making love. Use of earth and water has been mentioned, blowing air, and placing in sunlight for the fire element. Never place a crystal or gemstone in an actual flame to cleanse it. However, moving it through the light and smoke of an altar candle (or incense smoke for air) purifies and clears it for healing and after.

For a new crystal never before used or bonded, salt or salt water is the place to start. Try the other methods later, as a crystal needs cleansing from time to time. One or a few methods become favorites. Use the methods one at a time; only one is needed for any particular clearing. When the quartz feels heavy, it needs clearing. There is no set time interval, and a crystal needs to be cleared in some form after every healing. Clearing the crystal is the equivalent of grounding at the end for the woman healer. For a new, unbonded crystal, visualize it made clean, clear, pure and ready to receive the healer's impressions and programming. For a bonded crystal, visualize only the dis-ease and negativity, the pain leaving it, the bonding and positive images remaining. Sense the crystal washed and shining, sparkly, new, vibrant and ready, then take it to the altar to begin the bonding.

A new crystal should be consecrated to its intended use. In this case it's for healing, and the dedication can be formal or not, with or without a fully cast circle. In a ritual way, invoke the goddess and ask her help and presence. Use a bit of chalice water, sprinkle it on the stone or stones and say, "I dedicate this crystal to the goddess as a tool for healing." You can do this using only water, or you can use any or all of the other elements as well. Drawing it through incense smoke dedicates the quartz to air, the east and the east's corresponding goddesses. Sprinkling salt or earth on it dedicates it to the Earth, earth goddesses and the north; sprinkling with water dedicates the stone to the west, water, and ocean goddesses of various names. In each case, state aloud what the quartz is for, as this programs the crystal for its future use.

If wanting to reprogram the stone, clear it in any of the previous methods and rededicate it. A crystal's programming can be left flexible by making an open-ended dedication: "I dedicate this crystal to the goddess, to work for my good and the good of all," and *will* the intention into the stone each time it's used. This works very well, but don't neglect the clearing from time to time. In doing consecrations, invoke goddesses of any name and aspect to match the stone's dedication, and rededicate it from time to time when it feels right. Programming is a process of creative visualization, as is so much of healing and women's spirituality work.

A cleared and dedicated quartz crystal is ready to be bonded, to be taught to resonate with the healer's individual aura and to work with her needs. This basically means that she keeps the crystal present in her aura, on her body, handling it and sensing it often. By day she carries it in a left-hand pocket or wears it in a drawstring bag around her neck, next to her skin. By night she places it under her pillow, holds it in her left hand while she sleeps, or puts it on her altar till the morning. Bonding is a process of giving and receiving between the woman and the stone. The crystal absorbs the woman's energy and stores it and tunes its resonance to her aura; it becomes fully sensitive to energy changes and the woman's direction, visualization and programming. When stroked, held or squeezed, the quartz releases electricity and energy. The healer also bonds herself with the crystal or crystal pair, learning its vibration rate, feeling it in various situations, along with its colors, moods, weight, shape, sounds. Hold it in the left hand to receive energy from it, in the right to send impressions or direction to or through the stone. With a pair, keep them on the sides they fit best, and they will tune to you and each other in polarized ways.

Bonding is a pleasant process, and the healer feels herself growing more psychically sensitive, sleeping better, dreaming deeper, becoming more calm and grounded as she makes the crystal or crystal pair her own. No one else should touch the quartz at this time until it is fully bonded, and the process takes about a month of constant presence in the aura. Even after this, no one should touch the crystal unless the owner feels good about it. She may need to keep it hidden from others or ask them not to touch, as crystals are beautiful and attract everyone. If others handle the stone, clear it of their energies. This is not to suggest that someone else's energies are negative, only to emphasize that in bonding you put only your energies into the crystal.

During the bonding process, begin gradually using the crystal or crystal pair. Altar and ritual work are a good place to start; color work and meditation, healing later. Do meditation work holding the crystal in the left hand or one in each hand. Do color meditations, drawing the various colors in through the crystal and the left, sending the colors back to the Earth or universe through the right side or crystal in the right hand. Hold the crystal when doing breathing exercises. Begin biofeedback work.

Biofeedback is a basic self-healing technique making use of meditation states, crystals, and the polarity magnetic flow that draws energy or colors in through the left and releases it through the right side of the body, in through the crown and out through the foot or root chakras, or in through the feet and out of the body through the crown. The energy flows of the beginning chakra meditations are bio-feedback work, using the basic polarity and magnetism of woman's body and the Earth for deep relaxation and energizing. To do this for crystal healing, use clear quartz and colors to change moods, relax, lower blood pressure, and alter heart rate and breathing by setting up polarity.

Hold a crystal in the left hand. To get warm, draw red in through the crystal, circulate it through your body, and release the color to the Earth or sky. For cooling, draw in blue or green, circulate and release it the same way. Another means of cooling is to draw blue in through the left hand, while placing the crystal on the right, and visualize heat leaving the body through the crystal and right hand. The point of the crystal is toward the fingers, or point it at the Earth to absorb the excess heat and change it into useful energy. Using a single crystal or a crystal pair both work well.

For pain, visualize blue or green entering the body through the left side and the crystal on the left, traveling to and through the pain area and breaking up the pain. See the pain as fragments touched by crystal light and blue, swept away and out of the body by the flow leaving from the right side. See the energy changed for recycling as it enters the Earth or sky.

For insomnia, draw in violet or rose warm sleepiness through the crystal, circulate it through the body, and releasing the excess through the crown chakra. See tension dissolving into fragments washed away by the polarity flow. Slow your breathing and heart rate by pranayama work.

To energize, draw in orange and yellow through the stone, circulate it, raise breathing and heart speed, and release the excess. Use the crystal or crystals to draw or send, as crystals both send and receive. This is the beginning of crystal self-healing. Be sure to ground when finishing.

Clear the crystal at the end of healing, but be careful not to strip its new bonding from it. Avoid harsh salt or salt water at this stage. Blow through the stone instead; place it on an altar or in the Sun for awhile, or try rose petals. Running water is good, but when using it visualize only the pain leaving the crystal and bonding with the healer remaining strong. Bonding is a teaching process for both the crystal and the woman healer. They learn from each other at this time, and learn to tune fully to each other's energies and auras. The bonding is fragile only at the beginning; in time it becomes almost permanent.

In pain situations, the polarity circle of drawing in energy and seeing the pain fragments leave with the excess energy or color is a basic one, variable for many self-healings and healing with others' needs. For other pain uses, hold a crystal in each hand and enter the meditative state. Visualize being fully well and cast an aura of gold light around the self and the crystals. Send the pain into the stones with both hands. It takes several minutes, but the crystals become hot by the end of it and the pain is gone. Visualize sending a one-way energy flow from the pain area to the stones. Be sure to clear the crystals afterwards in running water. Hold them in the water point downwards until they feel cold again, and the pain is washed down the drain. This works for sending away headaches, fatigue, anxiety, muscle pain or tension, for insomnia. Do deep and rhythmic breathing during the process.

Another pain technique comes from DaEl. Hold a crystal in the left hand, and feel energy build in it in the same way as rubbing the hands raises energy in laying on of hands. When the energy rises, continue holding the crystal in the left, and place the right palm over the pain area. Keep the hand there gently for some time.[14] The left hand and crystal in it do not touch the floor or other parts of the woman's body. The menstrual cramps, body pain, tension or headache ease and leave within half an hour, usually faster. When used with pranayama breathing and color transmission, the healing is faster yet. The crystal can also be rested on the pain area, and laying on of hands done with both palms, if the area for self-healing is within reach. This works for any situation that laying on of hands is used for, and also works in doing healing with others.

In laying on of hands or psychic healing with others, hold a crystal in each hand, or use only one in the right hand to send pranic energy. Use the crystal as a magick wand, a crystal ray device or laser for transforming pain, changing dis-ease to well-being. In doing aura assessments, hold the crystal in the left hand to receive impressions. In sending color or light doing "tinker-woman" distant healings, hold the crystal in the right again to send. Clear quartz crystal greatly increases the power of laying on of hands or psychic healing. It focuses energy intensively, in waves or sometimes bursts of healing light, and increases the strength of visualizations, color transmissions, and "tinkering."

In this work for yourself or others, distant or present, hold the crystal over the pain area, rotating it *clockwise* in a spiral motion over the woman's body. The crystal point faces the woman being healed. Stroke the aura with the crystal, or spray the aura with crystal light and color to energize and protect. When doing an aura assessment, use a flow of crystal energy to fill or change the spots that are different, moving the crystal in a rotating clockwise spiral. Visualize as usual and send color. For a chakra reading, use this rotating motion to dissolve blocks or "goo" in a chakra, to send light or brighten and polish a center. Use the crystal as a "tinker-woman" tool. See pain, goo, blocks or different spots drawn into a crystal held in the left hand. Feel the stone grow heavy and cloudy with it, grey with it, until the pain or blocks are gone from the chakra. Clean the crystal after the healing. Blow through it after clearing each center, and run it under tap water at the end. With water flowing over and through the downward pointed quartz, visualize the grey and heaviness leaving it, the crystal washed clear, cold and bright again.[15] Be sure to ground.

If an image of the crystal as a healing laser is empowering for her, the healer can make a crystal into a healing wand.[16] Using a one-foot piece of copper plumbing pipe, ¾" in width, splay one end (or both for two crystals) by cutting into the pipe ends crossways. The cuts divide the end or ends of the pipe into quarters, about one to 1½" deep. Bending the splayed ends with pliers to fit a crystal closely at the base, glue the crystal into the rod, with the point protruding from the top of the copper pipe. Use a crystal at each end, or cap one end of the tubing. Rods and caps are available in plumbing and hardware stores, and some stores will do the cutting. Use a pipe length that feels comfortable to hold, a foot to eighteen inches long seems best. Decorate the outside of the copper tubing. Wind it with satin ribbon, tie streamers of ribbon or beads to it. Make it a thing of individual beauty and creativity. Consecrate the tool to the goddess and dedicate it to healing work.

Crystal tools are useful in healing and ritual, and are good transmitters of pranic energy. Some women enjoy using them, while most healers prefer the closer feeling of direct use of the palms without the sending rod. Michael Smith suggests leather to wrap the outer pipe with, but if you are unwilling to take an animal's life, a contradiction in healing, substitute ribbon or cloth. Copper contains both feminine lunar and masculine solar energies. Artists such as Uma

Silbey are making these rods from pure silver and using the feminine aspect totally for them. They are sometimes available for purchase at the vendors' areas of women's music festivals and pagan gatherings by various artists, and are beautiful, powerful things. When choosing one ready-made, choose as in choosing a crystal. Accept a tool only if it feels right, feels positive, powerful, and good to hold. Use the palm chakras to sense the tool's energies, and rely on intuition. Clear, dedicate and bond it on an altar and in the healer's hands.

Women can tap into crystal energy for self-healing by doing meditation work or ritual while seated inside a circle of crystals. The stones point inward toward you for energizing or healing energy, point away to remove pain or do banishing work. Such rituals are good when connected to the Moon's phases. On waxing Moons, do healing rituals that increase—increase energy, increase well-being, increase a particular color or color aspect in the woman's unseen bodies. On Full Moons do healing that culminates—brings dis-ease up and out, brings regeneration, fills the woman's bodies with goddess healing. Draw down the Moon for the goddess-within. Full Moons are good times for formal healing rituals. On waning Moons, do banishings, crystal healing that dissolves and disperses negativity. Send pain away, and see it enter the crystal, or the Earth or sky to be transformed there. End dis-ease, end pain, end excesses, and break negative habits. Use crystals in each hand, in the right or left hand, or as a protective healing circle to channel the energies of the goddess Moon, of the Earth and sky, and of woman's unseen bodies. Cast a circle with crystal light, and use the healing rod or stone as a magick wand.

A simple banishing that works well with chronic pain is to tape a seed crystal, a tiny chip or point, to a pain area at the time of the waning Moon. Leave it taped there for three nights, then bury the quartz in the Earth. Visualize the pain entering the crystal, being buried with the crystal, and waning with the waning Moon.[17] When the New Moon comes, the pain is gone with the new cycle. In a variation of this, tape tiny seed crystals in a circle around a wound or pain area, for example a painful knee. Place points inward, facing the pain area, and use laying on of hands/pranic healing over the dis-ease. Leave the crystals on overnight, then do healing again in the morning and bury the seed crystals in the ground. Visualize the pain entering the crystals, leaving the knee new and whole again. The tiny crystals are lost to the process, but so is the pain.

To do chakra balancing with crystals, use a technique suggested by healer David Speer.[18] Have the woman being healed lie down and relax completely, directing her through pranayama breathing and/or body tension/release and into the meditative state. Holding a crystal in each hand (double terminated ones are especially powerful for this), rotate them clockwise over a pair of chakra centers as given below, until intuition senses that each pair of centers is balanced. Two centers are balanced at once. While rotating the crystals, visualize the color for each chakra entering it and brightening it. The healer can balance both chakra pairs at once, or hold one hand and crystal steady while energizing the other of the centers and then reverse it. The rotating motion of the hands and crystals is always clockwise, moving to the left in a spiral.

First balance the belly chakra with the brow center. The colors here are: belly chakra—orange, and brow center—indigo. Send each chakra its color, visualizing it entering the center with spiraling motion through the crystals. When the energy fades in the palms and crystals and both centers are balanced, move to the next pair of centers. The time this takes varies. Be aware of all impressions, and pay close attention to the woman's responses. The second pair of centers is the root and the crown: root center—ruby red, and crown center—violet. Clear light also works for the crown center, a rainbow lotus with a golden center, if the healer is attracted to it. The third pair to balance is the solar plexus and the throat, clear, bright yellow with clear, bright blue. The last center is the heart, which can be balanced with either the brow or crown. Send the heart chakra clear green or loving rose through the crystals. The centers are always balanced in these pairs and in this order.

When working with the heart chakra in any form of healing, the woman being healed sometimes experiences a release of emotions. She laughs or cries, gets very quiet or active, screams, is distraught, turns over into a fetal position, gets angry, or needs to be hugged and held. The healer's place in this is to comfort and assist her, accepting her totally. Explain to her what's happening, that she's releasing blocks and deep-seated pain that need moving before healing occurs. Assure her that nothing's wrong with releasing it, if the emotions or their intensity are disturbing her. Assure her that she's safe and cared about, and that it's okay to cry, to talk about her feelings if she chooses. It's okay to be angry. Hands touching the brow and heart chakra or doing the cradle movement are especially comforting at this time. When the woman is calm again, stroke her aura and smooth it, send her rose colored light. When she relaxes, she may feel warm or cold. Cover her if she needs it, keep her comfortable and don't leave her alone. Releasing moves a lot of dead issues and makes room for well-being, and the healer assists without judging or trying to prevent it. Be compassionate but remain detached, not allowing the woman's pain to overly affect you, letting it flow through if it does. Remember to use a grounding cord and let go of the energy, remember to adjust your belly chakra to a comfortable opening. Heal with heart and hands.

After a chakra balancing, with or without emotional release, if the woman wants to sleep, she should be allowed to. Whether she feels this or not, encourage her to get up only slowly, to remain lying still for awhile. The woman can be dizzy or suddenly feel light or very heavy. Her aura is different than it was before starting, and the weight of old blocks and the issues of years are gone. The feeling is a pleasant but different one, and the healer urges the woman to go with it, to accept and enjoy it and not to rush the process. The feeling is part of the healing taking place. The woman can use grounding techniques to return to now more quickly. Remember to remove negativity from your hands and crystals and to ground yourself. The process of balancing the chakras in pairs can be done without crystals but takes longer, and crystals add energy and colors that hands alone can't seem to match.

A similar technique in crystal healing is to place a clear quartz crystal on each chakra of the woman being healed. This is called laying on of stones and is also used with gemstones. The woman is lying on her back and in the meditative state, and you work above her slowly and with gentle motions. Place single terminated stones with all of the points facing in the same direction, or a series of double terminated ones end to end. If the crystal points face the woman's crown, she experiences an uplifting feeling from the healing, energizing and with possible psychic experiences and awakening. If the crystals point toward her feet, the healing is more grounding, calming and settling. Double terminated crystals establish an energy flow that runs in both directions, a polarity channel.

Place a crystal on each chakra, starting with one below the

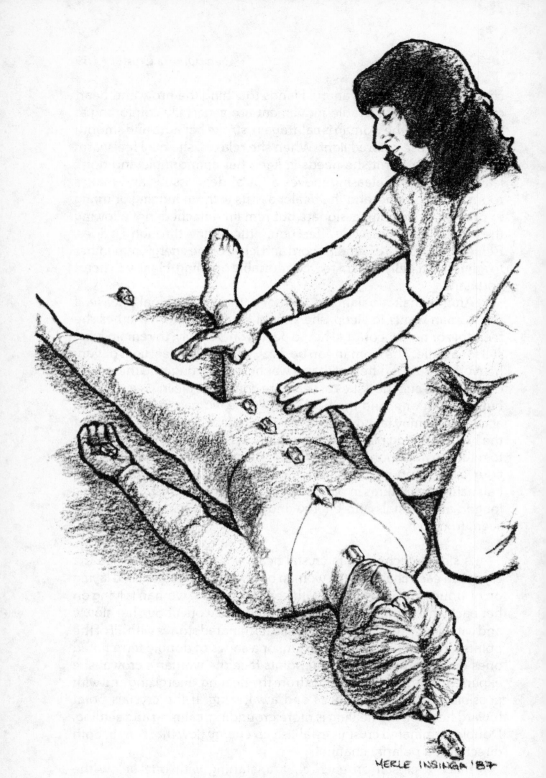

Crystal Healing

woman's feet and one at her transpersonal point, beyond her crown. Put a crystal in each of her hands. Place a quartz resting on her root chakra, on her belly between root and navel, just above her navel for the solar plexus, in the hollow of her breastbone for the heart, at the base of her throat, on her forehead, and at the top of her head. (This one is resting on the floor or table where the woman lies).

The woman relaxes completely and does rhythmic breathing while you use laying on of hands (either holding crystals or not), usually without touching, over the chakras. Move from crown to feet, opening each center, holding your hands over each until the healing sensations fade. Flick off negative energy from your hands before moving to the next chakra. Moving from feet to crown could raise kundalini energy. If you feel Shakti awakening with this, stroke the woman's aura along the spinal line or the line of chakras at the front from crown to feet, not touching her physically, and gently push kundalini back down again to the root chakra. With each chakra opened from head to foot by pranic healing, visualize the bright, clear color of the center as you work with each. Clear and stroke the woman's entire aura, sweeping hands from head to foot at the end of the healing. Then withdraw from the woman's aura and ground, while the woman remains quiet with the crystals still on her centers. When she is ready to move, remove the crystals, and the woman moves slowly for awhile. The exercise is a powerful chakra balancer, and calms, grounds and vitalizes. It relieves pain, and is good particularly for chronic back pain. The woman walks and holds her body differently at the end, is more centered and connected with her body and the goddess Earth.

The healer with crystals uses the meditative state or grounding and centering with all healings. While deep meditation is not required (as is also true for laying on of hands work), connection with the goddess *is*. The woman being healed, if she is receptive, aids the healing process by doing deep breathing and grounding and centering herself as well. The healer can lead her into this, but if the woman is unaware or unreceptive, continue the healing anyway. In most cases, consciously or not, the woman being healed is in an alpha state by the end of the work. Take care to protect yourself from absorbing the woman's pain, use a grounding cord, and cast light around yourself and the woman being healed. Talk to and reassure the woman being healed where this is needed, and you will intuitively know when to be quiet. Paying attention to the woman's responses is a major thing in crystal healing and in laying on of hands, and the healer finds her intuition heightened while she's doing healing. At the end of the work, she casts light around herself and around the woman being healed, and breaks contact. The woman being healed is encouraged to rest and may be sleepy. Ground, wash hands in tap water, clear your crystals by blowing through them or running in water. Use visualization and colors in every aspect of the healing process; crystals transmit these things well, and they are vital tools for controlling and using healing energy.

The woman who begins using crystals finds herself drawn to them constantly and finds the right healing crystals drawn to her. Some women in the presence of a quantity of crystals want to sleep, or are blissed out with the experience of crystal energy. Some women want to own every crystal they see, but realize that no one actually owns a crystal, which is a piece of the goddess Earth and a living Being. Some women take long periods to bond a clear quartz to their satisfaction and use, while others bond a crystal—any crystal—simply by holding it. Some women are drawn to very clear stones and others to clouded or rainbow ones. Some prefer larger crystals, others smaller. Most women find that in owning and using a crystal they are being taught by it constantly, and never want that crystal away from them once they bond it. They find their lives made more positive and well, increasing in joy and well-being, increasing in women's intuition, after dis-covering clear quartz crystal energy.

Occasionally a woman's crystal leaves her, or becomes uncomfortable to use or hold. If she hasn't physically lost it, she doesn't want it with her, even when it's been with her continually for years. Women change and so do stones, and the crystal that wants to leave will do so. The woman loses it, and though she's done that and found it again a dozen times, this time it's really lost. Perhaps she feels compelled to give it to someone, not understanding *why* at the time. She may forget to take it with her in the mornings as she usually does, and leave it on her altar instead. She may be drawn to another stone, forgetting the first one.

When a crystal feels uncomfortable, the first thing to try is clearing it. If lighter methods fail, try burying it in the ground for three days, or use salt as a last resort. Give the crystal a rest by not using it for awhile, not carrying it in the woman's aura. The woman using a different stone may or may not return to the first one again. The crystal may have taught all it chooses to, and wants to move on. When the time and next woman who needs it occur, the woman knows and gives the crystal. In the meantime, she has another crystal to teach her further; she has what she needs and flows with it. Even the woman who has no easy access to sources for clear quartz finds she has the stones she needs, and when she needs them. Native American shamans call clear quartz crystals "living stones," and the woman who is a crystal worker learns to trust their responses.

Healers who want their crystals always with them do this in a variety of ways. Wearing it on a necklace is the simplest way to keep a smaller crystal always in the aura. Wear the stone next to the skin point down for grounding and balancing, and use a chain length that puts the quartz over a chakra that needs it most. Throat, heart and solar plexus are all possible. For wearing, use stones that are capped with pure metals, silver or gold, and capped without piercing the stone. Wire-wound is better than gluing, but gluing is better than drilling. A mounting cap open at the top allows energy to flow freely.

Single terminated crystals worn point down are calming, but worn point upward are usually too spacey to wear all the time. They energize and raise power, but can be unsettling and over-sensitizing. This is also true of double terminated crystals worn as necklaces. Another way to carry a crystal over the heart is in a small drawstring bag made of natural materials.

Crystals worn on bracelets can be used to channel energy, sending and receiving, depending upon which arm the jewelry is worn. Crystals as rings, the stone mounted open so the crystal touches the skin, are good channeling focuses for laying on of hands/pranic healing work. A crystal held in a headband over the brow chakra (stone touching the skin or just over it) induces psychic experiences and women's intuition during healings.[19] The tool is too powerful to wear outside of ritual or healing work.

A good and easy way to keep clear quartz in the aura is to carry it in a left-hand pocket. Crystal filters and magnifies all sensations entering the woman's aura by this. It sensitizes her and protects her, and makes her more aware of every energy nuance and impression in her surroundings. Worn on the right side a crystal is grounding; worn on either side it is balancing and calming. Holding the stone in either hand from time to time is soothing and feels good, particularly in the left receiving hand, and a crystal's sensations in the palm are always comforting and joyous. Instant biofeedback is a plus of having stones in easy reach, and this can be done anywhere. If more than one crystal is carried or the stones are carried with other gemstones or pocket objects, wrap them in soft cloth to protect them from chipping and scratching. Natural fabrics are best, and silk is an energy insulator. A chipped crystal that develops sharp edges can be ground down on concrete, but seeing sparks come from a bonded stone while doing it is unsettling, and the crystal is changed and feels different afterwards. Crystals tend to change and flow with their users, and often a new chip or change in quartz reflects changes in the woman's life and Be-ing. A stone can crack or break after an especially intense healing, but this is rare. The dis-ease enters the quartz and the stone can't withstand it. The crystal is sacrificed, but the woman owes her healing to it. This also happens with gemstones.

Use this chapter and book only as a beginning, a basis for where to start in using crystals. So much of women's healing is individual work, and two women's ways of doing the same thing can vary greatly. Just as different women have affinities to different crystals or prefer different colors to send in healing, so do different methods work for different women. One woman sends energy with her left hand and receives it from her right, while another woman sends with her right and receives from her left. Most women heal with their palm chakras, but some heal powerfully through their fingertips. For some women, use of positive and negative polarity charges has to be precise, but other women ignore the charges completely and get good results.

If intuition says use red, do it. If intuition says use the right hand though the book says use the left, do that. If intuition says pick one crystal and leave the other one, follow that, too. In virtually every instance, woman's aura intuition is her best guide and teacher, and no given method is always the right one. For women who work with spirit guides, what to do "just comes" and has no explanation she can give, but she uses it and it works for her effectively. The issue is never the technique, but always the results. Use imagination, women's intuition and the goddess-within to determine how to heal. A book only reflects the methods that work traditionally or for the author, and is only a starting place. Women use what works for them.

The more a woman uses crystals in healing work, the more she learns *how* to use them. Crystals are great teachers in healing, and valuable tools. Women who are drawn to them often won't heal without them, though women who are not attracted to crystals know that healing doesn't require them to work. Healings with and without crystals are done in mostly a similar process, but the techniques, results, energy flows and sensations are all enhanced and different with clear quartz added. Women make use of crystals' healing properties, their ability to send and receive, magnify and store energy and colors to enhance and develop their healing work. Crystals are beautiful to see, hold and use, and things of great beauty and power-within, and they attract many women, reflecting women's goddess selves. The wonder, brightness, power and joy of clear quartz crystal is a goddess' gift to women's healing and self-healing, and to women's well-being.

FOOTNOTES

1. DaEl, *The Crystal Book* (Sunol, CA, The Crystal Co., 1983), p. 13.

2. Michael G. Smith, *Crystal Power* (St. Paul, Llewellyn Publications, 1985), p. 137.

3. Robert Bodoh, *Discover Quartz* (Bodoh Crystals, 565 Academy Dr., Edgerton, WI 53534), 1984 flyer.

4. Michael G. Smith, *Crystal Power,* p. 137.

5. *Ibid.*, p. 137-138. Also Uma Sita Silbey, "Crystal Tools, Not Toys," in *Magical Blend Magazine* (POB 11303, San Francisco, CA 94101), Issue 13, May 1986, p. 34.

6. Randall and Vicki Baer, *Windows of Light: Quartz Crystals and Transformation* (San Francisco, Harper and Row Publishers, 1984), p. 3-5.

7. Katrina Raphaell, *Crystal Enlightenment* (New Aurora Press, 1985), p. 8-9.

8. Robert Bodoh, *Discover Quartz,* flyer.

9. Katrina Raphaell, *Crystal Enlightenment,* p. 53-78.

10. DaEl, *The Crystal Book,* p. 14-15.

11. See Diane Stein, *The Women's Spirituality Book* for more on clear quartz crystal, including non-healing uses.

12. Serenity Peterson, *Crystal Visioning, A Crystal Workbook* (Nashville, TN, Interdimensional Publishing, 1984), p. 7-8.

13. Korra Deaver, Ph.D., *Rock Crystal: The Magic Stone* (York, ME, Samuel Weiser, Inc., 1985), p. 53.

14. DaEl, *The Crystal Book,* p. 67.

15. Uma Sita Silbey, "Natural Quartz Crystal Healing Ritual", in *Circle Network News* (POB 219, Mt. Horeb, WI, 53572), Fall, 1984, p. 13.

16. Directions are from Michael G. Smith, *Crystal Power,* Chapter Two. Dedicate this tool to healing and to peace; it's very powerful.

17. Suggested by healer Tyshe Moonfeather, at her Michigan Women's Music Festival workshop, August, 1983.

18. Personal communication and teaching. This is wonderful to experience and to do.

19. See Michael G. Smith, *Crystal Power,* Chapter Four for construction suggestions.

Beginning Gemstones: The Root Chakra

THE WOMAN who has bonded and worked with clear quartz crystal knows most of the techniques for using colored gemstones in healing. Clear quartz is more versatile than any single gemstone, but colored stones are more specific, go directly to the heart of dis-ease and change it in the etheric double and the chakras. Work with gemstones is based on work with colors and chakras, and their energy is the energy of color healing intensified. Clear quartz crystal sends all colors; gemstones send their own. Clear quartz is programmed; gemstones come with set programming. In some ways gemstones are simpler to use and in some ways more complex, but they are as powerful for their uses as is clear quartz. In using clear quartz, the direction for healing comes from the healer's hands and aura through the stone—and this is also true in gemstones. In using colored stones, the skill is in the healer's ability to analyze and assess auras and chakras to choose the correct gem energy. Many of the techniques for healing and self-healing (once analysis is made) are the same as in using clear quartz crystal.

Gemstones are minerals found in the Earth, with the exception of the few gem materials that are of marine, plant or animal origin (coral, pearl, jet, amber, ivory). Any ornamental stone is a gemstone, and the line between precious and semi-precious gemstones is a fuzzy one. In general, stones that are used faceted in jewelry work are considered precious gemstones. These are powerful for healing, but so are the less expensive semi-precious stones. Semi-precious stones are cheaper and more easily available, and are the basis for most women's gemstone healing work. Faceted gemstones are crystalline in form and many semi-precious stones are crystalline, while other healing gemstones are not. Mineral gemstones (gemstones of non-organic origin), are formed by volcanic action, intense pressure, heat and melting, or by sedimentation affecting chemical properties. Crystalline gemstones all involve heat formation, as do most that are noncrystalline. Found underground, most gemstones are mined from surrounding rock structures, brought to the surface for sorting, grading, polishing, cutting, tumbling or faceting. Hardness, designated by the Moh's scale that grades from one to ten, is a factor. The harder the stone, the less fragile it is, and the more cutting and working it's able to withstand. The softer the stone, the more likely it is to break in preparation, carrying or in use. Notice the hardness designations and be prepared to protect from crumbling, chipping or breaking stones with low numbers. Precious or semi-precious, soft or hard, gemstones are living Be-ings from the goddess Earth, and are beautiful, positive, powerful healing tools.

Colored gemstones contain piezoelectric energy, but most bond to a specific chakra frequency rather than to the entire aura. Healers make use of the chakra affinity and the stones' color transmission. Gemstones are healing-specific: a stone great for headaches can be ineffective for indigestion or ovarian cysts. A stone that calms is not the same one to use for energizing. Hot stones, warm colors, cannot be programmed for cooling. Where clear quartz crystal is used for all occasions, only lapis lazuli and chrysocolla come close to this of all the colored gems, and even these have specific uses. The woman who uses colored gemstones for healing work uses her stone for a specific purpose or chakra. If she depends on colored gemstones for a variety of healing work, she has a variety of different gems to work with, and she knows the attributes and correspondences for each. As in any form of women's healing, these attributes are slightly different for different women, and women's intuition is necessary with knowledge for using them best.

The difference in gemstones' piezoelectricity from that of quartz means that the healer has less bonding to do with a new stone, but the process of starting gem use is the same. The woman chooses her gemstones in the same way as she chooses her quartz crystal, by feel, and finds them from the same sources. Museum gift shops and rock shops are good places to find gemstones cheaply, as are the women's music festivals. Gemstone jewelry is popular right now, and strands of gemstone beads or chips can be found in department stores. The healer clears the stone after healing with it. Sea salt and salt water are good general clearing agents, as are sunlight, running tap water and placing on an altar. There is less aura individuality to make the bonding fragile between woman and stone, but stones can be drained by repeated uses. A new colored gemstone is consecrated at the altar to healing. The woman bonds it by holding it and keeping it with her when she needs its energies. The bonding is less specific than for crystals, and it takes less time.

Gemstones used for healing work have no need to be jewelry quality, and with that choice they are surprisingly inexpensive. Raw rubies and emeralds in tiny chips sell for as low as two dollars, and most uncut stones sell for under ten. Healing gemstones can be used as totally raw chunks or crystals, as tumbled pieces, as gemcut and faceted, as strung beads or as jewelry set and mounted—whatever appeals to the woman using them. Be aware of the energies of metals when using mounted stones. Where stones are not crystalline, tumbled pieces and beads have a finish between raw and gemcut. They have polish and refined quality and color, without looking or feeling tampered with. Compared to jewelry-cut stones, the tumbled ones are inexpensive: a necklace string of rose quartz or aventurine beads or chips is under twenty-five dollars, and a tumbled single piece of these costs from twenty cents and up. As in every case in women's healing, the healer chooses what works for her, what appeals to her, what she is drawn to, and what feels good in her hands. She wears in her aura only stones that attract her, and that harmonize with her needs.

The size of healing gemstones is optional and open to individual choice as well. A quarter-inch ruby chip can be extremely powerful for energizing, and so can the six-inch chunk of amethyst put under the bed for calming and insomnia. Tiny stones are easily lost and hard to hold onto in healings; pieces too large are awkward or heavy to hold. Small stones can be necklace-mounted easily if wished, with a silver cap and some glue or silver wire winding. The parts are available at jeweler's supplies and arts and crafts stores. Medium sized gemstone pieces of an inch or two are comfortable for holding in the palms or carrying in pockets or drawstring necklace bags. Larger ones work to change the energies of entire rooms. Whatever their size, gemstones are powerful for healing.

Colored gemstones come in two basic forms: crystalline or non-crystalline/matrix. Crystalline structure is the symmetrical shape seen in clear quartz. Other crystalline gemstones are the colored quartzes: citrine, amethyst, rutile quartz, smoky quartz (rose, blue or green quartzes are matrix). Topaz, garnet and tourmaline are crystalline stones, as are others of the precious gems like sapphire, ruby, emerald, diamond, and aquamarine. These are the stones that are often faceted when jewelry-cut. Clear quartz is hexagonal, and other gemstones have other shapes in their crystalline structures—octagonal, tetragonal, isometric, trigonal, orthorbhombic, monoclinic, and triclinic.[1] The crystalline shape directs the stone's energy-sending pattern and capability, and faceted or not crystalline gems are considered the purest energy transmitters and transmitters of color. They are also the stones most sought after for jewelry. The natural uncut crystals of many of these are very beautiful, and their energies are intense and positive whether raw or worked.

The other major form is called matrix. These are the stones that are noncrystalline, and come from the Earth as chunks, rather than as crystals or geometric forms. Some of these include rose, blue or green quartz, lapis lazuli, agate, carnelian, jasper, jade, turquoise, rhodochrosite. Polishing and tumbling, cutting into shapes, brings out the color and beauty of these stones for jewelry use. They are not faceted and are usually opaque. Much bead jewelry is from matrix stones, gem carvings and relief work, talismans, and gemstones cut into objects—fetishes, statues, altar tools, eggs, pyramids and cups. Crystalline stones have been used for these, but are more expensive and are usually harder to work with. The Mexican marble onyx animals and ashtrays sold in the southwest United States to tourists is an example, and pipestone and turquoise fetish animals are used by some Native American peoples. Strings of gemstone beads or chips in lapis, malachite, tiger eye, rose quartz, aventurine, hematite and jade are matrix/noncrystalline stones used as jewelry, and are also healing gemstones. Some of these beads and carvings can be expensive, depending on the rarity of the stone, the artwork, popularity, mining techniques, type of store and distance of origins. No tumbled or raw matrix stone pieces, single uncarved gemstones of an inch or so size, should cost more than five dollars and may cost under a dollar. Probably the most expensive of these is lapis lazuli, which should still be in this range or close to it. Most noncrystalline gemstones are at the lower end of this price range; try museum giftshops for availability.

A final form of gemstone is those that are not stones at all, but are of animal, vegetable or marine origin. Stones are formed in the Earth by combinations of heat and pressure on their chemical compounds, and they are of mineral/earth compositon. Amber is a material that is nonmineral formed from the fossilization of pine tree resin, a vegetable compound. It often includes bits of leaf, stem or trapped insects, and has a texture and energy that is definitely different from stone. Jet is compressed coal, fossilized wood is plant matter. Coral is the calcium building of tiny marine animals, and is polished for jewelry work. Pearl is the reaction of the pearl oyster to an irritant inside its shell. Ivory is animal bone, the tusk material of elephants or tusk-bearing pigs.[2] Though not actually stones, these materials are classed as gemstones and are used in gemstone healing. They are valued as jewelry, but at usually less value or price than the faceted crystalline gemstones, and put on a par with some matrix stones for cost. Amber and coral are major healing and protection energies.

The colors of gemstones are caused by their chemical compositions. Metals that absorb portions of the light spectrum are present in the stones, allowing some colors to be visible and others to remain unseen. The colors involved here are the light colors of the chakra rainbow, and the metallics present in gemstone composition are: chrome, iron, cobalt, copper, manganese, nickel and vanadium.[3] These are in very small quantities. The type of metal determines which colors of light are absorbed and which are radiated. In the case of some colored quartzes, it is heat and not chemicals that make the colors. Natural radiation makes clear quartz into smoky quartz, and natural heat makes amethyst into citrine. When buying smoky quartz, particularly, watch for a brown color that's transparent or translucent, rather than dark black that is not. Some smoky quartz being sold is human-made, irradiated. Some citrine being sold is amethyst heated in ovens. Held in the palms, the tampered stones feel hurt or burnt, and are not effective for healing work. If all the colors of light pass through a stone it is colorless; if all are absorbed, the stone is black. The light vibration rates in between, affected by metals, chemicals or heat, are what's visible as gemstone color.

Crystalline gemstones carry their energies and colors intensively, often in bursts or waves of strong power that add light to the aura as a whole, along with meeting resonance in the chakras. Matrix stones are softer and gentler in their actions, working with steady energy to transmit their colors and qualities to the chakras specifically. The nonmineral gemstones are whole aura substances, with coral also specific for the belly chakra, amber for the solar plexus, jet for the root. Chakra specific stones have great power for healing and transformation. In comparison of clear quartz crystal with other gemstones, gems generally are less powerful than clear quartz, but are more powerful in specific ways. The healer makes use of the stones' individual attributes and uses those attributes where they are needed.

Being chakra specific and operating on the aura level of the etheric double, gemstones in healing are used by putting their energies and light into a woman's physical aura. This means carrying, wearing or placing them on the body. Wearing a necklace is the most familiar— a single stone pendant or string of gemstone beads. Earrings are popular as are rings, and the stone's backing should be open to the skin. Gemstone bracelets can be used to transmit colors and healing energy, and they work for some women more than for others. Settings of silver are cool and flowing, lunar and feminine, while gold settings are hot and energizing, solar, and copper combines both. Silver is recommended in healing, while alloys of other metals than gold, silver or copper are not.

Holding a gemstone in the left hand to receive its energy is a method of using gemstones for healing. The stone can be kept in a left side pocket, present in the aura, and cradled in the palm when needed. A personal choice for gemstone work and one that is very powerful is to sleep holding the needed gemstone in the left hand. Deep relaxation opens women's unseen bodies to accepting gemstone or healing energy, and sleeping with the stone admits a maximum amount of this. Gemstone energy and color can be magnified by holding a clear quartz crystal in the same hand with the stone. The woman doing this dis-covers that the stones stay with her after doing it for a few nights. If she loses them in the sheets they haven't gone far, and after awhile she doesn't lose them at all. She is aware of the changes being made in her aura by the stones, pays close attention to them, and if a stone becomes too powerful, or she has had enough of it, she puts it back on her altar. If not sure of what she needs, she uses the stone she is drawn to, and when she is no longer drawn to it or the stone won't stay with her, she stops.

In magnetizing water/gemstone elixirs, place the gemstone you wish to transmit into the glass before using your palms over it. When you magnetize the water, send the color that matches the stone and your healing needs. When magnetizing cloth, hold a gemstone on top of the cloth you are energizing, and again transmit the color through the stone. Using clear crystal with the gemstone amplifies the healing energy.

In laying on of hands or psychic healing, use a gemstone in your right hand to transmit its color and attribute to the woman you are healing. In the laying on of stones chakra balancing given in the clear quartz chapter, substitute or add a gemstone for each chakra, a stone that matches that chakra. Place the stones on the front of the woman's body, while she is lying down, then use clear quartz crystals in your hand or hands to balance the centers. For each chakra, send the color and attributes of the stones, visualizing the gemstone energy going into the chakras to clear, brighten and vitalize them. A woman needing work for a specific chakra can have only the stones for that center placed on her body, on that chakra, and use laying on of hands with or without a crystal to transmit the stones' colors in a healing. Surrounding the chakra and the gemstones on it, optionally use a circle of clear quartz crystals to magnify and intensify the energy.[4]

The art of laying on of stones is practiced by healer Katrina Raphaell, who traces the skill to Atlantis, and to India, Egypt, South America and Tibet.[5] For a chakra balancing layout, she suggests:

> Point a single quartz crystal at the top of the head; place an amethyst on the third eye, aquamarine at the throat, rose quartz at the heart, malachite on the solar plexus, citrine quartz on the navel and smoky quartz on the pubic bone.[6]

Her stones for the crown and third eye differ slightly from their chakra positions in this book. To change this if wished use a fluorite on the third eye, and move the amethyst to the crown, the clear quartz crystal above the head. Spiritual body aura levels and their gemstones tend to overlap. Use what stones you are drawn to, what sytems, colors, gem correspondences that work best for you individually. Put another clear quartz at the feet, and one in each hand.

In single chakra healing to balance the root center, use black tourmaline, smoky quartz or tourmaline quartz on the pubic area, surrounding the gemstones with clear quartz crystals that point to the black stones. To energize the belly center, use carnelian, red/brown agate and orange coral. For the solar plexus, place amber, citrine quartz or a topaz crystal above the navel area, surrounded by clear quartz crystals. In each case, use laying on of hands over the stones, and the surrounding clear quartzes are optional.

For a woman experiencing heart loss or emotional pain, use rose quartz on her heart chakra. Place one or more rose quartz pieces, or rest a string of rose quartz beads on her breastbone and surround the area with a circle of clear quartz crystals. The points of the crystals face the rose quartz. Do laying on of hands. Other stones for heart pain are pink or watermelon tourmaline, green aventurine, green fluorite, or green or rose jade. In working with the heart chakra, be ready for emotional release in the healing. Green aventurine, jade and rose quartz are the most comforting of the stones to use, and rose quartz is recommended for its gentleness. Katrina Raphaell suggests a stone layout using either one kind of gemstone or several different gemstones that correspond to the same chakra. Place them in a pleasing pattern over the center, with or without quartz crystals.[7] When using a variety of stones, be aware of which stones energize and which calm, and use all of the same quality needed. Mixing types can cause the stones to neutralize each other.

If the woman needs to talk about her pain, her throat center is activated by placing a piece of lapis lazuli, chrysocolla or other throat chakra gemstone on it during the heart healing. Use a clear quartz crystal (a double terminated one is good) between the woman's heart and throat, pointing to both chakras. Another version of this is to place a clear quartz crystal on the throat center.[8] To activate the third eye, use the same process with moonstone or a clear or indigo fluorite octahedron on the brow chakra. To calm a woman or induce sleep, use pieces of amethyst on her crown or third eye, or place pieces of amethyst on her crown, third eye and solar plexus. Remembering the complementary colors, too much solar plexus yellow is reduced and balanced with violet or violet gemstones. Use clear quartz with this if wished. Stones carry a doctrine of signatures: their appearance—in this case colors—directs their uses.

A further idea for laying on of stones for a very simple chakra balancing is to use stones taken from the Earth, any stones from the ground, gemstones or not; the smooth ones are most comfortable to use. Place a stone on each chakra, then do laying on of hands and aura stroking and balancing. This is a good exercise for grounding the root chakra and for calming. Stones come from the goddess Earth, and even the most mundane have healing qualities. In grounding emotional or physical pain, any stone will do, too. Hold it in the right hand and send the pain into it, then clear the stone of pain before returning it to Earth. Use visualization to clear the stone, or running water, seeing negativity transformed into useful energy. After any healing, ground the energies and clear the stone/s. During any gem-stone healing, use the same procedures and protections as with clear quartz crystal, laying on of hands or psychic healing. Remember the meditative state, the grounding cord, aura of protective light, and grounding with hands to the Earth at the end.

Use of stones found on the ground for healing or laying on of stones leads into work with specific gemstones for each chakra. This begins with the root center. Briefly, the root center is the survival center, and its colors are red and black. An increase of red energy means an increase of survival energy and sexual/affectional vitality; a decrease or balancing of the red energy with the black gemstones reduces the root chakra's "running on survival," and aids grounding, stability, security, rootedness, centering and release of pain. Green and green stones are complementary to red, and soothe red as well. Root chakra red is life force energy, the ability to stay alive to create new lives; root chakra black is the womb, woman's connection with the goddess Earth, with being part of her, and of the continuity of life, death, after-life and rebirth.

Red is hot and heats; it stimulates, increases blood circulation and metabolism, the building of red blood cells. It activates and rouses, increases fertility, and stimulates the liver and uterus. Red stones are used for dis-eases such as AIDS, leukemia, cancer, neuralgia, frostbite, exhaustion, over-exposure to cold, and burnout. Black stones cool and calm. Where red stones transmit incarnation, the black stones transmit karma. Black helps with pain, fear, aids steadiness, abstract thought, physical control, drug issues and detoxification, pain, stress and staying power.[9] Where a woman is too nervous or angry, too volatile for use of red stones, substitute the black ones for red energy healing. The etheric double ribbon is both red and black when women see it, and the physical aura level is both colors. Some black gemstones raise karmic issues, other lives, and work to be completed in this life.

Though in laying on of hands or psychic healing the healer seldom uses black light, the black gemstones are powerful and positive for healing work. Black contains all colors of the chakra rainbow, absorbs all colors of the aura and transmits all colors into the woman's etheric double. Black light is not sent traditionally in healing, mainly because of patriarchal thought-form connotations of it. Black in a racist and misogynist society is a death color, a depressive and awesome color, a negative one. It is woman's taboo womb, unknown, unspoken of, dark and feared by men to invoke. Black light, coming from women's awareness, however, is an absorber and dissolver of negativity and used for grounding and connecting with the Earth. Black stones are matter instead of light, and are new to women, free of negative thought forms, and free to carry the positive of the black Earth, black night, the dark goddess, the beautiful black womb to women's chakras and bodies. Like their duality counterparts, the all-colored white stones and clear crystals, black gemstones are immense-ly powerful.

Women using black stones, any gemstones, need to know their attributes, to respect their strengths and use their abilities. The triad to red and white in the life force, black gemstones are the Earth womb and the karmic positive darkness, the bridge between lives and beginnings, the connection with the goddess Earth as the mother of all, and women's connection with all peoples as one. When doing psychic healing or laying on of hands, seldom send black light, but when doing gemstone healings use the positive black stones. In sending light with black gemstones, send red light, or the red/black of the etheric double ribbon, or send clear/rainbow light instead in most cases.

Gemstones for the root chakra begin with black stones and continue into red ones. The root chakra is the closest center to the physical body, and root chakra gemstones are concerned with the physical, women's relationship with dense earthly life and its manifestations. Black gemstones for the root chakra include smoky quartz, black tour-maline, tourmaline quartz, obsidian/Apache tears, black onyx, jet and hematite. The red root chakra gemstones that follow these are bloodstone/heliotrope, red garnet, ruby and red jasper.[10]

Smoky quartz is the best known of black gemstones in women's healing, a brown to black form of clear quartz crystal, colored by natural radiation. The stone is crystalline and beautiful, found in Pennsylvania and Scotland, Switzerland, Brazil and Colorado. A very black variety of the stone is called morion, and in Scotland smoky quartz is called cairngorm. Very light smoky quartz is erroneously called smoky topaz; look for it in strings of necklace beads.

Too much of the smoky quartz available is irradiated deliberately in a cyclotron to turn it dark. Be aware of this, and be suspicious of a stone that looks burnt or very black, as most natural smoky quartz is golden brownish. One natural source for very dark smoky quartz is Colorado, but natural smoky quartz does *not* come from Arkansas— irradiated clear quartz does. Most of the true smoky quartz available in the United States comes from Brazil, particularly Minas Gerais. In Russia, where clear quartz is less common and more valued, smoky quartz was baked in bread for oven heat to turn it clear.[11] Here, there is much more clear quartz available, and since smoky quartz brings higher prices, the tampering is done.

Use palm sensitivity to feel the crystal's energies when choosing smoky quartz, and choose the stone that feels good for healing. An irradiated stone can look natural but feels hurt and burnt. If chosen, it can be helped with clearing methods; use intuition. Smoky quartz is also available with rutile inclusions, fine metallic hairs or wisps inside the stone that magnify and electrify its energy. Like clear quartz crystal that it's a colored variety of, smoky quartz is listed as a 7 on the Moh's scale of hardness that runs from 1 to 10. The hardest gemstone energy is diamond, listed as a 10.

Natural smoky quartz is a basic grounding stone, highly recom- mended for sedating, relaxing, purifying and stabilizing. It stimulates the desire for life, survival and continuance, helps with the courage to make changes and break bad habits, stimulates positive self-image/ self-acceptance. Smoky quartz is used for any sort of stress, depression, fear or panic, including personal fears of inadequacy. It aids any sort of survival fears from stagefright to threat of attack, and is a powerful protection stone that has been used as such in wartime. The woman in self-healing sends the stone her pain through the right hand, or draws its energies into her aura through the left. She wears it, holds it, or carries it in a pocket.

Take smoky quartz to bed and hold it while entering sleep to calm, aid insomnia, soothe fatigue, dissolve negativity of all sorts. It aids in assimilation and digestion, and helps in cases of gas, intestinal disturbance, diarrhea. Use it to bind the self to the earth plane, for spaciness of all sorts, for psychic elimination of old issues and for exhaustion. When not needed for healing, put it aside. Slept with, the stone can induce disturbing dreams at times not needed, and can awaken past life experiences. Mellie Uylert says that carried unneeded, it stimulates gloominess.[12]

Smoky quartz is a good meditation stone, aiding the alpha state and good to use for self-hypnosis and hypnosis. It gives a sense of pride and self-pride, a sense of steadiness and being here, helps when women feel they can't meet ideals, and helps with recycling, trying again and rejuvenation.[13] Rutile smoky quartz (smoky quartz containing natural needles of metallic fiber) is particularly powerful and electric. Women with drug issues or smoking use rutile or plain smoky quartz to help them detoxify their bodies, to go through withdrawal and remain clear. Body weight issues and suicidal tendencies are helped by smoky quartz, as is premenstrual syndrome and the after-effects of abortion. The stone is calming, comforting, aids sleep and is stabilizing for anyone drawn to it, is particularly helpful in crisis situations, and is helpful with emotional or physical trauma. Smoky quartz balances the root chakra and connects the root to the crown, the physical to spiritual realms, the self to the goddess and goddess-within. It's a powerful and positive tool in women's healing, a stone that stimulates hope and eases fear and pain.

Black tourmaline is another root chakra stone that aids in making changes and transformations. It grounds and deflects negativity, and is used as a protection stone. Black tourmaline transforms internal negativity, changes and releases it, and protects against negative energies entering from the outside. The stone is found in Germany, the United States, Africa, the Urals and Madagascar; in the United States it occurs (in all colors) in California, Maine, New York, Connecticut, and Colorado. Another name for black tourmaline is schorl, and it measures 7-7½ in hardness on the Moh's scale. One of the stone's major properties is its magnetism and electricity. Rubbing a black tourmaline rod with wool cloth or heating it raises static electricity and causes a positive charge at one end, a negative charge at the other. The Dutch who first imported tourmaline from Africa used this magnetism to draw ash from smoking pipes. The woman healer makes use of its polarities to draw negativity and dis-ease from the chakras, holding a black tourmaline rod over a blocked chakra and rotating it counter-clockwise to open the blocks.[14] The stone is particularly good for this in the lower centers, and like smoky quartz it connects the physical with the spiritual in women's bodies. Use it with clear quartz crystal, or in the form of tourmaline quartz, which has black tourmaline needle inclusions that occur naturally in quartz crystal.

Black tourmaline is a grounding stone, and a good one. It reduces anger, resentment, jealousy and insecurity, and grounds and eases neuroses and obsessions. Working with the intestinal tract—the root center is the center for elimination—black tourmaline treats diarrhea, constipation and intestinal blockages, balances the physical elimination system and processes. Like smoky quartz it's a meditation stone. Wearing black tourmaline is like wearing a protective shield, and Julia Lorusso and Joel Glick recommend it for those drawn to it.[15] Thelma Isaacs says that black tourmaline should not be worn directly on the body.[16] In personal experience, carrying it in a pocket works very well.

Katrina Raphaell uses black tourmaline in laying on of stones to direct energies from higher aura levels and chakras into the physical body. She uses it to direct negativity out of the body, placing black tourmaline rods at the feet and knees in stone layouts.[17] Tourmaline quartz is also used for this, combining the energies of all-color clear quartz with the all-color black energies of the root center. The combination works with opposites and balances them, uses black tourmaline's magnetic properties increased by the polarity and aura resonance of clear quartz. Old habits and patterns are broken by this for new growth and positive change. Both tourmaline quartz and black tourmaline deflect and change negativity, and are good for grounding and nervousness, for too much root center red. Black tourmaline balances the root center, and tourmaline quartz connects the root to the crown. Clear crystal is a stone for the crown and transpersonal point.

A root chakra black stone that enters into karmic and subconscious issues is *black obsidian*. Obsidian has a powerful polarity to clear quartz crystal, is recommended to be used with it,[18] and brings to light things hidden inside. The stone illuminates truth, and not always gently. It shows the woman using it her inner self, both her weaknesses and strengths, explodes fantasies and dreams for realities. Such realities can be harsh, and the woman working with obsidian is warned to go gently with it. Use it only for short periods, and paired with clear quartz, as crystal helps with processing the insights. Black obsidian is a volcanic lava formation, a crystal formed too quickly to develop facets. It is a form of natural glass as is clear quartz. An alternate name for it is Apache tears or Navaho tears. It's found in Utah, Oregon, Arizona and Nevada in the United States, and in Mexico, Siberia and Hungary. The stone was known to ancient Rome, and occurs in solid black with a silver or gold cast or in form of lighter flower patterns on a dark background. This type of patterned gemstone is called snow-flake obsidian.

Like the other black gemstones, obsidian is used for grounding and stabilizing and it activates the root chakra and collects its scattered energies. The stone stimulates inner and outer sight, and is good for eye problems, for not-seeing to avoid the pain of truth. A psychic mirror, obsidian magnifies delusions and weaknesses and reflects them back on the woman using it for her knowledge and work to change them. Fears can be intensified, illusions exposed. There is a subconscious awakening. Karmic issues are raised, the third eye/brow chakra activated and connected to the root, and work themes carried from one life to the next. This is a very powerful stone with potential for positive cleansing and transformation. The stone aids concentration and meditation, is used for scrying, and is a teacher of inner truth and understanding. It absorbs negativity and shows it equally with positive forces, the dualities as one. By exposing dark-ness it opens up light, and the woman choosing to work with it knows when to stop and go on.

Katrina Raphaell calls black obsidian "one of the most important teachers of all the New Age stones."[19] Similar to black tourmaline and smoky quartz, obsidian is involved with survival, with drawing the body and spirit together. It brings energy from all the other centers into the root chakra, and brings the energy of the inner subconscious out to the rational mind. The stone is the duality of the goddess, stating that black and white, night and day, inner and outer, negative and positive are both at once, and that neither half of the pair is complete or whole alone.

Lee Lanning and Nett Hart posit obsidian as the volcanic fire symbol of women's sexuality,[20] women as the unknown, the inner, the womb, the lunar, the subconscious. With discussion of the con-notations of black as a color in patriarchy, and women's association always with the black unknown, the concept fits well with Raphaell's analysis of black obsidian. Entrance into the labyrinth, the womb, the subconscious self and the darkness is always frightening, but women do it every day with perfect trust. Women who are this inner darkness know its secrets and truths as the sources of Be-ing and goddess. The labyrinth of darkness is women's mysteries, the mysteries of birth, death and rebirth, of incarnation and reincarnation. Given these pathways to the center/source, obsidian is perhaps the spirit guide for the journey to the goddess and goddess-within. Women enter it with respect for higher power and knowledge, and use the forces wisely, safely and well.

Black onyx is another root center stone, one that has been used for 5,000 years in engravings and cameos for jewelry and healing. The stone comes in black, brown or other colors and is a form of chalcedony/agate, colored in layers. Brazil, India, the Malagasy Republic and Uruguay are sources, with the best for jewelry said to come from Brazil. True onyx is not to be confused with marble onyx, the striated cream and green Mexican marble that's sold as carvings in the southwest United States. Mellie Uyldert connects black onyx to the sign of Capricorn and the planet Saturn, and designates all of the black gemstones to Saturn. Black in onyx is the most powerful of its colors for healing, and Serenity Peterson recommends it used with quartz crystal and with silver.[21] Rhiannon McBride pairs onyx with pearl for women, with diamond for men,[22] stones of the crown or transpersonal point.

Black onyx is a protection stone that absorbs and transforms negativity without storing it. It's a stone to use for dealing with stress, aids inspiration, stabilizes the emotions, stimulates seriousness, perseverance, and the will. It helps to settle karmic debts before age thirty.[23] For women with a strong Saturn in their horoscopes, black onyx is a positive, protective and strengthening stone. For women who have weaker Saturn influences in their chart, the gemstone can attract negativity—gloominess, harshness, poverty and relationship breakups.[24] The guideline here is in what feels right. Women who are drawn to a particular stone are virtually always in need of it and benefit from its use. For women drawn to using black onyx, it brings spiritual, moral and physical strength, wisdom, temperance, courage, purpose, reserve and protection from harm.

The major healing use of black onyx is in releasing, using its powers of separation in positive ways. A stone of balancing, it helps in times of mourning or grief and has been used for that for centuries. Onyx also helps in leaving or ending a negative relationship, or recovering from one. It prevents others from draining a woman's energies. Onyx aids the skin, nails and hair, is helpful for heart disease and hearing problems related to stress, separation and letting go. The stone is used also by athletes for physical stress and strength. It's a healing stone for ulcers and watery eyes, pus, blood circulation and protection from accidents. Black onyx absorbs but does not transmit negativity and is a record keeper for the wearer's physical herstory.[25] Use the stone in psychometry.

The differences in the black stones' reactions to negativity is interesting. Smoky quartz dispels negativity, black tourmaline deflects it, obsidian absorbs and draws it in, and black onyx absorbs but does not store it, and transforms it to balance. Of the remaining black stones in this section, jet repels negativity, and hematite transforms it. All of these are methods of balancing the root chakra, the center closest to the dense physical level. The woman choosing a black stone accepts the one she is drawn to, and works with visualization and healing to flow with the stone's energies for her needs.

Another healing black gemstone is *jet,* a stone of importance for the matriarchal Pueblo peoples of Native America. In Pueblo silver work, particularly Zuni, jet is the material used to symbolize the earth element, the body, the womb and the pre-emergence underworld. It's the stone of the kiva, the resting place between lives from which emergence comes through the sipapu/womb. Jet is a gemstone that is not stone, but has organic origins. It's a form of compressed coal, which is fossilized wood. Like tourmaline, jet heated or stroked develops an electrical charge, positive and negative polarity. The stone is found in Utah and Colorado, as well as in England, Germany, France and Spain. Its traditional use has been in mourning jewelry.

Jet in women's healing is another stone of releasing. It repels negativity and aids letting go, aids acceptance of the karmic cycle of birth, death and rebirth. It helps in the ending of relationships, dispels depression, worry and fear. For women who fear thunderstorms, jet is comforting.

Because of its softness (2½-4 Moh's scale) and organic composition, jet has been used for healing in powdered and burnt forms. Early and traditional uses of gemstones ingest powdered stones frequently for healing, but modern uses prefer absorbing only their energies, not their physical matter. The closest to this practiced today is in magnetizing gemstone elixirs or essences, where the energies of the stones are transmitted to water and the water is drunk medicinally. The gemstone remains intact and is used again unharmed. Using laying on of hands over a glass of clear water containing a gemstone is to make a gemstone elixir, and sunlight or moonlight are other methods of creating them.

In powdered forms taken in wine or water, or mixed with a bees-wax salve for external use, jet has been used for toothaches and to treat skin tumors. Powdered and burnt, the stone emits heavy fumes that are used to dispel dis-ease and negativity and for protection. It was used as a fumigant, to repel contagion and fever, and was known in Europe during the plague. The smoke was also used for epilepsy, hysteria, dropsy, headaches, hallucinations, lymphatic swelling and stomach dis-eases.[26]

The mining and working of jet has been known since the Bronze Age, and was a major industry in early twentieth century England when jet was a popular jewelry stone. Soft and porous, jet is easily scratched in jewelry, and feels warm to the touch.[27] Women use it to connect with the karmic cycle, to release grief and let go, and to repel sadness. For the Native American Pueblo peoples, jet is an element of the life force, of women's womb and source emergence.

Thelma Isaacs lists *hematite* as another earth energy root chakra stone used by the Pueblo Indians.[28] She notes it as being worn with turquoise, probably as a protector and balancer, a connector with the Earth and sky. Hematite is a shiny metallic substance, black nodules in a red/black base material. The nodules are used in jewelry making, and the water that aids in the cutting turns blood red from the process. The Dutch name for this stone is bloodstone, but it is not called that in the United States, and should not be confused with the green and red stone known here as bloodstone or heliotrope. Hematite is found in the United States, as well as in England, New Zealand, Germany, Spain, Brazil, Norway and Sweden. Its hardness is 5½-6.

Hematite was known to ancient Greece and Rome as a charm against bleeding, and for protection from wounds and danger. It was a warriors' stone, offering courage and endurance. In ancient Greece, the women's-equality Spartans considered childbirth comparable to war, requiring as much courage, endurance and strength. Hematite then is a stone for birth and delivery, dealing with the incarnation issues of the other black gemstones, and preventing hemorrhaging in childbirth. Mellie Uyldert suggests its other uses in lowering high blood pressure, for bloodshot eyes and blood vessel hemorrhages in the eyes, for muscle cramps, ulcers and the kidneys and bladder.[29]

The gemstone aids quiet sleep, reduces inflammation, calms, grounds, relaxes and reduces emotional upsets. Held in the right hand, it is used to "focus energy patterns and emotions for better balance between the mental, physical and spiritual."[30] A balancer, it transforms negativity and connects the energies of the root chakra with the energies of the other centers, and connects the four bodies. Hematite carvings have been found in ancient Egypt, where the stone was used mainly for bleeding, and at archeological sites in Babylon, Mexico and South America.[31] In jewelry hematite is used in intaglios, talismans and beads. Thelma Isaacs says that its healing effects become negative if worn too long, or worn unneeded. Combining the energies of red and black, though black predominates, hematite is a general grounder and balancer for the root chakra, and the last covered of the healing black gemstones.

The other color of the root chakra, the color first associated with it in meditation and color work, is red. Red gemstones are powerful transmitters of life force energy and incarnation. Rather than grounding and balancing as the black stones are, red gemstones for the root chakra are rousing and energizing. When used in healing, they should not be used with a woman who is volatile, angry or resentful, highly nervous or restless, or having high blood pressure. Use the black stones instead, or complementary color green ones, to give her balancing and life energy without adding to her pain. The red stones are best for heating and vitalizing, for helping with exhaustion, overexposure to cold, poor blood circulation, low blood pressure, the uterus. They aid in fertility and conception difficulties and bring on menstruation. Red stones help the blood. Ruby is the most passionate and volatile of the red stones, garnet the gentlest and most balanced in effects. Red jasper stabilizes and heals the aura, and bloodstone/heliotrope purifies and offers long life. Bloodstone is not solely a red energy stone, but participates in root chakra balancing. The red stones are powerful and positive for healing, are the life force emerged and incarnated from the dark womb, are the unknown inner labyrinth brought to the physical side of the life cycle.

The uses of *bloodstone,* an opaque, noncrystalline dark green stone interspersed with glowing red flecks, are close to the uses for hematite. Despite the European name for hematite being bloodstone, the stones are not the same, and another name for red and green bloodstone is heliotrope. Bloodstone is used to heal wounds, for external and internal bleeding, to prevent hemorrhaging in surgery and childbirth, and to aid easy childbirth delivery. It's a major blood purifier, induces courage and helps the blood transporting abilities of the heart. Bloodstone's power is the life force red carried by the regenerating green complement of the heart chakra. The stone is a form of jasper, found in India, Australia, Brazil, China and the United States. In jewelry work, it takes a high polish and is used for intaglios and carvings. In hardness it is 6½-7 on the Moh's scale, as hard as quartz.

Bloodstone offers healing for wounds, bleeding, fevers and inflammations, and it offers long life. The root center is physical survival, and blood circulation is circulation of the life force through the physical body. Bloodstone cleanses the blood and stimulates the blood purifying organs, the kidneys, liver and spleen. It detoxifies the blood, aids iron deficiency and anemia, and raises oxygen levels in the red blood cells. Where there is blood congestion, clots, blocked arteries or poor circulation, use bloodstone over the area in laying on of stones.[32] For external wounds, Mellie Uyldert dips a bloodstone in cold water and places it on the spot to stop bleeding.[33] Also use it for nosebleeds and varicose veins, hemorrhoids, insect and scorpion bites. Wherever the blood or blood circulation are involved, bloodstone is useful. Elimination is another function of the root chakra, as is reproduction, and bloodstone is used for the intestines and stomach, for calcium in the bladder and urinary cystitis, especially when hemorrhagic. Bloodstone purifies, strengthens, stops bleeding and regenerates from the root chakra level. Edgar Cayce used it as a major healing stone.[34]

Bloodstone is a charm for agriculture, helpful to women on the land. It protects crops, plants and animals, and encourages growth. An inherited bloodstone carries with it the help of the foremother it belonged to. It aids concentration and meditation, gives prophetic dreams and visions of the past and future. The stone encourages unselfishness, idealism and wisdom, and makes the wearer invisible.[35] For grounding or decision making, hold bloodstone in the left hand to help. For women with heavy menstrual flows, bloodstone decreases it, and helps to balance the functioning of the uterus. Though the flecks of red in bloodstone are tiny, they are powerful, and the complementary green is a balancer. This is a major root chakra red stone.

The gentlest of red gemstones, and a personal favorite, is *red garnet*. Garnet is the blanket name for several different minerals with similar composition: garnet, pyrope, almandine, spessartite, grossularite. It's a crystalline stone, best known for its glowing dark red color, but occurring also in greens, oranges and violet. Red and red/brown garnets work well with the red root chakra, the ones leaning more toward orange with the belly center, and greens or yellow/greens with the heart and solar plexus as complements to red and balancers. Violet garnets are crown center stones. Wispy streaks in the gemstone are mostly seen as grey or black, but white streaks also occur. Colorado, Arizona and Greenland are sources for red garnet, as well as Africa, Czechoslovakia, Australia, Sri Lanka and Brazil. The red crystals come in interesting geometric shapes, embedded in other stone. Garnet is one gemstone best used cut and polished, and strings of the tiny beads are the easiest way to use it. A choker-length strand should be about twenty dollars through gemstone dealers or even department stores. The stones can be used loose if wished.

Garnet is classic red energy. It warms and aids blood circulation, rouses sexuality, and heals the reproductive system and the heart. The stone is a balancer of yin/yang energy, and when the woman is ready for it, helps in the rise of kundalini energy. Garnet opens the third eye, raises depression, draws and enhances love and peace. It's a stone of patience and persistence, vitality, courage and women's sexual power.

In the healing of dis-ease, garnet is positive for uterine, vaginal and reproductive problems, for any blood circulation ills. Garnet purifies the blood, and helps with inflammations, infections and skin dis-eases.[36] Use garnet in cases of frostbite, anemia, over-exposure to cold, paralysis, neuralgia, and for the calcium deposit dis-eases of arthritis and bursitis. Use garnet anywhere that warmth is called for. The stone has a positive effect on balancing the reproductive organs and hormones. It helps with menstrual cramps, eases menstrual flow, and helps women trying to conceive. Garnet also opens and balances sexuality.

Mellie Uyldert says that wearing garnet attracts love, and that widows in Italy wear it for this.[37] She lists garnet as a friendship stone, but also warns that they can break up love affairs. The stone has sexual energy, but when combined with its attribute of stubbornness, it can be volatile. For women alone, garnet draws peace and the ability to use aloneness in positive ways. It draws sexual love and soul-mates to women seeking them. Garnet gives women will and confidence, persistence, pride and success, and gives them constancy of purpose in a love affair or not.

Garnet is a happiness stone, one of the most positive known for depression, loneliness, and heart pain. Its warmth is comforting, calming and glowing, peaceful and soothing. Garnet is a stone for winter, much too warmth-generating to use in summer heat. It aids cold feet and cold bodies on cold nights. Garnet is a gift for a friend feeling down, something to always raise a smile. It's a protection from outside negativity and a transformer of negativity from within. Garnet prevents nightmares and stimulates good health, protects in travel and from lightning, and stimulates the imagination and fancy in thought forms of love. Garnet enhances meditation work and visualization ability.

Energizing and grounding at once, warming and comforting, garnet is a prime example of a women's healing gemstone. Julia Lorusso and Joel Glick list it as a prime balancer of root chakra sexuality and reproduction. Red and green garnets used together (or red garnet and green peridot), are positive for creating any sort of duality balance or polarity in women's bodies.[38] They suggest that the darker the stone's color, the closer its function to the physical level, and the lighter colors reach higher aura bodies. For an inexpensive and relatively easy-to-find gemstone, garnet does a lot of positive things and is important to women's healing. Women using it for love are aware of its one negative feature—its persistence and power that can be carried too far—and make use of garnet for happiness, warmth, protection and for love.

Red stones to most women mean *ruby,* the most precious for jewelry and best known of the root chakra stones. Ruby is a strong, hot stone for healing, with great stimulating attributes. Despite its high price and value when jewelry cut, raw pieces of it sell for as little as two dollars in rock shops and museums. Healing stones have no need to be jewelry quality or gem cut. Even the smaller pieces of a stone as powerful as ruby are positive and useful for healing work, and ruby has been known as a healing stone throughout time. Found in Thailand, Burma, Sri Lanka, India, Afghanistan, Australia, Brazil and Rhodesia, ruby is also found in some surprising places, including North Carolina. It often appears with other gemstones: beryls, garnets, moonstones, sapphires, tourmalines and topazes. Arizona ruby or cape ruby are not ruby but garnet, and before 1800, ruby and garnets were classed together, thought to be the same stone grouping.[39] After diamond, ruby is the hardest of the gemstones, measuring 9 on the Moh's scale. Diamond is 10, and clear quartz crystal has a hardness of 7. Ruby is a crystalline gemstone.

Ruby is a hot, intense, volatile stone. Held in the left hand it emits short, intense bursts of stored heat and red energy for absorption into the root chakra. It's a stone of incarnation, bestowing long life, happiness, life force energy, strength, health and protection. It draws loyalty and courage, invulnerability, passionate love and self-love. Ruby is the most intense of the purifying stones, a cleanser for the blood, blood vessels, and blood purification organs. It's a stone of the uterus and birth, and a stone of the life force heart. It stimulates sexuality, mental concentration, the emotions, physical vitality and energy, immunity to dis-ease. It brings on menstruation and labor, and Mellie Uyldert uses it to prevent miscarriages.[40]

Any dis-ease where life force energy is needed is helped by ruby. Tuberculosis, AIDS, anemia, leukemia, cancer, are all treated with ruby intensity. Use it for the liver and kidneys, the adrenal glands, snakebite and blood poisoning. Use it for heart regeneration and to break up blood clots. Uyldert suggests ruby for pain, bleeding and fever,[41] in the homeopathic sense of like healing like, but personal work suggests to use stones that cool and sedate. Rubies are used to rouse passion, love in all forms, sexuality, the connnection with and love of the goddess. This is a root chakra stone that affects all the aura levels and connects the crown with the physical center, the divine with dense matter energy.

Ruby is great for exhaustion, depression and burn out, for women who are run-down from any disease, but it's not for use with women experiencing too much red energy. Ruby amplifies emotions, and if the woman being healed is anxious, restless or emotionally in pain, ruby is not the stone to use. Red energy is active and intense, can be angry or jealous, and ruby in these cases adds to the problem. Thelma Isaacs warns against using it under severe mental or emotional stress,[42] as ruby energy under stress is hard to channel.

Use ruby for the down-side of manic depression, for chronic tiredness, for warming. It opens and heals the physical body, and changes love from the personal to the universal. The woman who uses ruby with unselfish motives becomes more open and giving, more loving, and with greater emotional strength. The woman who uses it selfishly learns that ruby passion can warm or burn, and risks harm by misuse of it. Ruby is an Aries stone, ruled by Mars. As a meditation stone, it helps women's self-image and ego, and stimulates positive self-love. Ruby is an intense gemstone energy.

One more red gemstone is *red jasper,* a stone far less volatile than ruby. After the intensity of ruby energy, red jasper is earthbound, a calming and stabilizing stone. Jasper is found in a variety of colors and worldwide, and red jasper was known to the writers of the Old Testament, to ancient India, Egypt and presumably to the matriarchies. It's a form of chalcedony, and bloodstone/heliotrope is a jasper. The stone is found in Ontario, Germany, Russia, India, Sicily, France and the United States, and is not considered a precious stone. Its noncrystalline opaque structure makes it seen most often cut and polished in ovals (cabachons). The spots and streaks in it are interesting and attractive, and where wood is petrified, jasper is often the agent. Colors are usually dark. The red/brown forms are called silex, and a form of light colored jasper is tinted blue and sold as Swiss lapis, an imitation of lapis lazuli. Its hardness is 6½-7.

Red jasper is a grounding and calming stone that stabilizes and gives connection with the Earth. It's a good stone to use for purifying the blood, and draws energy steadily, without over-exciting or overwhelming. Red jasper is used for upset stomachs and menstrual cramps, cystitis and bladder infections, for conception and morning sickness in early pregnancy. It works on the liver, kidneys and gall bladder, and enhances the sense of smell, the sense correspondent to the root chakra. A stone of the life force red, but, unlike ruby, a grounded one, it helps to repair the aura after surgical or other trauma.[43] Serenity Peterson uses it with crystal and sets it in silver mountings.

A connector with incarnation and the physical, use red jasper for epilepsy and to prevent miscarriage. It draws unselfishness in women who wear it, and is used for tuberculosis, cancer and other wasting dis-eases.[44] Its major use has been from antiquity in preventing vomiting and queasiness, and in soothing the stomach and nerves. Thelma Isaacs suggests its use in magnetized water or as a necklace at the throat chakra to change vibrations rising from lower centers.[45] Jasper's energy transmission remains close to the the dense body in vibration and effects. For women who are drawn to it, jasper has strong healing uses.

In the case of red or black gemstones, of all gemstones, women use the stone or stones they are drawn to. If jasper is unappealing to her, garnet may be attractive, or ruby or smoky quartz. A stone a woman is drawn to usually has healing benefit for her. A stone she is not drawn to likely does not. Sense the gemstone energies, and use them while needed, but when the stone becomes unattractive, gets lost in the sheets or forgotten on the altar, its usefulness for the time is ended. Women know what they need, and follow it—use women's intuition. If a stone becomes uncomfortable to use, put it down. If carried in a pocket or kept with her, the woman is aware of subtle mood changes and feelings. Such feelings are often because of the gemstone/s energies and influence. She pays attention to them, and uses them positively for her needs. In laying on of stones, the gemstone that keeps bouncing off, getting lost on the ground, won't stay in place, either belongs elsewhere on the body or is a stone to take away for that healing.

All of the colored gemstones are magnified by using clear quartz crystal with them. In the case of ruby, this probably is not wanted, but in other stones it may be. Again, use intuition. One suggestion for self-healing is to keep the gemstone in the left hand and a crystal in the right, or hold both together in the left palm. Relax and absorb the energies. Remember that gemstones need clearing, though less often than quartz crystal. Clear them after healings, and use water or salt if they feel heavy. Sometimes a depleted stone needs time on an altar to restore it to strength. Occasionally a stone is sacrificed to a particularly intense healing when it cracks or shatters.

The next chapters consider gemstones for the other chakras. Chapter Eight is the belly and solar plexus, the gemstones for healing work at those centers. See the chart at the end of this book for a summary of gemstones and their uses for all the chakras.

FOOTNOTES

1. Walter Schumann, *Gemstones of the World* (New York, Sterling Publishing, 1984, original 1977), p. 16-17.

2. *Ibid.,* p. 216-224.

3. *Ibid.,* p. 27. Most technical statistics and places of origin for gemstones in the book are referenced from Schumann.

4. Katrinna Raphaell, *Crystal Enlightenment: The Transforming Properties of Crystals and Healing Stones* (New York, Aurora Press, 1985), p. 40-41.

5. *Ibid.,* p. 8-9.

6. *Ibid.,* p. 39.

7. *Ibid.,* p. 40.

8. *Ibid.*

9. Mellie Uyldert, *The Magic of Precious Stones* (Great Britain, Turnstone Press, 1981), p. 60.

10. Major references for gemstone attributes in this book come from: Thelma Isaacs, *Gemstones, Crystals and Healing* (Black Mountain, NC, Lorien House, 1982), p. 30-98; Julia Lorusso and Joel Glick, *Healing Stoned* (Albuquerque, NM, Brotherhood of Life, 1985, original 1976), p. 27-80; Rhiannon McBride, Charlene Deering, Louise Devery and Amber K, "Occult Uses of Gemstones," in *Circle Network News* (POB 219, Mt. Horeb, WI 53572), Summer, 1982, p. 12; Serenity Peterson, *Crystal Visioning: A Crystal Workbook* (Nashville, TN, Interdimensional Publishing, 1984), p. 41-60; Katrina Raphaell, *Crystal Enlightenment: The Transforming Properties of Crystals and Healing Stones* (New York, Aurora Press, 1985), p. 78-164; Gemstoned Ltd., *Crystal Essence* (New York, Gemstoned, Ltd., 1984), pamphlet; and Mellie Uyldert, *The Magic of Precious Stones* (Great Britain, Turnstone Press, 1981), p. 82-156. Place origins and geologic material come from Walter Schumann, *Gemstones of the World,* (New York, Sterling Publishing, 1984, original 1977), and from Mellie Uyldert. Other sources are referenced, and much material comes from personal work and experimentation.

11. Mellie Uyldert, *The Magic of Precious Stones,* p. 104.

12. *Ibid.,* p. 103. Much of the reference for smoky quartz is from Uyldert.

13. Katrina Raphaell, *Crystal Enlightenment,* p. 91.

14. *Ibid.,* p. 132.

15. Julia Lorusso and Joel Glick, *Healing Stoned* (Albuquerque, NM: Brotherhood of Life, 1985, original 1977), p. 77.

16. Thelma Isaacs, *Gemstones, Crystals and Healing* (Black Mountain, NC, Lorien House, 1982), p. 93.

17. Katrina Raphaell, *Crystal Enlightenment,* p. 132.

18. *Ibid.,* p. 93-100. Much of the material for this gemstone comes from Raphaell's work.

19. *Ibid.,* p. 93.

20. Lee Lanning and Vernette Hart, *Ripening: An Almanac of Lesbian Lore and Vision* (Minneapolis, Word Weavers, 1981), p. 60.

21. Serenity Peterson, *Crystal Visioning, A Crystal Workbook* (Nashville, TN, Interdimensional Publishing, 1984), p. 54.

22. Rhiannon McBride, "The Occult Lapidary: Black Onyx," in *Circle Network News* (POB 219, Mt. Horeb, WI, 53572), Spring, 1984, p. 8.

23. Mellie Uyldert, *The Magic of Precious Stones,* p. 92.

24. *Ibid.*

25. Rhiannon McBride, "The Occult Lapidary: Black Onyx," in *Circle Network News,* Spring, 1984, p. 8.

26. Thelma Isaacs, *Gemstones, Crystals and Healing,* p. 64.

27. Mellie Uyldert, *The Magic of Precious Stones,* p. 147-148.

28. Thelma Isaacs, *Gemstones, Crystals and Healing,* p. 60.

29. Mellie Uyldert, *The Magic of Precious Stones,* p. 124.

30. Thelma Isaacs, *Gemstones, Crystals and Healing,* p. 60.

31. Mellie Uyldert, *The Magic of Precious Stones,* p. 124.

32. Katrina Raphaell, *Crystal Enlightenment,* p. 139.

33. Mellie Uyldert, *The Magic of Precious Stones,* p. 103.

34. Thelma Isaacs, *Gemstones, Crystals and Healing,* p. 81.

35. This list of attributes is from Mellie Uyldert, *The Magic of Precious Stones,* p. 103.

36. *Ibid.,* p. 121.

37. *Ibid.*

38. Julia Lorusso and Joel Glick, *Healing Stoned,* p. 37.

39. Walter Schumann, *Gemstones of the World,* p. 82.

40. Mellie Uyldert, *The Magic of Precious Stones,* p. 114.

41. *Ibid.*

42. Thelma Isaacs, *Gemstones, Crystals and Healing,* p. 46.

43. Serenity Peterson, *Crystal Visioning,* p. 51.

44. Mellie Uyldert, *The Magic of Precious Stones,* p. 102.

45. Thelma Isaacs, *Gemstones, Crystals and Healing,* p. 82.

Colored Gemstones: The Belly and Solar Plexus

THE BELLY and solar plexus centers (the abdominal chakras located below and above the navel) are the colors orange and yellow. The centers correspond with the *emotional body* (orange/belly) and the *lower mental level* (yellow/solar plexus) of a woman's aura. Both are warm, stimulating colors for centers concerned with digestion, sexuality, emotions, assimilation and nurturance. The belly chakra is the center for sexual and generative energies, sexual feelings and actions. It corresponds to the ovaries in women and the spleen in men; the pancreas in some healing systems. When the center is in balance, women are in touch with their emotions and flow with their feelings in positive ways. Not enough orange is repression, drying, hardening—dis-eases like sexual dysfunction, hardening of the arteries, arthritis, and emotional and physical coldness. Pride, warmth, creativity, positivity, caring and sexual balance are the harmony of orange and the belly chakra.

Orange is a healing color, sending vitality and well-being to a woman who is run-down and helping her to resist and fight dis-ease, tiredness and physical weakness. This is a hot temperature color, almost as hot as red. In healing it sends warmth, nurturing and solar energy, helps with exhaustion, depression and burn out.

Correspondent with the emotional aura body, orange intensifies all emotions and images and should not be used where this is not wanted. As in using red, avoid orange with women who are angry or

195

distraught. Lung dis-orders are treated with orange and orange gem-stones, as are sexuality and sexual dysfunction problems, menstrual cramps, ovarian cysts and ovulation difficulties. Orange gemstones bring on menses, purify the kidneys and urinary tract, warm arthritis, aid breathing, increase breast milk (some indigo and opaque white stones do this also), and stimulate the thyroid. Some of the functions of orange and orange gemstones overlap those of red, and many of the functions of orange are also held by its complementary colors blue and indigo.

Yellow gemstones correspond to the solar plexus chakra, the bodies' distribution center for prana, nutrition and mental under-standing. The center and color correspond to the lower mental body. This is the major center for energy and vitality, a solar center as is orange. Kama-manas, emotion linked with mind, is centered here, which is the ability to visualize and to transmit desire to the bodies above and below it. Prana enters and is distributed from here, and women's intuition and psychic skills are maintained and distributed from the solar plexus. Too much yellow is nervousness/ungrounded-ness, indigestion, eating and anorexia/bulemia dis-orders, mental and psychic instability. Not enough yellow energy is lethargy, apathy, chronic tiredness, laziness, diabetes, and weight gain. Yellow gem-stones are used to create a balance in this center, and equilibrium and harmony of all sorts are solar plexus, or solar plexus combined with belly or heart chakra based.

Yellow in gemstone healing is a stimulant. It dispels fears and tiredness, lifts depression, stimulates the voluntary and involuntary muscular and nervous system, the lymphatic system, digestive tract, and the mind. Mental activity is located in the solar plexus and the will, and yellow stimulates learning, studying and writing. Yellow and the solar plexus are connected with the adrenal and endocrine glands in some systems, the pancreas in others (some correspondences place the adrenals at the root center and the pancreas at the belly). The color is not for use with women who are anxious and ungrounded; use the complementary colored violet stones instead. Yellow's elec-trical counterpart gold is in an all-aura healing color, repairing and rejuvenating, a major general healing color (as is orange) for some healers. Topaz and amber are gold energy gemstones.

Yellow gemstones for the solar plexus include citrine/yellow quartz, tiger eye and golden beryl. Malachite and peridot, yellow/

green gemstones, overlap the solar plexus with the heart chakra. Some of the green stones designated for the heart center overlap with the solar plexus, and some of the rose heart chakra stones (watermelon tourmaline, rhodochrosite) also connect the energies of the solar plexus and heart centers and stimulate both. Gemstones for the belly chakra include orange forms of gemstones known less for this color: orange garnets, orange calcite, orange sapphire, fire agate and the form of citrine that's naturally orange in color. These are less easy to find available. The most popular and most used orange energy gemstones are carnelian, orange/red coral, jacinth and orange/brown agate.

Belly chakra gemstones begin with *carnelian*, the most versatile of the easier to find orange gemstones. Carnelian is a form of chalcedony, an opaque matrix stone traditionally used for talismans against depression and dementia.[1] Other names for it are sard, sardius and cornelian, as well as carnelian agate. The stone comes from Brazil and Uruguay, with the best for jewelry work said to come from India. The darker red/brown carnelian most often known as sard comes from Asia Minor. Carnelian colors run from light peach through deeper oranges and orange/brown shades. The stone was known to the writers of the Old Testament as part of the high priest/high priestess' breastplate of power. Mellie Uyldert connects it with blood ties and the obsession with blood purity of the Old Testament patriarchs.[2] With these concepts transformed into goddess themes of oneness and community, carnelian suggests the tribal connectedness of women, the sharing of emotional, physical, mental and spiritual ties that transcend male notions of nationalism, race or hierarchy. Katrina Raphaell, noting that carnelian is composed of the same SiO_2 that quartz crystal is, considers it an important form of quartz though noncrystalline.[3] She calls it a stone that's evolved and grown over the ages.

Carnelian as a healing stone is used for menstrual cramps and to bring on menstruation. It aids sexual function and orgasm, conception and fertility by purifying the blood and the sexual hormones. It stimulates and opens the belly chakra, the center for sexuality and feeling. Katrina Raphaell suggests wearing it over the pelvic area for these uses.[4] As a blood purifier, the stone is also a protection against blood poisoning and the "evil eye" of negativity. Mellie Uyldert uses it homeopathically for fevers, infections, nosebleeds, wounds, sores and anger,[5] rather than the more generally used cooler stones. The healer experiments and learns how carnelian works for her individually. Personal choice uses blue stones for these, but women use what works for them, and uses vary. Stones that are positive for one woman may not attract another, but be aware that carnelian's hot color is an emotional stimulant.

Carnelian's warmth is soothing and good for neuralgia and arthritis, dis-eases that are cold and need warming. Use it in combination with "tinker-woman" psychic healing for arthritis, flooding the pain area after "tinkering" with carnelian orange light. Hold a carnelian in the right hand and send healing light through it. Lethargy and muscle spasms react to carnelian energy, and it stimulates the sense of taste, the sense correspondent to the chakra. Carnelian helps nightmares, confusion and absentmindedness, and helps women see into the past.[6] It holds attention to the *now* for work in manifesting goals, while recycling past lives and past experiences for stronger understanding. The stone aids mental ability, cures madness, and stimulates creative visualization; it deepens concentration. It's a tonic for the blood purifying organs, the liver, gall bladder, bloodstream, pancreas and for the reproductive organs, ovaries and uterus.

Serenity Peterson notes carnelian's electromagnetism and sees it as a powerful stimulant of kundalini energy, both causing Shakti to rise and opening the chakras as she does so.[7] She sees carnelian as a physical and astral/emotional level aura filter against toxins and blocks, and recognizes the stone's great healing power. Carnelian stimulates the voice for eloquence and expression, and is a healer of the lungs and respiratory system.[8] Use it to loosen phlegm for the entire breathing tract, from the sinuses down, and for asthma, pneumonia, colds and epilepsy. Carnelian's stimulation of the lower digestive system also makes it useful as a laxative. This is a very stimulating, warm to almost hot gemstone. For women who need the stone's qualities but not its energizing, look to orange's complement, the blue and indigo gemstones instead.

An orange/red gemstone known worldwide for its protection abilities is *coral*. The stone is not a stone, but of marine animal origins: the calcium skeletal deposits of tiny sea polyp organisms. Orange/red coral is known worldwide, was known to ancient Greece and is one of the four element gemstones of Pueblo Indian symbolism. Of

Top Row: Jet, Obsidian, Smoky Quartz, Black Tourmaline, Hematite
Bottom Row: Red Jasper, Garnet, Rough Ruby, Bloodstone

Top Row: Tiger Eye, Amber, Red-Orange Agate
Bottom Row: Carnelian, Topaz, Golden Beryl, Citrine

Top Row: Aventurine, Malachite, Raw Emerald, Jade
Bottom Row: Green Tourmaline, Peridot, Watermelon Tourmaline

Top Row: Rose Quartz, Rhodochrosite, Turquoise, Aquamarine,
    Chrysocolla
Bottom Row: Lapis Lazuli, Sodalite, Two Fluorites, Amethyst

Top Row: Tree Agate, Moss Agate, White Chalcedony, Tourmaline
    Quartz
Bottom Row: Selenite, Raw Opal, Moonstone, Rutile Quartz

Left:
    Single Terminated Quartz

Right:
    Double Terminated Quartz

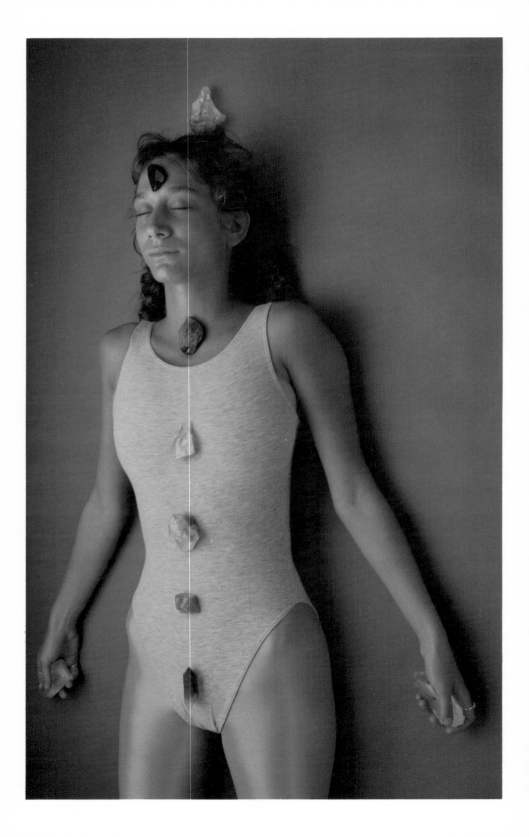

the four colors used for the directions in the Hopi/Zuni Road of Life: coral, jet, abalone, and turquoise, only turquoise is actually a stone. Coral is the warm energy of the Sun, and the southern direction.

Orange/red coral is found in Hawaii, Polynesia, Japan and the Mediterranean. It comes in other colors than orange; notably pink, white, black and blue, but orange/red coral is the color predominantly used in healing and in jewelry. Pacific branch coral is the kind most valued by Native American artists and silversmiths. Brittle and difficult to work with, coral is used in pierced branch pieces that are strung on necklaces and made into beads and rings. The famous Zuni inlay work of the southwest United States uses coral as thin mosaic chips, often in combination with the other three element gemstones. Coral's chemical composition is calcium carbonate, $CaCO_3$, and its hardness is a low 3-4 of the Moh's scale. It's opaque and noncrystalline in form.

In Rome and Holland, coral was worn almost universally by women as an antidote to anemia,[9] and in Italy as a protection charm against accidents and the "evil eye" of negativity. It was a stone used especially to protect children. Edgar Cayce used it to attune people with the creative Be-ing of the universe,[10] a use the Pueblo Indians make of all four of their elemental gemstones. The orange of the stone when worn against the skin both warms and is warmed. After a few minutes of wearing orange coral, the stone becomes body temperature and feels like flesh itself. Thelma Isaacs lists its uses for stopping bleeding, curing insanity, and bringing wisdom. It's a charm against depression and a stimulant to the blood and heart, a blood purifier and protector against poisoning. Like other orange gemstones, coral stimulates sexuality and aids infertility. It helps with bladder infections, and lung problems, including congestions and whooping cough, coughs and asthma. Use it for weakness and emaciation, for indigestion, eye problems, arthritis, and other calcium deposit dis-eases of the joints. Use it for cheering and against fear.

Orange/red coral is another gemstone used in earlier times by taking internally, used powdered in wine or water for those rich enough to afford it. In the Middle Ages, ground coral was taken for

> asthma, obesity, anemia, jaundice, eye troubles, urinary tract diseases, constipation, fevers, indigestion, loss of appetite, cough, emaciation and rickets, and increase of beauty.[11]

In salves, powdered coral was mixed with ground pearl for ulcers, scars and the eyes. Ingested, pearl and coral were used for colic and to prevent vomiting[12]—coral is calcium carbonate. Modern uses of gemstones and gemstone substances seldom take them internally. Try making a gemstone elixir instead, drinking water magnetized by laying on of hands with a piece of red coral in the water, or wear a string of coral beads or branches next to the skin. Coral is a gemstone that absorbs energies (unlike carnelian that radiates it), removing impurities from the blood and aura. Wear it at the pelvic area for menstrual, ovarian or sexual difficulties, to stimulate sexuality and orgasm, or to conceive. Coral, as other gemstones, should only be worn or used by women who are drawn to its energies. For women who are attracted to it, it's a powerful, warming and energizing stone.

A quieter, more stable orange gemstone for the belly chakras is *orange/brown* agate. The stone is a balancer more than a stimulant, carrying attributes of the more active orange stones but without their restless intensity. A massive member of the jasper and chalcedony group, it comes in an almost endless variety of patterns and beautiful forms. Traditional uses for agate, a layered stone, have been in cameos and intaglios, and carved into decorative objects, talismans and fetishes. Sources for orange/brown agates are Germany, Uruguay, Brazil, Italy, China, Mexico and the United States. These are fascinating stones to see, each unique in its patterns and color layers. They are the lining material of geodes and tumble nicely into lovely-to-hold stones for the palms. They are hard stones, 6½-7 on the Moh's scale, and durable.

Lee Lanning and Nett Hart say this about agates:

> We can't resist picking up an agate—its clarity and fluid order are present in even the tiniest chip. We collect them; they are said to promote grace, good health, happiness, intelligence, longevity. A person who looks upon an agate tells the truth and is aided in remembering. We are getting more honest every day.[13]

Agates are grounding and gentle. They are protection stones, stones for courage and acceptance, for overcoming obstacles, for eloquence, and for finding treasures and gaining inheritances.[14] They give strength, grace, victory and attunement with the goddess Earth.

Use orange/brown agates for the same uses as other belly chakra stones, but with much more stability and calming. Use it for stress, athletics and childbirth, for menstrual cramps, for stomach dis-eases of a physcial rather than emotional nature, to banish fear and protect children from falls. It protects from storms and aids children in teething, protects vision, and prevents nightmares.[15] Agate aids vitality without causing ungroundedness, helps vision and hearing, heart problems, the hair. A blood purifier, it stimulates blood circulation, aids blood dis-eases and anemia, and prevents poisoning. Orange/ brown agates are not overheating in their warmth and are used for fevers. They stimulate intelligence and seriousness, aid physical and emotional balance, and are used for epilepsy.

Serenity Peterson calls agate a grounder that gives a solid physical base for higher energy levels to flow through. She says that it clarifies truth, then makes truth easier to accept.[16] It stabilizes the emotions and the emotional/astral body, stabilizes sexuality and reproduction. Grounding, stabilizing and protecting are its major attributes. Of the orange belly chakra gemstones, orange/brown agate is the gentlest and least volatile.

Other gemstones for the belly chakra are orange stones less easily available from routine sources. These are all crystalline and include the orange varieties of garnet (spessartite and hessonite), Madeira citrine, which is an orange form of the usually golden citrine quartz, orange sapphire and orange calcite. Wulfenite, a very soft stone occasionally used in jewelry, is another orange crystalline gem. Jacinth, an orange form of zircon, is also called hyacinth and comes from Southeast Asia, from Vietnam, Cambodia, Burma, Thailand and Sri Lanka, also from Australia, France and Tanzania. Healers use jacinth for insomnia, blood purification, and protection from poisoning. Thelma Isaacs calls it a stone of independence and self-reliance, and lists healing and quieting the spirit as its major attributes. She uses it for lung dis-orders, polio and tuberculosis, says that it protects travelers, protects from lightning, strengthens the heart, aids insomnia and increases immunities, and protects from injuries and wounds.[17] Mellie Ulydert uses jacinth to open psychic sight.[18] It aids astral projection (a solar plexus attribute; gemstones for the chakras tend to overlap), creative visualization and the liver. Healers seeking jacinth (hyacinth or orange zircon), be aware that the stone is often sold in human-made imitations.

When working with any gemstone whose qualities are unknown,

be aware of the doctrine of signatures. This means that a stone's appearance gives clues to its uses. Color is the major attribute to follow with this. If an unknown gemstone is orange, sense it with the palms and experiment with its energies, and decide if orange energies are needed for healing. The healer that does this learns what a stone does and what energies it carries. Experiment slowly, and avoid using the stone for healing till its properties are known. Personal best method for understanding a new gemstone is to hold it in the left hand when going to sleep. Pay careful attention to the impressions and sensations, subtle mood changes and vibrations that come from the stone while relaxing with it. In no case continue using a stone that feels negative.

Gemstones for the solar plexus include stones that are golden, yellow and yellow/green. The golden stones, topaz and amber are highly electrical and powerful, with intense healing energies. Yellow gemstones are warm and solar, containing less of the magnetic polarity and volatility of the golden stones. They store and transmit energy, digestion, nutrition and assimilation to all of the unseen bodies, and have physical, emotional, mental and psychic effects. Yellow energy is prana, the fuel that powers the energy spaces between atoms and that connects the four bodies, the levels of the aura. Prana is the electricity and magnetic polarity of the aura, and yellow gemstones distribute and balance that life energy for women's health and well-being.

Yellow gemstones include citrine quartz, tiger eye and golden beryl, all yellow or yellow/brown stones. Yellow/green gemstones for the solar plexus overlap with the heart chakra, particularly malachite and peridot, but other green and yellow/green gemstones listed for heart center healing overlap also. In some systems it is the solar plexus (the rational mind and carrier of kama-manas) that is seen as connecting the physical, emotional and mental aura bodies with the inspirational and spiritual levels, and in other systems the connecting chakra is the heart center, the higher mental body. Both are central and vital chakras, the solar plexus involved with distributing energy and rational knowledge, and the heart center involved with the distribution of feeling for others, connectedness, creativity, love, healing, abundance and openness.

Some stones listed for either the heart chakra or solar plexus are gemstones that connect the two centers: the lower with the higher unseen bodies, the rational and physical with the intuitive and inspirational. A balance between the physical and spiritual, the Earth and sky, a connection and harmony among all of the bodies, is necessary for women's peace and healthy well-being. Connecting gemstones include malachite and peridot (listed for the solar plexus) and rhodochrosite and watermelon tourmaline (listed for the heart). Citrine is another connective gemstone, though a solar plexus yellow stone with yellow gemstone qualities.

Yellow and golden gemstones are used for energy and warmth, and stimulate the nerves and mind. They are involved with manifesting the unseen onto the earth plane; thought into concrete action and object. Gold is a faster vibration of yellow energies, more electrical than warm, and reaching a higher octave of aura levels. Yellow is cheering and clarifying, imparting self-confidence and positive thinking, psychic balance and personal power-within, direct action and the will. Most yellow and golden gemstones aid the sense of sight, the sense correspondent with the chakra. The solar plexus is also the center for psychic sight, the distribution of psychic abilities and impressions to the chakras that specialize in them, and is the center for seeing and physical vision, and also the mental ability to understand and process ideas. Solar plexus yellow and yellow gemstones are both mental and emotional stimulants, carriers of kama-manas. For very anxious women, the color may not be positive on all occasions. In healing, if a woman needing yellow or golden energy is too ungrounded or energized by it, try the color's complement, violet, instead.

Topaz is the most electrical and magnetic of the golden gemstones for the solar plexus. Like amber and the tourmalines, it's an electrically charged stone, possessing polarity and static magnetism that charges the entire aura and aura bodies. Julia Lorusso and Joel Glick describe topaz as an "electrical coagulant," with charges that "stimulate rather than sedate."[19] The gem is a major one for treatment of exhaustion, depression and depletion, and for vitalizing because of this aura electricity. Its hardness is 8.

Topaz is *not* yellow quartz, the citrine it's often mistaken for. Another name for citrine is Scotch topaz, which is incorrect. Topaz has also been mistaken for yellow sapphire, sometimes called Oriental topaz, and for heated amethyst that turns golden. Gold topaz or

Madeira topaz are names for heat-changed amethyst, and are not true topaz. Topaz comes in golden, orange/golden or red/golden colors and in brown, pink, blue, light green and clear. Rhiannon McBride identifies true topaz by its slippery feel and luster.[20] True golden topaz and citrine are very different in their properties; topaz magnetism and electricity are not present in citrine/yellow quartz. True topaz is found in Brazil, Sri Lanka, Germany, Burma, South Africa, Ireland, Australia and Japan, and in the United States in Maine, New Hampshire, Connecticut, Utah, California and Colorado. Despite its status as a precious gemstone, raw crystals sell for under ten dollars, and do not have to be jewelry quality for healing.

The electricity of topaz is highly energizing and warming. Several sources list the calming of insomnia, tension and tension headaches among its healing uses (Isaacs, McBride, Uyldert), while other sources list the gemstone as energizing and not for use in anxiousness or stress (Lorusso and Glick, Peterson). The stone's ability to create lightness of moods and raise depression, to strengthen, love and brighten make it positive for most women and most situations. If ungroundedness is an issue, trust individual intuition and reactions. Topaz is an aura protector against negativity, encouraging joy and positivity in all who use it. It radiates energy and light.

Topaz is one of the stones to use in sending gold in healing. Hold it in the right hand and use it as a magick light wand to send protection and wellness in psychic healing work. Hold it in the left hand to draw its energies inward for self-healing. Even a very small topaz crystal is highly powerful. Mellie Uyldert lists topaz as a stimulant of the liver and the blood. She uses it for blood circulation dis-eases, for varicose veins, hemorrhoids, blood clots, thromboses, hemorrhages.[21] She also lists topaz as a stone for true friendship and to calm anger, for chastity, and says that in thunderstorms its magnetism excites psychic sensitivity and restlessness. Use topaz for the urinary tract and kidneys, as an aphrodisiac (contradicting Mellie Uyldert), and for sexual dysfunction.[22]

Other uses for topaz are in stimulating the intellect, for writers, scientists and artists. It aids abstract thinking and creativity, innovativeness, helping to bring artistry from the mental level to concrete physical form. Topaz banishes fears, including fears of death and darkness, and at time of death aids the transition. It's a stone of trust, protection and strengthening on mental, emotional and physical body levels. It aids the eyes, appetite and digestion, the processing of ideas and nurturance, and dispels negativity, shock and pain. Rhiannon McBride suggests placing a topaz under the pillow at night to heal anger or nervous/emotional dis-ease, to release stress and tension, rengenerate physical, mental and emotional energies.[23] Along with these uses, Thelma Isaacs lists topaz for dis-eases of the teeth and bones, and for the lungs.[24] She uses it for the spleen, pancreas, kidneys, bladder, urinary tract dis-eases and asthma.

A chakra balancing exercise from Rhiannon McBride:

> Sit or lie comfortably, then beginning with your foot chakras, simply hold the topaz gently to the center of each bare foot for a few minutes. Feel the release and the gentle filling with clean energy which immediately follows. Next do your palm chakras, then your root, pleasure, solar plexus, heart, throat, third eye (you may want to try the bridge of your nose on your way up), and finally your crown chakra. You will probably feel different intensities of release, cleansing and charging energies in each of your centers—stronger where you needed more. This is a good clue to further balancing yourself in other ways. This exercise can be very uplifting and leaves one feeling clear headed and *good!*[25]

Gemstones that are electrical and magnetic in their properties are stones to use for drawing out—drawing out negativity, exhaustion, dis-ease, tension. When using them in this manner, the healer makes sure to cleanse and clear them often. Topaz is a stone to use for this, dispelling and dissolving negativity. This is a powerful and positive healing gemstone.

Another gemstone that protects the entire aura with gold energy is *amber.* Not actually a stone, amber is fossilized pine resin, fifty to sixty million years old. Inclusions of plant matter, pine needles, flowers or bits or bark are frequent, as are inclusions of trapped insects in the resinous material. Amber has a feel to it distinctly different from other gemstones, is warm to the touch, and feels almost the consistency of hard rubber. Legends variously attribute amber to the tears of Isis or of Freya, the goddess' teardrops landing in the sea turned to gemstones. Amber is found along the Baltic coast in the sea bed, and in Sicily, Rumania, Spain, Burma, Canada, the United States and the Dominican Republic. It is probably the oldest material used for jewelry and carvings, and one of the earliest healing gemstones. Very soft, it lists only 2-2½ on the Moh's scale.

Amber is another electrical stone, developing polarity when rubbed. Use it to draw out negativity or pain, remove dis-ease from any of the chakras and from the aura bodies. The stone absorbs negativity into itself, and needs to be cleared frequently. Used often for healing, amber becomes cloudy. Katrina Raphaell places amber pieces over any organ that needs healing or energizing.[26] It draws out negativity and draws in energies from higher centers to the dense physical level. The stone is energizing without being unsettling, vitalizing and stabilizing at once. Like other gemstones of the three lower chakras, amber warms. Drawing heat into itself, amber retains it to the point where the stone is actually flammable. After healing, clear it in cool water to release absorbed heat.

Traditional and modern uses for amber involve protection, protecting the aura from trauma, negativity, contagion and dis-ease. Repairing the aura bodies, it dispels pain and is a general healing and well-being stone. It's a protector against infections and the "evil eye" of negativity, used for casting spells, and against accidents. Healing the aura and the physical body, amber helps women who are suicidal and helps with the phantom pain of amputated limbs. It casts an aura of gold protective light around the woman who wears it in a necklace, and transmits the healing properties of gold in psychic healing or in laying on of hands. Julia Lorusso and Joel Glick say that amber's electricity resonates with brain wave patterns and aids the endocrine system that in turn directs the root, belly, solar plexus and heart chakras. These develop the chakras, opening blocks and obstacles for the rise of kundalini safely.[27] Redder shades of amber are especially good for this.

In healing physical dis-ease, use amber for depression, hysteria, lung dis-eases, ear and hearing problems, the skin and hair, asthma, bronchitis, toothache and cutting teeth in infants, intestinal dis-ease, urinary infections, poisoning, giddiness and malaria.[28] Thelma Isaacs lists amber worn as a necklace to protect the throat and for calming. She lists its uses for goiter, coughs, ulcers, heart dis-ease, hay fever, throat growths and asthma.[29] Other traditional amber uses were internal ones, either as an oil or ground into powder. Mixed with honey and rose oil and ingested, amber was a remedy for the eyes and ears, for earaches and deafness. It was made into a salve for burns, boils and ulcers in external use, and drunk in water for fever, dysentary and stomach aches, for liver and kidney dis-ease.[30]

Modern major uses for amber are external ones. Amber is used for calming and quiet warming on cold nights, for returning energy and vitality to a woman depleted and stressed, for general protection and harmony, and for cheering. Use it for respiratory and digestive/eliminative dis-orders. Amber is a good luck stone and a gemstone of well-being, peace and women's healing energy.

Yellow gemstones have similar but less intense properties, more physical level properties, than the golden stones. They are stimulants for the mind and nervous systems, aid in digestion and digestive disorders, nausea, constipation and diarrhea, ulcers and upset stomachs. They reduce fat and obesity, reduce anxiety and help the user to accept feelings.[31] Among these stones are citrine quartz, tiger eye and golden beryl. Yellow/green stones also with these qualities, plus heart chakra qualities, are malachite and peridot.

Citrine quartz is representative of yellow gemstone energy. It brings warmth, openness, strength and eloquence, and aids in times of exhaustion and depletion. Connecting the heart and solar plexus, it bridges the lower and higher mental bodies, the rational and intuitive/creative mind. It connects the dispassionate intellect and logic with the openness and empathy of the feeling heart. Use citrine for digestion and the digestive organs and dis-eases. It aids the gall bladder, colon, liver, kidneys, and purifies the entire digestive and urinary tracts.[32]

Natural citrine quartz is a relatively rare crystalline stone, with most yellow quartz available being heat-treated amethyst or smoky quartz. Temperatures of 572°-772°F turn smoky quartz yellow, and temperatures of 878°F are enough to change amethyst from its violet color. A red tint and streaking identifies heat-changed stones, as true citrine quartz is clear and lemon colored.[33] Other yellow gemstones are confused with citrine, especially yellow beryl, topaz and yellow tourmaline. Names for it like Bahia topaz, Scotch topaz, gold topaz and Madeira topaz are misleading—citrine and topaz are diffferent stones, and citrine is much less expensive than topaz. Natural citrine quartz is found in Ceylon and Brazil, Spain, Russia, France and Scotland, as well as on Pikes' Peak in Colorado. Chemically, citrine is clear quartz crystal colored by iron and heated naturally underground.

As a form of clear quartz, citrine contains the aura resonance and piezoelectric magnetism of clear quartz crystal. It enters a woman's aura, and its vibrations match aura frequencies to make citrine a powerful gemstone for healing. It magnifies and enhances trance states, transforms sexual energy from the physical to spiritual levels, focuses and enhances mental activity, knowing and intellect, and sharpens perception and clarity. Citrine is a good stone to use for the writer or teacher, for any form of studying or learning activities. It sharpens both mental and psychic sensitivity and aids astral projection.[34] Citrine is a purifier of the mind and of the organs of digestion, and it removes wastes and toxins from the blood.

Mellie Uyldert uses citrine/yellow quartz to raise depression and stimulate blood circulation, as well as to stimulate clear thinking and the nervous system.[35] Serenity Peterson uses it for physical and emotional grounding, to strengthen the will and balance the solar plexus chakra. She says that it opens the consciousness, makes the user accepting of change and new ideas, and broadens reality. Emotional warmth, open giving, the will and physical strength are some of its attributes.[36] Use citrine held in the hand in meditation to sharpen and stimulate creative visualization and color work. Sending citrine in healing is to send its properties and also to resonate them with the woman's aura who is being healed. Hold it in the left hand or use it over the solar plexus with clear quartz or other yellow/gold gems in laying on of stones. Wear it on a necklace for an aura of protection and to dissolve negativity. Citrine quartz is a warming and energizing yellow stone.

Katrina Raphaell uses citrine for manifesting, for making wishes and transmitting them clearly so they become real on the physical plane. Other gemstones that do this are peridot and green tourmaline. The means of citrine's strength in this is in its attunement to woman's aura for clarifying and projecting. She warns that used selfishly, this power of visualization and manifestation can have negative results,[37] and an old adage in the goddess craft is, "Be careful what you wish for, you may get it." The solar plexus is the center for materiality, and the heart is the place of abundance. These things are positive, but women know too that there are other levels to reality, other wealths that complement the physical/material. Use citrine quartz and the solar plexus chakra for nourishment and abundant manifesting, but recognize when to give and to let go as well. Another craft adage is, "What you send out returns threefold."

Raphaell finds this balance through pairing the solar plexus and the crown chakra, mentality and manifestation with the goddess, as dualities working together. In laying on of stones, using a citrine at both the solar plexus and the crown is a way of uniting the centers.[38] She uses it at the heart, solar plexus and belly chakras to connect feeling, mind and sexuality and to energize all three, and uses it over areas of dis-ease to aid digestive problems. Citrine works on both physical and unseen levels, as do most gemstones. It helps in physical dis-ease and in its inner cause, and is a strengthener of psychic digestion and assimilation along with their physical body counterparts.

Use citrine quartz to adjust and adapt, to process changes and eliminate the waste. It helps women to flow with life's changes, instead of being stuck in the status quo. It aids self-confidence, trust and security, particularly in interpersonal relationships, in business and teaching, learning and the family.[39] Citrine cheers, protects, purifies, balances and stimulates.

Tiger eye is a yellow/brown gemstone, another gemstone for use at the solar plexus. Its appearance and uses are similar to hawk's eye and the stones are found together. Tiger eye is hawk's eye in iron oxidized form, and both are found in South Africa, Western Australia, Burma, India and California. Tiger eye is brown and golden, while hawk's eye has a blue/green sheen. Both are fibrous forms of massive quartz, with the appearance of an animal's shining eye in the surface fibers. The stones are opaque, with a hardness of 7.

The gemstone's appearance of an eye suggests its use by the doctrine of signatures. Tiger eye is a protection stone, used for repel-ling the "evil eye" and for protection from negativity and from things without. The stone is also used as protection and healing for eye dis-ease and sight. Like other solar plexus gemstones, tiger eye aids clear-seeing in the physical and psychic sense, deepening perception and clarity of understanding what's seen. Above all, it helps women to see themselves, for insight into both work areas and strengths.[40] Changes and transformations come from inner knowledge.

Tiger eye is soothing as a stimulant, and aids in the manifesting of ideas and visualizations into reality. It helps in recognizing past life connections to others and in recognizing karmic ties between women. Serenity Peterson uses it for separating important from unimportant desires and issues, and for making use of this knowl-edge, giving women the strength to take charge, the strength to act surely. Again the reminder of, "Beware of what you ask for," since with tiger eye and other yellow stones, the woman gets it. With the will rooted in the solar plexus chakra, tiger eye strengthens and energizes woman's sense of will and purpose. It helps attain goals by taking direct action and by knowing when to act or wait.[41] It stimulates and strengthens power-within.

A lower mental level gemstone working primarily on the physical dense body, tiger eye in healing is used for asthma and lung diseases, for purification of the blood and digestive organs from alcohol or drugs. Lorusso and Glick minimize tiger eye's effectiveness as being purely physical and without the power to make itself felt strongly enough.[42] For women attracted to it, however, the stone is positive and helpful, stimulating sight, visualization, digestion, the mind and understanding, protecting and strengthening the mental aura. It energizes woman's self-confidence and sureness, purifies, and repels negativity, while aiding the ability to know what to go for. This is a very magickal solar energy stone. Julia Lorusso and Joel Glick predict that tiger eye is only beginning in its development as a New Age gemstone. They envision the stone becoming crystalline and translucent in ages ahead, retaining its shine and the shining eyes within it, while adding a deep red color.[42] Stones develop and change through the ages, and women using gemstones for healing work develop and change as well.

While major sources list citrine, topaz and amber primarily for yellow and gold gemstone energies, other less known stones are available. These range from yellow diamond, a golden and highly electrical gemstone, to soft minerals like yellow sulphur. Yellow tourmaline is a solar plexus gemstone, as are brazilianite, sphene, yellow barite, yellow sapphire, yellow jade and periclase. Tiger eye is a more common yellow gemstone but is considered a stone less major than citrine, amber or topaz. Yellow or *golden beryl* is another of these lesser known but more available solar plexus gemstones for healing.

The beryl family includes emerald, alexandrite and aquamarine, and the crystalline stones called beryl are those of any color but green (emerald), green/violet (alexandrite, very rare), or aqua (aquamarine) in the beryl grouping. Yellow or golden beryl is found in Sri Lanka and Namibia. As with other yellow gemstones, golden beryl is confused with topaz, citrine, golden peridot and yellow tourmaline, but is not the same. Seers use beryl to scry the future by looking into its color changes and crystalline depths. Mellie Uyldert lists golden or yellow beryl as a protection stone for sailors and adventurers, and for mouth, jaw, throat and digestive dis-eases, dis-eases of the stomach and liver.[43]

In the work of Thelma Isaacs, golden beryl is a yellow energy gemstone connecting the mental bodies, the lower rational mind with the higher intuition, the solar plexus with the heart. It brings peace of mind and giving from the heart, and is a steady rather than powerful gemstone energy. It stimulates the adrenals, purifies the digestive system, and sharpens the intuition and the mind. Isaacs recommends wearing golden beryl at the solar plexus or navel area for short periods,[44] with positive uses in laying on of stones in the solar plexus area. Julia Lorusso and Joel Glick list yellow or golden beryl as a relatively new gemstone, still evolving into healing power, and places its use and emphasis on non-physical aura levels, particularly in balancing the higher and lower mental bodies.[45]

As do other yellow gemstones, golden beryl works on the digestive system, on the sight, inner sight and intellect. It stimulates wisdom from the higher mental level, stimulates understanding and brain power, and aids visualization and manifesting. Golden beryl is a general stimulant, energizing and cheering with solar energy, with prana, and is a stone to use for exhaustion or depression. Stimulating the solar plexus as a psychic center, golden beryl increases psychic abilities and the woman's ability to process and understand psychic knowledge. Yellow gemstones aid all forms of physical and non-physical nourishment and their intake into the bodies, from food to prana to psychic energy. Use golden beryl for acceptance of feelings, to stimulate the pancreas, help upset stomachs, aid constipation, diarrhea, ulcers, nausea and obesity.[46] Women who are drawn to this gemstone experiment with its properties and learn its uses for their needs. Hold it in the left hand for meditation work, hold it in front of a candle flame and scry through it, carry it in a left pocket or take it to bed to learn its qualities. Written material on the less known gemstones particularly is open to re-visioning and dis-covery, to women's intuition and healing work.

Gemstones and crystals connect women's unseen bodies with the dense physical level, for healing and well-being to take place in the energy spaces between atoms and in the cells themselves. Several of the yellow gemstones connect the mental bodies, the solar plexus with the heart, and some yellow/green gemstones, though green is the heart center color, are listed traditionally as solar plexus stones and do the same. Malachite and green peridot are two listed as solar plexus gemstones, and other green and rose gemstones with the attribute of connecting are listed as heart chakra stones. The yellow/

green color of malachite and peridot places them in a position of being neither heart center green nor solar plexus yellow or gold. Instead they partake of both, balance both, and connect the chakras.

While the heart is usually accepted as the center that connects the three spiritual levels with the lower aura bodies (etheric double, emotional body, lower mental body), the solar plexus is responsible for nourishment distribution to all the centers. It transmits energy and information, and is sometimes listed as the connecting chakra, the bridge between the higher and lower aura levels. Malachite and peridot are yellow/green connecting stones that bridge the solar plexus and heart centers, the lower and higher mind, and share properties common to both chakras. In the higher aura levels, from the higher mental body (heart chakra) upward through the crown and trans-personal point, gemstones often overlap centers and connect, balancing and bridging between two or more centers. The upper centers are the higher mind (heart chakra), the lower spiritual (throat), middle spiritual (brow chakra or third eye), higher spiritual (crown center) and the transpersonal point beyond the physical body. Heart chakra gemstones are discussed in Chapter Nine.

Malachite is a yellow/green gemstone for the solar plexus/lower mental level that connects the lower and higher minds. Used in ancient Egypt for eye dis-eases, psychic sight, for channeling energies from the unseen to the seen, and for manifesting, malachite is one of the oldest of healing gemstones. The stone is massive and soft, only 3½-4 on the Moh's scale that lists quartz as 7 and diamond, the hardest gemstone substance, as 10. Malachite is found in Russia, the Urals, Zaire, Australia, Chile, Rhodesia, South Africa and in the United States in Arizona. Modern major deposits and mining are from Zaire. Along with jewelry and amulets, malachite is used in carvings and objects, jewel boxes, ashtrays, eggs and figurines. Russian tsars used malachite slabs to panel palace walls. The stone is dis-tinctively patterned, clear opaque green with striations and concentric rings of darker green, eyes, circles and whorls. In meditation work, the patterns draw the user into labyrinths and other worlds. The stone is seldom found in solid coloring. Ground malachite is used as paint pigment, and was used for eye shadow in ancient Egypt. In amulet form, malachite was used in Greece, Rome and Egypt as a protection from negativity and the "evil eye," particularly for children, a protection against lightning and nightmares, and was carried to cure vomiting.[47]

All of the solar plexus attributes of yellow gemstones are attributes of malachite, plus other attributes that link it to the heart chakra. Malachite is a purifier of the digestive system, used for the gall bladder, liver, pancreas and spleen. Stimulant and calming at once, it's a balancer of blood sugar and bile levels.[48] A stone of solar plexus nourishment and heart chakra flowing, malachite increases breast milk, balances irregular menstrual cycles, and is used for asthma, colic, epilepsy, joint pain, rheumatism, and spasms in the stomach, muscles and heart. Malachite purifies the blood against poisons and toxins, regulates blood pressure, and helps toothaches. In its heart chakra attributes, it regenerates the heart physically and emotionally, regenerates the nerves and body tissues, soothes, calms and heals wounds. Use it for vitality and easing stress, for the nervous system, and for degenerative nerve dis-eases such as multiple sclerosis. Mellie Uyldert uses malachite to inspire hope, ease longings, and comfort love-loss, other heart center uses, and for intuition and fidelity in love.[49]

Malachite is a psychic mirror, comparable to obsidian, bringing buried feelings and issues out for looking at consciously. It opens the blocks for knowing and processing. Though gentle, the stone is powerful and women are urged to respect its strength. Malachite energy is balancing and peaceful, but facing repressed emotions is not always easy, if often necessary for a woman's well-being. The insights gained from using malachite are catalysts for change. Use the stone for short sessions, in meditation or taken to bed, processing the knowledge before going further. Malachite magnifies moods, both positive and negative, and awareness of moods is urged when using it. The stone is particularly good for women who are very mental, but who tend to block out or lose touch with feelings. The healings that occur with malachite come from deep within.

Katrina Raphaell uses malachite over dis-ease areas in laying on of stones, to draw out negativity and to surface the inner reasons for dis-ease.[50] The stone is absorbent of negative energy and needs to be cleared often, but is too soft a material for salt or salt water. Running water and sunlight are good cleansers, as are marigold petals, rose petals or herbs, and Raphaell suggests clearing malachite by placing it on a clear quartz crystal cluster for several hours. Without frequent clearing, malachite becomes dull and loses healing strength. Emotional blocks from within surface with using malachite, blocks to inner harmony and balance, repressed emotions, unprocessed hurts or angers. It releases diaphragm tension for deeper breathing and connects the solar plexus to the heart center, the lower and higher mind levels, by way of deeper breath.[51] Malachite aids inner and psychic clarity and self-knowledge, and connects and grounds unseen energies with the physical. Its leaf green color suggests its uses in grounding and regeneration, since green is the color of abundance, nourishment and the growing, blooming Earth.

Serenity Peterson uses malachite as a general and heart healer, to draw negativities from the lower chakra levels, from the etheric double, belly chakra and solar plexus (the physical, emotional and lower mental bodies). She sees it as a stone to repair, heal and strengthen the aura at all unseen levels, and as a bridge between woman's self and her spirit guides. Malachite aids both the rational and intuitional mind, offers emotional understanding and inner strength, connects the mind to feelings, and feelings to inspiration and intuition.[52] The unseen becomes visible and wishes manifest with malachite, a New Age stone for women's healing. Malachite found in combination with chrysocolla is the Israeli Eilat stone, a stone of harmony and peace. Malachite found with azurite is a powerful soother and regenerative healer.

Even closer to the heart is *peridot,* a yellow/green stone also known as olivine or chrysolite, and sometimes as peridotite. This leaf-green crystalline gemstone can be confused with other clear green gemstones, particularly with tourmaline, emerald and green beryl. Uncut, its waxy clarity contains and reflects shimmering lights, and is soothing and joyous to simply look at. A brittle stone, it breaks easily, and is a stone that can be shattered by intense healing work. Not a rare or expensive material, peridot is mined on the Island of St. John in the Red Sea, in Burma, Australia, Brazil, Russia, South Africa, Norway and Zaire. In the United States, peridot is native to Arizona, Hawaii, New York State, and New Mexico, and in Canada is mined in British Columbia. Chakra correspondences vary for peridot: Thelma Isaacs lists it for the spiritual body levels, Katrina Raphaell for the heart and solar plexus, Julia Lorusso and Joel Glick for the heart and solar plexus, and Mellie Uyldert for the solar plexus totally. The stone is the only gemstone material found in meteorites, and may be a material not of this planet. Its hardness is 6½-7.

Peridot comes in two colors, golden and yellow/green, with the green most available and most used for women's healing. Mellie Uyldert calls the golden variety a stone of the Sun, and gives it solar plexus attributes of healing eye dis-eases and inspiring psychic sight and clairvoyance. It may have been the stone that Pliny called topaz. Yellow/green peridot was brought to Europe by returning Crusaders who confused it with emerald. Both colors for Uyldert aid inner and physical vision, are mood elevators, give eloquence and inspiration, and dispel illusions.[53]

Personal work with green peridot finds it calming, cheering, soothing and balancing. The stone calms the heart and emotions, eases sleep, relieves anxiety, and aids in manifesting physical work into material abundance. Partaking of solar plexus yellow nourishment and heart chakra green abundance and regeneration, a gift of a peridot is a gift for drawing prosperity and peace. Carry it in a left-hand pocket or wear it as a necklace and keep it close. With a peridot in the aura, there is enough—the woman finds a job and better than she's hoped for, gets a raise, finds a twenty dollar bill on the street, hits the lottery or otherwise increases her potentials for prosperity where none seemed possible. Examples repeat and become magick, and prosperity gained is for the good of all, with loss or disharmony to none. For women whose health issues are related to poverty and its stress, carrying or wearing a peridot is highly recommended. Use it to aid creative visualization and for manifesting wishes on the earth plane.

As a solar plexus stone, yellow/green peridot is a tonic to well-being, balances the endocrine system and adrenals, and releases and balances nervous tension. It aids both the rational/intellectual mind and the intuitional/inspirational higher mind. As a heart chakra stone, peridot cleanses negativity, draws joy and peaceful balance, and neutralizes the too-much-red of anger or jealousy. It helps with hurt feelings, helps self-image and self-love, and Katrina Raphaell says it helps to hold relationships together.[54] A gentle and powerful balancer between the solar plexus and the heart, peridot helps to heal and connect both chakras. It connects the mind with feelings, vision with inner sight, nourishment with abundance. Use it with garnet for yin/yang balancing or the balancing of any pairs of dualities or opposites. Peridot connects physical with mental and spiritual health and well-being.

In dense body healing, use peridot to soothe digestion and for digestive upsets and dis-eases. Wear it as a necklace on a long chain to hold it low near the navel. It helps ulcers and colitis, spastic or inflamed bowel conditions, constipation, the spleen. Julia Lorusso and Joel Glick recommend peridot for "emotional con-stipation,"[55] and for the form of mental retardation that comes from chemical imbalance. The stone is a cleanser and purifies the blood and heart, is good for lung congestion, fevers, inflam-mations and as an antiseptic. It vitalizes, soothes and protects the physical organs as well as the aura bodies. Along with solar plexus digestion and mentality, it aids and soothes the heart, inspiration, intuition and emotions. Lorusso and Glick list peridot as a major healing gemstone of fabled Atlantis and of the South American Aztec, Inca and Toltec goddess societies that are believed to have been Atlantis survivors (with Egypt).[56] Thelma Isaacs lists peridot primarily as a protection stone, of the most use to spiritually developed women who are clear minded and sensitive enough to benefit from its subtle vibrations. Peridot is a gentle stone, of easy intensity, that achieves quiet balancing and healing.

Yellow/green solar plexus gemstones merge with gemstones and healing for the heart chakra. While solar plexus issues are digestion, intellect, sight, energy and nourishment, the heart center is simply a higher vibration of these attributes, plus others. The heart chakra balances giving and abundance, transmitting and receiving the abundance of higher nourishment than the physical, the nourishment of love for the self and others. It operates from intuition and inspiration, from the higher mind. The green, rose and aqua gemstones of the heart chakra develop these issues more fully, while solar plexus gold, yellow and yellow/green gemstones are their mental and more earthly counterparts.

FOOTNOTES

1. Walter Schumann, *Gemstones of the World* (New York, Sterling, Publishing Co., 1984, original 1977), p. 126.

2. Mellie Uyldert, *The Magic of Precious Stones* (Great Britain, Turnstone Press, 1981), p. 91.

3. Katrina Raphaell, *Crystal Enlightenment* (New York, Aurora Press, 1985), p. 139.

4. *Ibid.*

5. Mellie Uyldert, *The Magic of Precious Stones*, p. 92.

6. Julia Lorusso and Joel Glick, *Healing Stoned* (Albuquerque, NM, Brotherhood of Life, 1985, original 1976), p. 61.

7. Serenity Peterson, *Crystal Visioning, A Crystal Workbook* (Nashville, TN, Interdimensional Publishing, 1984), p. 46.

8. Mellie Uyldert, *The Magic of Precious Stones*, p. 92.

9. *Ibid.*, p. 154.

10. Thelma Isaacs, *Gemstones, Crystals and Healing* (Black Mt, NC, Lorien House, 1982), p. 43.

11. *Ibid.*, p. 44.

12. *Ibid.*

13. Lee Lanning and Vernette Hart, *Ripening: An Almanac of Lesbian Lore and Vision* (Minneapolis, MN, Word Weavers, 1981), p. 60.

14. Mellie Uyldert, *The Magic of Precious Stones*, p. 90.

15. Thelma Isaacs, *Gemstones, Crystals and Healing*, p. 80-81.

16. Serenity Peterson, *Crystal Visioning*, p. 41.

17. Thelma Isaacs, *Gemstones, Crystals and Healing*, p. 97-98.

18. Mellie Uyldert, *The Magic of Precious Stones*, p. 11.

19. Julia Lorusso and Joel Glick, *Healing Stoned*, p. 73.

20. Rhiannon McBride, "The Occult Lapidary: Topaz, Stone of Love and Light," in *Circle Network News* (POB 219, Mt. Horeb, WI 53572), Fall, 1983, p. 4.

21. Mellie Uyldert, *The Magic of Precious Stones*, p. 118.

22. Gemstoned Ltd., *Crystal Essence* (New York, Gemstoned Ltd., 1984), unpaged pamphlet.

23. Rhiannon McBride, "The Occult Lapidary: Topaz, Stone for Love and Light," in *Circle Network News*, Fall, 1983, p. 4.

24. Thelma Isaacs, *Gemstones, Crystals and Healing*, p. 91.

25. Rhiannon McBride, "The Occult Lapidary: Topaz, Stone of Love and Light," in *Circle Network News*, Fall, 1983, p. 4.

26. Katrina Raphaell, *Crystal Enlightenment*, p. 136.

27. Julia Lorusso and Joel Glick, *Healing Stoned*, p. 28.

28. Mellie Uyldert, *The Magic of Precious Stones*, p. 151.

29. Thelma Isaacs, *Gemstones, Crystals and Healing*, p. 31.

30. *Ibid.*, p. 30-31.

31. Ida Shaw, workshop handout, National Women's Music Festival, May, 1986.

32. Walter Schumann, *Gemstones of the World*, p. 120.

34. Gemstoned Ltd., *Crystal Essence*, unpaged pamphlet.

35. Mellie Uyldert, *The Magic of Precious Stones*, p. 101.

36. Katrina Raphaell, *Crystal Enlightenment*, p. 87.

37. *Ibid.*, p. 87-88.

38. *Ibid.*, p. 87-88.

39. *Ibid.*, p. 88-89.

40. Mellie Uyldert, *The Magic of Precious Stones*, p. 104.

41. Serenity Peterson, *Crystal Visioning*, p. 58.

42. Julia Lorusso and Joel Glick, *Healing Stoned*, p. 59.

43. Mellie Uyldert, *The Magic of Precious Stones*, p. 107.

44. Thelma Isaacs, *Gemstones, Crystals and Healing*, p. 37-38.

45. Julia Lorusso and Joel Glick, *Healing Stoned*, p. 38.

46. Ida Shaw, workshop handout.

47. Walter Schumann, *Gemstones of the World*, p. 176.

48. Gemstoned Ltd., *Crystal Essence*, unpaged pamphlet.

49. Mellie Uyldert, *The Magic of Precious Stones*, p. 132.

50. Katrina Raphaell, *Crystal Enlightenment*, p. 144.

51. *Ibid.*, p. 144-145.

52. Serenity Peterson, *Crystal Visioning*, p. 53.

53. Mellie Uyldert, *The Magic of Precious Stones*, p. 128.

54. Katrina Raphaell, *Crystal Enlightenment*, p. 149-151.

55. Julia Lorusso and Joel Glick, *Healing Stoned*, p. 53.

56. *Ibid.*

Colored Gemstones: The Heart and Throat Chakras

IN THE religion of the Hopi Road of Life, the heart is the place where the Earth and sky meet, the physical and spiritual become one. In the ancient Hebrew Qabala that recognizes ten major chakras, the heart is located between severity and mercy, the chakra centers of the shoulders, and it balances these qualities. Love and compassion, and the oneness of the physical, emotional, mental and spiritual bodies are the themes of the heart chakra and of heart center healing. The heart is the higher mind, the place of inspiration and intuition beyond rational understanding, the place of formless thought and imagination. From this place, the healer reaches upward and downward for unity, harmony and wholeness, for woman's well-being that encompasses all of her unseen levels and the seen. The healer works with her heart chakra wide open, and all healing and self-healing takes place there. She opens her throat center next to communicate heart chakra caring.

The heart represents compassion for the self and for others, and its colors are green, rose and blue/green. Green denotes giving, abundance, sympathy and success. Rose soothes the nervous system, is love and positive self-love, the ability to care. Clear aqua or blue/green overlaps the heart with the throat chakra, merges caring with creativity and expression as natural outcomes of heart center opening. Blue/green is soothing, strengthening, healing, freeing and stabilizing. Of the three colors, green and blue/green are cooling, with green the most neutral in temperature and use of all the healing color spectrum. Blue/green is colder. Rose for the heart is slightly warming, but much less so than the hot colors of the lower chakras, and the heart and throat colors are all soothing shades. The heart corresponds with woman's sense of touch and the throat with her sense of hearing: the woman who reaches out to touch others also hears their needs. In healing, the two chakras are linked.

Half of heart healing is learning self-love, a pre-requisite for loving others; loving both self and others is needed for opening the throat. If the heart is constricted by pain or worry, there is loss of connectedness with feelings. An unopened heart results in not feeling good enough in the self and in distrust of others. In the case of the throat, if the throat center is too far closed, the inability to express and release heart-felt feelings prevents the free flow of energy throughout the bodies, and the woman doesn't hear others' needs or her own. The release of heart emotions opens creativity and communication of all sorts from the throat center. It aids expression, sincerity, self-confidence and self-reliance. A balancing and opening of both chakras brings peace and blessings to a woman healer and helps to make her whole. Joy, beauty, contentment, self-acceptance, love, giving and receptivity are heart center attributes, and the throat communicates and expresses them, moves them freely throughout Be-ing.

Green gemstones in the heart center heal and calm tension. They are antiseptic and cooling to use for inflammations, fevers, infections, wounds, sunburn and burns. They are regenerating stones, building and repairing muscles and tissues, are good for the nerves, eyes and heart. Use green gemstones for ulcers, stress and high blood pressure, to calm and soothe physically and emotionally. Use them for flu, headaches, neuralgia, migraines, venereal and heart diseases, stomach ailments and cancer.[1] Green is the color of abundance, and stimulates healing of every sort; it's springtime and new life, and its complementary color is red and the life force. Green healing gemstones include emerald, green jade, green aventurine and the green and watermelon tourmalines that overlap with the solar plexus. Malachite and peridot, yellow/green gemstones listed with solar plexus healing, are also healing for the heart, as are the blue/green or aqua gems that overlap with the throat center.

Rose colored gemstones for the heart chakra include rose quartz, pink and watermelon tourmaline, and rhodochrosite, as well as rose jade and rose coral, dolomite and kunzite, pink carnelian, rhodonite and the pinker shades of precious opal. Rose gemstones are for heartache, loneliness and love-loss, for drawing love and positive self-love, and drawing the goddess within. They are warming, soothing, cheering and comforting for depression and grief. Rose gemstones stimulate the thymus for creativity, opening, joy and trustfulness. In physical healing they help with hearing and deafness, skin ailments, palsies, kidney trouble, and all heart dis-eases and heart pain (physical or emotional). Use rose gemstones for trauma, cancer prevention, and recovery from child-abuse, and with tourmalines or rhodochrosite to connect solar plexus energy and intellect with heart center giving, empathy, intuition and abundance. A rose gemstone aura sent in healing and self-healing comforts, warms, loves, protects and cares. Rose gemstones bring hope, harmony, happiness and balance, and rejuvenate the entire nervous system with peace. Sending rose energy in healing work sends love and a glow of joy, connects the woman being healed with her spirituality, mind, feelings and body as one Being, with her self and others as goddess.

Green and rose heart center stones overlap with the throat center's blue/green or light blue ones for healing. The release, communication and expression of heart feelings is necessary for woman's well-being and good health. Words that can't be said, angers and emotions that can't be or aren't expressed and released, are the classic causes of sore throats and throat growths, of ulcers, cancer, skin dis-eases and more. Speaking out is taking risk in a patriarchal world, where anger is strong for women and expressing it often has cost. Speaking anger can risk job loss, risk a business deal, risk a love affair, risk rejection or retaliation. But angers and emotions held within block the free flow of energies throughout the body, keep energies stuck in negative ways and turn pain destructively on the self. Releasing and expressing anger is an issue for women and women's health, learning to re-cognize and speak individual needs, feelings and pain in safe and positive ways, keeping communications open and flowing between individuals. An open throat chakra is the means of expressing the emotions and love of an opened heart, and preventing pain from becoming stuck or becoming dis-eased. Much of healing involves opening and releasing both centers. When the throat and heart are open, anger and emotions are freed. Sincerity, self-confidence, self-reliance and the ability to accept and give love are made possible.

Blue/green gemstones overlap and balance the heart and throat chakras, while the truer blue stones overlap the third eye. Both colors ease worry and the over-active mind, and are calming and relaxing. Blue and blue/green cool, reduce high blood pressure, reduce inflammations, fevers, swellings and infections, soothe burns and stress, and heal wounds. Blue/green stones are especially good to use with headaches, and the difficult to heal migraines and high blood pressure that are systemic and emotional dis-eases of patriarchy. Blue gemstones are good for all physical healing, for relieving pain, reducing bleeding, inducing sleep and disinfecting, as well as for sore throats and to stimulate communication, expression and creativity. Some blue/green gemstones are turquoise, chrysocolla and aquamarine. Some darker blue gemstones overlap with the healing stones of the brow center. These throat and brow center energies are discussed in the next chapter.

Rose gemstones for heart chakra healing begin with *rose quartz,* the most representative and universally positive of heart healing stones. A massive form of quartz crystal, rose quartz is light to strong pink in color and usually translucent to opaque. Crystalline forms are possible but rare, and rutile forms and star rose quartz occur. Clearer stones can be faceted, but most rose quartz is found as beads, chips or tumbled pieces, sometimes carved into ornaments, and often left raw in chunks. The stone is found in Brazil, the Malagasy Republic and Madagascar, and in the United States. It is common in California. The light pink color can fade in direct sunlight, and rose quartz used for healing should not be cleared by this method. As a form of clear quartz, the color caused by inclusions of manganese, rose quartz is a stone that resonates with woman's aura for deep and personal healing. Its energies contain great sweetness: its planet is Venus, the goddess of love, and its zodiacal correspondence is Virgo,[2] belonging to the huntress Diana or Artemis, the free woman. Rose quartz in healing is an opener of the heart.

Use rose quartz to draw love; the energy that all life flows from. Put it on an altar to Oshun or Aphrodite, Venus or Artemis or Sappho Use it with pink candles treated with rose oil, a vase of pink roses, and rosebud incense. The woman who asks for love in her life both gives and receives it and she finds it within: rose quartz shows her the way. Carry it in a mojo bag or in a left-hand pocket. Sleep with a rose quartz egg and a clear quartz crystal to bring love into a woman's life.

Rose quartz energy works two ways, and this is its power. The stone draws love from without while opening it from within, and one does not exist without the other. Self-love in women is a positive attribute, something denied to women by the attitudes of patriarchal societies and religions. Self-love is positive, beautiful and empowering, and from it comes love and compassion, empathy and caring for others. From it comes love of the goddess, since the goddess is within. Rose quartz stimulates love of self, others and the goddess, and an appreciation of the beauties of the goddess Earth. It stimulates an open heart for trust and giving, for the ability to heal the self and others. Comforting, caring, contentment, receptivity, creativity, honesty and joy are attributes of rose quartz healing.

Many women are raised with fear and pain, and the inability to express love, the repressions of a male society embarrassed by emotion and afraid of it. Too many children are unwanted or abused, or are taught that love is reserved for only one lover or partner, and love for others is repressed into suspicious competition. The women's movement has taken on these attitudes and made great progress, but much work remains, and scars in women's lives run deep. Taught from childhood that emotion is private, crying is shameful, talking about feelings is trivial, much is repressed and held in. Opening the heart with rose quartz is to access and reach deeply. The stone opens nearer blocks then deeper ones, always with great comforting and gentleness, wrapping the woman using it in a rose warm blanket of love. Hurts are surfaced, looked at, accepted and released; the heart is opened to new giving and receiving.

Using rose quartz in healing releases depression and every sort of heartache. Use it for loneliness, heart loss, love loss, and grief. The process of healing deep hurts is a slow one, and emotional release occurs. When using rose quartz in healing work or laying on of stones with others, be prepared to be there and to comfort. When using rose quartz alone, be aware of heightened sensitivity and vulnerability; the woman gives herself caring and understanding. Tears come and it's okay. At these times, keep a piece of rose quartz in the aura to comfort, heal and help.[3] Acceptance, inner peace and self-fulfillment,

an opening to love and self-love, to beauty and to joy are the outcome of rose quartz release and healing.

Physical heart dis-ease is literally a broken heart, and rose quartz
is a healer for these ailments. It helps high blood pressure, nervous
tension, stress and heart pain, and it soothes, warms and eases. Use
rose quartz for the throat, ears and hearing, sinuses, the kidneys,
palsies and anemia.[4] Use it for expression, singing and speaking, eloquence and to bring loving dreams. The stone's very gentle vibrations are especially positive for healing children, for childhood and
adolescent emotional and physical pain. Rose quartz is comforting
for any age, and in aging it brings peace and reduces wrinkles.[5]

The sweetest natured of healing gemstones, rose quartz stimulates forgiveness, acceptance, love for self and others, for the goddess, and stimulates universal love. Through emotional healing,
heart chakra opening, release and balancing, it offers peacefulness
and joy, sensitivity to the beauties of Be-ing.[6] Rose quartz teaches
women to give and receive love in perfect trust.

Rose quartz is an emotional aura and heart chakra gemstone,
and *rhodochrosite,* another rose healing stone, is a connector of the
heart and solar plexus. Rhodochrosite works through both chakras
to balance them, and to balance and integrate the three higher with
the three lower aura and chakra levels. The three aura levels closest
to the dense physical body are the etheric double (root chakra),
emotional/astral body (belly chakra) and the lower mental (solar
plexus) body. Meeting at the heart, the higher mental level, the three
upper levels and chakras are the three levels of the spiritual body, the
throat, brow and crown centers. Woman's physical essence, the lower
aura and chakra levels, often suffer from patriarchal preoccupations
with living in the mind and spirit only. This is a split that did not exist in
the matriarchies, but happened as part of the splitting of dualities in
patriarchal religions, attempts to separate women from their bodies
and power-within. Modern women and women's spirituality include
in their re-claiming the re-claiming and re-valuing of the body and
emotions, woman's womb and woman's intuition, re-cognizing their
oneness and wholeness with the mind and spirit. Women's health
and well-being depends on this unity, and rhodochrosite is a gemstone that stimulates it.

Rhodochrosite is a pink to salmon-colored massive gemstone.
Its name is Greek and means "rose red," and Inca rose is another

name for the stone, which comes from its appearance in the abandoned Inca silver mines. Major sources for rhodochrosite are Argentina and Colorado. The stone is layered and striped with white, appearing to be formed in tree-ring like patterns. It's a soft stone, 4 on the Moh's scale of hardness, and its color is caused by manganese, as is the pink color of rose quartz. One of the more expensive healing gemstones, rhodochrosite is usually available in raw, rough pieces, but is used in jewelry, beads and carved ornaments as well. The darker orange to almost red shades are more often used in jewelry work. It is sometimes seen in unpolished slabs. Katrina Raphaell recommends the rarely found orange crystals for cancer and liver treatment, and uses them in an elixir for this.[7] Rhodochrosite is only beginning to be dis-covered as a stone for women's healing, and is a powerful and positive energy.

The stone has heart center and solar plexus center correspondences. Along with opening and balancing these two chakras and the higher and lower mental bodies, rhodochrosite integrates the physical, emotional and mental with the inspirational and spiritual aura layers. It's a stong transmitter of energy and aura fields, an electrical conductor. Rhodochrosite's patterns and lines suggest the unseen bodies that exist and operate behind and along with seen levels.[8] Mellie Uyldert sees this stone as a protective filter, good for confusion and mental disturbance, incoherence and anxiety. She suggests it for psychics who wish to reduce the "vibes" for a time of rest,[9] and sees it as a stone of the astral plane.

In healing for the solar plexus and the heart, use rhodochrosite for heart attributes of acceptance, clarification, forgiveness, eloquence and creative thinking, for feeling and giving love, for emotional healing release and opening the heart center.[10] Use it for healing of the nails, hair, skin and feet, for palsies and ulcers, multiple sclerosis and Parkinson's dis-ease, for growth and growth hormones (thymus). In solar plexus attributes, use rhodochrosite for the eyes and eyesight, for removing toxins from the blood and digestive system, for the liver, asthma, breathing, lung and digestive systems, for constipation, to stimulate the mind and brain, the pituitary gland, and to dry excess mucous in the lungs and sinuses. Use rhodochrosite to open the healing chakras in the palms of the hands. The stone holds energy and directs it.

Katrina Raphaell suggests using rhodochrosite with malachite in laying on of stones, placing both in the solar plexus area to direct energies from the higher centers to the lower ones. She uses smaller rhodochrosite pieces at the eyes to improve vision, particularly for the "not wanting to see" types of eye and vision dis-eases. The stone aids acceptance, interpretation and assimilation of what is seen.[11] As women become more in touch with their bodies seen and unseen, and learn to re-claim, love and unify all aspects of Be-ing in themselves, rhodochrosite is a gemstone increasingly important in women's health.

Other heart chakra gemstones are *pink, watermelon* and *green tourmaline,* three gemstones of the tourmaline grouping that also includes black tourmaline or schorl for the root chakra. Tourmalines are crystalline gemstones for bright colors ranging from clear and transparent to opaque and black, with all of the colors and ranges in between. The stones are found in a variety of locations, including South Africa and Brazil, (watermelon and pink tourmaline), Sri Lanka (green), the Malgasy Republic, Mozambique, Angola, Australia, India, Burma, Thailand, Russia and Switzerland (black). In the United States, tourmalines are found in California, Maine, New York, Connecticut and Colorado. The stones can be cut and faceted for jewelry, and single-colored varieties are less common than the two or more colored ones. Tourmaline wands of up to a foot long are found in South America, contain a range of colors in a single wand, and are very powerful for healing.[12] Tourmaline measures 7-7½ in hardness.

A major attribute of the tourmaline grouping is its polarity and magnetism: when rubbed or heated, the stones develop a definite electrical charge, positive on one end and negative on the other. In healing this is used to draw out negativity, and tourmalines channel electrical aura energy, raise vibrations of energy for vitality, growth, protection and healing. All of the colors of tourmaline cast an aura of brightness and protection around the woman using them, protect in aware daylight and in astral sleep, and in addition transmit the attributes of their individual colors. They enhance personal radiance and charisma, transmit warmth, electricity and the life force. They have an up-reaching energy flow that raises moods and vitality, and even helps with physical balance.[13] Katrina Raphaell uses them in laying on of stones to raise energy flows from physical to spiritual levels, and to connect and balance between any two pairs of chakras.[14] Thelma Isaacs says that tourmalines should not be worn on the body, but no other source agrees.[15] Julia Lorusso and Joel Glick, as well as Katrina Raphaell, praise it as among the most powerful and positive of healing gemstones, channeling light, healing and balance to a woman's aura.

While all three of the tourmalines in this section are heart chakra gemstones, *pink tourmaline* is most specifically a heart center energy. Also called rubellite, pink tourmaline works with other rose gemstones to open and balance the heart, draw love, self-love, friendship and universal love. Use it for calming, mood elevation, to ease fears and induce peaceful, protected sleep. It helps in the balancing of relationships with others, brings harmony in love affairs, and is also a healer for women in the helping fields against burn out.[16] With tourmaline's attribute of casting an aura of protection around the user, pink tourmaline casts a rose colored aura of love, of giving and receiving, openness, joy and trust, compassion, unselfishness and enthusiasm.

Katrina Raphaell uses pink tourmaline in laying on of stones in triad with rose quartz and kunzite:

> Rose quartz first focuses on the development of self-love which Kunzite then activates and makes ready for external expression. With this foundation prepared, pink Tourmaline can then exert its influence to make a glorious offering of that love to the world.[17]

She uses pink tourmaline as a stone of manifesting, of bringing love and self-love from within to a place of giving and reaching out to others. Since what's sent out returns threefold by goddess law, the giver of love receives it. Pink tourmaline, like rose quartz, dissolves holding back, transforms the fear that blocks and freezes free expression of the heart. Like rose quartz, pink tourmaline can cause healing by emotional release,[18] and is a stone to use for heartache, loss and grief, a comforting and protective gemstone that soothes all pain with gentleness and love. When the woman using pink tourmaline is the most vulnerable, the stone's circle of protection and compassion is at its strongest. For heart center healing and woman's well-being, pink tourmaline is a major gemstone.

Watermelon tourmaline is composed of a green outer layer or rind around a rose core or center. The green skin is often thin, with the rose predominant, but some pieces show a fairly even mix of the colors throughout. The gemstone in healing combines pink tourmaline energies with that of green tourmaline, and is both a heart center and solar plexus gemstone, a balancer between the upper and lower triads of centers. Green is success, balance, stability and regeneration energy, and these combined with the love and positive self-love of rose are a powerful healing team.

Lorusso and Glick use watermelon tourmaline as a balancer of metabolism (solar plexus) and the endocrine system, a balancer of the chakras, and a connector of the physical, emotional and mental to the higher mental and spiritual centers. They note its use particularly in balancing sexuality, and in stabilizing the yin/yang polarities that exist in everyone. Protecting and altering cell structure, the healing that takes place from cell level regeneration and the blueprint of cell replacement is a function of watermelon tourmaline, suggesting its use as a preventive for cancer and an aid to cancer healing. The protective shield that's a tourmaline attribute in all its colors is made use of here.[19]

The dual heart colors of watermelon tourmaline make it a general harmonizer. In another solar plexus and heart center blending, the stone stimulates balance between the lower and higher mind, the rational and imaginative for creativity and art. The colors energize the heart chakra and the kama-manas/desire-mind. The stone's green rind is an emotional healer and the pink transmits and receives love. Katrina Raphaell uses watermelon tourmaline for heart chakra healing, to repair weariness and heartache, heart soreness and heart loss. She notes its lightness and sense of humor that inspires awareness of the beauties in life and gives the courage to open up again and go on.[20] Combining the heart center colors of rose and green, the attributes of love and growth, with tourmaline's circle of protection, watermelon tourmaline is another gemstone for healing and woman's well-being.

Green tourmaline, also called verdelite, begins the discussion of green gemstones and color in heart chakra healing work. Green is the color of new growth and spring, and is a stabilizing, cleansing, cooling and calming color in healing work. It's used for infections and bacteria, reducing fevers, swellings and inflammations, lowering blood pressure, raising moods and for opening the abundance and giving that comes from the heart.[21] Green is a universal healing color, safe and positive to send in any healing work; it soothes and heals for virtually any dis-ease. Green tourmaline is representative of green healing energy, working through the nervous system to calm, balance and stimulate new growth.

Like peridot, which it works well with, green tourmaline draws success, prosperity and manifesting of wishes on the material plane. Like peridot, too, it's a cooling and soothing gemstone, a stabilizer and balancer of emotions. Both a heart and solar plexus gemstone, green tourmaline balances the rational and creative mind and balances the lower chakras with the higher levels. The solar plexus as the place of will is tempered with heart center wisdom,[22] and peace of mind results. The stone calms the nerves and is used for all nervous and nerve center dis-eases, for nerve regeneration and opening the channels and meridians of the nerve paths.[23]

Use green tourmaline for fatigue and regenerating exhaustion. Use it to draw prosperity and creativity, as an aura protection against negativity, and to enhance creative visualization and manifesting.[24] Use it to open the heart, heal heart dis-eases, digestive dis-eases and upsets, to purify and balance the blood, for intestinal obstructions and constipation, for the teeth, bones and for varicose veins.[25] Use it to calm and reduce fear and anxiety and to open the heart to accepting and giving love. Use it for bacterial dis-ease healing, to reduce fevers, pain and inflammations, for flu and colds, for general healing and vitalizing, and to lower high blood pressure. The protective shield of tourmaline becomes an all-aura healing and energizing with green tourmaline energy. Wear green, pink or watermelon tourmaline in a mojo bag or carry it in a left-hand pocket, sleep with it in the left hand, use it in laying on of stones, or wear it as jewelry. Use tourmaline rods in psychic healing to send its qualities and colors.

Green gemstones symbolize serenity, and *emerald* is the archetype of green gemstone healing. While Thelma Isaacs lists it as a solar plexus gemstone, and there are overlapping qualities, emerald is basically a heart center energy. A stone of Venus and the South American love goddess Esmeralda from which it was named, emerald is an astrological correspondent to Taurus, Libra or Cancer,[26] and is dedicated to peace, fidelity and the loving open heart, to beauty and psychic sensitivity.

Emeralds are among the oldest of healing gemstones, known and valued by ancient Egypt, and Cleopatra's emerald mines near

Aswan, active in 50 B.C., are still known. The stone has been used as a healer throughout herstory and listed among the most monetarily valued of gemstone materials worldwide. It was one of the stones of ancient India and known to the Old Testament. It is a member of the beryl family, and aquamarine, alexandrite and beryl are of the same composition as emerald, differing primarily in color. The distinctive pure green coloring is caused by vanadium or chromium, and emeralds are crystalline and very hard, measuring 7½-8 on the Moh's scale.

Emeralds are mined in Brazil, Columbia, South Africa, India, Austria, Norway, Pakistan, Australia, and in the United States in Maine, Connecticut and North Carolina. Major gem quality deposits are in Columbia, Africa and Brazil. The stone is also synthesized in laboratories, but human-made gemstones are not positive for healing work. While cut and faceted emeralds and emerald jewelry can sell for thousands of dollars, raw emerald crystals are quite inexpensive, and can be found in rock shops and museums for as little as a dollar or two. Serenity Peterson recommends faceted emeralds for healing use,[27] but uncut and unpolished raw stones are also positive and powerful. For a woman drawn to uncut emeralds, they have an inexpensive, beautiful and healing energy. Emeralds have been confused with green tourmaline and peridot, stones that share the rich color and many of the same healing properties.

Meditation with emerald brings peace, patience, calming and heart opening love and joy. It's a stone of the goddess Moon, the lunar feminine of water and oceans, and whole realms and seas are evoked by looking into it in candle light. Thelma Isaacs says use emerald on waxing of Full Moon phases, and that green in a gemstone means growth, birth and abundance. Traditional uses for emerald are to preserve marriages and relationships by protecting fidelity. The stone is said to balance physical sexuality with emotional and mental love, and to cloud when a partner is unfaithful. It also clouds around poisons. In ancient Egypt, emeralds carved with the sign of Isis were worn to prevent miscarriages and to ease labor and delivery. All life emerges from the womb and the sea. The green soothing and regeneration of emerald is used for exhaustion and the eyes, for strengthening the aura in dis-ease and tiredness, to ease sleeplessness and nightmares, and to stimulate prophecy and prophetic dreams. It's a traveler's protection stone, especially for ocean travel, and a healer for epilepsy, blood toxins and bleeding.[28] Emerald is a promoter of gentle and gracious aging and of the appetite.

Mellie Uyldert lists emerald as a stone for the solar plexus, heart and throat, a connector of the lower and higher mind with the lower spiritual body, inspiring intellect, creativity and expression.[29] Thelma Isaacs lists it as a solar plexus gemstone, healing for the eyes, digestive system, liver, spleen, gall bladder, pancreas and adrenals, but also gives it the heart chakra attributes of drawing love, lifting depression, calming and balancing the emotions, and for all healing, aura protection and strengthening. She lists it as a remedy for demon possession, for heart dis-eases and the spine.[30]

A connector of the lower and higher mind, and a connector of the three lower with three upper chakras, emerald has the ability to stimulate and open all of the chakras at once, not as a purifier in the solar plexus sense, but as a stone that takes power in a purified aura.[31] Serenity Peterson, and Lorusso and Glick list emerald as a heart center energy exclusively, with all of the attributes of other green gemstones. The peace, love and calming of this stone inspire heart center qualities of harmony, positivity, wisdom, love, self-knowing and stable balance for all who use it. Emeralds soothe pain and are antiseptic and healing, repairing and rejuvenating for the aura and all the chakras. They cool fever and dis-ease, balance blood pressure and the nervous system, heal the heart physically and emotionally to establish order from chaos, and well-being from pain. Sending emerald in psychic healing, placing it in the aura or using it for meditation, sends the power of new growth and oceans, the green antiseptic soothing of dis-ease, and the peace of mind that transmits healing for body, emotions, mind and spirit.

With emerald, another ancient healer is precious *jade*, the prosperity and healing virtue stone of China. Jadeite is an alternate name, and nephrite is not jade, though similar in composition, but healing uses class jadeite, nephrite and jade together as they are used interchangeably. The name jade is from the Spanish *piedra de ijada*, hip stone or colic stone. It was used in South and Central America at the time of the conquistadors' intrusion to protect against kidney disease. The stone, for its nonbrittle hardness (6½-7), was used in early patriarchy for weapons, probably in the matriarchies for tools, and was considered more precious than gold in the goddess religions of China and Central America. Burma is the major mining source for jade today, and jade is found in China, Guatemala, Japan, Mexico, Canada, Greece, New Zealand, and in California, Alaska and Wisconsin in the United States. In green jade, chromium or iron causes the coloring, and jade is also pink, blue, red, violet, salmon, yellow, cream and brown. It's a noncrystalline gemstone energy.

Precious jade is the gemstone of China, though most Chinese jade today is imported for carving there from Burma. It symbolizes the five major virtues of the goddess Kwan Yin—mercy, modesty, courage, justice and wisdom. The stone used in carvings, beads or any form of jewelry, used tumbled or raw, is a charm for long life, fertility, protection, childbirth, prosperity and good luck.[32] Jade dispels negativity, bringing peaceful tranquillity to the woman that holds it or that wears it in her aura. Its soft, smooth texture is calming to touch, and it harmonizes and stabilizes feelings and emotions. It connects the heart and solar plexus chakras, the rational and intuitive mind, and has attributes for both centers.[33] Jade salves the nervous system and the eyes and is calming, stabilizing and grounding. It aids meditative states, gives wisdom and clear and perceptive thinking, removes blocks in the heart and solar plexus, stimulates healing abilities and compassion, and aids mental and physical strength.[34]

Thelma Isaacs, in her collection of sources, lists jade for peace and resolving problems, for emotional expression and heart healing, and places the various colors on the chakras that match them. She uses jade for bladder, urinary and kidney dis-eases, digestion and the eyes, for long life and easeful death, and for loyalty.[35] She uses red jade for defining emotional problems and anger, orange for learning about vitality issues and correcting them, yellow jade for the solar plexus, for digestion, bile and constipation, blue for soothing the mind, salmon jade to stimulate the adrenals, and lavender jade for love and emotional balancing.[36] Lorusso and Glick use cream jade for the eyes and nervous system, and yellow-brown jade for the liver.[37] The stone in all its colors brings issues and problems to the surface and offers the peace and wisdom to resolve them. A stone of the Chinese goddess of healing mercy, it's a gemstone of women's healing that has always been re-cognized as a healing stone.

Green aventurine is a heart chakra gemstone, a member of the quartz grouping that overlaps the throat chakra for healing. The stone comes in two similar appearances, a dark bottle green that's slightly metallic, and a lighter green shade containing inclusions of metallic darker green. In the lighter shade, the inclusions are feathery or leafy looking and caused by green mica. The color of this is green watered to almost aqua, and this particular shade has attributes similar to rose quartz for the heart, or aquamarine for heart and throat. Darker aventurine is more common, and is often seen in tumbled pieces at museum giftshops. It has basically heart center healing uses, and can be confused with jade. Both light and darker colors are used similarly to jade in beads and carvings. Both aventurine shades are noncrystalline forms of quartz, and are more brittle than jade or nephrite. Other spellings of the name are adventurine or aventurine quartz. Further colors are gold with brown in the lighter form, and blue metallic for the darker. Blue aventurine is a throat center gemstone that stimulates creativity and expression. Aventurine is found in Nepal, India, Brazil and Russia.

Aventurine with its soothing green color is primarily a heart center gemstone. It brings luck and surprises in love, games and adventures, and aids independence and originality. Mellie Ulydert lists aventurine (lighter and darker shades) for skin dis-eases,[38] which are attributed at the source to lack of love, and are a heart center healing issue. In the case of the lighter green especially, aventurine is similar in energy to rose quartz or aquamarine for calming, comforting and emotional healing. It's a cooler energy than rose quartz in temperature, bringing harmony and balance, peace and tranquillity, an easing and soothing of emotions. Use it for migraines at the end of the cycle, for headaches, sore throats, high blood pressure, the heart, eyes and hair, for self-love, loneliness and heart loss. Aventurine opens the heart and soothes a wounded heart, calms after emotional release, and stimulates talking about and expressing hurts to heal them. The stone is not quite as powerful emotionally as rose quartz, but may be more soothing. Its aqua/green color with feathery inclusions and bits, or green with metallics, is tranquilizing to look into and meditate with.

In a time of stress, while holding in my left hand a string of light aventurine beads just dis-covered and purchased, the stones darkened in color while I held them. The shade changed from a nearly ice green (the inclusions had faint shadows inside the beads) to a vivid aqua with inclusions deeper and more defined in a period of half an hour. On putting the beads down, the heightened coloring mostly remained, lightening slightly when the beads were cool again. Further holding over several days and in sleep turned them slightly darker each time and then they remained the same; very aqua but turning slightly lighter when cold. In each case of holding the beads, calming and healing occurred slowly and with gentleness, a little more each time. Cried, calmed and talked about, the problem was resolved.

Aventurine is a soothing energy that calms, balances and releases tensions. Its ability with the emotions makes it a heart center gemstone, and its color bordering on aqua overlaps with the throat center by aiding the expression of hurts to heal them. The stone opens both heart and throat, and is gentle for both.

While the lighter green aventurine moves in color and healing uses toward aqua or blue/green, it's still primarily a heart center green gemstone. Aquamarine, turquoise and chrysocolla are three blue/green stones, overlapping heart and throat healing and participating almost equally in both chakras. The throat chakra is the place of hearing and speaking, creativity and originality, the expression and release of emotions and communication. A blocked throat center is a given in patriarchal living, where frustrations are great and the risks of speaking out are high. The throat center is the lower spiritual aura body, and corresponds with woman's creativity. Opening throat center blocks allows for the release and expression of feelings awakened by opening the heart, and inspires creative work of all sorts to follow. Blue/green or light blue gemstones are good for the eyes, ears, nose and throat and their dis-eases, for swelling, fevers, inflammations, infections and burns. Blue/green stones are the best choices for vascular problems, heart dis-eases, headaches and migraines, high blood pressure, joint dis-eases that need cooling, and all stress issues of expressing and releasing emotional situations. The color for the throat chakra is clear light blue, but most throat center gemstones overlap with either heart center green (the blue/green stones) or the indigo (darker blue) gemstones of the brow chakra. Aquamarine, turquoise and chrysocolla are discussed here, and throat center gemstones overlapping the brow center are discussed in the next chapter.

Aquamarine is a lovely blue/green crystalline gemstone, one of the loveliest in women's healing. A member of the beryl grouping, the stone is the same in composition as the emerald, alexandrite and precious beryl, differing only in color. Formed in hexagonal rods, it is usually translucent, but can be transparent or opaque. The coloring is from iron, and though aquamarine colors can range from colorless/ clear to deep blue, the aqua blue/green tints are best for heart and throat chakra healing work. Dark aquamarine, of a darker blue color and less easily available, is a brow center gemstone. Though comparatively expensive, raw one-inch rods of good-colored aquamarine should cost about ten to twenty dollars. The stone's name means "sea water" in Latin, and its most desired color is the blue/green tint of the sunlit sea. Aquamarine is found on all continents, with mines in Brazil being the most prominent. The stone is mined in Australia, Russia, Sri Lanka, India, Africa and in several states of the United States: in Colorado, Connecticut, California, Maine and North Carolina. The color is distinctive, but can be confused with blue topaz.

Aquamarine is strengthening and healing. In meditation it draws the user into the waves and colors of the living sea, the peace, beauty and tranquillity of Yemaya or Tiamat at quiet rest. The stone is calming and balancing, stimulating oneness with the creative goddess and goddess-within on physical, emotional, mental and spiritual aura levels. Aquamarine is an opener of the heart and throat, stimulating emotional understanding and its expression and release. Self-knowledge is an outcome of using aquamarine, carrying it in a left-hand pocket or left hand, or wearing it as a necklace over the heart. The stone gives purpose and direction, and protection to women vulnerable to emotion while learning to express it. Traditionally, aquamarine is a physical protection for sea travelers. Its tranquilizing ability calms fears, protects vulnerability and increases intelligence. Stomach, liver, jaw and throat healing are among traditional uses.[39] Sources conflict as to chakra correspondence. Some author/healers overlap solar plexus and heart, while others the heart and throat. Personal work suggests that the heart and throat are effective, but women experiment and use what works for them. There are attributes for all three chakras.

Innocence, openness, receptivity and purity are descriptions of aquamarine healing, and women drawn to this stone encourage these qualities with it. Playfulness and fidelity, love for friends and in relationships, and psychic/mystic ability are stimulated by wearing aquamarine in the aura. Dis-eases of the neck, head and mouth are helped with aquamarine, as are laryngitis, coughs, swollen glands, toothaches and earaches, as well as stomach dis-eases and upsets.[40] Aquamarine for the eyes helps in soothing and accepting what is seen. Use aquamarine for headaches and migraines, for vascular diseases. It stimulates both the thymus (heart chakra—growth and immune system) and thyroid (throat) glands,[41] and eases the tightness and choking of not being able to get the words out. A peace-drawing relaxant, aquamarine is positive for anxiety and insomnia, for performers' stagefright, and aids flowing, giving and speaking out gently on any occasion.

Lorusso and Glick see aquamarine as a filter and purifier of emotions, similar but less powerful than emerald. It aids imbalances of any sort on the physical, emotional or mental levels, physically through the glands. They suggest charging aquamarine before healing by wrapping copper wire around it and placing it in direct sunlight for eight to twenty-four hours.[42] Copper is an electrical conductor for the prana, light and warmth of the energizing Sun, and it combines solar and lunar energies. Serenity Peterson uses aquamarine to enhance meditation and spiritual awareness, and to manifest throat center creativity on the earth plane. She recommends faceted stones, but women use what works, and have great success with raw crystals. Use it with clear quartz to amplify and focus aquamarine healing. Migraines are among the hardest of dis-eases to treat in women's healing, and aquamarine is effective and positive for them. The stone as a calmative and balancer has no equal, and matches green aventurine in this. It stabilizes impressions and emotions and aids in their expression for self-knowledge and release.

As jade is the most valued gemstone in China, *turquoise* is the primary healing and precious gemstone of southwest Native America, and also of ancient Persia/Iran. The name comes from the European origins of turquoise popularity; it was brought from Turkey during the Crusades and called Turkish stone. The Navaho name for turquoise means "sky stone." It's a wedding stone in Russia, and in the Orient it was used to protect horses and their riders; the Arab world uses turquoise for meditation.

Turquoise is a soft, opaque, massive gemstone, listing 5-6 on the Moh's scale of hardness. It's absorbent and scratches easily, and almost any influence—water, chemicals, light, soap, oils or perspiration—affect and change the color, particularly where the stone is unpolished or unglazed. Colors range from sky blue to aqua to light green, and veins or matrix of other minerals and metallics add to its interest and healing. Turquoise is found in the southwest United States, and also in Iran, Afghanistan, Australia, Tibet, Israel, Mexico and Egypt. Over 6,000 years ago, turquoise was mined in the Sinai. For the Egyptian women healers of that time, turquoise was the place where heaven and Earth meet, where past and present lives connect, and where the physical and spiritual become one. It was valued with malachite and lapis lazuli for its blue/green color.

In the southwest United States among Pueblo and Navaho peoples, turquoise is also a connector of Earth and sky, a connector of its wearer to Earth and universal energies. It's the elements of earth and air, has affinity to the blue of water, and is the only one of the four elemental gemstones (coral, jet, abalone, turquoise) that is actually a stone. In healing, turquoise connects the spiritual bodies with the other levels of existence: the physical, emotional and intellectual. A stone of balance, protection and love that overlaps the heart and throat (in some sources heart only, and in others heart, throat and solar plexus), turquoise is a stone that connects the three lower and three upper chakras, the seen and unseen bodies of woman's aura.

Protection, tranquillity and serenity, knowing woman's value and part in the universal plan are attributes of healing with turquoise. The gem is calming, balancing and grounding, a heart soother and opener of heart and throat blocks. It combines woman's will with her ability to open and give love. Great wisdom and understanding of the self and others, compassion for others is a turquoise attribute as is the openness to give and the ability to express caring in giving.[44] Thelma Isaacs recommends wearing turquoise as a necklace between the heart and throat centers for the ability to give service to others. She also uses it held in the left hand, or worn as a ring or bracelet on the left hand or arm, for personal serenity, spiritual sensitivity and inner understanding. In jewelry settings, the stone works best with silver.

Turquoise is a stone of prosperity and luck, and Native Americans use it as a guardian in death, for the period between lives.[45] It's a stone of remembrance of past lives and past life loves and inspires romantic love, particularly in karmic reunions. It aids fidelity and long-term love in friendships and relationships. The stone absorbs negativity, to the point of even being shattered by it in protection of its wearer.[46]

In physical healing, use turquoise for all health and prosperity, for peace of mind, release of tensions, grounding and balancing, and high blood pressure. Use it for the eyes, especially eye inflammations, all sorts of inflammations, fevers, swellings, wounds,[47] and the easing of headaches and migraines. Julia Lorusso and Joel Glick use turquoise for the lungs and respiratory system, solar plexus healing, but note it as an ancient gemstone losing its powers and chrysocolla becoming its successor. For those drawn to it, however, turquoise retains great healing ability. It stimulates breast milk, protects against falls and depression, absorbs trauma and shocks of all sorts, works well in cooling and in soothing burns, calming digestive upsets and spasms, and lessens asthma and epilepsy.[48]

Connecting woman physically and spiritually with the Earth and sky, turquoise grounds her feet in the physical plane and her Be-ing in the universe and goddess creation. It's a stone of Spider Woman, whose thread of life connects all that lives with her essence. Turquoise aids heart ailments and heart loss and stimulates imagination, creativity, hearing, inspiration and physical all-healing. Bluer forms are more overlapping with the throat center, while greener stones are centered in the heart and overlap the solar plexus.

The last heart/throat healer and blue/green gemstone is *chrysocolla* that Julia Lorusso and Joel Glick lists as an upcoming gemstone energy evolving to replace turquoise (as previously mentioned). Chrysocolla is a massive and opaque blue/green gemstone often mistaken for turquoise, but differing in chemical composition. Its streaks and matrix are green or white, and the stone's blue to green color is brighter in general than is most turquoise. Chrysocolla is a soft gemstone, only listing 2-4 on the Moh's scale. It's mined in Arizona and Nevada, and in Mexico, Russia, Chile and Zaire. Found mixed with quartz, it's called chrysocolla quartz, and found with turquoise and malachite is the Israeli Eilat Stone. Eilat stone is a deeper green color, interspersed with blue. Neither Serenity Peterson or Mellie Uyldert discusses chrysocolla, and Thelma Isaacs discounts it as a healer except to conjecture that it may be the unknown stone that Edgar Cayce incorrectly called lapis.[49] Katrina Raphaell, Julia Lorusso and Joel Glick, and personal experience all value this gemstone highly, and dis-cover it to be a major healer. Katrina Raphaell uses the translucent and more rare gem quality chrysocolla, gem silica, in her healing. This is mined in New Mexico and South America, and is less easy to find than the massive form.

A personal experience: at a time of writer's block and anxiety,

I was drawn to buy a small piece of chrysocolla at a museum gift shop. The price was a dollar for a porous, foamy looking piece about an inch round, crumbly, irregularly shaped and of a lovely bright aqua color. Holding the stone in my left hand while working, it took less than half an hour to calm and ground fully, release all nervousness and a headache, slow breathing and heart rate, and begin writing again.

The stone held at night aids insomnia, soothes and eases restlessness for peaceful sleep. A definite feeling of throat chakra tingling and opening accompany its use, comparable only to using lapis lazuli—another of the more powerful healing gemstones. Chrysocolla is a heart center opener and soother, an opener of throat chakra creativity and inspiration, and a physically and emotionally calming gemstone for the intellect and nervous system (solar plexus). It bridges daily consciousness to creative/meditative awareness and peace, connecting the lower three with the upper three chakras and aura bodies.

Lorusso and Glick recommend chrysocolla as a gemstone elixir or ingested as a crumbled powder for these dis-eases. Use it for arthritis and joint problems.[50] Lorusso and Glick also recommend chrysocolla for the solar plexus, to ease fears, anxieties and guilt, and prevent ulcers and digestive upsets. They note that the stone will be re-cognized for cancer therapy, particularly in karmic origin cancers.[51]

Katrina Raphaell, who has great regard for gem silica/chrysocolla, calls it a feminine lunar gemstone, representative of the calm giving of such goddesses as Yemaya, Mary or Kwan Yin. She uses the stone for drawing peace and the goddess-within, for the qualities of patience, compassion, forgiveness and tolerance for others and the self. A women's gemstone is used for women's healing, and Raphaell recommends chrysocolla for menstrual cramps and backaches, and for premenstrual syndrome nerves and depression. She uses it for healing after miscarriages, abortions, hysterectomies, and during and after childbirth for emotional and physical healing.[52] With its qualities of healing internally and emotionally, for easing fear, guilt, pain and anger/rage, the stone would also be helpful in rape recovery or recovery from other abusive situations.

In heart center work, use chrysocolla or gem silica/chrysocolla to balance the emotions and open the heart. Like rose quartz, it sweetens emotions, releases anger, and soothes grief and emotional pain into understandintg, acceptance and self-acceptance. It helps in the ability to feel compassion for others, and universal love. Katrina

Raphaell uses chrysocolla as a representative stone of peace, for peace of mind and heart, and the peace that is harmony with others and with the natural flowing of the Earth and universe. Use translucent gem silica for scrying and clairvoyant sight, and this or opaque forms of chrysocolla for meditation work. It activates the transpersonal point center beyond the body, the center of goddess consciousness.[53]

In physical healing, use chrysocolla for infections, wounds, burns, fevers, as an antiseptic and generally soothing all-issue healer. Use it to calm and release tension, lower blood pressure, treat insomnia, headaches and migraines. As a throat center gemstone, chrysocolla opens intuition and creativity, and is a throat and voice healer. It also stimulates the thyroid, and eases neck and shoulder pain from muscle tension. Use it for all types of spasms; for epilepsy, asthma, ulcers, multiple sclerosis, nervousness, to release guilt, for digestive problems, and to connect the physical, emotional and intellectual bodies and chakras with the spiritual levels and the goddess.[54] A gemstone of women's healing, chrysocolla/gem silica is a goddess gift to women, worthy of much further work and dis-covery.

Gemstones for the throat chakra are also overlapping energies for heart and sometimes solar plexus healing. The solar plexus and the heart, the rational and intuitive mental bodies, merge in healing with the throat center's creativity, an expression of the knowledge of the two chakras below it and the brow above it. The throat is the lower spiritual body, and much of women's healing involves an opening of the spiritual, while unifying spirituality with the physical, emotional and mental levels of Be-ing. Heart and throat center gemstones work together in this for women's well-being. The throat/brow center gemstones of the next chapter merge with gemstones for the brow and crown chakras, the transpersonal point, to connect woman's unified Be-ing with the goddess and goddess-within.

FOOTNOTES

1. Mellie Uyldert, *The Magic of Precious Stones* (Great Britain, Turnstone Press, 1981), p. 58.

2. *Ibid.,* p. 100.

3. Katrina Raphaell, *Crystal Enlightenment* (New York, Aurora Press, 1985), p. 139. Raphaell's work with rose quartz is sensitive and beautiful, and personal experience verifies her findings. The stone is the author's healing favorite.

4. Gemstoned, Ltd., *Crystal Essence* (New York, Gemstoned Ltd., 1984), unpaged pamphlet. Note the throat center attributes here.

5. Ida Shaw, workshop handout, National Women's Music Festival, 1986.

6. Serenity Peterson, *Crystal Visioning, A Crystal Workshop* (Nashville, TN, Interdimensional Publishing, 1984), p. 56.

7. Katrina Raphaell, *Crystal Enlightenment*, p. 120.

8. Julia Lorusso and Joel Glick, *Healing Stoned* (Albuquerque, NM, Brotherhood of Life, 1985, original 1977), p. 66-67.

9. Mellie Uyldert, *The Magic of Precious Stones*, p. 125.

10. Most of these attributes are from Katrina Raphaell, *Crystal Enlightenment*, p. 117-120, and from Gemstoned Ltd., *Crystal Essence*, pamphlet.

11. Katrina Raphaell, *Crystal Enlightenment*, p. 120-121.

12. *Ibid.,* p. 128-129.

13. Mellie Uyldert, *The Magic of Precious Stones,* p. 136.

14. Katrina Raphaell *Crystal Enlightenment,* p. 126.

15. Thelma Isaacs, *Gemstones, Crystals and Healing* (Black Mountain, NC, Lorien House, 1982), p. 93.

16. *Ibid.*

17. Katrina Raphaell, *Crystal Enlightenment,* p. 130.

18. *Ibid.,* p. 130-131.

19. Julia Lorusso and Joel Glick, *Healing Stoned,* p. 74-75.

20. Katrina Raphaell, *Crystal Enlightenment*, p. 133-134.

21. Ida Shaw, workshop handout.

22. Julia Lorusso and Joel Glick, *Healing Stoned*, p. 76.

23. Katrina Raphaell, *Crystal Enlightenment*, p. 129-130.

24. *Ibid.*

25. Thelma Isaacs, *Gemstones, Crystals and Healing*, p. 93.

26. Mellie Uyldert, *The Magic of Precious Stones,* p. 110.

27. Serenity Peterson, *Crystal Visioning*, p. 49.

28. Mellie Uyldert, *The Magic of Precious Stones,* p. 110.

29. *Ibid.*

30. Thelma Isaacs, *Gemstones, Crystals and Healing*, p. 35-36.

31. Julia Lorusso and Joel Glick, *Healing Stoned*, p. 34.

32. Mellie Uyldert, *The Magic of Precious Stones,* p. 130.

33. Julia Lorusso and Joel Glick, *Healing Stoned*, p. 39-40.

34. Serenity Peterson, *Crystal Visioning*, p. 50-51.

35. Thelma Isaacs, *Gemstones, Crystals and Healing*, p. 62-63.

36. *Ibid.*

37. Julia Lorusso and Joel Glick, *Healing Stoned*, p. 40.

38. Mellie Uyldert, *The Magic of Precious Stones*, p. 97.

39. Thelma Isaacs, *Gemstones, Crystals and Healing*, p. 34-35.

40. Mellie Uyldert, *The Magic of Precious Stones,* p. 110-111.

41. Gemstoned Ltd., *Crystal Essence*, unpaged pamphlet.

42. Julia Lorusso and Joel Glick, *Healing Stoned*, p. 28-29.

43. Mellie Uyldert, *The Magic of Precious Stones*, p. 134.

44. Thelma Isaacs, *Gemstones, Crystals and Healing*, p. 94-96.

45. *Ibid.*

46. Mellie Uyldert, *The Magic of Precious Stones*, p. 133.

47. Thelma Isaacs, *Gemstones, Crystals and Healing*, p. 95.

48. Julia Lorusso and Joel Glick, *Healing Stoned*, p. 79.

49. Thelma Isaacs, *Gemstones, Crystals and Healing*, p. 39.

50. Gemstoned Ltd., *Crystal Essence,* unpaged pamphlet.

51. Julia Lorusso and Joel Glick, *Healing Stoned,* p. 30.

52. Katrina Raphaell, *Crystal Enlightenment,* p. 102-103. Much of the reference for chrysocolla/gems silica is from Katrina Raphaell and personal work.

53. *Ibid.,* p. 103-105.

54. *Ibid.,* p. 104.

Colored Gemstones:
Spiritual Body Centers

IN THE spiritual body—the chakras and aura levels involving the throat, brow, crown and transpersonal point—the gemstones overlap. While blue and blue/green stones are classed usually as throat center gemstones, the major blue/indigo healers (lapis lazuli, sodalite, fluorite, blue sapphire) are brow chakra energies that often activate both throat and third eye. Opaque or translucent white gemstones for the brow center also are crown chakra designates— moonstone, white precious opal, chalcedony, moss agate and beige selenite. The place of merging between the centers is not a clear one. The most representative crown chakra gemstone, amethyst, is listed variously as a crown or brow chakra energy. Crown and transpersonal point energies also overlap, and some systems combine them as one center. The all-aura clear/rainbow/white gemstones—zircon, diamond, rutile and clear quartz crystal—are transpersonal point gemstones or crown center ones. They contain all of the colors of the aura spectrum rainbow, and are used for all-aura healing. While the chakras and their gemstones are organized in as logical a sequence as possible here, the healer realizes this overlapping and uses the material in ways that work best for her.

The reason for the overlap is the close interconnectedness and progression of spiritual body qualities. The lower spiritual level, the throat chakra, corresponds with hearing (admitting others into one's consciousness), and the speaking, expression and creativity coming

245

from the heart and the spiritual that make this a two-way admission. Physical ears and hearing are only one level of doing this. The quality of an individual woman's spirituality is expressed from her throat center. The center's color is light blue, overlapping to blue/green in interaction with the heart, and overlapping to indigo/darker blue in interaction with the brow. The throat represents the Crone in the Maiden/Mother/Crone triad.

The indigo brow chakra is involved with woman's universal connection to others, her sense of oneness with the Earth and all that lives, of being part of the whole. This represents the Mother, and is an increase in awareness from the hearing and speaking of the throat center. Brow chakra healing involves sight and psychic sight, along with all other senses, on the level of non-physical sensitivity. Spiritual knowing is a major activity and result of an open brow center, the extra-physical sight of the third eye that is vision and intuition combined with certainty and wisdom. This level is a step beyond that of the intuition/inspiration/imagination of the throat chakra.

Developing the brow or third eye is to develop inner knowledge, psychic sensitivity and interconnectedness with others. Creative visualization, seeing auras, and empathy/telepathy links are located here. An open heart and third eye together are powerful and essential for psychic healing—compassion and knowing, giving and wisdom. Third eye healing includes relief of fear and pain, sedating, calming, positivity, slowing blood flow, building immunity and white blood cells, fighting infection and accepting reality. Indigo and white gemstones for third eye healing decrease rate of breathing and metabolism and cause contracting, drying, thickening and hardening. Eyes, ears, nose and lungs are all brow center healings, as are asthma, bronchitis, tuberculosis and pneumonia. Hearing loss, mental and nervous dis-orders, upset stomachs and nervous system dis-eases of epilepsy, multiple sclerosis, Alzheimer's dis-ease, manic-depression and Parkinson's dis-ease are all brow chakra healings.[1] Indigo is a highly electrical energy that is also (along with the light blue and blue/green of the throat chakra) a complement to orange. Opaque white gemstones are soothing energies, building immunities, white blood cells and psychic openness, fostering interconnection with others and connectedness to the goddess/source, and functioning as psychic reality mirrors. They also stimulate breast milk and fertility, a reflection in women of the goddess as nourisher of the universe.

For the violet crown center, the major healing gemstone is amethyst, but other crown chakra energies are shared with the brow and transpersonal point. The line between indigo and violet is a thin one, and the opaque white gemstones bridge the two levels. Some chakra systems use white with a golden center for the crown chakra color, and some systems combine the crown and transpersonal point. Where the brow chakra is interconnection with others and the Earth, the crown chakra is woman's interconnection with the goddess and Be-ing, her participation in creative divinity. Pure knowing and pure intuition— brow center attributes on a higher level—are crown center attributes. Meditation, trancework, spiritism, and connection with spirit guides are located on these levels, with the crown being the highest level of psychic development skills. This is the level of the Maiden.

Crown center healing involves calming, purifying and centering, reducing stress and all nervous system dis-eases, healing tumors, injuries and dis-eases of the head and brain. High blood pressure, headaches and insomnia are violet crown chakra healing, and white crown gemstones slow the motor system and heart rate, decrease glandular activity, and stimulate the spleen and immune system. Violet and white gemstones decrease sexuality and sensitivity to pain, aid colds and sinus conditions, meningitis and spinal dis-eases, hair loss, concussion and brain dis-eases[2]—as do indigo gemstones. Connection with the crown center is connection with the goddess, and healing from this place comes direct from the source. Profound changes and deep inner peace are a result of crown center opening and healing, of becoming a channel through all the chakras from head to feet. The connection with the goddess, the Hopi concept of *kopavi* or African theme of the *sekpoli,* is total harmony, creativity, well-being and peace, a oneness of the seen and unseen, of the physical, emotional, mental and spiritual.

Since the transpersonal point is beyond the body but is part of the body's aura, healing for this center is combined with the crown. Its clear/rainbow color is the crystalline energies of zircon, diamond and rutile quartz, and the all-healing clear quartz crystal that brings gemstone work back full circle. These gemstones work with the entire aura field, rather than a particular place on the physical body. They contain all colors for all the levels, and work on a level beyond the seen. White gemstones in a higher octave are the clear/rainbow ones, and connection with the goddess taken to the higher level of

the goddess herself is transpersonal point energy and gemstones.

Transpersonal point healing is a question, since beyond the
dense physical and with no physical correspondents, and beyond the
connection with the source to the source herself, there can be nothing less than well-being. The woman connected with and open to the
all-colors of the transpersonal point is a channel for health and healing energy in herself and for others. Partaking of the goddess and
open to her, she is the goddess-within. All of women's spirituality
reaches toward this place, the free channel of energy and connection
with the goddess, the Maiden, Mother and Crone as one unity and
thought form. This is also the unity of the four bodies in women and is
kundalini opened safely and positively. The throat, brow, crown
and transpersonal point gemstones and chakras offer healing on
spiritual levels, aiming for the direct interconnection and working
with the goddess.

Gemstones for the spiritual body begin with *lapis lazuli,* a blue/
indigo gemstone for the throat and brow chakras, the lower and middle
spiritual levels of the Crone and Mother. Lapis, along with amethyst
and chrysocolla and after clear quartz, is the most representative of
healing gemstones, an all-healer more versatile than any other of the
colored gemstones, and is known as a healer throughout herstory.
This was a stone of Isis for the women of ancient Egypt, along with
malachite and turquoise. Sky and water colors are sacred to the
goddess, connectors of the spiritual with the earthly, and carved
yonis of lapis lazuli were offerings of respect to the goddess and the
feminine in ancient Egypt and Assyria. Mellie Uyldert notes that lapis
lazuli is a gemstone devoted to Mary,[3] its color often the color of her
robe in paintings, and researchers believe that Mary was derived
from Isis/Ishtar. Lapis Lazuli is a love-drawing gemstone, also
dedicated to Venus/Aphrodite.

A massive, noncrystalline, opaque gemstone ranging from light
to indigo blue, lapis is also called lazulite and is confused with sodalite
that it's chemically related to. The stone is identified from sodalite by
its golden pyrite inclusions. Sodalite's inclusions and streaks are
white, and sodalite is a deeper, greyer blue. Of healing gemstones,
lapis lazuli is relatively rare and highly valued both for jewelry and
healing. It's expensive as well, and less easy to find than many other
gemstones. Afghanistan is the major source for high quality,

magnificently blue lapis, and deposits in Russia and Chile are less valued because they are not so evenly blue in color. The blue in these is grainy and broken up by white calcite. The stone is also found in Burma, Mexico, Egypt and the Andes. Swiss lapis is not lapis lazuli, but a form of jasper dyed for the blue and gold-flecked appearance of it. Needless to say, jasper and lapis have different healing qualities. The name lapis lazuli is Arabic, and means "blue stone." It measures 5-6 on the Moh's scale.

Lapis lazuli is an overall toner and all-healer. Its lovely clear blue color is extremely powerful in cooling and calming, and for infections, swelling, wounds, inflammations and bacterial dis-eases. It's the most major gemstone for reducing pain and for use on burns, sunburns, earaches, fevers and blood dis-eases. Send it in psychic healing and use it with clear crystal; wear it on a necklace near the throat to open the throat chakra and the brow center/third eye.[4] It aids expression, speech, hearing, eloquence, self-confidence, singing, writing and all forms of creativity. Wearing lapis as a necklace, the throat center tingles as does the brow. It stimulates the thyroid and endocrine glands and balances all energy transmission throughout the bodies, opens, purifies and balances all of the chakras, aura levels and meridians. It stimulates and balances the central nervous system, the spinal column, nerves and brain—the seen and unseen bodies' entire electrical network.[5] The stone also effects kundalini. A feeling of overall excitement, joy, well-being and positive, hopeful energy results from wearing lapis lazuli.

As a meditation tool, lapis opens psychic abilities, the third eye, clairvoyance and clairaudience, and aids in creative visualization for use in telepathy and psychic healing. Empath/telepath links are increased with lapis, though more so with moonstone. Wear it on a headband over the brow to increase ESP and instant knowing. It stimulates spirituality, and brings out qualities from within, enhances women's creativity and her feeling of interconnection with others and the Earth. The brow chakra has no recognition of negativity, and lapis dispels negativity, heals dis-ease and raises moods.[6] Hold it in the left hand or place it over the area to dispel physical pain. Use it for headaches and migraines, and to bring a mood of calm, harmony and peace. Its ancient altar uses carved as women's genitals suggest it for women's healing, for birth and birth recovery, for menstruation, menopause, abortion recovery, hysterectomy, rape recovery. It's a stone positive for incest survivors, and multiple sclerosis.[7] Katrina

Raphaell suggests its use as an aura cleanser to release past pain, and for this advises lapis used with other healing stones. Green aventurine, rose quartz or amethyst are suggested, as lapis lazuli in this releases the subconscious for other stones to do the healing.[8]

For Mellie Uyldert, lapis is a protection stone and a stone of friendship, to draw love and heal love loss. It brings kindness and cooperation, harmony in relationships, strengthens the will, and aids insomnia. She uses it for shyness, to prevent strokes, for the heart, blood and spleen, for epilepsy and the skin. As an elixir, she uses lapis as an eyewash.[9] One of the most powerful of healing gemstones, lapis lazuli was known to ancient healers and is known in women's healing today.

Sodalite is listed in some sources interchangeably with lapis, and contains a number of shared properties with it, but is not the same. A member of the lapis lazuli family, it differs from lapis chemically and in inclusions, and does not often contain the pyrites that lapis is known for. Streaks are white calcite, and the stone is smoother grained and deeper blue. Sodalite is found in Brazil, Canada, Namibia and the United States, and is much less rare and less expensive than lapis. Serenity Peterson and Thelma Isaacs classify it with and the same as lapis lazuli, while personal experience finds it very different. Julia Lorusso and Joel Glick discount its properties as being similar but denser than lapis. They note its use in metabolic deficiencies, metabolism and glandular balance, and recommend it for diabetics, as it balances the Islets of Langerhans.[10] Use it with clear quartz crystal to amplify and intensify sodalite's healing power. As an indigo gemstone, sodalite has the cooling, drying and anti-inflammatory attributes of lapis. Use it for wounds, infections, inflammations, burns and swellings, for blood and vascular dis-eases, for headaches, sinus conditions and high blood pressure.

A grounding, calming and centering gemstone energy, sodalite clears the mind for deeper and more wise thinking. It aids logic along with opening third eye intuition, stabilizing mental processes and aiding the shift from emotional to rational/reality thinking. Use it for intellectual understanding of emotional situations and for self-knowing. For women who are oversensitive or who over-react emotionally, sodalite is positive and grounding. Katrina Raphaell uses sodalite to clear old mental patterns, opening the way for new habits and thought forms.[11] The stone, like lapis lazuli, is a purifier, and healer/writer Phyllis Galde recommends it for "radiation healing, nausea, raising consciousness and spiritualizing emotions."[12] Use it for inner sight, perspective, logic and understanding, for third eye wisdom and knowing, and for multiple sclerosis. Sodalite is powerful and positive for women who are drawn to it. The stone is more for brow than throat chakra healing.

The most representative indigo gemstone for the brow chakra is *blue sapphire,* though the stone the ancients called sapphire was often lapis lazuli. Colors range from very light blue to deep indigo, merging into violet. Sapphires also come in other colors: yellow, orange, green, pink and black, and are healers for the chakras that the colors match. Ruby is red sapphire, the difference in composition is only in the color. Iron and titanium are the coloring agents in blue sapphire, while ruby's red color is from chrome. Both are corundums, as are other colors of the sapphire/ruby grouping. For brow center healing, the darker blues are most powerful, while lighter blues overlap with the throat chakra. Sapphires are less rare and less expensive than rubies, and are found in Australia, Burma, Sri Lanka, Thailand, India, Africa, Cambodia, and Montana in the United States. Star sapphires are found in Finland. The stone is very hard, 9 on the Moh's scale; only diamond is harder. A crystalline gemstone, sapphires can be confused with blue tourmaline, and have also been synthesized.

Blue sapphire is a widely used healing gemstone, an opener of the brow chakra with throat center qualities. Its attribute of astringent, electrical cooling works for fevers, infections, burns, swellings and inflammations. In throat center healing, it inspires creativity and friendship, soothes sore throats, earaches and throat coughs, and inspires spirituality and spiritual expression. As a brow chakra gemstone, sapphire reduces bleeding, dispels negativity and depression, aids in circulatory and vascular dis-eases and heals the senses. It's a gemstone for quiet, spirituality-minded women, the scholars, priestesses and poets, bringing them harmony, clarity and peace.[13] Sapphire is positive for the nervous system and for mental and nervous healing, for the energy field of the aura as a protector and sealant. It raises energy levels, soothes the adrenal glands, stabilizes heart rate, and draws power-within, courage, devotion and psychic knowing.[14] For Serenity Peterson, blue sapphire connects the higher mind (heart chakra) with the spiritual centers (throat, brow, crown), and is a cleanser and purifier.[15]

Mellie Uyldert says blue sapphire should be worn constantly as a necklace by those who are drawn to it.[16] Thelma Isaacs uses it as a ring to draw off negativity, but says never as a necklace, as it draws in negativity from others.[17] Women who choose a particular gemstone energy dis-cover how best to use it for their needs. Follow women's intuition. Where the stone is of darker blue, indigo is a color that cannot express negativity in any form, dispelling it rather than drawing or sending it.

Blue sapphire for Uyldert brings innocence, purity, optimism and joy, calms the nerves, and aids thinking and concentration. It's a binding love token for fidelity and long-term relationships, a stone of love, truth, faith, prophecy, peace of mind and imagination. Sapphire clears thinking and aids understanding and wise knowing, and is a good meditation stone. In physical healing, she uses it for nose-bleeds, hemorrhages, eye problems and vision, for asthma, ulcers, insomnia, the heart and blood, neuroses, and mental/nervous calming.[18] Use it for degenerative nerve and nervous system dis-eases, for mental confusion and delusion, for migraines. Multiple sclerosis, Alzheimer's dis-ease and dementia are indigo sapphire healing, and indigo gemstones are positive for dispelling pain and fear.

Three varieties of sapphire are included here: blue, indigo and blue star sapphire. For Julia Lorusso and Joel Glick, star sapphires have a more subtle energy form than clear blue sapphire, and in the clear sapphires they value the darker blues/indigos most. They consider the lighter clear blues as a different stone entirely from clear indigos, and use them for mood raising, optimism and meditation, for the throat center rather than the brow. They see the darker-than-indigo black sapphire as mutant and negative,[19] while Thelma Isaacs uses black sapphire as an all-aura protection stone and for grounding. She says star sapphires work on the chakras, and clear indigo sapphires on the aura as a whole, the lighter blue gems on the higher mental (heart) plane.[20] Many of the all-healing qualities attributed to lapis lazuli are also present in blue sapphire.

Another brow chakra healing energy, and unique in its mineral form, is *fluorite*. Cleaving naturally into translucent or transparent crystal octahedrons, the form of a double pyramid, fluorite occurs mainly in indigo, purple, gold and white—all brow and crown center colors—as well as less often in blues, greens, oranges, reds and pinks.

Colors are solid or mixed and spotted inside a crystal. The stone is also found in crystalline clusters, and in jewelry can be cut, shaped and faceted. The stone is soft for jewelry use, 4 on the Moh's scale, and is brittle and fragile. Fluorite octahedrons are commonly available at museums and rock shops, and sell for a couple of dollars; sizes of crystals vary. They are easily glued to mountings for pendant and pendulum use, or carried in a left hand pocket to influence the aura. Fluorite is found in West Germany, England and in the United States.

Of the major references used for gemstones in this book, only Katrina Raphaell works seriously with fluorite, though Julia Lorusso and Joel Glick mention its grounding and transmuting properties. Personal experience has had great success with fluorite, in psychic opening, grounding, and the calming that comes from awareness of a universal plan. Of the four major fluorite colors, all are brow chakra energies or brow and crown chakra mergings. A feeling of connected-ness to others and the goddess, of being a positive and right part of the whole, comes from wearing fluorite on a necklace or holding it in the left hand. Fluorite octahedrons in a left pocket stimulate the feeling of walking in a protective shell, almost of being invulnerable, invisible if wished, and of being surrounded by indigo/purple light. Held in front of a lighted candle and scryed through, fluorites are an empowering meditation tool, with positive journeys and insights gained from working with them. The colors and markings inside their translucence, or their translucence alone, are always interesting and expanding. Meditation with fluorite is a healing for stress situations, aids problem solving, and is calming before sleep.

Katrina Raphaell, in *Crystal Enlightenment*, uses fluorite as a balancer of polarities of all sorts, and an integrator of knowledge and wisdom for an outcome of grounding and peace. Fluorite connects the experience of the goddess with daily living, for creative Be-ing on the physical plane and the ability to distinguish reality from illusion. For healing, Raphaell uses fluorite octahedrons and clusters for mental and nervous disturbances and brain wave/brain pattern dis-eases (epilepsy, Parkinson's, stroke prevention). It develops concentration and intellect along with expansion of consciousness and spirituality: she calls it the "genius stone."[21]

Of the four most common fluorite colors:

Blue is the color of inner peace, mental calmness and serenity.
Purple represents the devotional aspect of a mind that is focused

on and committed to spirit. Gold is the color of wisdom and understanding, where the mind merges with infinity and still maintains individual expression. White is the color of purity and oneness. . . . [22]

All are useful in brow chakra/crown connecting, and in laying on of stones are useful on all of the upper chakras, the throat (try a lighter blue one), brow (try darker blue/indigo), and the crown (use violet, white or gold above the head). For a balancing exercise in laying on of stones, Raphaell suggests holding a fluorite octahedron in each hand and placing one over each eyebrow.[23] The result is a feeling of calm centeredness and great peace.

For a fuller laying on of stones with fluorite, she uses seven stones, a larger one at the hairline on the center forehead, smaller ones over each eyebrow, larger ones at the throat and navel, and two smaller ones at the root chakra.[24] These stimulate conscious and subconscious knowing, expression of higher consciousness, and direction of higher consciousness into the physical. Other layouts with fluorite might include pink or green octahedrons at the heart chakra (very soothing), or where the colors are available, using them to match each center. Put clear quartz crystals or white octahedrons in each hand. Violet/indigo fluorites at the solar plexus are calming and harmonizing for women who are stressed or anxious—balance them with indigo and violet fluorite crystals at the brow and crown. Design an all-chakra laying on of stones using indigo, violet, gold and white octahedrons with clear quartz crystals. The clarity and peacefulness of mind that fluorite brings, the feeling of protection and being taken care of, the help in problem solving, has to be experienced to be appreciated. Less involved in physical dis-ease than in the mind, brain and spiritual centers, fluorite octahedrons bring spiritual-level healing.

Opaque or translucent white gemstones are energies that bridge the third eye/brow with the crown center. While various sources conflict in chakra designations, listing various stones as being for the crown or the brow, the overlap is an important function of all of them to emphasize. White gemstones listed here are moonstone, white/precious opal, white chalcedony/moss agate, and off-white selenite/desert rose. These are brow center energies in their opening of the third eye for awareness, understanding, and psychic sensitivity, and crown chakra gemstones for their connecting to oneness and the goddess. Peace of mind, spiritual strength, universal detached love, the balancing of emotions, and inner nourishment and knowing are attributes of these gemstones.

Moonstone is the precious stone of India, a stone of Cancer or Libra in the zodiac, and a gem of the feminine goddess of lunar energy. A member of the feldspar grouping, it's a translucent cream or colorless stone with a sheen to it like moonlight. Asterism/cat's eyes are possible, and the coloring varies from pearly grey, to white, to slightly peach. It can be confused with chalcedony, and moonstone is mined in India, Burma, Sri lanka, Australia, Brazil, Switzerland and the Malagasy Republic, and is found in several states in the United States. Hardness is 6-6½ on the Moh's scale, fairly hard after the softness of fluorite (4), and although used for jewelry and considered a precious gemstone, it is inexpensive in the raw state. Moonstone in jewelry is usually cut into oval/cabochon form and highly polished, but raw moonstone is powerful, beautiful and positive for healing—and quite cheap.

Meditation with moonstone calls into consciousness the three-form moon phase goddesses, Diana/Selene/Hecate, the waxing, Full and waning Moon. These are woman as goddess in her ages and contradictions, Maiden/Mother/Crone. The goddess is all-giver/birther and all-taker/death, and her opposites and phases are truths and necessary. Moonstone is a balancing energy between the opposites/polarities/triads/dualities in women's Be-ing. It's a stone for meditation on the wheel of life, for knowing, understanding, appreciating and flowing with it, and for learning to balance and reconcile the phases in the self. Moonstone stimulates awareness and self-awareness, opens psychic sensitivity more powerfully than any other of the brow or crown chakra gemstones. It neutralizes negativity by awareness.

Moonstone is a psychic mirror (its other names are dreamstone and hopestone), and in Vicki Noble's words, "What you hope for, you also fear."[25] Hopes, fears and dreams are from the lunar subconscious, the non-verbal, intuitive woman's unseen self, and moonstone amplifies these and makes them felt in the rational mind. This is positive if used positively for a journey of dis-covery into the labyrinth, but negative if the knowledge is feared or resisted. Women using moonstone use mood awareness with it, avoiding it when feeling angry or negative, or using it in these times actively to dispel negativities and to calm them. Connected to the Moon, moonstone waxes and wanes in her phases, and with women's physical and emotional lunar cycles. Use it for clarity of mind, astral and earthly sensitivity, to protect and strengthen the aura or inner journeys.[26] Use it for calming, hope and inner peace, and for accepting/recognizing realities.

A gemstone of the Moon is a woman's healing gemstone, and moonstone helps in balancing women's menstrual and hormonal cycles in menarche, menstruation and menopause. It aids the endocrine and pineal glands, and is a lymphatic cleanser for stimulating the immune system. It protects the astral/emotional aura body, and helps to both stabilize emotions and connect them to spiritual Be-ing. Over-reaction and over-emotion, being swung by emotional or hormonal tides, is balanced by using moonstone.[27] Use it for premenstrual syndrome and irregular cycles, for difficult menstruation, for going through menopause, and for soothing emotionally during any stress. Use it for nervousness on the Full Moon or depression on the waning Moon, and for manic-depressive syndrome—moonstone is a balancer. Use it to stimulate psychic experiences, for psychometry and meditation during the dark Moon phase, for far-seeing and clairvoyance at the Full Moon.

White gemstones stimulate breast milk and white blood cells, fertility and immunity against dis-ease. In Arabia, moonstone is a talisman for women's fertility, sewn into clothing, and is hung on fruit trees in blossom for plentiful fruit.[28] Use moonstone for immunity and strengthening when tired or run down, when recovering from dis-ease, for dropsy, tuberculosis, cancer, degenerative cell or nerve dis-eases, for multiple sclerosis. Try it for sinus conditions and for colds, and for any dis-ease of the eyes and senses, for insomnia,[29] and to stimulate vivid dreams and lucid dreaming. Hold it in the left hand or place it under the pillow when going to sleep, particularly from the Full to New Moon phase.

Mellie Uyldert uses moonstone to favor new love, for inspiration, success and the development of love, for the hope of love. It separates illusion from reality, enemies from friends, false from true love situations. Held in the mouth, it separates true from false actions and makes the distinctions clear, impresses priorities on the consciousness while allowing the rest to fade.[30] It helps in finding purpose and direction, in problem solving and decision-making. Uyldert credits moonstone to the zodiac sign of Cancer, while Katrina Raphaell credits it to Libra. The Moon in her balance, power, flowing, phases and peaceful life cycles is symbolized by moonstone in women's healing.

Three less re-cognized white gemstones for the brow and crown are white chalcedony, moss agate and selenite. Chalcedony is a confusing grouping, as it includes agates and jaspers in a variety of colors with a variety of chakra designations and healing uses. *White chalcedony* and *moss agate* are the specific stones here, but other forms and colors are carnelian (belly chakra), blue lace agate (throat), chrysoprase (heart center), onyx and heliotrope/bloodstone (root), and all the other agates and jaspers used for healing. White chalcedony is a fibrous form of micro-crystalline quartz that resembles moonstone for its sheen and translucent coloring. Its hardness is 7 on the Moh's scale, and it's found in several states in the United States, in California, Colorado and as part of the petrified forests of Arizona, plus in Brazil, India and Iceland. Another name for it is white carnelian, and translucent forms are called Oriental chalcedony, while opaque ones are called Occidental chalcedony. The stone is never found clear.

Mellie Uyldert calls white chalcedony "mother stone," and uses it as a stone for healing and nourishment. She uses it to stimulate breast milk and maternal feelings, a mirror in women of goddess nourishment from the universe. She uses it for binding broken bones and wounds, to stop bleeding, and to protect against poisoning and hypnosis.[31] A white healing gemstone of the crown and third eye, white chalcedony calms and raises moods, helps insomnia, physical healing, and aids in coherent thinking. It stabilizes the emotions, raises vitality and immunity, and offers strength in times of emotional need. White chalcedony is a protection to travelers and from natural disasters, a good luck and good health stone. It aids truthfulness in relationships, victories in legal matters, promotes chastity and sobriety, and heals the throat. The stone is antiseptic and purifying, holds and sends properties transmitted into it, and is a shield and cleanser against negativity, a shield from the stresses and pain of the outside world.[32] Connection with others in impersonal/univeral ways and connection with psychic and physical nourishment are chalcedony attributes, as is receptivity to psychic experiences and psychic/aura/emotional protection.

Moss agate is a white chalcedony with darker streaks and

inclusions, mossy dark cloud forms inside the light, translucent gemstone. The composition is $SiO_2 + H_2O$, the silicon dioxide of chalcedony and clear quartz crystal, plus water. Hardness is 6½-7. Moss agate is a semi-precious crystalline gemstone valued primarily for jewelry making, where chalcedony is used for jewelry, talismans and carvings. It's found in Brazil, China, India, Uruguay, West Germany, and in the United States in Utah, Wyoming, Colorado, Montana, Oregon and Idaho. The inclusions are caused by later-filled pockets of steam during the stone's magma formation.

Personal experience has had great success with moss agate, a very beautiful gemstone, worn as a rectangular polished piece set in a silver ring. The stone is a crown and brow center opener that connects the spiritual to the physical, the sky to the Earth. Several root chakra gemstones bring energy upward from the root to the crown, but moss agate works in the other direction, bringing the crown center's expansive energies downward to the physical. An opener of psychic and healing intuition, moss agate is an aura protector that neutralizes fears and survival fears, and opens the mind and Be-ing to new ideas.[33] It balances logic with intuition and spirituality with earth plane living. As a meditation stone and for scrying by candlelight, the mossy forms, lines and lights inside the gem invoke feelings of connectedness, of being a part of the goddess' plan, of inner peace, perfect trust and inner knowing. The clouds lead the mind into astral realms and expand consciousness, bringing that awareness from altered states into daily life. Using it eases emotional pain, aids creative visualization, and increases trust and strength for earthly survival.

Moss agate stimulates universal love and healing love, rather than personal or emotional, and is positive as a connector to spirit guides, to opening or ongoing communications with unseen entities. The stone is enlightening, calming, an aura protector and draws luck. It reduces fevers and aids sobriety and sexual temperance.[34] Julia Lorusso and Joel Glick list moss agate as a devolving gem material and give it no healing uses. They recommend it for connection to nature spirits and for connection with the land and agriculture.[35] Most other sources ignore moss agate and chalcedony or list them together with other agates, not separating their healing properties. Personal experience sees great power and potential in this gemstone, and for women who are drawn to moss agate or white chalcedony, the stones are positive and worth learning more about.

Selenite or *desert rose* is another crown and third eye energy that has been mostly ignored by healers, but that needs dis-covery and re-claiming. A crystalline form of gypsum and very soft (Moh's hardness, 2), it's a brown to colorless transparent gemstone found in crystals or massive lumps. The lumps are interesting, balls of buff-colored material with crystalline ridges, resembling roses from the barren desert. The stone is too soft for jewelry work. Selenite is found worldwide with deposits in Canada, England and Mexico, Oklahoma, New York, Texas, Iowa, Nevada, California and Michigan. Its chemical composition is 79 percent calcium sulfate and 21 percent water, $CaSo_4 + 2H_2O$. Another name for it is specular stone, and crystalline selenite has been used in the past to make eyeglasses. The material is inexpensive and found in museum gift shops.

Stimulating goddess nourishment spiritually and physically, beige selenite is classed with the white crown and brow center gemstones. A woman nursing her fourth child didn't have enough milk. A bruja gave her a ball of selenite, telling her to wear it in a mojo bag between her breasts. Her milk increased to abundance and remained so as long as she wore the bag and gemstone. A selenite ball is calming and soothing, easing fear and emotional pain, quieting for worry and an over-active negative imagination. It slows breathing rate and metabolism, balances anxiety reactions, gives a sense of peace and well-being protection, and aids mental concentration.

Katrina Raphaell, the only one of the major gemstone references for this book to discuss selenite, uses the crystalline form in meditation for clarity, inner truth and self-knowing. She designates it a crown center gemstone for expanded awareness and brain function, for connection with the source, spirit and enlightenment. She uses it for mental states and mental clarity, calming and inner truth, rather than for physical healing. Able to record and store impressions and information, use selenite for psychometry, telepathic communications, and to develop psychically. The stone is white light/rainbow clarity, the knowing of all colors; it aids confusion and confused mind dis-eases, and brings peace of mind.[36]

Selenite's high calcium content and the common use of gypsum in plaster of Paris suggests selenite/desert rose for use in calcium deficiency dis-eases such as osteoporosis and for healing broken bones. British healer James Sturzaker uses it interchangeably with moonstone, recommending selenite for bleeding, fevers, burns and ulcers, cancer and dropsy, and as an all-aura protector from harm. Under specular stone, it's listed as a remedy for wrinkles.[37] The material is interesting visually and to hold, and is another gemstone energy demanding women's use and study. The name selenite connects it to the goddess Moon.

White/precious opal is a stone usually designated for crown chakra healing, a white gemstone overlapping with the brow but containing all colors of the spectrum rainbow and with conflicting designations by healers. Precious opals, any with color play, are commonly called fire opals, but only the red/orange opals are fire opals. Precious opals are white or black, and include gemstones with the changing lights and colors unique to opal. White precious opal is the stone considered here, while black precious opal (having a blue or green background, rarely actually black) has also crown and brow chakra attributes. Opals are found in Australia, Honduras, Czechoslovakia, Mexico, Brazil, Guatemala, Japan, and in Nevada in the United States. White precious opal for jewelry use comes mainly from Australia and Brazil. The stone is 5½-6 on the Moh's scale, but is quite fragile because of its high water content, 6 to 34 percent. The water easily evaporates, leaving the stone dull or shattered. Heat, cold, pressure, bumping can destroy opals, while storing in oil or moist cotton helps to prevent the water content from evaporating. The stone is brittle and very fragile in jewelry, and expensive in jewelry, but raw chips are sold inexpensively in rock shops. Synthetic and fake opals are common.

Ancient Greece and Rome valued opal highly for prophecy and truth perception, and it's a stone of hope, loyalty, purity and good fortune in the Orient. In Europe, opal is considered to be bad luck, and in the United States it's said to be negative if it isn't the individual's birthstone (October). Opal contains all the colors of the chakra rainbow, opening and stimulating each of the centers. How the user responds to this stimulation is her personal choice, whatever her birth month, so that if she is able to harmonize her physical, emotional and mental reactions to the stone's harmony with the universe, the gem can only be positive. Precious opal is a psychic mirror that amplifies the wearer's traits and attributes, whatever they may be. Like moonstone, it brings needs and problems into woman's consciousness,[38] and using it with awareness and mood awareness is recommended. If approached to gain all-aura balance and harmony, to focus awareness on moods and issues for work and positive change, opal is a transformative gemstone energy and is beneficial. If approached out of harmony and allowed to stimulate out of harmony centers and reactions, opal can be negative. The positivity or not is with the user, not the gemstone.

As in any gemstone for healing, the clearest indication of a stone's benefit is in woman's intuition. If the woman is drawn to opal, it is positive for her to use it. If she is not, or if she has had enough of its energies, she knows to put it aside. Women are drawn to the energies of their own healing needs, and the stones themselves teach how to use them.

Mellie Uyldert attributes opal's bad press to an unlucky opal ring in the Spanish Court, and also to its power in stimulating kundalini.[39] With patriarchy's distrust of the sexual aspects of kundalini rising and of its spiritual aspects of goddess and power-within, the origins of opal as a negative energy become understandable. The stone absorbs and returns deceit and dishonesty—or purity and positivity—and is operative in karmic debts. When obtaining a gemstone that others have used or worn, clear it thoroughly, and dedicate it to positive uses.

Opal is a spiritually purifying gemstone, useful in meditation work, for attunement, sensitivity, receptivity, and for becoming a channel of healing and the goddess. Approached for these things, the stone is positive and extremely powerful. Looking into its colors and lights enhances meditative states and a woman's connection with the feminine and the goddess. She sees herself flowing as a channel of energy from the Earth to the sky, with no separations between her Be-ing and the goddess universe. Opal stimulates the pineal and pituitary glands, the brow and crown chakras, and connects the mental bodies to the spiritual. It acts as a tuner, magnifier and harmonizer, and aids psychic development, spiritual development and clairvoyance. It creates a longing and pursuit of the ideal.[40]

In healing work, precious opal aids the senses and the eyes, but has few physical body attributes. It sharpens memory, aids mental confusion, and stimulates clarity of mind and purpose.[41] It shatters mental illusions for new growth, aids in creative visualization and color work, stimulates high forms of creativity, and opens spiritual awareness. Serenity Peterson uses opal for women who feel themselves too earth bound, but avoids it for women who need grounding.[42] Use opal for innocence and achievement, soothing emotional anger, preventing infection, easing stress, worry or depression, and for strengthening the heart.[43] Patriarchal taboos are often a warning-away from the goddess and from women's feminine power. If menstruation, birth and women's sexuality are "evil" in male HIStory, the "evil" of a gemstone as lovely as opal is in question. A stone that connects women's Be-ing with the goddess and goddess-within is worth investigating. Use it positively and receive positivity from using it.

The crown chakra's major color correspondence is violet, and *amethyst* is the representative violet gemstone. There are few gemstones of this color: alexandrite is highly expensive, and purple garnets are hard to find, violet sapphire, spinel and zircon are not easily available, and stones like tanzanite and iolite are not generally known. Amethyst and violet shades of fluorite are the basic crown chakra energies for this color. A form of quartz crystal, amethyst has the piezoelectric properties of clear quartz and was known to ancient women for its healing abilities. The name is Greek and means "without alcohol," and amethyst traditionally is a sobriety stone. Found in geodes as clusters, in single or double-terminated points and massive forms, raw amethyst crystals or tumbled pieces can cost under a dollar and are easily located. In jewelry, the stone is faceted, but is also used tumbled, as beads, chips and carved.

Amethyst is found in Brazil, Uruguay, Africa, Mexico, Bolivia, Canada and in other countries. Canadian amethyst from Thunder Bay, Ontario is different for healing from the commoner Brazilian amethyst; it contains high levels of red energy. Greenland amethyst is strongly blue. Amethyst interspersed with white bands of chalcedony is called amethyst quartz, and occurs in France, Germany, Brazil, Namibia and the United States. When found in crystals, amethyst points are usually small and the color is darkest at the tips. Clear the stone by other means than sunlight, because amethyst fades.

For women who are anxious, fearful or ungrounded, or where insomnia is an issue, amethyst is a major stabilizer, grounder, and sedative. The combination of colors that make violet—red and indigo—balance the root chakra with the brow and crown, the physical with spiritual aura bodies. The color and gemstones are a balancer for too much solar plexus yellow, for lack of concentration, diabetes, sleep dis-orders, eating dis-orders and urinary problems. Use amethyst for nervous and mental healing, for migraines and headaches, stress, fear, emotional calming, for the eyes, lungs and respiratory system, asthma and allergies, sinus problems and glaucoma. Use it as a blood purifier and for circulatory dis-eases, for blood clots, gout, building white blood cells, fighting alcoholism, for nightmares and to inhibit sexuality.[44]

Amethyst is a balancer of the aura, an integrator of the physical, emotional, mental and spiritual levels. It raises vibrations from the physical to the spiritual, including and harmonizing all of the aura bodies as it does so. Transformation and spiritual cleansing, stabilizing and all-aura protection are the result. The woman using amethyst feels stronger on every level, more certain and confident, more attuned to who she is and what her purpose in this life is. Her connection to the goddess Earth and goddess universe, to power-within and goddess-within are more sure. Amethyst is a major healer for neuroses and psychoses, for depression, anxiety and the central nervous system because of this integrative ability. It offers the strength and emotional certainty for breaking negative habits and addictions, and for going through personal change.[45] It offers spiritual and psychic development, an increase in idealism, an easier and deeper access to meditative states, and a positive outlook. Amethyst promotes all healing and raises the vibrations of molecules for healing from the cell-source and unseen levels. Use it for palsies, multiple sclerosis, Parkinson's and degenerative nerve dis-eases, and for brain tumors.

Because of its partial red energy, amethyst is sedating and energizing at once, a contradiction especially felt when using Canadian amethyst. Julia Lorusso and Joel Glick note this and recommend amethyst for some psychoses, particularly for catatonic and manic-depressive states, but find it disturbing for some other states. In cases of paranoia or chemical-imbalance mental dis-eases, they warn against amethyst (try malachite).[46] Healers are sensitive to gemstone actions and re-actions and pay attention to their energies. Amethyst is a stabilizer for kundalini energy.

Mellie Uyldert uses amethyst for creativity and creative thinking, for spiritual and psychic development and cleansing, and for meditation. In physical healing, she uses it for venereal dis-eases and childbed fever, for neuralgia, hallucinations, "hatred and rage," for homesickness, skin dis-eases, blood dis-eases, fear, grief, dropsy and color blindness.[47] Katrina Raphaell uses amethyst for humility and trust in the universe/goddess, to calm the mind and for deeper understanding and wisdom. She uses it both for grief and to aid the transition into death, for terminal illness in the self or a loved one. Use amethyst to calm temper, anger and hot-headedness, ease tension and tension headaches/migraines, to ease worry and overwork, burn out and being overwhelmed.[48] Katrina Raphaell uses amethyst with rose quartz for soothing the mind and heart at once. Use it also with clear quartz crystal, to enhance and amplify amethyst, and personal experience finds it calming with aquamarine.

Wear amethyst on a necklace below the heart chakra for solar plexus grounding and balancing; many women wear it continually in their auras. Choose a crystal mounted point downwards or a polished unfaceted oval. Place a cluster or chunk of raw amethyst under the bed, or a smaller piece under the pillow for sleep and protected dreams. A piece on an altar or held in the left hand (or each hand) enhances meditation. Use amethyst in a left-hand ring for drawing its energies in, in a right-hand ring for sending amethyst in healing. Keeping amethyst in a room makes it a protected, calming place to be, but put it aside for love-making. In laying on of stones, use it anywhere there is pain or an area needing balance, particularly the solar plexus and spiritual chakras. After clear quartz crystal and with lapis, amethyst is the most major stone in women's healing.

Crown chakra gemstones, with the notable exception of amethyst, move away from physical healing. They have karmic, psychic and psychological attributes for healing on unseen levels, and have all-aura attributes. The transpersonal point is located beyond the physical body entirely, and its healing uses are mainly esoteric. The transpersonal point gemstones, often combined with crown chakra healing designations, are clear/rainbow/white gemstones, crystalline electrical energies that radiate all colors and specifically affect the aura field. They influence all of the chakras, rather than a single center. Representative gemstones include clear zircon, diamond and rutile quartz, and the most major healing gemstone of all, clear quartz crystal. Any survey of healing gemstones for woman's chakras and aura bodies returns ultimately to clear quartz crystal.

Clear zircon is a stone often used as a substitute for diamond and without a high reputation of its own, but it has healing uses. Zircon in colors (orange, green, yellow, red, violet) is a correspondent for each color's chakra, and colorless/clear/rainbow zircon is a gemstone for the crown and transpersonal point. The stone is double-refracting (diamond is single) and hard, 6½-7½ on the Moh's scale, but not as hard as diamond, which is 10. Zircon is brittle and easily damaged, as diamond is not, and is far less expensive than diamond. The stone is found in Southeast Asia and Sri Lanka, in Australia, Tanzania and France. Blue and colorless zircons are sometimes produced by heating red/brown or grey/brown ones to tempertures of 1500-1800°F. Green zircons are the most rare color. Zircons are cut like diamonds in the faceted brilliant cut, and are sometimes called matura diamonds. All the colors of zircon can be labeled jacinth. There are synthetic varieties and heat-treated ones, but natural zircon when found is more than imitation diamond.

Thelma Isaacs called clear zircon a stone of independence and self-independence. She notes that it emits low levels of natural radiation that affect the aura field and four bodies. Natural radiation should not be confused with the Three Mile Island variety. In healing, use zircon for the lungs, for polio and tuberculosis. It's a purifier and healer of the aura, bringing peace of mind and healing to the spirit. It's a stone for women who are quiet of nature, despite its flashiness. Zircon is an all-aura protection stone against contagion and infection, lightning, wounds and injuries, particularly for travelers. Use it for insomnia, calming and sedating,[49] for a protection charm, heart stimulant and to prevent nightmares.[50]

Julia Lorusso and Joel Glick list zircon as a stone that is evolving, but give it no healing properties at the present time.[51] Mellie Uyldert considers primarily the orange zircon or hyacinth, noting it as a liver stimulant for the belly chakra. She notes zircon in general as a spirituality opener, a stimulant of dreams and dream-thinking/picture-thinking, and a connector to spirit guides, all crown center/transpersonal point attributes. Zircon stimulates astral projection, a solar plexus-located psychic skill.[52] Rhiannon McBride calls clear zircon a wishing stone, in keeping with its creative visualization attributes, and a stone of protection and power. She says that it attracts money, and notes its clear and positive energy.[53] Less expensive than diamond and having a resurgent popularity in the last few years, clear/rainbow zircon is a stone meriting women's investigation as a healer.

The first gemstone most women are aware of is *diamond;* it pervades patriarchal society as a metaphor for marriage and Western values. The stone is the most expensive and most familiar of gemstone materials, the hardest in composition (10 Moh's), and possibly the most powerful for both positive and negative energies. Only diamond cuts or polishes diamond, and diamond cutting began relatively recently, in 1456 in Belgium. The fates and fortunes of countless people and several nations have been involved in diamonds and the diamond trade, and the stone is mined primarily in South Africa. India, Brazil, Russia, Borneo and Australia are other sources.

Diamond is not a mineral, but is carbon (plant matter) crystallized under high pressure and heat. The stages that turn vegetable matter into diamond are: humis, peat, lignite, pit-coal, graphite and diamond. The sequence runs from darkness to brilliance, or Saturn to the Sun in astrology.[54] Stories abound of unlucky diamonds, fabulous in their value but appalling in their death and devastation. Other stories of diamond rings passed from daughter to daughter are completely positive ones, and are far more frequent. Diamond is a stone of fidelity, with its other side of possession, and a stone of wealth (physical and spiritual), with its other side of greed. As in other gemstone energies, there is choice.

Like opal, diamond contains all the chakra colors, and like clear quartz or zircon is an all-aura energy. The dualities in diamond come from how its intense power is used, its ability to absorb, retain and transmit energy, any energy indiscriminately. Clear diamond is the strongest energy absorber of the gem world and the strongest energy transmitter. It takes in and magnifies within whatever it finds, whoever is wearing or using it, and sends that energy outward. It retains impressions and is extremely hard to clear of its patterning.[55] If the wearer or user is positive, the gem increases her positivity and transmits it, holding it for the next who wears the stone as well. If the wearer or user is negative, greedy, possessive or going through great pain, diamond absorbs, holds, magnifies and transmits that, too, both for its present user and for women who will use the stone after her. A diamond that's worn retains a pattern of the life force of the woman wearing it.

Representative gemstone of the transpersonal point, a positive diamond is involved with pure knowing and pure spirit. Used unselfishly it brings peace and long life, spirituality and connection with the goddess and goddess-within. It's an all-aura protection field and aura strengthener, eases fears and nightmares, draws fidelity in love, clears the skin and nourishes spiritual, mental, emotional and physical growth. It protects from physical attacks and injuries, and magnifies the healing attributes of other gemstones used with it.[56] Serenity Peterson recommends using diamond with amethyst or rose quartz, rather than the clear quartz usually used with other gemstones.[57]

Thelma Isaacs mentions emerald, and Julia Lorusso and Joel Glick recommend using yellow/brown diamonds with amber to create a powerful healing aura field.[58]

Gentler methods of clearing gemstones do not apply to diamond. If the energies are unknown, try burying it in Earth or dry sea salt before using, and choose a raw diamond or diamond jewelry with great care as to how it feels intuitively. Personal experience with a foremother's diamond have been totally positive; worn as a ring on the right hand, it magnifies and transmits healing energy.

A diamond without negativity repels negativity and protects the wearer from it. Not imprinted with pain, greed or possessiveness, it draws peace, serenity and innocence, joy and wealth, bonding and long-lasting in relationships.[59] Diamond is a catalyst and partakes of dualities and opposites; it is capable of great good and sometimes great misfortune, usually determined by the wearer herself. A diamond makes its wearer more of who and what she is, amplifying her positive or negative qualities. The stone increases endurance, develops courage and concentration, is a protector against poison and contagion, eases quarrels and stabilizes mental instabilities. It helps insomnia and prevents nightmares, strengthens the heart, helps gout, convulsions and delirium tremens.[60] The most familiar and most powerful of all healing energies, diamond used wisely is a benefit for the good of all.

One further healing gemstone for the crown and transpersonal point chakras, for all-aura healing, is *rutile quartz*. The stone is a form of clear quartz crystal, crystal containing metallic fibrous inclusions. The rutile appear like fine golden wires or hairs inside the stone. Rutile quartz can be clear quartz crystal, and usually is, but rutile also occurs frequently in smoky quartz and sometimes in rose quartz. Inclusions can be diffuse or more solid, appearing as a pattern or star inside the crystal. The metal is titanium and sometimes called Venus' hair, and rutile is found in Brazil, France, Norway and the United States. A form of quartz crystal, its hardness is 6½-7 on the Moh's scale.

The effect of rutilation varies from crystal to crystal. The first crystal ever personally seen or drawn to was a rutilated clear quartz, cut in a rather ugly cabochon/oval. The stone acted as an immense psychic opener, felt like tingly fireworks or bright shooting stars when held. Another rutilated clear quartz, a tumbled one, feels cool and flowing like a waterfall, while a large, raw rutile smoky quartz has become an altar image, and is powerful held for grounding and to ease fear. Rutile clear quartz prevents nightmares and stimulates dreams, including psychic and precognitive dreams and lucid dreaming. Rutile smoky quartz encourages very strange dreams. Either stimulates intuition, calms and sedates, and is a powerful enhancer of meditation states. In scrying, rutile opens connections with universal others, and aids in getting answers to the questions asked. A feeling of being surrounded by bright, protective electricity comes from using rutile clear quartz, holding it in the left hand, especially when sleeping.

Rutile in clear quartz is a highly amplifying energy that affects the entire aura field. The energy is active, electrical and usually hot, always intense and powerful. It's a reminder of power-within and the goddess-within, woman's connection with the goddess. It energizes and calms at once, raises psychic vibrations, and balances the aura and aura bodies. It aids nutrition assimilation, mental assimilation, psychic clairvoyance and telepathy, strengthens creative visualization and thought-form transmission. Rutile quartz strengthens immunity, slows aging and the dis-eases of age, and prevents and raises depression.[61] Mellie Uyldert suggests it for bronchitis, and Julia Lorusso and Joel Glick for balancing the etheric body centers, for endocrine and sexual imbalances, for neurological "wiring errors" like dyslexia, for fighting infections, rebuilding cells from the energy blueprint of well-being, and for raising body temperature. They note the increase in magnetism of a stone containing rutile inclusions; the metal fibers are conductors of strong electricity and polarity for healing.[62] Rutile fibers hold, store and transmit this electrical charge and magnify clear quartz crystal energy.

Used with or as clear quartz crystal, rutile quartz is a powerful healer. It has the piezoelectric effect of clear quartz crystal amplified, and holds a projection of any healing color or visualization to send in healing. It may be harder to control and send with than clear quartz. In most cases, inclusions that jewelers consider impurities add to the healing properties of a gemstone. This is also true for turquoise, and in rutile quartz the inclusions are a major benefit for women's healing. Rutile quartz works as an all-healing gemstone to cast an aura of peace and protection, and can be used in every way that clear quartz crystal is used for healing work.

Any healing survey of gemstones begins and ends with *clear quartz crystal*, the most versatile all-aura, all-chakra healing gemstone. Clear quartz *amplifies, holds and transmits energy* and is directed/ programmed by the woman healer for whatever visualization or color work, whatever psychic healing or "tinkering" she desires. The most totally positive, totally pure healing energy, clear quartz relieves physical and emotional pain, calms the nerves, balances dizziness and reduces bleeding, purifies, protects, sedates or energizes, and opens for a woman's well-being and good health. It works on the level of the seen and unseen bodies, on all the aura levels, and for all the chakras. It affects, develops and balances the physical, emotional, mental and spiritual bodies, unifies and integrates them for power-within and goddess-within on the Earth plane.

Stimulating cell regeneration in the blueprint of perfect health, clear quartz crystal repairs the cells, the energy spaces between atoms, the physical and non-physical planes of a woman's aura and Be-ing. Use it for peace, use it for self-confidence, use it for a positive balance between self-love and love of others/universal love, use it for connection and knowing of the goddess. The woman who works with clear quartz crystal finds herself an energy channel for healing, con-nected with the Earth and universe, connected with other women, and connected with the goddess and Be-ing. Whether she heals others or herself and uses the stone for laying on of hands, biofeed-back, psychic healing, "tinker-woman" healing, mental/creative visualization, color work or meditation, clear quartz crystal is the ultimate in gemstone healing energy. The woman who works with gemstones begins and ends with clear quartz crystal, and returns to its uses again and again.

Women's healing is a combination of methods, philosophies and psychologies that reach both the seen and unseen of women's Be-ing. It does not deny allopathic medicine, but says that male medicine's denial of women and its physical-only emphasis is incom-plete. No system that ignores the unseen energy levels of the body, that fragments the parts and body parts into lesser and greater worth, that denies the power and value of women's organs, intuition and experience can truly heal. Patriarchal medicine works on the dense physical level only, ignoring the other components. It rejects the part that emotions, mind and spirit have on women's health and it rejects women's natural functions and Be-ing as being health at all. This type of partial medicine treats symptoms, and "cures" or cuts out women's breasts and reproductive organs indiscriminately. Women's healing treats and respects women's Be-ing, all the levels of women's Be-ing, values and honors her sexuality and ability to give birth, her cycles of menarche, menstruation and menopause, and her unseen aura and intuition. Women's healing prevents dis-ease by changing the conditions that cause it.

The woman healer uses a variety of methods from this book and from other sources, uses her aura intuition and psychic sensitivity to heal herself and to help others. Gemstone and crystal healing is a part of women's healing, used with all methods to affect the four bodies, the chakra centers and the aura levels. The woman healer is a channel for the goddess and for power and goddess-within. She knows her healing power is a part of women's heritage and tradition. Healing deals with wellness, with creating and maintaining a balance and harmony in all of Be-ing, with helping women find wholeness and good health.

If, in our current state of knowledge, women's healing is not total health care for everyone, then neither is male/traditional medicine. A balance between the two would be an ideal state, using the best parts of science in a humane, respectful, women-oriented/people-oriented way along with women's skills for total health. Such a combination and synthesis of knowledge and a concentrated effort to gain more understanding is for the benefit of all, for women, children and men, for animals and the planet. Hopes are that this book will add to women's knowing, and open new ideas for further exploration of women's healing, the re-claiming of lost skills and adding to them. Hopes are that this book will make the day when healing and medicine work together happen sooner—for the peace, health and well-being of all.

Moon almost new in Leo, August 5, 1986
Blessed Be

FOOTNOTES

1. Mellie Uyldert, *The Magic of Precious Stones* (Great Britain, Turnstone Press, 1981), p. 59

2. *Ibid.,* p. 59-60.

3. *Ibid.,* p. 136-138.

4. Ida Shaw, workshop handout, National Women's Music Festival, 1986.

5. Gemstoned Ltd., *Crystal Essence* (New York, Gemstoned Ltd., 1984), unpaged pamphlet.

6. Thelma Isaacs, *Gemstones, Crystals and Healing* (Black Mountain, NC, Lorien House, 1982), p. 66-68.

7. Rhiannon McBride, Charleen Deering, Louise Devery and Amber K, "Occult Uses of Healing Gemstones," in *Circle Network News,* Summer, 1982, p. 12.

8. Katrina Raphaell, *Crystal Enlightenment* (New York, Aurora Press, 1985), p. 142.

9. Mellie Uyldert, *The Magic of Precious Stones,* p. 136-139.

10. Julia Lorusso and Joel Glick, *Healing Stoned* (Albuquerque, NM, Brotherhood of Life, 1985, original 1976), p. 72.

11. Katrina Raphaell, *Crystal Enlightenment,* p. 153.

12. Phyllis Galde, "Using Gems for Healing," in *The Llewellyn New Times,* (Llewellyn Publications, POB 64383, St. Paul, MN 55164-0383), Issue 863, May-June, 1986, p. 10.

13. Thelma Isaacs, *Gemstones, Crystals and Healing,* p. 47-48.

14. Gemstoned Ltd., *Crystal Essence,* unpaged pamphlet.

15. Serenity Peterson, *Crystal Visioning, A Crystal Workbook* (Nashville, TN, Interdimensional Publishing, 1984), p. 58.

16. Mellie Uyldert, *The Magic of Precious Stones,* p. 115.

17. Thelma Isaacs, *Gemstones, Crystals and Healing,* p. 48.

18. Mellie Uyldert, *The Magic of Precious Stones,* p. 115.

19. Julia Lorusso and Joel Glick, *Healing Stoned,* p. 70.

20. Thelma Isaacs, *Gemstones, Crystals and Healing,* p. 47.

21. Katrina Raphaell, *Crystal Enlightenment,* p. 106-107.

22. *Ibid.,* p. 107-108.

23. *Ibid.,* p. 111

24. *Ibid.*, p. 42-43.

25. Vicki Noble, *Motherpeace: A Way to the Goddess Through Myth, Art and Tarot* (San Francisco, Harper and Row Publishers, 1983), p. 233.

26. Thelma Isaacs, *Gemstones, Crystals and Healing*, p. 52-53.

27. Julia Lorusso and Joel Glick, *Healing Stoned*, p. 46.

28. Mellie Uyldert, *The Magic of Precious Stones*, p. 141.

29. Gemstoned Ltd., *Crystal Essence*, unpaged pamphlet.

30. Mellie Uyldert, *The Magic of Precious Stones*, p. 141.

31. *Ibid.*, p. 93-94.

32. James Sturzaker, *Gemstones and Their Occult Powers* (London, Metatron Publications, 1977), p. 32-33.

33. *Ibid.*, p. 19-20.

34. *Ibid.*

35. Julia Lorusso and Joel Glick, *Healing Stoned*, p. 63.

36. Katrina Raphaell, *Crystal Enlightenment*, p. 151-152.

37. James Sturzaker, *Gemstones and Their Occult Powers*, p. 86-87, and 66-67.

38. Thelma Isaacs, *Gemstones, Crystals and Healing*, p. 84.

39. Mellie Uyldert, *The Magic of Precious Stones*, p. 98

40. Thelma Isaacs, *Gemstones, Crystals and Healing*, p. 84.

41. *Ibid.*

42. Serenity Peterson, *Crystal Visioning*, p. 55-56.

43. James Sturzaker, *Gemstones and Their Occult Powers*, p. 70-72.

44. Thelma Isaacs, *Gemstones, Crystals and Healing*, p. 77-78.

45. Ida Shaw, workshop handout, and Gemstoned Ltd., *Crystal Essence*, unpaged pamphlet.

46. Julia Lorusso and Joel Glick, *Healing Stoned*, p. 55.

47. Mellie Uyldert, *The Magic of Precious Stones*, p. 96.

48. Katrina Raphaell *Crystal Enlightenment*, p. 78-81.

49. Thelma Isaacs, *Gemstones, Crystals and Healing*, p. 97-98.

50. James Sturzaker, *Gemstones and Their Occult Powers*, p. 95-96.

51. Julia Lorusso and Joel Glick, *Healing Stoned*, p. 72.

52. Mellie Uyldert, *The Magic of Precious Stones*, p. 117-118.

53. Rhiannon McBride, Charleen Deering, Louise Devery and Amber K, "Occult Uses of Gemstones," in *Circle Network News*, Summer, 1982, p. 12.

54. Mellie Uyldert, *The Magic of Precious Stones*, p. 144.

55. Serenity Peterson, *Crystal Visioning*, p. 48.

56. Thelma Isaacs, *Gemstones, Crystals and Healing*, p. 50.

57. Serenity Peterson, *Crystal Visioning*, p. 48.

58. Julia Lorusso and Joel Glick, *Healing Stoned*, p. 51.

59. Rhiannon McBride, Charleen Deering, Louise Devery and Amber K, "Occult Uses of Gemstones," in *Circle Network News*, Summer, 1982, p. 12.

60. James Sturzaker, *Gemstones and Their Occult Powers*, p. 39-40.

61. Phyllis Galde, "Using Gems for Healing," in *The Llewellyn New Times*, Issue 863, May-June, 1986, p. 10.

62. Julia Lorusso and Joel Glick, *Healing Stoned*, p. 58-59.

APPENDIX I

THE USES OF HEALING GEMSTONES

GEMSTONES FOR THE CHAKRAS

THE USES OF HEALING GEMSTONES[1]

Stone	Color	Chakra	Healing Uses
Smoky Quartz	Black	Root	Calming, sedating, stabilizing, for fear, panic, depression, survival, body image, drug issues, spaciness, fatigue, stress, digestion, elimination, gas, bonds to Earth, meditation, PMS, quit smoking
Black Tourmaline	Black	Root	Grounds, calms, steadies, reduces anger, jealousy, insecurity, resentment, transforms negativity, protection shield, magnetizes, draws out dis-ease, eases neuroses and obsessions, diarrhea
Tourmaline Quartz	Black/White	Root	Grounds, calms, connects root with crown, balances, breaks old habits, protects, magnetizes, opens chakra blocks, deflects negativity, intestinal system
Obsidian (Apache Tears)	Black	Root	Grounds, stabilizes, calms, collects spaciness and scattered energies, a psychic mirror, eyesight and inner sight, karmic, entrance into the labyrinth/womb, magnifies fears and illusions
Onyx	Black	Root	Protection, stress, karmic debts, stabilizes, strength, courage, temperance, releasing, letting go, seriousness of purpose, will, grief, skin, nails, hair, heart, hearing, ulcers, pus
Jet	Black	Root	Grounds, calms, protects, repels sadness and negativity, grief, letting go, dispels depression, fear, worry, fevers, epilepsy, contagion, toothache, skin tumors, hysteria, headaches, dropsy
Hematite	Black/Red	Root	Grounds, calms, relaxes, courage, prevents hemorrhaging, ulcers, muscle cramps, childbirth, bloodshot eyes, kidneys and bladder, hysteria, focus energy and emotions, high blood pressure, sleep
Bloodstone/Heliotrope	Red/Green	Root	Grounds, calms, stops bleeding, childbirth, wounds, inflammations, fevers, blood purifier, courage, decision making, constancy, blood circulation, anemia, red blood, the heart, kidneys, liver, spleen, hemorrhoids, insect bites, cystitis, heavy menstruation

THE USES OF HEALING GEMSTONES (Continued)

Stone	Color	Chakra	Healing Uses
Red Garnet	Red	Root	Happiness, power, possessions, peace, patience, sexuality, constancy, balance, inspiration, cleansing, renewal, birth, menstruation and life passages, blood, fertility, arthritis
Ruby	Red	Root	Energizing, warming, labor and menstruation, fertility, uterus, depression, exhaustion, blood circulation, sexuality, heart, liver, kidneys, cancer, AIDS, tiredness, self-image, ego, love
Red Jasper	Red	Root	Calming, grounding, energizing, aura repair after trauma, vomiting, morning sickness, blood purifier, menstrual cramps, bladder infections, gall bladder, liver, stabilizing, epilepsy
Carnelian	Orange	Belly	Cure madness, bring on menses, orgasm, reproduction, sexuality, menstrual cramps, blood purifier, stimulates emotions, lungs, constipation, mental ability, creative visualization, warms, liver, gall bladder, pancreas, ovaries, kundalini energy, joint dis-eases, arthritis, allergies
Coral	Orange/ Red	Belly	Stimulant, anemia, cures madness, remedies poisons, the blood, protection, reproduction, menstrual cramps, bleeding, heart, depression, warms, protection, sexuality, infertility, lungs, arthritis, indigestion, coughs, asthma, cheering, removes fear, lungs, allergies
Agate	Orange/ Brown	Belly	Balancing, emotions, stability, childbirth, menstrual cramps, stomach dis-eases, protection, fear, falls, teething, vision, hearing, heart, blood purifier, fevers, epilepsy, grounding
Jacinth	Orange	Belly	Insomnia, blood purification, protection from poisoning, polio, TB, lung disorders, lightning, insomnia, wounds and injuries, psychic sight, visualization, the liver, quieting
Topaz	Golden/ Yellow	Solar Plexus	Stimulant, energizing, protection, depression, fear, death, intellect, insomnia, blood, urinary, kidneys, lungs, veins, friendship, calms anger, sexual dysfunction, trust, shock, dispels negativity, brightens, nervous dis-ease, stress, bones

Stone	Color	Chakra	Healing Uses
Amber	Golden/Yellow	Solar Plexus	Protection, calming, infections, ears, vision, ulcers, bleeding, teeth, pain, negativity, stimulant, yin/yang balance, warming, stabilizing, suicide, amputations, kundalini, depression, lungs, skin, hair, asthma, urinary and intestines, poisoning, throat
Citrine Quartz	Yellow	Solar Plexus	Stimulant, cheering, purifier, protection, clarity, color work, psychic and sexual energy, digestion, assimilation, urinary, bladder, kidneys, liver, the will, colon, visualization, mind, trance states, self-confidence, relationships, writing, studying, allergies, eating disorders
Tiger Eye	Yellow/Gold	Solar Plexus	Stimulant, cheering, purifier, protection from things without, protection from evil eye, sight, eye dis-eases, perception, clarity, understanding, digestion, drug and alcohol, karmic ties, visualization, purpose, the will, intellect, understanding
Golden Beryl	Yellow	Solar Plexus/Heart	Stimulant, cheering, energizing, purifier, scrying, protection, mouth, jaw, throat, digestion, diabetes, liver, stomach, mind, peace of mind, connects solar plexus and heart, intellect, sight, intuition, understanding, solar energy, exhaustion
Malachite	Yellow/Green	Solar Plexus/Heart	Stimulant, soothes, eyes, psychic sight, connects seen to unseen, protection, absorbs negativity, gall bladder, liver, pancreas, nerves, irregular menstruation, asthma, epilepsy, colic, joints, spasms, purifies blood, nerve dis-eases, magnifies moods, hope, hypoglycemia, allergies, dyslexia
Peridot/Olivine	Yellow/green	Solar Plexus/Heart	Stimulation, calming, balancing, prosperity, happiness, clarity, purification, digestion, sight, clairvoyance, eloquence, ulcers, bowels, constipation, blood, heart, fever, lung congestion, inflammation, antiseptic, protection, spleen, intellect, anxiety
Rose Quartz	Rose	Heart	Heart, emotions, release, acceptance, love and self-love, warms, positive outlook, forgiveness, joy, oneness, emotional pain, throat, heart, ears, nose, sinuses, kidneys, hypertension, palsie, love of others, love of goddess, trust, giving, honesty, aging, recovery from abused childhoods

THE USES OF HEALING GEMSTONES (Continued)

Stone	Color	Chakra	Healing Uses
Rhodochrosite	Rose	Heart/Solar Plexus	Balance upper with lower chakras, protection, filter, confusion, anxiety, acceptance, love, forgiveness, emotional release, eyes, heart, skin, nails, hair, palsies, ulcers, growth, liver, blood, digestion, cancer, asthma, lungs, intellect, mucous, constipation
Pink Tourmaline	Rose	Heart	Love, self-love, friendship, universal love, calming, depression, ease fears, peaceful sleep, relationships, harmony, protection, emotional burnout, joy, trust, giving, heartache, past sorrow
Watermelon Tourmaline	Rose/Green	Heart/Solar Plexus	Metabolism, endocrine system, harmonizer between chakras, love, cell regeneration, yin/yang polarity, protection, charisma, art, the mind, creativity, heartache, love loss, sense of humor
Green Tourmaline	Green	Heart/Solar Plexus	Calms, balances, nerves, nervous system healing, prosperity, flu, manifesting, visualization, stabilizes emotions, will-wisdom, protection, heart, digestion, intestines, purify blood, veins, constipation, teeth, bones, reduce fears and anxiety, draw love, gall bladder
Emerald	Green	Heart	Love, peace, serenity, beauty, fidelity, psychic sensitivity, joy, meditation, calming, emotions, childbirth, poisons, eyes, aura, exhaustion, growth, insomnia, epilepsy, bleeding, aging, heart, digestion, pancreas, depression, all-healing, nerves, fever, pain, prevents miscarriage
Jade	Green	Heart/Solar Plexus	Calming, tranquillity, virtues, long life, protection, fertility, childbirth, prosperity, luck, nervous system, eyes, meditation, wisdom, problem solving, strength, bladder, kidneys, urinary
Green Aventurine	Green	Heart/Throat	Calming, love, peace, independence, originality, luck, stress, skin, eye, hair, migraines, headaches, high blood pressure, cools, love loss, loneliness, self-love, meditation, tranquilizing, adventures, travel

Stone	Color	Chakra	Healing Uses
Aquamarine	Blue/Green	Heart/Throat	Calming, soothing, purity, love, meditation, throat, protection, direction, purpose, self-knowledge, expression and release, eyes, fears, intelligence, stomach, liver, jaw, teeth, glands, throat, coughs, acceptance, imbalances, awareness, creativity, migraines
Turquoise	Blue/Green	Heart/Throat	Cooling, protection, calming, soothing, meditation, prosperity, love, karmic love, trauma, tension, high blood pressure, eyes, fevers, inflammations, swellings, breast milk, wisdom, lungs, asthma, heart dis-ease, wounds, burns, migraines, headaches
Chrysocolla	Blue/Green	Heart/Throat	Cooling, calming, writer's block, soothing, nervousness, headaches, migraines, tension, arthritis, cancer, peace, menstrual cramps, premenstrual syndrome, abortion, birth, hysterectomy recovery, forgiveness, emotional balance, anger, fevers, burns, infections, throat, thyroid, voice, asthma, digestion, epilepsy, meditation, incest recovery, mastectomy recovery
Lapis Lazuli	Blue/Indigo	Throat/Brow	Cooling, all-healing, psychic development, infections, pain, fevers, swelling, inflammation, burns, blood, heart, throat, creativity, expression, speech, senses, nervous system, spine, calming, insomnia, depression, migraines, protection, purifies, women's healing, incest recovery, prevent strokes, eyes, epilepsy, multiple sclerosis
Sodalite	Indigo	Brow	Calming, grounding, cooling, metabolism, glandular balance, mind, wisdom, stabilizes mental processes and emotions, understanding, self-knowledge, clears old patterns, radiation, nausea, psychic vascular, wounds, inflammations, lungs, sinuses, headaches, endocrine balance, PMS, irregular menses, multiple sclerosis
Blue Sapphire	Indigo	Brow	Cooling, insight, perception, clarity, joy, protection, peace, fevers, infections, burns, swellings, inflammations, pain, fear, throat, senses, negativity, vascular and circulatory, nervous, purifier, mood raiser, intellect, concentration, devotion, love, multiple sclerosis

THE USES OF HEALING GEMSTONES (Continued)

Stone	Color	Chakra	Healing Uses
Fluorite	Indigo/ Violet	Brow/ Crown	Protection, meditation, calming, grounding, psychic awareness, connectedness, stress, insomnia, mental/nervous, intellect, brain, brain waves, epilepsy, stroke prevention, Parkinson's, screens empathy
Moonstone	White	Brow/ Crown	Calming, psychic development, balancing, polarities, self-knowing, irregular menstruation, premenstrual syndrome, endocrine, pineal, lymph cleanser, white bood cells, hopes and dreams, mirror, immunity, emotions, fertility, cancer, nerve dis-eases, colds, dreamwork
White Chalcedony	White	Brow/ Crown	Calming, breast milk, healing bones, wounds, bleeding, poisoning, maternal feelings, depression, insomnia, coherent thinking, psychic opening, emotional strength, immunity, vitality, emotions, osteoporosis
Moss Agate	White/ Dark	Brow/ Crown	Calming, meditation, scrying, psychic opener, inner peace, connectedness, astral realms, visualization, universal love, healing love, spirit guides, agriculture and the land, emotions, fevers, fear, sobriety, chastity, new ideas, aura protector
Selenite/ Desert Rose	White/ Cream	Crown	Calming, breast milk, easing fears, fevers, pain, emotions, slows metabolism, peace, mental concentration, meditation, brain function, confusion, mental clarity, calcium deficiency, telepathy, inner knowing, broken bones, osteoporosis, bleeding
White Opal	White/ Colors	Crown	Connection with goddess, clairvoyance, innocence, purity, loyalty, achievement, truth, inner reality, confusion, eyes, heart, purpose, focuses issues, kundalini, harmony, mirror, meditation, creativity, visualization, color work, clarity
Amethyst	Violet	Crown	Calming, sedating, insomnia, sobriety, meditation, nerves, headaches, migraines, tension, stress, diabetes, lungs, eyes, asthma, allergies, sinuses, blood purifier, nightmares, gout, blood clots, spirituality, psychic, positivity, concentration, creativity, anger, grief, burn out, worry, death, stress

THE USES OF HEALING GEMSTONES (Continued)

Stone	Color	Chakra	Healing Uses
Zircon	Clear	Trans-personal Point	Sedating, all-aura healer, protection stone, insomnia, peace, heart stimulant, polio, tuberculosis, lungs, independence, self-independence, spirit healer, contagion, infections
Diamond	Clear	Trans-personal Point	Positive/negative, fidelity, wealth, pure knowing, all-aura, insomnia, night-mares, courage, endurance, strength, peace, eases fears, skin, growth, protection, magnifies, catalyst, concentration, poisoning, contagion, heart, convulsions, gout
Rutile Quartz	Clear/ Smoky	Trans-personal Point	Magnifies clear crystal healing, psychic opener, calms, warms, insomnia, dreams, intuition, scrying, balances, nutrition, telepathy, aging, immunity, infections, dyslexia, depression
Clear Quartz Crystal	Clear	Trans-personal Point	All-healing

¹Sources: Thelma Isaacs, *Gemstones, Crystals and Healing* (Black Mt, NC, Lorien House, 1982), p. 30–98; Julia Lorusso and Joel Glick, *Healing Stoned* (Albuquerque, NM, Brotherhood of Life, 1985, original 1976), p. 27–80; Rhiannon McBride, Charleen Deering, Louise Devery and Amber K, "Occult Uses of Gemstones", in *Circle Network News*, Summer, 1982, p. 12; Serenity Peterson, *Crystal Visioning* (Nashville, TN, Interdimensional Publishing, 1984), p. 41–60; Katrina Raphaell, *Crystal Enlightenment* (NY, Aurora Press, 1985), p. 78–164; Gemstoned Ltd., *Crystal Essence* (NY, Gemstoned Ltd., 1984); pamphlet; Mellie Uyldert, *The Magic of Precious Stones* (Great Britain, Turnstone Press, 1981), p. 82–156.

GEMSTONES FOR THE CHAKRAS[1]

Root	Belly	Solar Plexus	Heart	Throat	Brow	Crown/Trans-Personal Point
Smoky Quartz	Carnelian	Topaz	Malachite	Aquamarine	Lapis Lazuli	Moonstone
Black Tourmaline	Coral	Amber	Peridot	Turquoise	Sodalite	Chalcedony
Tourmaline Quartz	Red/Brown Agate	Citrine	Rose Quartz	Chrysocolla	Blue Sapphire	Moss Agate
Obsidian	Fire Agate	Tiger Eye	Rhodochrosite	Amazonite	Fluorite	Selenite
Onyx	Orange Zircon	Golden Beryl	Pink Tourmaline	Blue	Moonstone	Opal
Jet	Orange Citrine	Malachite	Green Tourmaline	Aventurine	Chalcedony	Amethyst
Hematite	Jacinth	Peridot	Watermelon Tourmaline	Lace Agate	Moss Agate	Clear Zircon
Bloodstone	Brown Jasper	Yellow Jade	Emerald	Lapis Lazuli	Azurite	Diamond
Garnet	Phantom Calcite	Yellow Diamond	Green Jade	Sodalite	Star Sapphire	Rutile Quartz
Ruby	Poppy Jasper	Chrysoberyl	Jadeite	Blue Topaz	Dark Aquamarine	Clear Quartz
Red Jaspar	Wulfenite	Demantoid	Nephrite	Celestite	Blue Spinel	Alexandrite
Red Spinel	Salmon Jade	Hawk's Eye	Green Aventurine	Blue Quartz	Blue Zircon	Violet Garnet
Rhodonite	Orange Sapphire	Brazilianite	Aquamarine	Benitoite	Zoisite	Iolite
Magnetite	Orange Calcite	Apatite	Turquoise	Lazulite	Lazulite	Violet
Lodestone	Orange Fluorite	Sulphur	Chrysocolla	Variscite	Kyanite	Tourmaline (Rubelite)
Red Zircon	Fire Opal	Yellow Calcite	Crysoprase	Smithsonite	Aragonite	Tanzanite
Black Star Sapphire		Aquamarine	Green Quartz	Gem Silica	Blue	Ulexite
Red Fluorite		Green Tourmaline	Kunzite	Eilat Stone	Tourmaline	Violet
Red Jade		Green Calcite	Rhodonite	Malachite/Chrysocolla	Malachite/Azurite	Fluorite
		Yellow Zircon	Dolomite	Malachite/Azurite	Selenite	Pearl
		Green Zircon	Pink Beryl	Blue Zircon	Opal (White)	Sugilite
		Yellow Tourmaline	Morganite	Blue Fluorite	Opal (Black)	Violet Jade
		Yellow Sapphire	Pink Sapphire		Fire Agate	Amethyst
		Yellow Fluorite	Green Sapphire			Quartz
		Sphene	Rose Jade			Violet Zircon
		Yellow Barite	Rose Coral			Violet
		Periclase	Green Fluorite			Sapphire
			Pink Carnelian			

APPENDIX II

BIRTHSTONES

ZODIAC GEMSTONES

PLANETARY GEMSTONES

BIRTHSTONES[1]

Month	William Fernie	Thelma Isaacs (Ancient Rome)	Walter Schumann (English-Speaking Countries)	Walter Schumann (German-Speaking Countries)
January	Jacinth, Garnet	Garnet	Garnet	Garnet, Rose Quartz
February	Amethyst	Amethyst	Amethyst	Amethyst, Onyx
March	Bloodstone	Bloodstone	Aquamarine	Aquamarine, Red Jasper
April	Sapphire, Diamond	Sapphire, Lapis	Diamond	Quartz Crystal, Diamond
May	Emerald	Agate	Emerald	Chrysoprase, Emerald
June	Agate, Chrysoprase	Emerald	Pearl	Moonstone, Pearl
July	Carnelian, Ruby	Onyx	Ruby	Carnelian, Ruby
August	Sardonyx	Carnelian	Peridot	Aventurine, Peridot
September	Peridot, Sapphire	Peridot	Sapphire	Lapis Lzuli, Sapphire
October	Aquamarine, Opal	Aquamarine	Opal	Opal, Tourmaline
November	Topaz, Chrysoberyl	Topaz	Topaz	Tiger Eye, Topaz
December	Turquoise, Malachite	Ruby	Turquoise	Turquoise, Zircon

[1]Sources: William T. Fernie, MD, *The Occult and Curative Powers of Precious Stones* (San Francisco, Harper and Row Publishers, 1973, original 1907), p. 37; Thelma Isaacs, *Gemstones, Crystals and Healing* (Black Mountain, NC, Lorien Press, 1982), p. 104; Walter Schumann, *Gemstones of the World* (New York, Sterling Publishing Co., 1977), p. 232.

ZODIAC GEMSTONES[2]

Sign	William Fernie	Thelma Isaacs	Walter Schumann	Mellie Uyldert
Aries (3/21–4/20)	Bloodstone	Ruby, Bloodstone, Red Jasper	Red Jasper, Red Carnelian	Jasper, Ruby
Taurus (4/21–5/20)	Sapphire	Golden Topaz, Coral, Emerald	Orange Carnelian Rose Quartz	Sapphire, Rose Quartz, Lapis Lazuli
Gemini (5/21–6/20)	Agate	Clear Quartz, Aquamarine, Carbuncle	Citrine, Tiger Eye	Citrine, Clear Quartz, Aquamarine, Tiger Eye, Cat's Eye
Cancer (6/21–7/20)	Emerald	Emerald, Moonstone	Aventurine, Chrysoprase	Emerald, Peridot, White Serpentine, Chalcedony
Leo (7/12–8/22)	Onyx	Ruby, Amber, Sardonyx	Clear Quartz, Golden Quartz	Golden Quartz, Almadine, Peridot, Diamond
Virgo (8/23–9/22)	Carnelian	Pink Jasper, Zircon, Turquoise	Yellow Agate, Citrine	Carnelian, Agate, Sardonyx
Libra (9/23–10/22)	Peridot	Opal, Diamond	Smoky Quartz, Orange Citrine	Emerald, Jade, Aventurine, Nephrite, Orange Sapphire
Scorpio (10/23–11/22)	Aquamarine	Agate, Garnet, Topaz	Blood-Red Carnelian, Sard	Garnet, Hematite, Beryl, Pyrope, Spinal Ruby

ZODIAC GEMSTONES (Continued)

Sign	William Fernie	Thelma Isaacs	Walter Schumann	Mellie Uyldert
Sagittarius (11/23–12/21)	Topaz	Amethyst	Blue Quartz, Chalcedony	Topaz, Jacinth
Capricorn (12/22–1/20)	Ruby	Beryl, Jet, Black Onyx, White Onyx	Onyx, Quartz Cat's Eye	Smoky Quartz, Onyx, Jet
Aquarius (1/21–2/18)	Jacinth, Garnet	Blue Sapphire	Hawk's Eye, Turquoise	Turquoise, Malachite, Amazonite
Pisces (2/19–3/20)	Amethyst	Diamond, Jade	Amethyst, Amethyst Quartz	Amethyst, Opal, Moon- stone, Rhinestone

[2]Sources: William T. Fernie, MD, *The Occult and Curative Powers of Precious Stones* (San Francisco, Harper and Row Publishers, 1973, original 1907), p. 45; Thelma Isaacs, *Gemstones, Crystals and Healing* (Black Mountain, NC, Lorien House, 1982), p. 101; Walter Schumann, *Gemstones of the World* (New York, Sterling Publishing Co., 1977), p. 232; Mellie Uyldert, *The Magic of Precious Stones* (Great Britain, Turnstone Press, 1981), p. 27–28.

PLANETARY GEMSTONES[3]

Sun	Moon	Mercury	Venus	Earth	Mars
Diamond	Moonstone	Citrine	Rose Quartz	Aventurine	Ruby
Quartz Crystal	Chalcedony	Topaz	Blue Sapphire	Peridot	Garnet
Sunstone	Rhinestone	Yellow Sapphire	Nephrite	Green Jade	Red Jaspar
Ruby	Opal	Peridot	Emerald	Bloodstone	Lodestone
Topaz	Selenite	Quartz Crystal	Lapis Lazuli	Moss Agate	Fire Opal
Chrysoberyl	Pearl	Aquamarine	Turquoise		Amethyst
Emerald	Labradorite	Chalcedony	Orange Sapphire		Bloodstone
Garnet	Emerald	Amazonite	Hyacinth		Carnelian
Opal	Turquoise	Turquoise	Aquamarine		Coral
Pink Tourmaline	Rhodochrosite	Chrysocolla	Chrysoprase		Watermelon
Sulphur			Diamond		Tourmaline
Citrine			Moonstone		
			Pearl		
			Green Tourmaline		
			Pink Tourmaline		
			Kunzite		

PLANETARY GEMSTONES (Continued)

Jupiter	Saturn	Uranus	Neptune	Pluto
Jacinth	Onyx	Turquoise	Amethyst	Bloodstone
Topaz	Jet	Malachite	Opal	Pyrope
Orange Carnelian	Spinel Ruby	Amazonite	Coral	Dark Red Agate
Carbuncle	Blue Sapphire	Opal	Aquamarine	Almadine
Emerald	Carnelian	Tourmaline	Chrysocolla	Amber
Beryl	Chalcedony	Amethyst	Chrysoprase	Amethyst
Amethyst	Aquamarine	Chrysocolla	Emerald	Carnelian
Lapis Lazuli	Blue Spinel	Chrysoprase	Fire Agate	Fire Agate
Blue Sapphire	Amber	Fire Agate	Jade	Garnet
Chrysocolla	Bloodstone	Spectrolite	Spectrolite	Spectrolite
Chrysoprase	Coral	Lapis Lazuli	Malachite/Azurite	Malachite/Azurite
Pink Tourmaline	Diamond	Malachite/Azurite	Moonstone	Malachite
Watermelon Tourmaline	Garnet	Clear Quartz	Pearl	Moonstone
Sodalite	Jade	Topaz	Pink Tourmaline	Clear Quartz
Azurite	Smoky Quartz	Celestite	Sugilite	Smoky Quartz
	Malachite	Aquamarine	Fluorite	Ruby
	Peridot			Green Tourmaline
	Green Tourmaline			Watermelon Tourmaline
				Obsidian
				Selenite
				Diamond

[3]Combined sources: Julia Lorusso and Joel Glick, *Healing Stoned* (New Mexico, Brotherhood of Life, 1985, original 1976), p. 24; Katrina Raphael, *Crystal Enlightenment* (New York, Aurora Press, 1985), P. 156–159; Walter Schumann, *Gemstones of the World* (New York, Sterling Publishing Co, 1977), p. 232; James Sturzaker, *Gemstones and Their Occult Powers* (London, Metatron Publications, 1977), p. 113–114; Mellie Uyldert, *The Magic of Precious Stones* (Great Britain, The Turnstone Press, 1981), p. 26–27. Only recognized, dis-covered planets are listed, and sources are combined.

APPENDIX III

GEMSTONE REMEDIES

GEMSTONE REMEDIES[1]

Abortion Recovery Smoky Quartz, Chrysocolla, Lapis Lazuli

Aging Rose Quartz, Emerald, Selenite, Rutile

Alcohol Recovery Amethyst, Smoky Quartz, White Chalcedony, Tiger Eye, Moss Agate

Anemia Bloodstone, Ruby, Orange/Red Coral, Red/Brown Agate, Rose Quartz, Garnet

Anger Black Tourmaline, Topaz, Malachite, Peridot, Red Jade, Chrysocolla, Amethyst

Appetite Topaz, Emerald, Golden Beryl (eating disorders), Amethyst (to decrease)

Arthritis Carnelian, Chrysocolla, Orange/Red Coral, Malachite, Lapis Lazuli

Asthma Carnelian, Amber, Orange/Red Coral, Topaz, Tiger Eye, Malachite, Rhodochrosite, Turquoise, Chrysocolla, Sapphire, Amethyst

Bladder and Kidneys Hematite, Jade, Bloodstone, Ruby, Topaz, Red Jaspar, Orange/Red Coral, Amber, Citrine, Rose Quartz, Nephrite, Amethyst

Bleeding (to decrease) Lapis Lazuli, Moonstone, Amethyst, Emerald, Bloodstone, Hematite, Chrysocolla, Sodalite, Sapphire, White Chalcedony, Selenite

Blood Purifying Carnelian, Ruby, Bloodstone, Orange/Red Coral, Topaz, Citrine, Malachite, Rhodochrosite, Emerald, Green Tourmaline, Lapis Lazuli, Sodalite, Sapphire, Amethyst

Breast Milk Selenite, Turquoise, Carnelian, Malachite, Moonstone, White Chalcedony

Broken Bones Topaz, Selenite, Green Tourmaline, White Chalcedony

Burn Out Ruby, Garnet, Carnelian, Orange/Red Coral, Chrysocolla, Amber, Topaz, Pink Tourmaline, Green Jade, Orange Jade, Moonstone, Amethyst

Burns Chrysocolla, Turquoise, Emerald, Aquamarine, Lapis Lazuli, Sodalite, Sapphire, Selenite, Amethyst

Calming Amethyst, Smoky Quartz, Black Tourmaline, Hematite, Tourmaline Quartz, Red Jasper, Red/Brown Agate, Amber, Malachite, Jade,

GEMSTONE REMEDIES (Continued)

Calming (Continued) Eilat Stone, Malachite/Chrysocolla, Peridot, Rose Quartz, Pink Tourmaline, Emerald, Green Tourmaline, Green Aventurine, Aquamarine, Turquoise, Chrysocolla, Fluorite, White Chalcedony

Cancer Ruby, Red Jasper, Watermelon Tourmaline, Rhodochrosite, Chrysocolla, Moonstone, Selenite, Rose Quartz (prevention)

Child Abuse Recovery Rose Quartz, Green Aventurine, Kunzite, Pink Tourmaline, Watermelon Tourmaline, Green Fluorite, Chrysocolla

Childbirth Hematite, Bloodstone, Ruby (brings on labor), Red/Brown Agate, Emerald, Jade, Chrysocolla, Lapis Lazuli, Jacinth, Malachite

Circulation Black Onyx, Bloodstone, Garnet, Ruby, Carnelian, Red/Brown Agate, Topaz, Citrine, Sapphire, Emerald, Amethyst, Chrysocolla

Colds/Sinus Carnelian, Rose Quartz, Rhodochrosite, Green Tourmaline, Sodalite, Moonstone, Amethyst

Conception Garnet, Ruby, Red Jasper, Carnelian, Jade, Orange/Red Coral, Rhodochrosite, Moonstone

Constipation Carnelian, Yellow Tourmaline, Peridot, Green Tourmaline, Golden Beryl, Yellow Jade

Cooling Peridot, Green Aventurine, Turquoise, Green Tourmaline, Emerald, Aquamarine, Lapis Lazuli, Chrysocolla, Sodalite

Degenerative Nerve Dis-eases Malachite, Azurite, Azurite/Malachite, Malachite/Chrysocolla, Rhodochrosite, Watermelon Tourmaline, Green Tourmaline, Chrysocolla, Lapis Lazuli, Sapphire, Sodalite, Azurite, Fluorite, Moonstone, Amethyst

Depression Smoky Quartz, Black Tourmaline, Garnet, Ruby, Carnelian, Orange/Red Coral, Topaz, Citrine, Peridot, Golden Beryl, Rose Quartz, Emerald, Green Aventurine, Pink Tourmaline, Turquoise, Chrysocolla, Lapis Lazuli, Sapphire, Moonstone, White Chalcedony, Amethyst, Rutile Quartz

Diarrhea Smoky Quartz, Black Tourmaline, Tourmaline Quartz

GEMSTONE REMEDIES (Continued)

Digestion Green Tourmaline, Peridot, Topaz, Amber, Orange/Red Coral, Citrine, Tiger Eye, Golden Beryl, Rhodochrosite, Emerald, Jade, Yellow Jade, Turquoise, Chrysocolla

Drug Issues and Smoking Smoky Quartz, Rutile Quartz, Jet, Tiger Eye, Amethyst

Emotional Pain Smoky Quartz, Black Onyx, Hematite, Garnet, Rose Quartz, Red/Brown Agate, Topaz, Peridot, Eilat Stone, Pink Tourmaline, Black Tourmaline, Watermelon Tourmaline, Green Fluorite, Green Tourmaline, Emerald, Jade, Green Aventurine, Aquamarine, Turquoise, Chrysocolla, Sodalite, Sapphire, Amethyst, Moss Agate

Epilepsy Red Jasper, Carnelian, Red/Brown Agate, Malachite, Emerald, Turquoise, Chrysocolla, Lapis Lazuli, Fluorite, Amethyst, Diamond

Exhaustion Ruby, Carnelian, Orange/Red Coral, Topaz, Red/Brown Agate, Amber, Citrine, Emerald, Golden Beryl, Green Tourmaline, Moonstone, Orange Jade, Lapis Lazuli

Eyes Obsidian, Orange/Red Coral, Red/Brown Agate, Topaz, Tiger Eye, Hawk's Eye, Golden Beryl, Malachite, Peridot, Rhodochrosite, Emerald, Jade, Aquamarine, Turquoise, Sapphire, Lapis Lazuli, Moonstone, Opal, Amethyst

Fear Smoky Quartz, Black Tourmaline, Bloodstone, Orange/Red Coral, Red/Brown Agate, Topaz, Pink Tourmaline, Green Tourmaline, Jade, Aquamarine, Chrysocolla, Sodalite, Sapphire, Moss Agate, Amethyst, Selenite, Diamond

Fevers Bloodstone, Carnelian, Red/Brown Agate, Peridot, Green Tourmaline, Emerald, Aquamarine, Turquoise, Chrysocolla, Lapis Lazuli, Sodalite, Sapphire, Selenite, Moss Agate

Gall Bladder Carnelian, Citrine, Malachite, Emerald, Green Tourmaline

Grief Rose Quartz, Black Onyx, Jet, Amethyst, Pink Tourmaline, Watermelon Tourmaline, Black Tourmaline, Chrysocolla

Headaches	Jet, Topaz, Rose Quartz, Green Aventurine, Emerald, Aquamarine, Turquoise, Sodalite, Chrysocolla, Lapis Lazuli, Sapphire, Amethyst
Hearing	Red/Brown Agate, Amber, Rose Quartz, Aquamarine, Turquoise, Lapis Lazuli, Moonstone, Chrysocolla
Heart Dis-ease	Black Onyx, Ruby, Garnet, Bloodstone, Orange/Red Coral, Red/Brown Agate, Jacinth, Amber, Malachite, Peridot, Emerald, Jade, Green Aventurine, Rose Quartz, Aquamarine, Turquoise, Chrysocolla, Lapis Lazuli, Sapphire, Zircon, Diamond
Heart Healing (Emotional)	Black Onyx, Garnet, Malachite, Peridot, Rose Quartz, Pink Tourmaline, Watermelon Tourmaline, Green Tourmaline, Emerald, Jade, Green Fluorite, Green Aventurine, Aquamarine, Turquoise, Chrysocolla, Sapphire
High Blood Pressure	Hematite, Malachite, Green Tourmaline, Emerald, Green Aventurine, Rose Quartz, Aquamarine, Turquoise, Chrysocolla, Lapis Lazuli, Sodalite, Sapphire, Amethyst
Immune System	Ruby, Amber, Moonstone, White Chalcedony, Amethyst, Zircon, Diamond, Rutile Quartz, Sodalite, Lapis Lazuli
Incest Recovery	Lapis Lazuli, Chrysocolla, Sapphire
Infections	Carnelian, Amber, Peridot, Emerald, Green Tourmaline, Aquamarine, Chrysocolla, Lapis Lazuli, Sodalite, Sapphire, Opal, Amethyst
Inflammations	Hematite, Bloodstone, Peridot, Emerald, Green Tourmaline, Turquoise, Chrysocolla, Lapis Lazuli, Sodalite, Sapphire
Insomnia	Smoky Quartz, Hematite, Jacinth, Topaz, Rose Quartz, Pink Tourmaline, Emerald, Aquamarine, Chrysocolla, Lapis Lazuli, Sapphire,Moonstone, White Chalcedony, Amethyst, Zircon, Diamond
Intellect	Topaz, Citrine, Golden Beryl, Peridot, Rhodochrosite, Watermelon Tourmaline, Emerald, Jade, Aquamarine, Turquoise, Chrysocolla, Sapphire, Fluorite, Moonstone
Liver	Carnelian, Jacinth, Topaz, Citrine, Golden Beryl, Malachite, Rhodochrosite, Emerald, Yellow/Brown Jade, Aquamarine

GEMSTONE REMEDIES (Continued)

Menopause	Moonstone, Lapis Lazuli, Rose Quartz
Menstrual Cramps	Carnelian, Bloodstone (decrease flow), Ruby (brings on), Garnet, Red Jasper, Red/Brown Agate, Chrysocolla, Lapis Lazuli, Moonstone, Malachite, Sodalite
Mental Confusion Disorders	Carnelian, Orange/Red Coral, Rhodochrosite, Lapis Lazuli, Azurite, Sapphire, Selenite, Opal, Amethyst
Migraines	Chrysocolla, Aquamarine, Turquoise, Lapis Lazuli, Amethyst, Sodalite, Sapphire, Green Aventurine
Miscarriage (Prevent)	Ruby, Red Jasper, Emerald, Aquamarine
Miscarriage (Recovery)	Chrysocolla
Morning Sickness (Nausea)	Red Jasper, Amethyst, Malachite, Sodalite, Golden Beryl
Multiple Sclerosis	Lapis Lazuli, Sodalite, Blue Sapphire, Moonstone, Amethyst
Neuralgia	Ruby, Garnet, Carnelian, Amethyst
Pain	Smoky Quartz, Amber, Green Tourmaline, Emerald, Lapis Lazuli, Chrysocolla, Topaz, Amethyst, Sapphire, Clear Quartz Crystal
Pancreas	Carnelian, Topaz, Golden Beryl, Malachite, Emerald, Sodalite, Amethyst
Premenstrual Syndrome	Smoky Quartz, Chrysocolla, Moonstone, Amethyst, Black Tourmaline
Rape Recovery	Lapis Lazuli, Chrysocolla, Black Tourmaline
Reproductive Organs	Garnet, Ruby, Carnelian, Red/Brown Agate, Chrysocolla, Lapis Lazuli, Black Tourmaline
Respiratory System	Carnelian, Orange/Red Coral, Jacinth, Topaz, Amber, Tiger Eye, Peridot, Rhodochrosite, Turquoise, Amethyst, Zircon, Chrysocolla
Shock	Topaz, Smoky Quartz, Rutile Quartz, Chrysocolla, Turquoise
Skin, Nails, Hair	Black Onyx, Amber, Rhodochrosite, Green Aventurine, Rose Quartz, Amethyst, Watermelon Tourmaline, Lapis Lazuli, Diamond
Spine	Emerald, Chrysocolla, Lapis Lazuli, Selenite

GEMSTONE REMEDIES (Continued)

Stagefright Smoky Quartz, Aquamarine, Amethyst

Stomach Jet, Red Jasper, Red/Brown Agate, Golden Beryl, Bloodstone, Malachite, Aquamarine

Stress Smoky Quartz, Black Onyx, Black Tourmaline, Topaz, Amber, Malachite, Rose Quartz, Green Aventurine, Aquamarine, Emerald, Red/Brown Agate, Jade, Turquoise, Sodalite, Lapis Lazuli, Chrysocolla, Sapphire, Fluorite, Moonstone, White Chalcedony, Opal, Selenite, Amethyst

Surgical Recovery Amber, Smoky Quartz, Red Jasper, Lapis Lazuli, Chrysocolla

Swelling Peridot, Emerald, Green Tourmaline, Aquamarine, Turquoise, Chrysocolla, Lapis Lazuli, Sapphire, Sodalite

Teeth Topaz, Amber, Malachite, Green Tourmaline, Aquamarine

Throat Amber, Golden Beryl, Rose Quartz, Chrysocolla, Blue Aventurine, Lapis Lazuli, Aquamarine, Turquoise, Sapphire, White Chalcedony

Ulcers Black Onyx, Jet, Hematite, Bloodstone, Black Tourmaline, Amber, Golden Beryl, Peridot, Emerald, Rhodochrosite, Aquamarine, Sapphire, Chrysocolla, Selenite

Warming Ruby, Garnet, Carnelian, Amber, Topaz, Citrine, Rutile Quartz, Diamond, Orange/Red Coral

---

[1]Mixed sources. Use Clear Quartz Crystal for all healing, as well.

BIBLIOGRAPHY

Baer, Randall and Vicki, *Windows of Light: Quartz Crystals and Transformation* (San Francisco, Harper and Row Publishers, 1984).

Besant, Annie, and C.W. Leadbeater, *Thought Forms* (Wheaton, IL, Quest/Theosophical Publishing House, 1969, original, 1901).

Bibb, Benjamin O. and Joseph J. Weed, *Amazing Secrets of Psychic Healing* (New York, Parker Publishing Co., Inc., 1976).

Bodoh, Robert M., *Discovering Quartz* (565 Academy Dr., Edgerton, WI, 53534), Pamphlet, 1984.

Buckland, Raymond, *Practical Color Magic* (St. Paul, Llewellyn Publications, 1985).

Budapest, Z., *The Holy Book of Women's Mysteries, Part II* (Oakland, CA, Susan B. Anthony Coven No. 1, 1980).

Coddington, Mary, *In Search of the Healing Energy* (New York, Destiny Books, 1978).

DaEl, *The Crystal Book* (Sunol, CA, The Crystal Co., 1983).

Daly, Mary, *Beyond God the Father: Toward a Philosophy of Women's Liberation* (Boston, Beacon Press, 1985, original, 1973).

Daly, Mary, *Gyne/cology: The Metaethics of Radical Feminism* (Boston, Beacon Press, 1978).

Deaver, Korra, Ph. D., *Rock Crystal, The Magic Stone* (York Beach, ME, Samuel Weiser, Inc., 1985).

Denning, Melita and Osborne Phillips, *The Llewellyn Practical Guide to Astral Projection* (St. Paul, Llewellyn Publications, 1984).

Denning, Melita and Osborne Phillips, *The Llewellyn Practical Guide to Creative Visualization* (St. Paul, Llewellyn Publications, 1983).

Fernie, William T., M.D., *The Occult and Curative Powers of Precious Stones* (San Francisco, Harper and Row Publishers, 1973, original, 1907).

Galde, Phyllis, "Using Gems for Healing," in *The Llewellyn New Times* (Llewellyn Publications, POB 64383, St. Paul, MN 551614-0383), Issue 863, May-June, 1986, p. 10.

Gardner, Kay, "A Chart of Color, Sound and Energy Correspondences:, in *The Rose Window* (Healing Through the Arts, POB 399, Stonington, ME 04681), Spring, 1983.

Gardner, Kay, "A Rainbow Path" (Ladyslipper Records, POB 3124, Durham, NC 27705), 1984.

Gearhart, Sally, "Womanpower: Energy Re-Sourcement," in Charlene Spretnak, Ed., *The Politics of Women's Spirituality* (New York, Anchor/Doubleday Books, 1982), p. 194-206.

Gemstoned Ltd., *Crystal Essence* (New York, Gemstone Ltd., 1984), pamphlet.

Glendinning, Chellis, "The Healing Powers of Women," in Charlene Spretnak, Ed., *The Politics of Women's Spirituality* (New York, Anchor/Doubleday Books, 1982), p. 280-293.

ordon   i   ard *Your Healing Hands* (Santa Cruz, CA, Unity Press, 1978).

Griffin, Susan, *Woman and Nature: The Roaring Inside Her* (San Francisco, Harper and Row Publishers, 1978).

Isaacs, Thelma, Ph.D., *Gemstones, Crystals and Healing* (Black Mountain, NC, Lorien House, 1982).

Kilner, W.J., *The Aura* (York Beach, ME, Samuel Weiser, Inc., 1984, original 1911).

Krieger, Dolores, Ph.D., R.N., *The Therapeutic Touch: How to Use Your Hands to Help or to Heal* (New Jersey, Prentice-Hall, Inc., 1979).

Lanning, Lee and Vernette Hart, *Ripening: An Almanac of Lesbian Lore and Vision* (Minneapolis, Word Weavers, 1981).

Leadbeater, C.W., *The Chakras* (Wheaton, IL, Quest/Theosophical Publishing House, 1985, original 1927).

Leadbeater, C.W., *Man Visible and Invisible* (Wheaton, IL, Quest/ Theosophical Publishing House, 1980, original 1925).

Lorusso, Julia and Joel Glick, *Healing Stoned* (Albuquerque, NM, Brotherhood of Life, 1985, original 1976).

Mariechild, Diane, *Motherwit: A Feminist Guide to Psychic Develop - ment* (Trumansburg, NY, The Crossing Press, 1981).

McBride, Rhiannon, "The Occult Lapidary: Black Onyx," in *Circle Network News* (POB 219, Mt. Horeb, WI 53572), Spring, 1984, p. 8.

McBride, Rhiannon, "The Occult Lapidary: Topaz, Stone of Love and Light," in *Circle Network News* (POB 219, Mt. Horeb, WI 53572), Fall, 1983, p. 4.

McBride, Rhiannon, Charleen Deering, Louise Devery and Amber K, "Occult Uses of Gemstones," in *Circle Network News* (POB 219, Mt. Horeb, WI 53572), Summer, 1984, p. 12.

Meek, George, *Healers and the Healing Process* (Wheaton, IL, Quest/Theosophical Publishing House, 1977).

Miller, Roberta DeLong, *Psychic Massage* (San Francisco, Harper and Row Publishers, 1975).

Noble, Vicki, *Motherpeace: A Way to the Goddess Through Myth, Art and Tarot* (San Francisco, Harper and Row Publishers, 1983).

Noble, Vicki and Jonathan Tenney, *The Motherpeace Tarot Playbook: Astrology and the Motherpeace Cards* (Berkeley, CA, Wingbow Press, 1986).

Ouseley, S.G.J., *Colour Meditations, With Guide to Color Healing* (Essex, England, L.N. Fowler and Co., Inc., 1981, original 1949).

Ouseley, S.G.J., *The Power of the Rays: The Science of Colour Healing* (Essex, England, L.N. Fowler and Co., Inc., 1981, original 1951).

Ouseley, S.G.J., *The Science of the Aura* (Essex, England, L.N. Fowler and Co., Inc., 1982, original 1949).

Peterson, Serenity, *Crystal Visioning, A Crystal Workbook* (Nashville, TN, Interdimensional Publishing, 1984).

Powell, A.E., *The Etheric Double, The Health Aura of Man* (Wheaton, IL, Quest/Theosophical Publishing House, 1983, original 1925).

Powell, A.E., *The Astral Body* (Wheaton, IL, Quest/Theosophical Publishing House, 1982, original 1927).

Powell, A.E., *The Mental Body* (Wheaton, IL, Quest/Theosophical Publishing House, 1984, original 1927).

Powell, A.E., *The Causal Body and the Ego* (Wheaton, IL, Quest/Theosophical Publishing House, 1978, original 1928).

Ramacharaka, Yogi, *The Science of Psychic Healing* (Chicago, Yogi Publication Society, 1937, original 1909).

Raphaell, Katrina, *Crystal Enlightenment: The Transforming Properties of Crystals and Healing Stones* (New York, Aurora Press, 1985).

Rindge, Jeanne P., "The Use of Non-Human Sensors," in George W. Meek, Ed., *Healers and the Healing Process* (Wheaton, IL, Quest/Theosophical Publishing House, 1977), p. 130-146.

Schumann, Walter, *Gemstones of the World,* (New York, Sterling Publishing, 1984, original 1977).

Sheely, C. Norman, "Postcript," in George W. Meek, Ed., *Healers and the Healing Process,* (Wheaton, IL, Quest/Theosophical Publishing House, 1977), p. 265-266.

Sherwood, Keith, *The Art of Spiritual Healing* (St. Paul, Llewellyn Publications, 1985).

Silbey, Uma Sita, "Crystal Tools, Not Toys," in *Magical Blend Magazine,* (POB 11303, San Francisco, CA 94101), Issue 13, May, 1986, p. 34.

Silbey, Uma Sita, "Natural Quartz Crystal Healing," in *Circle Network News* (POB 219, Mt. Horeb, WI 53572), Fall, 1984, p. 13.

Smith, Michael G., *Crystal Power* (St. Paul, Llewellyn Publications, 1985).

Starhawk, *Dreaming the Dark: Magic, Sex and Politics* (Boston, Beacon Press, 1982).

Stein, Diane, *The Kwan Yin Book of Changes* (St. Paul, Llewellyn Publications, 1985).

Stein, Diane, *The Women's Spirituality Book* (St. Paul, Llewellyn Publications, 1986).

Sturzaker, James, *Gemstones and Their Occult Powers* (London, Metatron Publications, 1977).

Teish, Luisah, *Jambalaya: The Natural Woman's Book* (San Francisco, Harper and Row Publishers, 1985).

Uyldert, Mellie, *The Magic of Precious Stones* (Great Britain, Turnstone Press, 1981).

Wallace, Amy and Bill Henkin, *The Psychic Healing Book* (Berkeley, CA, Wingbow Press, 1985, original 1978).

INDEX

This index was designed to aid the seeker in using this book as a reference. She should look for specific illnesses under their names and the general body region they affect.

STAY IN TOUCH

On the following pages you will find listed, with their current prices, some of the books and tapes now available on related subjects. Your book dealer stocks most of these, and will stock new titles in the Llewellyn series as they become available. We urge your patronage.

However, to obtain our full catalog, to keep informed of new titles as they are released and to benefit from informative articles and helpful news, you are invited to write for our bimonthly news magazine/catalog. A sample copy is free, and it will continue coming to you at no cost as long as you are an active mail customer. Or you may keep it coming for a full year with a donation of just $2.00 in the U.S.A. ($7.00 for Canada & Mexico, $20.00 overseas, first-class mail). Many bookstores also have *The Llewellyn New Times* available to their customers. Ask for it.

Stay in touch! In *The Llewellyn New Times'* pages you will find news and reviews of new books, tapes and services, announcements of meetings and seminars, articles helpful to our readers, news of authors, advertising of products and services, special money-making opportunities, and much more.

The Llewellyn New Times
P.O. Box 64383-Dept. 759, St. Paul, MN 55164-0383, U.S.A.

•   •   •

TO ORDER BOOKS AND TAPES

If your book dealer does not have the books and tapes described on the following pages readily available, you may order them direct from the publisher by sending full price in U.S. funds, plus $1.00 for handling and 50¢ each book or item for postage within the United States; outside U.S.A. surface mail add $1.00 extra per item. Outside U.S.A. air mail add $7.00 per item.

FOR GROUP STUDY AND PURCHASE

Because there is a great deal of interest in group discussion and study of the subject matter of this book, we feel that we should encourage the adoption and use of this particular book by such groups by offering a special "quantity" price to group leaders or "agents."

Our Special Quantity Price for a minimum order of five copies of THE WOMEN'S BOOK OF HEALING is $38.85 Cash-With-Order. This price includes postage and handling within the United States. Minnesota residents must add 6% sales tax. For additional quantities, please order in multiples of five. For Canadian and foreign orders, add postage and handling charges as above. Credit Card (VISA, MasterCard, American Express, Diners' Club) Orders are accepted. Charge Card Orders only may be phoned free ($15.00 minimum order) within the U.S.A. by dialing 1-800-THE MOON (in Canada call: 1-800-FOR-SELF). Customer Service calls dial 1-612-291-1970. Mail Orders to:

LLEWELLYN PUBLICATIONS
P.O. Box 64383-Dept. 759 / St. Paul, MN 55164-0383, U.S.A.

THE WOMEN'S SPIRITUALITY BOOK
by Diane Stein

Diane Stein's *The Women's Spirituality Book* is a work of insight and a much-needed addition to women's magic and ritual. Beginning with "Creation and Creation Goddesses" she enthusiastically informs the reader of the essence of women-centered Wicca, using myths and legends drawn from a variety of world sources to bring her work to life. Nonpatriarchal myths and tales are presented in the first half of the book, which leads the reader through the yearly progressions of rituals in some of the most complete descriptions of the Sabbats ever published.

The second half of the book is a valuable introduction to visualization, healing, chakras, crystal and gemstone magick. Subsequent chapters cover "transformational tarot" and Kwan Yin.

Diane Stein's *Women's Spirituality Book* is a tool for self-discovery and initiation into the Higher Self: a joyous reunion with the Goddess.

0-87542-761-8, 300 pages, 6 x 9, illus., softcover.   **$9.95**

THE KWAN YIN BOOK OF CHANGES
Diane Stein

The Kwan Yin Book of Changes places the ancient Chinese I Ching, a divinatory system much a complement to the tarot, in a context that women and men in touch with peace can relate to. The patriarchalism and rigidity of the traditional *I Ching* is exchanged for a women-only communal government and world, with situations and language relevant to modern occult women and to men who relate to the feminine aspects of themselves. The God/Emperor of traditional translations is replaced by the eminence of the Earth and the Goddess, and fate and predestiny give way to free will and choice. The Superior Man of the old versions is the Superior or Spiritual Woman in a system much more positive than any earlier *I Ching* translation.

As a divinatory tool, *The Kwan Yin Book of Changes* returns the Chinese *I Ching* to women's use, and is a tool of great power that is simple to use. The book stands the *I Ching* side by side with the tarot as an aspect of women's spirituality, and is a remembering of the submerged skills of women's matriarchy and culture.

0-87542-760-X, 256 pages, 6 x 9, illus., softcover.   **$9.95**

THE KWAN YIN WORKSHOP TAPE
by Diane Stein

Diane Stein's workshps on Kwan Yin lend a special magick to your working of the I Ching divinatory system. She gives suggestions for utilizing our own magick—free choice—in using Kwan Yin, and sends her special love to everyone in the listening audience. Questions asked during the workshop are those you wanted answered yourself. Gain new insights into this reclaimed divinatory approach to the Goddess.

L-764-2   **$7.95**

THE CRYSTAL HEALING WORKSHOP TAPE
by Diane Stein

Before modern medicine and technology started treating "symptoms," women were healers. Crystals, working components in modern "technological" equipment, are the tools of women's healing. Diane Stein dis-covers Crystal Healing, and the ability to share well-being through magickal stones. Audience participation in the workshop brings up several points of interest, and gives common examples of crystal experiences.

L-765-0   **$7.95**

RACHIDA FINDS MAGICK TAPE
by Diane Stein

Diane Stein has led hundreds of women in guided meditations to find the magick within themselves. One of her most popular and successful of these is *Rachida Finds Magick*, a tale of a young girl—the child and seeker within you—who leaves her home with her cat, and travels through the world to find magick.

Along the way, she meets people and animals who act as guides in her quest. She sees Baba Yaga, the witch of Russian fairy tales; Yemaya, the African mermaid Goddess of oceans, rivers, women and birth; Spider Woman, the Navajo and Hopi Goddess who brought culture to the people; Pele, the volcano Goddess of Hawaii; and The Snake Goddess of ancient Crete, who created all life.

Each of the Goddesses help Rachida discover secrets within herself in her own way, and they will help you, too, find the magick that is within yourself.

L-763   **$9.95**

GUIDED MEDITATIONS TAPE
by Diane Stein

Meditation on the Goddess Within helps you understand and reclaim the Goddess power—the power of creation and change—for yourself. In this meditation, you'll discover the Goddess, blend with Her, and She will give you a special gift, that of your true self.

Side two of this tape is *Meditation on the Chakras: The Rainbow*. In this meditation, you welcome light, color and peace into your essence with the seven rainbow colors of the Chakras, the natural power points on the body that relate both to body and spirit. Together, these colors are related to the oneness we have with the Earth and with the Goddess within.

L-762   **$9.95**

CRYSTAL AWARENESS
by Catherine Bowman

For millions of years, crystals have been waiting for people to discover their wonderful powers. Today they are used in watches, computer chips and communication devices. But there is also a spiritual, holistic aspect to crystals.

Crystal Awareness will teach you everything you need to know about crystals to begin working with them. It will also help those who have been working with them to complete their knowledge. Topics include:

•**Crystal Forms•Colored and Colorless Crystals•Single Points, Clusters and Double Terminated Crystals•Crystal and Human Energy Fields•The Etheric and Spiritual Bodies•Crystals as Energy Generators•Crystal Cleansing and Programming•Crystal Meditation•The Value of Polished Crystals•Crystals and Personal Spiritual Growth• Crystals and Chakras•How to Make Crystal Jewelry•The Uses for Crystals in the Future•Color Healing•Programming Crystals with Color•Compatible Crystals and Metals •Several Crystal Healing Techniques, including The Star of David Healing•**

Crystal Awareness is destined to be the guide of choice for people who are beginning their investigation of crystals.

0-87542-058-3, softbound, illustrated.   **$3.95**

EARTH POWER: TECHNIQUES OF NATURAL MAGIC
by Scott Cunningham

Magick is the art of working with the forces of Nature to bring about necessary, and desired, changes. The forces of Nature—expressed through Earth, Air, Fire and Water—are our "spiritual ancestors" who paved the way for our emergence from the pre-historic seas of creation. Attuning to, and working with these energies in magick not only lends you the power to affect changes in your life, it also allows you to sense your own place in the larger scheme of Nature. Using the "Old Ways" enables you to live a better life, and to deepen your understanding of the world about you. The tools and powers of magick are around you, waiting to be grasped and utilized. This book gives you the means to put Magick into your life, shows you how to make and use the tools, and gives you spells for every purpose.

0-87542-121-0, 250 pages, illus., softcover. $6.95

MAGICAL HERBALISM—The Secret Craft of the Wise
by Scott Cunningham

In Magical Herbalism, certain plants are prized for the special range of energies—the vibrations, or powers—they possess. Magical Herbalism unites the powers of plants and man to produce, and direct, change in accord with human will and desire.

This is the Magic of amulets and charms, sachets and herbal pillows, incenses and scented oils, simples and infusions and anointments. It's Magic as old as our knowledge of plants, an art that anyone can learn and practice, and once again enjoy as we look to the Earth to rediscover our roots and make inner connections with the world of Nature.

This is the Magic of Enchantment . . . of word and gesture to shape the images of mind and channel the energies of the herbs. It is a Magic for *everyone*—for the herbs are easily and readily obtained, the tools are familiar or easily made, and the technology that of home and garden.

This book includes step-by-step guidance to the preparation of herbs and to their compounding in incense and oils, sachets and amulets, simples and infusions, with simple rituals and spells for every purpose.

0-87542-120-2, 243 pages, 5¼ x 8, illus., softcover. $7.95

THE MAGICAL HOUSEHOLD
by Scott Cunningham and David Harrington

Whether your home is a small apartment or a palatial mansion, you want it to be something special. Now it can be with *The Magical Household*. Learn how to make your home more than just a place to live. Turn it into a place of life and fun and magic. You will learn simple magical spells that use nothing more than items in your house: furniture, windows, doors, carpet, pets, etc. The result is a home that is safeguarded from harm and a place which will bring you happiness, health and more.

ISBN: 0-87542-124-5, illustrated, paper $7.95